WARFARE IN HISTORY

The Soldier Experience
in the Fourteenth Century

T0374694

WARFARE IN HISTORY

ISSN 1358–779X

Series editors
Matthew Bennett, Royal Military Academy, Sandhurst, UK
Anne Curry, University of Southampton, UK
Stephen Morillo, Wabash College, Crawfordsville, USA

This series aims to provide a wide-ranging and scholarly approach to military history, offering both individual studies of topics or wars, and volumes giving a selection of contemporary and later accounts of particular battles; its scope ranges from the early medieval to the early modern period.

New proposals for the series are welcomed; they should be sent to the publisher at the address below.

Boydell and Brewer Limited, PO Box 9, Woodbridge, Suffolk, IP12 3DF

Previously published titles in this series are listed at the back of this volume

The Soldier Experience in the Fourteenth Century

Edited by

Adrian R. Bell and Anne Curry

with Adam Chapman, Andy King and David Simpkin

THE BOYDELL PRESS

First published 2011
The Boydell Press, Woodbridge
Paperback edition 2017

ISBN 978 1 84383 674 2 hardback
ISBN 978 1 78327 243 3 paperback

The Boydell Press is an imprint of Boydell & Brewer Ltd
PO Box 9, Woodbridge, Suffolk IP12 3DF, UK
and of Boydell & Brewer Inc.
668 Mt Hope Avenue, Rochester, NY 14620–2731, USA
website: www.boydellandbrewer.com

A CIP catalogue record for this book is available
from the British Library

The publisher has no responsibility for the continued existence or accuracy of
URLs for external or third-party internet websites referred to in this book,
and does not guarantee that any content on such websites is,
or will remain, accurate or appropriate

This publication is printed on acid-free paper

Contents

Contributors

Rémy Ambühl took his PhD at St Andrews and is now taking up a Leverhulme Early Career Fellowship at the University of Southampton. His research interests concern war and society in late medieval Europe. He has published several articles on ransoms and prisoners of war in the Hundred Years War and is currently preparing a monograph on this topic.

Andrew Ayton is Senior Lecturer in History at the University of Hull. His research publications have focused mainly on warfare, military organisation and military service in fourteenth-century England and continental Europe. He is also interested in east-central Europe and was editor of Pál Engel's *The Realm of Stephen*, the first large-scale general history of the medieval kingdom of Hungary to be published in English.

David Bachrach is Associate Professor of medieval history at the University of New Hampshire. He is a specialist in the administrative and military history of England and Germany. He has published several articles dealing with the military organisation, administration and armament of the armies of Henry III and Edward I. His publications also include *Religion and the Conduct of War c. 300–1215* (Woodbridge, 2003); and *Gesta Tancredi of Ralph of Caen: A History of the Normans on the First Crusade*, translation and commentary with Bernard S. Bachrach (Aldershot, 2005).

Adrian Bell is Professor of the History of Finance, ICMA Centre, University of Reading. He is interested in soldiery in the Hundred Years War and, together with Professor Anne Curry, led a research project 'The Soldier in Later Medieval England' which created a database of 250,000 service records between 1369 and 1453 which is available at www.medievalsoldier.org. His book, *War and the Soldier in the Fourteenth Century*, was published in 2004. Adrian is also interested in medieval finance and has published widely on this topic, including *The English Wool Market c. 1230–1327* in 2007.

Adam Chapman is a visiting fellow at the University of Southampton where he completed his doctoral research on the Welsh Soldier 1272–1422. His current research is on the effects of war on Welsh society in the later Middle Ages. He has published on the Welshmen in the Armies of Edward I as well as contributing to several articles produced as part of the AHRC Soldier in Later Medieval England project. A monograph on the role of the Welsh soldier in England's wars between 1277 and 1422 is under preparation.

Anne Curry is Professor of Medieval History at the University of Southampton, where she is also Dean of the Faculty of Humanities. She has published widely on the Hundred Years War, especially on the fifteenth-century phase, including Agincourt, and was also editor of the Henry VI section of the *Parliament Rolls of Medieval England*. She was co-director of the AHRC project 'The Soldier in Later Medieval England'.

Michael Jones, Correspondant de l'Institut, is Emeritus Professor of Medieval French History, University of Nottingham. He has published extensively on late medieval Brittany, most recently *Le Premier Inventaire du Trésor des chartes des ducs de Bretagne* (1395), *Hervé Le Grant et les origines du Chronicon Briocense* (2007) and 'Les comptes d'Auffroy Guinot, trésorier et receveur-général de Bretagne, 1430–1436. Édition et commentaire', *Journal des Savants*, Année 2010.

Andy King is a Research Fellow in History at the University of Southampton, and was a researcher on the AHRC project 'The Soldier in Later Medieval England'. He has published articles on the Northern Marches, Anglo-Scottish warfare, chronicles and castles in the fourteenth century, as well as an edition of Thomas Gray's *Scalacronica*. He is currently working on a textbook on England and Scotland 1296–1603.

Iain MacInnes is a Lecturer in Scottish History at the Centre for History, University of the Highlands. He completed his PhD, entitled 'Scotland at War: Its Conduct and the Behaviour of Scottish Soldiers, 1332–1357', at the University of Aberdeen in 2008, and hopes to produce it in the near future as a monograph. He has also written several articles on the subject of the Scottish Wars of Independence.

Guilhem Pépin is currently based at Oxford working on the AHRC-funded project 'The Gascon Rolls' which intends to publish both online and as a printed version summaries in English of the content of this largely unpublished source. He gained his Doctorate at the University of Oxford after having been a graduate student at St John's College, Oxford, and a student in the history faculties of Paris I – Sorbonne and Bordeaux. He is a specialist of the Anglo-French relationship during the later Middle Ages and works particularly on the history of the Anglo-Gascon duchy of Aquitaine (or Guyenne).

David Simpkin specialises in the military service and culture of the English aristocracy during the late thirteenth and early fourteenth centuries. He has also researched and published on English armies and soldiers during the Hundred Years War as a member of the recent Soldier in Later Medieval England project. He obtained his PhD from Hull in 2007 and is currently Honorary Visiting Fellow at the ICMA Centre, University of Reading.

Andrew Spencer was educated at King's College London, and Peterhouse, Cambridge. He is a British Academy Post-Doctoral Fellow and a Junior Research Fellow at Corpus Christi College, Cambridge. He has published on politics and warfare in the reign of Edward I.

List of Abbreviations

AHRC	Arts and Humanities Research Council
AN	Archives Nationales de France, Paris
Arch. Dépt.	Archives Départementales
BIHR	*Bulletin of the Institute of Historical Research*
BL	British Library, London
BnF	Bibliothèque Nationale de France, Paris
CCR	*Calendar of the Close Rolls (1272–1485)*, 45 vols (London, 1892–1954)
CDS	*Calendar of Documents Relating to Scotland*, ed. J. Bain, 4 vols (Edinburgh 1881–8)
Complete Peerage	*The Complete Peerage*, by G.E. Cockayne, revised and edited by V. Gibbs, H.A. Doubleday, Lord Howard de Walden and G.H. White, 13 vols (London, 1910–59)
CPR	*Calendar of the Patent Rolls Preserved in the PRO (1232–1509)*, 52 vols (London, 1891–1916)
EHR	*English Historical Review*
NAS	National Archives of Scotland, Edinburgh
ODNB	*Oxford Dictionary of National Biography*, Oxford University Press, online edn
Parl. Writs	*Parliamentary Writs and Writs of Military Summons*, ed. F. Palgrave, 2 vols in 4 parts (London, 1827–34)
PROME	*The Parliament Rolls of Medieval England 1275–1504*, 13 vols (general editor C. Given-Wilson) (Woodbridge, 2005)
Rot. Scot.	*Rotuli Scotiae in turri Londoniensi et in domo Westmonasteriensi asservati, 1291–1516*, ed. D. Macpherson, 2 vols (London, 1814–19)
Scotland in 1298	*Scotland in 1298: Documents Relating to the Campaign of Edward I in that Year*, ed. H. Gough (London, 1888)
TNA	The National Archives, Kew
TRHS	*Transactions of the Royal Historical Society*
VCH	*Victoria History of the Counties of England*

Introduction

There are few areas of medieval studies that have flourished so much in recent years as military history. This volume represents a further flowering. The seeds of its contents were sown at a conference held at the ICMA Centre, University of Reading, in July 2009. They germinated there thanks to the energetic discussion of all participants, have subsequently been nurtured and pruned by reviewers, and are now presented in full bloom as significant contributions to the study of the individual soldier in the fourteenth century.

From the outset, our intention had been to invite contributors carrying out grass roots research in archival, as opposed to chronicle, sources, so that the conference and any publications would be genuinely new and ground-breaking. This was a natural development of our own research project under the auspices of which the conference was held – 'The Soldier in Later Medieval England'. This project was funded by the Arts and Humanities Research Council (AHRC) for three years from 2006, with Adrian Bell and Anne Curry as co-investigators, Andy King and David Simpkin as research assistants, and Adam Chapman as doctoral student. Our aim was to produce an on-line searchable database of all soldiers known to have served the English crown between 1369 and 1453. This information was collected from a vast array of muster and retinue rolls held in English and French archives, and from the letters of protection and attorney which some soldiers took out to protect their domestic interests during their military service. The database currently includes over 250,000 service records as well as supporting materials. It was formally launched during the conference, and generated a huge amount of media interest worldwide. The project team found themselves being called out of the conference by their University media teams to give interviews on the *Today* programme on BBC Radio Four, on Five Live and on assorted local radio stations, as well as making international broadcasts in Canada, the USA and Australia. The project website was featured as the most shared site on the BBC Online front page, with an associated news story. This in turn was picked up by the national and international print media: we knew we had nowhere else to go when we were covered by the *Rocky Mountain Independent*! Over the following three months the site (www.medievalsoldier.org) enjoyed over three and a half million hits in addition to the many queries sent by family historians to the project team. It continues to be used widely by both professional and amateur historians. Some of this enthusiasm can be seen in the Soldier profiles written by a number of our users.[1] Several other publications

---

[1] See, for instance, the soldier profiles researched and written by David Large, David Judd, Randolph Jones and Richard Leathes on www.medievalsoldier.org.

have arisen out of the project:[2] a team-written monograph is close to completion, and a further collection of essays arising out of the conference, but focusing this time on weapons and military organisation, has been accepted for publication as a special issue of the *Journal of Medieval History* in 2011.[3]

The aim of this volume, then, is to bring together innovative and ground-breaking research on armies and combatants during the long fourteenth century, in keeping with the working principles of the 'Soldier in Later Medieval England' project. It is, therefore, appropriate that the collection begins with an ambitious and thought-provoking paper by Andrew Ayton, who takes as his theme 'Military Service and the Dynamics of Recruitment in Fourteenth-Century England'. Drawing on his own extensive researches on the armies of Edward III's reign, recent work on military service under Edwards I and II, the Court of Chivalry and the data collections produced and made publicly available during the 'Soldier' project, Ayton produces a coherent conceptual framework for understanding medium-term change and continuity in English armies of the period. Underpinning the analysis is a belief – fundamental to Ayton's work – that the best way to get to grips with the organisational complexities of these armies (which, during the century, evolved from a partly 'feudal' to a fully contractual form via a significant 'hybrid' stage) is by considering in detail the personal linkages that existed at retinue-level among individual combatants and their retinue leaders. By tracing the threads connecting single warriors to the sometimes vast armies assembled at muster via a number of intermediate recruitment stages, and by carefully unpicking the ways in which these connections became subtly (and sometimes drastically) altered over time as a consequence of both endogenous and exogenous stimuli, Ayton is able to weave together a convincing explanation for the increasingly fluid and unstable army compositions of the later fourteenth century. This is all the more valuable for the reason that, up until now, such over-arching causational models of development have been lacking, if only because of the gaps that until recently existed in the prosopographical data and analyses available on English fourteenth-century armies. In some ways, then, this paper is proof that 'military service prosopography' is now at a stage of facilitating

[2]   Including: Anne Curry, Adrian R. Bell, Andy King and David Simpkin, 'New Regime, New Army? Henry IV's Scottish Expedition of 1400', *EHR* 125, 517 (December, 2010), pp. 1382–413; David Simpkin, 'New Muster – Related Sources for Henry IV's Army in Scotland', *Archives* xxxv, 123 (2010), pp. 1–18; Andy King, '"What Werre Amounteth": The Military Experience of Knights of the Shire, 1369–1389', *History* 95, 320 (2010), pp. 418–36; Andy King, 'Sir William Clifford: Rebellion and Reward in Henry IV's Affinity', *The Fifteenth Century IX. English and Continental Perspectives*, ed. Linda Clark (Woodbridge, 2010), pp. 139–54; A.J. Chapman, 'Welshmen in the Armies of Edward I', in *The Impact of the Edwardian Castles in Wales*, ed. D. Williams and J. Kenyon (Oxford, 2009).

[3]   A follow-on to the 2009 conference was held as a strand within the annual Fifteenth Century Conference 2010, at the University of Southampton. Papers delivered at this event, and focused on fifteenth century armies, will form the core of a guest edited issue of the *Journal of Medieval Military History*, vol. IX (Woodbridge, 2011), eds Anne Curry and Adrian R. Bell.

broad comparative interpretations, something that can certainly only aid further debate, and of course research, in this area in future.

There then follow three papers looking at patterns of military service in Edwardian armies of the late thirteenth and early fourteenth centuries. Two of these focus on the English gentry, while the third considers the contribution to the war-effort made by an altogether more obscure group, the leaders of arrayed foot-soldiers.

Andrew Spencer takes up the theme of 'Gentry Enthusiasm for Edward I's Wars' during the years of most intense campaigning, 1296–1307. Utilising a sample of gentry, he seeks to ascertain whether the political unease of the final years of the reign had a negative effect on the gentry's willingness to take up arms. He finds that this was so, with levels of participation peaking for the Falkirk campaign of 1298 but much lower in years marked by political and military crisis, such as 1300, 1301 and 1306. Moreover, he finds that seldom can more than 40 per cent of the gentry of any given county be shown to have served on a particular campaign, with participation rates usually between 10 and 25 per cent. While acknowledging the incompleteness and limitations of the military service records, Spencer argues that these figures 'are not hugely encouraging for gentry participation', with particular groups, such as knights of the shire, showing lower levels of involvement than might be expected. Seeking to explain these trends, Spencer argues that the answer lies both in a general lack of gentry interest in the king's wars and, more specifically, a growing political hostility during the final years of the reign brought about by a combination of financial exhaustion and the browbeating tactics of an unswerving king. These growing tensions were, of course, to have dire consequences during the reign of Edward I's successor. Spencer demonstrates, however, that they were already apparent before Edward I's death, not least in the declining levels of military participation among the gentry.

Offering a different angle on a similar topic, David Simpkin explores patterns of gentry service during the reigns of Edward I and Edward II through an integrated study of the landholding and military service records. Seeking to move away from traditional studies that focus on the gentry at the level of the county or locality, Simpkin argues that the way forward might well lie in a more thorough exposition of the extant sources at national level and an examination of the gentry's socio-military networks across a broader canvas. This approach requires the computerisation of vast amounts of data. Simpkin makes a start by combining the full range of military service records at his disposal with the full set of landholding returns for the counties of Nottinghamshire and Cambridgeshire from the years 1285, 1302–3 and 1316. In drawing on evidence from the wapentakes and hundreds within these counties, Simpkin argues that it is possible 'to go beyond the rather static impression of social networks provided by the county towards an understanding of these networks that is more multi-dimensional and, consequently, realistic'. However, Simpkin's main aim is to highlight the potential benefits of a combined analysis of landholding and military service records and to draw attention 'to what might be made possible if such a study were extended to incorporate the landholding community of the greater part of the realm'. Utilising the evidence from Nottinghamshire and Cambridgeshire, Simpkin finds that the data throw up numerous interpretative difficulties due to the complexity of gentry landholding, the incompleteness of the source materials and the consequent inadequacies of focusing on only a couple of counties: a small piece of the jigsaw. Nevertheless, he argues that, from the evidence for Nottinghamshire and Cambridgeshire and the smaller administrative divisions within, there are good reasons for expanding this methodology. 'The way forward', Simpkin suggests, 'is through the study of social networks in a broader sense' than traditional gentry studies have allowed.

Staying with the theme of military service during the reign of Edward I, David Bachrach steps into largely uncharted territory by focusing on the military careers of, and levels of military professionalism among, the king's 'centurions'. Bachrach draws on 'a *corpus* of about two thousand documents dealing with Edward's campaigns, principally in Scotland during the last decade of his reign' in an attempt to find evidence of repeated service among the leaders of the king's infantry troops. Although many of the 1,200 *centenarii* in Bachrach's sample 'appear but a single time in the pay records examined thus far as leading infantry companies', nevertheless he finds considerable evidence of men 'leading infantry companies year after year, and in some cases for more than a decade'. This, he argues, supplies evidence of their military professionalism, a professionalism that is particularly evident among the leaders of crossbowmen. Within this body of professional 'centurions' were, on the one hand, men who served repeatedly in this capacity over a number of years and campaigns and, on the other, those who switched between service as 'centurions' and service as *soldarii* (paid fighting men who were not obligated to serve). Bachrach maintains that such distinctions in terminology were meaningful in denoting different types of soldier owing to the fact that clerks 'tended to use standardized terminology to describe military matters'. A third group of 'centurions' went on to serve as leaders 'of what appear to have been contract companies of professional foot archers'. Thus, there was more than one career path open to these men. Bachrach argues that repeated and varied service of this type among Edward's infantry leaders was crucial, as it enabled them 'to keep well-informed, through personal experience, about the state of political and military affairs in the regions in which he led his men'. In turn, this gave the men under their command greater confidence in the abilities of their leaders.

The papers in this volume have an integrity derived from their source base and their originality, but they range widely in time and space. We were keen to ensure a good geographical spread, as England's soldiers did not operate in a vacuum. The next three papers look at soldiery using a regional focus (as does the paper by Pépin), through England's closest neighbours, Scotland and Wales, and then focusing on the careers of the combatants at the battle of the Thirty in Brittany in 1351.

Iain MacInnes examines the support in Scotland on a regional level for Edward
Balliol after 1332, in the war he fought with English backing against David II, the
son of Robert Bruce. There were a number of Scottish magnates who had lost
their lands for their opposition to King Robert, and others who had submitted
to his allegiance only reluctantly, under force. Such men were ready to support
Balliol when he invaded. Nor were they necessarily alienated by his dependence
on Edward III's aid and his cession of much of southern Scotland to English
occupation. For some Scots the English were a lesser evil than the Bruce dynasty,
which still lacked legitimacy in the eyes of Balliol's supporters. It is of course
enormously difficult to uncover the motives which determined a man's allegiance,
and many Scots undoubtedly went over to Balliol out of cold calculation of what
would best serve their own interests. However, many of Balliol's supporters did
remain remarkably faithful to his cause, and some were never reconciled with the
Bruce party, eventually forfeiting their lands. All of this suggests a genuine and
deeply held loyalty to the Balliol cause, which has tended to be overlooked or
dismissed by historians. Finally, although support for Balliol was not necessarily
the same as support for the English, the failure of Balliol's kingship brought
some Scots into English service, and some such ended up pursuing careers as
English soldiers.

Chapman's paper considers the careers of the rather select group of Welshmen
who became knights in the fourteenth century. The role of the *Uchelwyr* (lit. High
Men), descended from pre-Conquest princes and nobility, in the society of post-
Conquest Wales has been a common feature in the study of the fourteenth and
fifteenth centuries. This has, however, largely focused upon their relative decline
in status rather than their importance as agents of the English crown. Since
Welshmen contributed to the wars of the three Edwards in Wales, Scotland and
France in enormous numbers, the contribution of their leaders should not be
underestimated. These men reflect the class who did well from the Conquest –
men who, during the wars between Llywelyn ap Gruffudd and Edward I, were
brought up in the English court and others, in the second half of the century,
who rose to prominence through their military ability, a fact celebrated in the
praise of poets and in the rewards of administrative office.

One of the great chivalric episodes of the fourteenth century forms the subject
of Michael Jones's paper. The 'Battle of the Thirty' of 26 March 1351 was a minor
skirmish which has entered into legend. The fight was unusual in that it was a
set-piece engagement fought, in answer to the challenge of Jean de Beaumanoir,
captain of Josselin, between thirty men, English, Breton and German, under
Robert de Bamborough, captain of Ploërmel, and thirty Bretons under Beaumanoir. The Bretons fighting against Bamborough's force represent not the elite of
the Breton nobility but provide, in microcosm, an indication of the experiences
of Breton troops in the wars of the fourteenth century. What this study reveals
are the bonds of kinship and camaraderie present in this group drawn from the
north of the duchy; many were to serve together in the same battles later in their
careers. Overall, the essay shows the importance not only of pre-existing links

but also those generated in war, and in this case, in victory. It is also unique in managing to mention the 'delectable' Nastassja Kinski and Don Bradman within a few pages of each other!

The volume concludes with three studies focusing upon detailed case studies of soldiers and taking alternative approaches to highlight the ups and downs of military careers in the late fourteenth century. Despite the overall emphasis of the volume on research in archival sources, it is not surprising to find the chronicles of Froissart surfacing on several occasions, given their continuing fascination and domination of all things to do with the Hundred Years War. One of the most intriguing passages is found in Book Three, where Froissart, during his visit to Orthez, 'interviews' a Gascon routier, the Bascot de Mauléon. Kenneth Fowler suggested in 2001 that the Bascot was 'possibly a figure of Froissart's imagination', on the grounds that he could not find mention of him in archival sources.[4] Pépin proves that the Bascot did exist. By a detailed study of a list of pro-English fortresses in Guyenne and of the financial records of the count of Armagnac flesh is put on his bones. The Bascot's career can be traced from the 1350s through service as a routier captain with the king of Navarre in Normandy in the 1360s; by the early 1380s he acknowledged the authority of the king of England and received pay from the count of Armagnac for guarding several castles. Furthermore, the Mauléon family is located and the linguistic context revolving around the term 'bascot' explained. Even if there remains doubt over how well Froissart might have understood the Bascot's version of French, we surely have here a real insight into the experience of a routier soldier as well as into Froissart's perception of him.

The plight of English prisoners in the 1370s is the subject of Rémy Ambühl's paper. Capture was an increasingly common hazard for English soldiers during this period of military reversal; and, indeed, some had the misfortune to be taken two or three times, or even more. As soldiers were allowed to keep the greater part of the ransoms of any prisoners they captured, so there was no obligation for the king to aid men who were themselves captured while in his service. Certainly, given the abject state of royal finances, aid for prisoners was always not forthcoming; and even when it was, grants of money could be distinctly parsimonious. Nevertheless, other less expensive forms of royal patronage might help to restore a captive's finances after he had ransomed himself, such as a marriage to an heiress or a grant of crown office. In the absence of direct royal aid soldiers could turn to their comrades or captains for help, but financial assistance would commonly take the form of a loan rather than an outright grant, still leaving the ransomed prisoner indebted. However, one means of turning military defeat to advantage was to demand the release of English captives as part of the terms for

---

[4] K. Fowler, *Medieval Mercenaries. I. The Great Companies* (Oxford, 2001), p. 14, n. 53.

the surrender of besieged towns to the French. And this implies a high degree of solidarity within the military community.

The final paper draws upon depositions of soldiers from the Court of Chivalry (as did the first paper) to develop case studies of the military career for English soldiers in the later fourteenth century. While previous studies and biographers have used these depositions perhaps uncritically, this essay measures these witness statements against the military service records held by the Exchequer and Chancery (and available online at www.medievalsoldier.org). These governmental sources also need to be treated with care, but the overall picture of military service seems to be accurately stated. If anything, the issue appears to be certain soldiers 'understating' their service in order to protect the interests of the plaintiff for whom they were speaking in the Court of Chivalry. From the resulting case studies, it can be shown that the average military career started early, lasted a good number of years, involved a variety of theatres and covered great distances, with travel as far as Jerusalem not being so uncommon an occurrence.

It only remains to acknowledge the help we have received in organising the conference and in preparing this volume. The conference ran smoothly and was blessed with a plethora of excellent papers, and the sessions were managed by a host of distinguished chairs. The discussion was always helpful and lively, and all participants were fully involved in the discussions both in the lecture theatre and spilling over into coffee breaks, lunch and dinner. We were also very pleased to welcome Robert Hardy as our special guest. The conference was kindly hosted within the ICMA Centre and we are grateful for being allowed use of this facility and the support of colleagues, including Liz Adams (who did the accounts), Leanne Ley (who did everything else) and Sam Gibbs and Tony Moore who gave voluntary help throughout. We will never forget the interactive, multi-media longbow demonstration organised by Randall Moffett and delivered by Mark Stretton, Nick Ashley and Glennan Carnie. Caroline Palmer of Boydell and Brewer generously gave her time to provide a bookshop at the conference and has worked closely with us to bring this book to fruition. The finished book also owes a debt of thanks to our panel of reviewers, including Andrew Ayton, Michael Prestwich, Michael Jones and Chris Given-Wilson, whose in-depth commentaries have focused and improved every essay in this volume. Finally, a memorable conference dinner was held at Miah's Garden of Gulab in Reading, and we are grateful for their patience and for graciously accommodating a rabble of medieval military historians who behaved little better than their fourteenth-century warriors.

1

Military Service and the Dynamics of Recruitment in Fourteenth-Century England

ANDREW AYTON

The study of military service in late medieval England, of the men who fought and of the circumstances and mentalities that caused them to take up arms, has been transformed in recent years. In 1994 it was possible to write that '[t]here are few aspects of medieval English history as worthy of investigation, yet as neglected, as military service'.[1] Indeed, the principal aim of the book that opened with these words was to establish methodological and interpretative foundations for the study of the armies and military communities of fourteenth-century England. Such foundation-laying could not have been achieved in an academic vacuum: it was preceded, accompanied and informed by a range of important work on late medieval military organisation and army recruitment.[2] But in the mid 1990s there was no immediate prospect that Philippe Contamine's magisterial *Guerre, état et société à la fin du Moyen Age* would be emulated in England. Since then, it is pleasing to report, purposeful advances have been made, notably two book-length military prosopographical studies[3] and the completion of the Soldier in Later Medieval England Project.[4] The latter has provided online access to all

[1] A. Ayton, *Knights and Warhorses: Military Service and the English Aristocracy under Edward III* (Woodbridge, 1994), p. 1.
[2] The pioneering work of J.E. Morris, R.A. Newhall, A.E. Prince and N.B. Lewis was followed up and extended in various ways by, among others, M.R. Powicke, Maurice Keen, James Sherborne, Ranald Nicholson, Michael Prestwich and Anthony Goodman, and then by a new generation, including Simon Walker, Philip Morgan and Anne Curry. For references, see Ayton, *Knights and Warhorses*, pp. 272–89 (Bibliography).
[3] A.R. Bell, *War and the Soldier in the Fourteenth Century* (Woodbridge, 2004); D. Simpkin, *The English Aristocracy at War: From the Welsh Wars of Edward I to the Battle of Bannockburn* (Woodbridge, 2008). Also, A. Ayton, 'The English Army at Crécy', in A. Ayton and P. Preston, *The Battle of Crécy, 1346* (Woodbridge, 2005), pp. 159–251; A. Curry, *Agincourt: A New History* (Stroud, 2005), chapter 3.
[4] See www.medievalsoldier.org.

surviving military service records for the period 1369–1453, a remarkable achieve-
ment, efficiently realised. Given that, elsewhere, similar datasets have been, or are
being, compiled for the preceding century, there is good reason to hope that an
appreciation of the importance of military service, through direct engagement
with the collective experience of those who fought, will now have altogether
more influence on research. Naturally, the most immediate impact will be on the
study of England's wars and the manpower, resources and institutions that were
employed to wage them. Reconstruction of military events, from major campaigns
to routine garrison patrols, should now be informed by prosopographical study
of the men involved. Viewing an army from the perspective of the biographies of
the men who served in it can be a first step towards transforming that army from
a characterless numerical abstraction, an accounting summary on a payroll, into a
vibrant social entity composed of a multitude of distinguishable individuals who
together give an ephemeral institution a distinctive collective identity. But the
benefits of knowing who served, when, where and with whom, should extend far
beyond the realm of 'military history' as traditionally understood. Recapturing
the martial service of individuals, groups and communities in England has implications for our understanding of politics, local and national; and, above all, it
can illuminate many aspects of social, economic and cultural life. Back in 1994
it was argued that '[t]here can be few major research undertakings in the field
of late medieval English history that would offer such wide-ranging benefits as
a full-scale reconstruction of the military community'.[5] While fulfilment of that
ambitious goal still lies some way in the future, the data upon which the necessary nominal record linkage and career reconstitution could be built is now far
more accessible than before.

Scholarly engagement with the administrative records that document military service in fourteenth-century England has, therefore, been gathering pace in
recent years. Accompanying and, indeed, contextualising this prosopographical
work has been a deepening understanding of army structures and organisational
change and a growing appreciation of the role played by particular sub-sets of the
population, the military communities, in influencing the structure and composition of those armies.[6] This paper focuses on a subject that should be at the very
heart of this burgeoning field of research: the dynamics of recruitment. It seeks
to identify and conceptualise the circumstances and forces that, individually and
through their interaction, contributed to, accompanied or were generated by the
recruitment of armies in late medieval England. In doing so, it adds a dynamic

---

[5]   Ayton, *Knights and Warhorses*, 2.
[6]   The 'military communities' of Edwardian England, which were communities 'of the mind
and of function, of shared mentality, skills and perhaps focus: of shared identity', are examined
in A. Ayton, 'Armies and Military Communities in Fourteenth-Century England', in *Soldiers,
Nobles and Gentlemen: Essays in Honour of Maurice Keen*, ed. P. Coss and C. Tyerman
(Woodbridge, 2009), pp. 215–39. The ground-breaking study of this phenomenon was
P. Morgan, *War and Society in Medieval Cheshire, 1277–1403* (Manchester, 1987).

dimension to a model, previously presented,[7] which attempts to capture the essence of the late medieval army by highlighting its distinctive characteristics, most notably the multi-faceted relationship that it had with the military communities from which its captains recruited their men. As we shall see, a conceptual grasp of the dynamics of recruitment provides the key to understanding the changing character of both armies and military communities during the 'long' fourteenth century. But as conceptual as that grasp needs to be, investigation of the dynamics of recruitment must also be grounded in the concrete prosopographical data that enable us to reconstruct, in as far as the surviving sources permit, the composition of army retinues over an extended period. It is with such prosopographical method, the patterns of service that are revealed by it and the mechanics of retinue formation that are essential to an understanding of those patterns that we shall begin.

*

By some margin the most fully documented of the major contingents in the English army that fought the battle of Crécy is the retinue that served under the banner of Thomas Beauchamp, earl of Warwick, the marshal of the army. For most of the retinues in that army, establishing the names of the combatant manpower is dependent upon three types of documentation: records connected with the issue of letters of protection; documents of various kinds generated by the implementation of a new, but short-lived, form of military assessment based on landed income; and charters of pardon, which are most accessible in their enrolled form.[8] The coverage of each of these categories of documentation is (for different reasons) no more than partial and each poses interpretative problems of a distinctive kind. Consequently, what emerges from correlation of these sources at retinue level are lists of names that are not only incomplete but also, in all likelihood, not consistently reliable. How we would welcome comprehensive retinue rolls like those that are available for the armies of 1387 and 1388, or even horse inventories of the kind that illuminate parts of those of the mid to late 1330s.[9] Unfortunately, with regard to the English armies that campaigned in France from 1337 to 1360, such records have survived only occasionally and the Crécy host is not one of those few well-documented occasions. Thus, although probably exceptional for that army, the materials that we have for Warwick's retinue certainly fall short, in terms of form and content, of a genuine retinue roll; and

<hr>

7   A. Ayton, 'From Muhi to Mohács: Armies and Combatants in Later Medieval European Transcultural Wars', in *Transcultural Wars from the Middle Ages to the Twenty-First Century*, ed. H.-H. Kortüm (Berlin, 2006), pp. 213–47 (241–7); Ayton, 'Armies and Military Communities in Fourteenth-Century England', pp. 231–6.

8   Ayton and Preston, *The Battle of Crécy*, pp. 198–9; A. Ayton, 'The English Army and the Normandy Campaign of 1346', in *England and Normandy in the middle ages*, ed. D. Bates and A. Curry (London and Rio Grande, 1994), pp. 253–68 (254–9).

9   Bell, *War and the Soldier*, pp. 52–68; Ayton, *Knights and Warhorses*, pp. 170–77.

in order to appreciate even this partial picture it is necessary to bring together documents that are dispersed in various record classes at the National Archives.

The most important group of documents consists of four items currently located in the files of warrants for protections and attorneys. Together they reveal both the structural make-up of the earl of Warwick's retinue and the place of many individual combatants in the hierarchy of relationships within that retinue. The core document of the group names the earl's principal lieutenants, his three bannerets, and specifies the number of men-at-arms serving in each of their sub-retinues.[10] Also named, in a left-hand column, are twenty knights with the number of accompanying esquires noted against each name (thirty in all),[11] and, in the right-hand column, a further list of thirty-one men (plus two unnamed 'compaignons'), who appear to be combatant esquires.[12] The knights and esquires serving in the sub-retinues of Warwick's three bannerets (or at least most of them) are listed on separate rolls that, in terms of provenance, do not seem to be closely related to the core document.[13] Of the three sub-retinue rolls, Sir Thomas Ughtred's appears to be the odd one out. Headed (in Latin) 'Names of the men-at-arms who are of the retinue of Thomas Ughtred', it lists, in addition to the leader, four knights and sixteen esquires, which is precisely the number that the core document specifies and perhaps suggests that the document is a form of retinue roll.[14] If so, it was also deemed useful to note the names of the men who were acting as attorneys for Ughtred and three of his knights. The roll of Sir Aimery St Amand's sub-retinue lists two knights and sixteen others; that of Sir Robert Scales, three knights and nine esquires.[15] Neither, therefore, is a full retinue roll. They, together with the core document, may have been connected with the time-honoured process whereby captains applied on behalf of their men for the issue of letters of protection, though if this is the case they do not mention it;[16] and, more importantly, a comparison of these rolls with the enrolled lists of protection recipients reveals much disparity in name spellings, suggesting that the former were not the documentary source for the latter. A

[10] TNA C 81/1742, no. 26. The bannerets' sub-retinues: Sir Thomas Ughtred (20 men-at-arms); Sir Aimery de St Amand (20 men-at-arms); Sir Robert Scales (15 men-at-arms).
[11] Sir Walter Dastyn is listed twice. Ten of the knights have two esquires and ten have one.
[12] It is likely that some or all of the 30 unnamed esquires are included among these 31 named individuals.
[13] The four documents display no consistency in language, format or name forms.
[14] TNA C 81/1741, no. 10. Although the document does not mention the earl of Warwick explicitly, correlation with other records allows us to link it to that earl's retinue with confidence.
[15] TNA C 81/1742, no. 25 (St Amand); C 81/1742, no. 31 (Scales). The former has been joined to the core document for Warwick's retinue in the National Archives file, the latter makes specific reference to service with the earl of Warwick.
[16] Ayton, *Knights and Warhorses*, pp. 157–62. We would not expect such documents to list all the men-at-arms in a retinue and, as the many surviving examples demonstrate, they had no common format.

characteristic that these three documents do have in common is that, to a greater or lesser degree, they were all used in connection with the new system of military assessment that was implemented at the time of the Crécy–Calais campaign. In each case, individuals whose names are 'pointed' or accompanied by annotations specifying counties are to be found on the Treaty Rolls with exonerations from the assessment.[17]

Taken together, these four documents supply the names of three bannerets, twenty-nine knights and seventy-two other men, though nine of the latter are illegible.[18] Comparison of these numbers with the manpower assigned to Warwick's retinue in the various post-medieval copies of the army payroll suggests that our nominal roll is far from complete.[19] The mounted archers who were attached to the retinue – in the region of 150 men – are wholly absent from our roll, and it may well be that it includes the names of no more than two-thirds of the men-at-arms who were actually serving under the earl's banner in 1346.[20] As we have seen, the bannerets' rolls omit very few names (five out of fifty-five), so in order to accommodate the greater part of the shortfall – perhaps a dozen knights and three dozen esquires – we need to turn to the core document for Warwick's retinue. The ratio of knights to esquires that we find there (1:1.5) suggests that some of the latter have not been named. The number of esquires assigned to individual knights, never more than two, also raises suspicions. Sir Robert Herle has two esquires, whereas in his indenture of retinue, dated 20 April 1339, it is stipulated that in wartime he would bring four to the earl's retinue.[21] If, as seems likely, most of the esquires listed on the core document were serving in the knights' companies, we would also need to allow for the earl's personal esquires, men such as John de Morehalle, who is described

---

[17]   Scales's roll is most clearly related to the military assessment: 8 of the 13 names on the roll are assigned to counties in which they were exonerated from their assessment in May 1346: G. Wrottesley, *Crecy and Calais from the Original Records in the Public Record Office* (London, 1898), p. 83 [henceforward Wrottesley]; TNA C 76/22, m. 22d. This applies to two names on St Amand's roll, which are also pointed (Wrottesley, pp. 83–4). Six of the names on the core document are pointed and they also have enrolled exonerations (Wrottesley, pp. 82, 84, 86).

[18]   Some of the other, partially illegible, names can be recovered by reference to other documents.

[19]   For the loss of the original *vadia guerre* and related accounts for the Crécy–Calais campaign (recorded in a book of foreign expenses for Walter Wetwang's term as Keeper of the King's Wardrobe) and for an assessment of the various surviving early modern transcripts of those accounts, see Ayton, 'The English Army at Crécy', pp. 160–62, 230–41.

[20]   See BL Harleian MS 3968, fos 114r–129r (at fo. 115r), which assigns to Warwick's retinue 3 bannerets, 41 knights, 106 esquires (in all, including the earl, 151 men-at-arms) and 154 mounted archers. The figures in College of Arms MS 2 M 16, the most widely used of the various imperfect early modern abstracts of Wetwang's payroll, include an implausibly high number of knights (3 bannerets, 64 knights, 131 esquires and 149 archers). Wrottesley, p. 193.

[21]   TNA C 81/1742, no. 26; 'Private Indentures for Life Service in Peace and War, 1278–1476', ed. M. Jones and S. Walker, *Camden Miscellany, XXXII*, Camden Fifth Series, iii (1994), no. 37 (pp. 70–71).

in another document as the earl's *vallettus*.[22] Some of the missing men can be identified by searching the other records that document military service at this time.[23] Thirteen can be found among those who secured letters of protection for service under Warwick's banner in the summer of 1346,[24] and one new name can be added from those who, at that time, were said to be fulfilling their military assessment in person.[25] This means that we have the legible names of 109 individuals, or perhaps about 70 per cent of the men-at-arms who were in pay in Warwick's retinue at the start of the campaign.[26]

The fact that Warwick's men were serving in the army's vanguard battle and, therefore, in the forefront of the fighting at Crécy confers upon them particular interest. To what extent was this a retinue of veterans, old hands at war who had brought to the fields of France a wealth of first-hand experience that, irrespective of the unprecedented scale and drama of this battlefield contest, would settle nerves and guide weapons? To what extent, moreover, had Warwick assembled a group of men who, whether through shared origins or comradeship in arms, were well acquainted with one another? Had he, indeed, managed to re-assemble a settled team of warriors, or at least a collection of settled teams that would mesh together to form an effective, composite force? Whether we can formulate convincing answers to these important questions depends upon how fully the military careers of the men who served under Warwick can be reconstituted. Owing to the methodological problems that beset prosopography of this particular kind – problems that arise from the incompleteness and uneven coverage of the sources and that attend any attempt reliably to link fragmentary scraps of information relating to the same person – the reconstitution of military careers can never be more than a partially successful exercise.[27] More can be learned of the careers of knights than of those of esquires. A man's earliest experiences of war are often poorly documented. Family members with the same forename may be difficult to distinguish in the records. We must be aware too that our records are not only incomplete, but inconsistently so from campaign to campaign. For example, while Warwick's retinue in 1345 is as well documented as its successor

[22] Wrottesley, p. 107 (for his enrolled protection, dated 20 June 1346, see 91).

[23] To maintain consistency of focus, records that might refer to men who had joined the earl's retinue during the later stages of what was a long campaign have been excluded from consideration.

[24] These include 1 man who certainly was a knight in 1346 and 2 others who were by 1347–8. All told, only 33 men intending to serve with the earl are identifiable through enrolled letters of protection: Wrottesley, pp. 91, 96 (incomplete); TNA C 76/22, m. 6.

[25] Of 25 men who have enrolled exonerations dating from before the embarkation for Normandy, only 2 do not appear in the TNA C 81 documents discussed above, and 1 of these has an enrolled protection. Wrottesley, pp. 81–6; C 76/22, m. 15d.

[26] Three bannerets, 30 (at most, 32) knights and 76 others, most of whom were combatant esquires.

[27] Ayton, 'The English army at Crécy', pp. 197–200.

in 1346 (we know the names of ninety-eight men),[28] of the ninety-two men-at-arms for whom he apparently received pay for the summer campaign of 1335 only two can be identified from enrolled letters of protection.[29] Awareness of these problems is essential but should not be disabling. It should influence approaches to analysis, ensuring that they exploit the strengths of the sources and not be unduly handicapped by their limitations; and it should inform assessment of the results, whether concerning individual careers or patterns of collective experience.

To begin with how experienced Warwick's men were in 1346: it can be shown that all three of his bannerets and over half of his knights had been campaigning since at least the mid 1330s, in most cases with some regularity.[30] Sir Thomas Ughtred, Warwick's lieutenant as sub-marshal of the army, was a veteran of Bannockburn (1314),[31] and while such martial longevity may have been exceptional in Warwick's retinue, there were many of the earl's men-at-arms at Crécy, knights and esquires, who had taken up the sword during the Scottish campaigns of the 1330s and brought that experience onto the continental stage. And, by 1346, Warwick's men-at-arms were also well acquainted with campaigning conditions in France. All except two of his knights had fought there before, the majority on at least two or three occasions. Such precision is not possible with the esquires as a group, but it is likely that the frequent service of a man such as Thomas Swathyng is indeed representative of many of his less well-documented comrades in arms. The other striking feature of Swathyng's career, that before joining the earl of Warwick's retinue in 1346 (via Scales's company) he had served repeatedly with the earl of Northampton,[32] is certainly typical of the period. For if we were to offer a career generalisation that applied to many – and perhaps most – of the men who served under Warwick's banner in 1346 it would stress loyalty rather than inconstancy. As a consequence, we would be justified in characterising the composition of the earl's retinue in the 1340s in terms of stability born of repeated service rather than discontinuity and rapid turnover. At one end of the spectrum was the loyalty of such men as Sir William Lucy and Sir Robert Herle, who had fought with the earl at every

---

[28] The materials for 1345 resemble those for 1346. A core document (TNA C 81/1742, no. 17) lists in a left-hand column, under 'Le counte de Warrewyk', 13 knights and 32 esquires, and in a right-hand column the sub-retinues of Sir Aimery de St Amand (3 knights and 10 esquires) and Sir Robert Scales (3 knights and 11 esquires), plus an extra knight. A separate roll (C 81/1741, no. 21) lists Sir Thomas Ughtred's sub-retinue (4 knights and 18 esquires).

[29] BL Cotton MS, Nero C VIII, fo. 236r; C 71/15, mm 27, 28.

[30] Seventeen of the 30 knights since at least 1337.

[31] A. Ayton, 'Sir Thomas Ughtred and the Edwardian Military Revolution', in *The Age of Edward III*, ed. J.S. Bothwell (York, 2001), pp. 107–32.

[32] 1336: TNA E 101/19/36, m. 5. 1337: *CPR, 1334–38*, 531. 1338: *Treaty Rolls, 1337–39*, ed. J. Ferguson (London, 1972), no. 653. 1340: C 76/15, m. 19. 1342: C 81/1735, no. 22.

opportunity during the previous ten years.[33] Indeed, at least five knights and five esquires had served unwaveringly with Warwick since 1336–7.[34] It is tempting to regard these men as the stable, reliable core within the earl's campaigning retinue and to do so would echo a long-established view of how such retinues were composed: that permanent retainers provided the 'nucleus around which ... less stable elements could collect'.[35] But closer scrutiny of the prosopographical data suggests a more dynamic model that recognises that, over time, the composition of a captain's war retinue would be subject to more complex evolutionary processes to which various forms of continuity and change contributed. If we were to hazard a descriptive term to sum up the collective state of such retinues it would be 'dynamic stability'. How it was that this collective state came about will be considered shortly. First, it is necessary to examine the evidence for repeat service under Warwick's banner.

How many of Warwick's Crécy men had served with him before and, indeed, how many remained loyal to the earl from one campaign to the next? Of the 109 identifiable individuals attached to Warwick's retinue in 1346, sixty-seven (61 per cent) were returning to his banner from the (admittedly abortive) expedition of the previous year. All told, seventy-one (65 per cent) of the earl's 'Crécy men' can be shown to have accompanied him on at least one previous occasion. As indications of the extent of continuity in the composition of Warwick's war retinues these figures are all the more striking because, as has been noted, they are based upon incomplete sources and, as a consequence, almost certainly fall short of the level of stability that actually existed. The collective experience of one consistently well-documented group within these retinues, the knights, certainly suggests that the actual level may have been higher. Of the twenty knights who are listed on the core document for the 1346 retinue, seventeen (85 per cent) had served with Warwick before, twelve of them (60 per cent) at least twice. Measurement of stability, and our interpretation of it, is affected not only by the available sources, but also by the vantage point from which the data are surveyed. In the case of Warwick's war retinues (in common with others), this is important because over time they fluctuated in size. Steady growth during the 1340s necessitated an influx of new recruits and, as a result, from the standpoint of 1345–6, the group of repeat-serving personnel, as a proportion of the whole retinue, diminished in size. But if, rather than using the expanded retinue of

---

[33] 1336: TNA E 101/19/36, m. 7d. 1337: E 101/20/17, m. 7d; 1340: C 76/15, mm. 25, 27. 1342: C 76/17, mm. 20, 39; E 36/204, fo. 88r. 1345: C 76/20, m. 11.

[34] Sir Ralph Basset, Sir Robert Herle, Sir William Lucy, Sir John Lisours, Sir Nicholas Peeche. William Bracebrigge, Philip Careles, William Carles, John Harleye, Thomas Henleye.

[35] N.B. Lewis, 'The Organisation of Indentured Retinues in Fourteenth-Century England', *TRHS* 4th ser. 27 (1945), pp. 33–4. Cf. G.A. Holmes, *The Estates of the Higher Nobility in Fourteenth-Century England* (Cambridge, 1957), p. 80. Until very recently it is indeed the instability of retinue membership, the 'strikingly rapid turnover', that has been emphasised: M. Prestwich, *Armies and Warfare in the Middle Ages: The English Experience* (New Haven and London, 1996), pp. 44–5.

1346 as the basis of measurement, we take up a different vantage point and look forward to 1346 from the past, it can be seen that nearly 70 per cent of Warwick's retinue personnel in 1345 returned in 1346, and that over half of those who can be identified as accompanying him to Brittany in 1342–3 served with him again in the mid 1340s.[36]

The extent to which the earl of Warwick's war retinues in the 1340s were settled in composition, with a significant proportion of his men offering him their services for a series of campaigns, was not exceptional for the period. Recent research has revealed such stability to have been a commonplace feature of retinues in mid-fourteenth-century English armies.[37] Indeed, more recently still, research independently conducted by David Simpkin and Andrew Spencer has uncovered the same phenomenon during the years of regular campaigning prior to the battle of Bannockburn.[38] What all this work has had in common is that it has focused on the service of retinue-based men-at-arms (knights, esquires and sergeants) in field armies, prosopographical work on other sections of those armies during the first half of the fourteenth century being hampered, to say the least, by the inadequacy of the surviving records. But it is noteworthy that studies of some of the pockets of evidence that are available have also drawn attention to stability in a variety of service contexts.[39] In this paper, however, we shall maintain our focus on retinue-based service in field armies, which is more consistently documented and which, from the middle of the century, became a particularly important organisational context for military service.

*

How is the retinue-level stability among men-at-arms that is observable in early to mid Edwardian armies to be explained and understood? It is necessary first of all to take account of long-term processes. During the reigns of the three King Edwards the forging of relationships between captains of comital and baro-

---

[36] In 1342–3 Warwick received pay for 96 men-at-arms, including 2 bannerets and 20 knights (TNA E 36/204, fo. 106r). Of 43 individuals whose names can be recovered from the records (E 36/204, fo. 88r; C 76/17, mm. 15, 16, 20, 24, 39; C 81/1742, nos 5, 7, 11, 12, 13, 14), 24 had returned to the earl's service in 1345–6. It is particularly notable that, of the 15 identifiable knights, at least 11 served with the earl in the mid-1340s.

[37] Ayton, 'The English Army at Crécy', pp. 205–15; Ayton, 'Armies and Military Communities', pp. 233–5.

[38] Simpkin, *The English Aristocracy at War*, pp. 119–41; A. Spencer, 'The Comital Military Retinue in the Reign of Edward I', *Historical Research* 83 (2008), pp. 46–59.

[39] For example, as Peter Konieczny has shown, repeat service was common in the contingents contributed to Edwardian armies by the city of London: P. Konieczny, 'London's War Effort During the Early Years of the Reign of Edward III', in *The Hundred Years War: A Wider Focus*, ed. L.J.A. Villalon and D.J. Kagay (Leiden and Boston, 2005), pp. 243–61. For stability of English garrison personnel in Scotland during the fourteenth century, see D.J. Cornell, 'Northern Castles and Garrisons in the Later Middle Ages', unpublished PhD thesis, University of Durham (2006).

nial status who needed to recruit retinues for the king's wars and those military
communities that came within their recruiting reach was an accompaniment to
– indeed, an integral part of – the 'militarisation' of the gentry. A process initi-
ated and sustained by direct engagement in war, militarisation effected a change
in outlook in those involved, individually and collectively, which in turn fuelled
further corporeal action. Thus, while the process of militarisation can be charted
in the tangible artefacts and semiology of aristocratic culture (in the evidence of
armorial dissemination, for example), the extent of it is most effectively substantiated by reference to the evidence of service actually performed. That evidence
is plentiful and what it reveals is the establishment of family traditions of
campaigning and the formation of a complex network of 'comradeship groups' at
local and regional levels, both of which were often closely associated with service
under the banners of particular noble lineages. Having been set in motion by
the wars of the first two Edwards, these processes gathered momentum during
the period of intensive campaigning in the 1330s and 1340s. This, then, is the
evolving socio-military context within which, as campaign followed campaign
and armies were raised and disbanded, clusters of knights and sergeants rode
together repeatedly and regularly serving captains were able to field retinues that
were, in part at least, settled in composition.

The relationship between, on the one hand, 'comradeship groups' and 'clusters of knights and sergeants' repeatedly riding together and, on the other, the
retinue-level stability among men-at-arms that has been observed in early- to
mid-Edwardian armies was fundamental. To understand the nature of that relationship we need to investigate the *mechanics of retinue formation*, which may
be defined as the various means and consequent processes, direct and indirect,
by which a captain assembled a retinue. They determined the structure and,
together with the captain's particular recruiting reach, shaped the operational
identity of the body of men serving under his banner; and, more generally, they
supplied the practical structures through which the dynamics of recruitment
operated. In retinue formation, a basic distinction is to be made between the
contributions made, firstly, by *groups* of men-at-arms and archers who joined
a retinue as members of contingents raised and led by bannerets, knights or
esquires, and, secondly, by *individuals* – generally esquires/sergeants and archers
– who had a direct attachment to the retinue captain. In practice, it is also necessary to distinguish, in the first category, between the miniature companies that
usually accompanied knights and the larger sub-retinues that a banneret might
contribute. The latter would in turn be composed of a combination of knightly
companies and individuals.[40]

In order to make such distinctions it is necessary to identify the hierarchy
of relationships that gave a retinue its particular structural character, and it

[40] As can be seen with particular clarity with the sub-retinue that Sir Thomas Ughtred
brought to Warwick's service in 1345. TNA C 81/1741, no. 21.

must be conceded that our documentary sources do not always make this easy.[41] Compiling a list of names for a retinue, using enrolled protections or, if we are lucky, a muster roll, is not the same as determining its structure. However, for the first half of the fourteenth century, revealing structural information can be found in a variety of documents, including a proportion of the surviving horse inventories. Take, for example, the retinue of 100 men-at-arms that the earl of Warenne led to Gascony in 1325. The size of the retinue and its period of service are documented by a pay roll,[42] while the names of about half of Warenne's men are recorded in documentation relating to the issue of letters of protection.[43] But it is only the earl's horse inventory that supplies a complete list of names organised in such a way as to reveal the internal structure of the retinue.[44] There were three sub-retinues, which altogether accounted for forty-four of the earl's 100 men-at-arms,[45] and twelve miniature companies, each led by a knight (the earl's 'bachilers'), which as a group provided a further thirty-six men-at-arms. Warenne's own 'esquiers' contributed the remaining 20 per cent of the retinue's combatant manpower. Thus, in order to assemble this retinue, Warenne had relied upon the efforts of a team of sub-contractors, three of whom were lesser captains in their own right. One of the sub-retinues contributed a quarter of the earl's manpower, while Warenne himself had a *direct* recruiting connection with only about a third of the men in his retinue. The extent to which the earl delegated the task of finding his rank and file men-at-arms to a team of subordinates is wholly typical of the period. There is, as we have seen, a similar pattern of delegation, involving three bannerets and twenty knights, in Warwick's Crécy retinue;[46] and, where the documentation permits, much the same can be seen elsewhere, though the relative contributions of contingents of different sizes to the mechanics of retinue formation did vary.

[41] For the later fourteenth century sub-contracts cast some light on the recruiting process as well as retinue structure, but survival of these documents is patchy at best. J.W. Sherborne, 'Indentured Retinues and English Expeditions to France, 1369–1380', in J. Sherborne, *War, Politics and Culture in Fourteenth-Century England*, ed. A. Tuck (London and Rio Grande, 1994), pp. 1–28 (25–8); A. Goodman, 'The Military Subcontracts of Sir Hugh Hastings', *EHR* 95 (1980), pp. 114–20; S. Walker, 'Profit and Loss in the Hundred Years War: The Subcontracts of Sir John Strother', *BIHR* 58 (1985), pp. 100–106.

[42] BL Additional MSS 7967, fos 40r–40v. Warenne was initially accompanied by the earl of Atholl, 2 bannerets, 23 knights and 74 esquires, but there was steady shrinkage in numbers from 13 June 1325 to 9 January 1326.

[43] TNA C 81/1741, nos 65–67; C 61/36, mm. 5, 7, 8; *CPR, 1324–7*, pp. 108–10.

[44] TNA E 101/17/31.

[45] Sub-retinues: David Strathbogie, earl of Atholl, with 2 knights and 7 esquires; Sir Ralph Cobham, banneret, with 7 knights (who brought 11 esquires) and 5 further esquires; Sir Ranulph Dacre, banneret, with 2 knights and 7 esquires.

[46] Our documentation does not allow precision, but it would seem that, taken together, the three sub-retinues led by bannerets supplied about a third of Warwick's men-at-arms, while the knightly companies probably contributed a rather larger proportion.

To recognise that, in assembling their retinues, captains relied heavily on engaging companies of various sizes that had been raised by others is important for several reasons. First, such recognition brings us closer to the realities of the recruitment process and highlights the distinctive network of relationships that this process laid down within a retinue: a network, derived from the social structure of military communities, in which comradeship groups provided the most immediate basis for identity and loyalty for many men; a network that became more complex and robust as a whole as the shared experience of campaigning encouraged a retinue-centred *esprit de corps*. Second, heavy reliance on pre-formed companies means that the retinue-level stability of personnel that is observable in early- to mid-fourteenth-century armies was not simply the consequence of a multitude of individual relationships between captain and soldier. Rather, to achieve that stability, much depended, firstly, on a captain's ability to retain the services, from campaign to campaign, of a settled team of bannerets and knights; and, secondly, on each of these leaders of sub-retinues and companies bringing to muster a group of men with whom they were acquainted and had served before. The ways in which a captain and his subordinates were able to maintain and sustain these loyalties merit our attention.

To begin with the captain: at the centre of his solar system, he knew that his gravitational pull affected his planetary lieutenants, but not necessarily their satellites. The strongest gravitational pull was, no doubt, exerted on those of his lieutenants who were indentured retainers. They could be relied upon to ride to war with him when called upon to do so and might also be required to bring with them a sub-retinue, or at least some additional manpower. Bannerets who were retained in this way would be expected to lead a company of twenty or even forty men-at-arms (in the later fourteenth century, with mounted archers).[47] More typical of the time was Sir Robert Herle's life contract with the earl of Warwick, which required him to serve with four men-at-arms.[48] Such documents do reveal something of how a magnate's recruiting needs and aspirations influenced the mechanics of recruitment; but – with some notable exceptions – it is unlikely that more than a small proportion of retinue-based manpower was raised as a result of fulfilment of the terms of long-term indentures.[49] For most captains, securing the repeated service of bannerets and knights who could be relied upon to contribute companies to their retinues was achieved not so much by enforcing formal, contractual agreements as by exploiting recruiting networks that had been built up over time, perhaps over generations: social networks of

---

[47] Jones and Walker, 'Private Indentures', nos 33–34 (pp. 65–68); Holmes, *Estates of the Higher Nobility*, pp. 122–3; S. Walker, *The Lancastrian Affinity, 1361–1399* (Oxford, 1990), pp. 47–8, and documentation cited there.

[48] Jones and Walker, 'Private indentures', no. 37 (pp. 70–71).

[49] See, for example, K. Fowler, *The King's Lieutenant: Henry of Grosmont, First Duke of Lancaster, 1310–1361* (London, 1969), pp. 181–6. For the uneven survival of such documentation, see Holmes, *The Estates of the Higher Nobility*, Ch. 3.

tenants, neighbours, family and friends, including long-standing comrades in arms.

The relationship between a captain's recruiting reach and the distribution of his estates (together with those of other men upon whose services he could rely) would bring to his retinue a degree of territorially related cohesion.[50] And yet because a magnate's sphere of influence was likely to be trans-regional, overlapping those of others and liable, over time, to shift in extent, a more complex social mix would be introduced into the composition of his retinue.[51] Indeed, the particularity of each captain's recruiting reach would give rise to retinues with correspondingly distinctive collective identities. It is in the light of how the mechanics of retinue formation operated within the scope of a captain's recruiting reach that we can see how he could achieve a settled retinue through the repeated service of bannerets and knights, even though the latter, when viewed as a group, were not necessarily bound by common characteristics such as shared regional origins. Warwick's retinue in 1346, in which the three bannerets, as well as most of the twenty knights who brought small companies, had served before, illustrates this rather well.[52] But, as diverse as their backgrounds might be, what the returning bannerets and knights had in common was a personal relationship with their captain and, thus, a shared loyalty that, with time, could develop into a retinue-based *esprit de corps*.

The terms of indentures of retinue offer evidence of how captains aspired to influence the composition of their war retinues, but they also leave us in no doubt as to the limits of that influence. The earl of Warwick might insist that Sir Robert Herle be accompanied by four *hommes darmes*, but could not insist on who they were. Quite as important to a captain as his lieutenants' loyalty was their capacity to inspire it in others. The leaders of sub-retinues and smaller companies would seek to base their recruiting on accessible social networks, much like their superiors in the command hierarchy, though on a smaller scale and at a more local level. It was at this level that comradeship groups within military communities were fostered and mobilised. Indeed, it was essentially through the mediation of these recruiting middlemen that magnates were able to gain access to local networks of manpower. The companies that were raised – often no more than a handful of men bound by ties rooted in kinship, neighbourhood or shared service – were the building blocks of Edwardian armies. The settled, cohesive nature of these companies, combined with the web of personal connections that was the essence of the hierarchy of command, provided a

---

[50] For example, Bell, *War and the Soldier*, pp. 117–25 (earl of Arundel).

[51] D.S. Green, 'The Military Personnel of Edward the Black Prince', *Medieval Prosopography* 21 (2000), pp. 133–52 (139–42); Walker, *Lancastrian Affinity*, pp. 31–8.

[52] Judging by the counties in which they held land, the three bannerets had no common regional interests: *Calendar of Inquisitions Post-Mortem*, 20 vols (London, 1904–95), XII, no. 412 (Scales), XV, nos 581–6 (St Amand). Ayton, 'Sir Thomas Ughtred'. Cf. the earl of Northampton's retinue in 1346: Ayton, 'The English army at Crécy', pp. 205–10.

foundation of stability and structural robustness for what was an intermittently mobilised and yet strongly characterised social and institutional phenomenon, the magnate's war retinue.

In highlighting the 'stability' or 'settled composition' of early- to mid-Edwardian army retinues, a phenomenon that, as we have seen, can be related to repeat service at two levels of recruitment, there is perhaps some risk of overstatement or, rather, of oversimplification. It goes without saying that neither a captain's 'team' of recruiting middlemen nor the composition of their companies would remain wholly unchanged from one campaign to the next. The incidence of casualties should not be ignored, though quite how numerous these were during this period has never been systematically investigated. Over time, some men would be incapacitated by ill-health or discouraged by advancing years. Others might switch allegiance in order to join a captain who needed to expand his retinue or build one from scratch.[53] And there would always be men whose personal circumstances – arising from the routine rhythms of gentry life, and the varied responsibilities and relationships that were at the heart of it – prevented them from answering the call. As all captains knew, these were the facts of life of managing a war retinue; and yet the withdrawal of a subordinate who had served loyally in the past would be felt, in the case of a banneret keenly. For, unless a relative or subordinate could step into his shoes, the contingent of men-at-arms (and, from the 1330s, archers) that he had brought to earlier campaigns would not now appear at muster, at least as an integral unit.

For a captain, finding a modest number of replacements would present few difficulties. But if he had to expand his retinue significantly he would probably need to look beyond the settled networks of social connections that he was accustomed to depend upon in order to secure the services of bannerets and knights who could supply companies 'off-the-peg'. In the early to mid fourteenth century this would not necessarily mean reaching out to distant corners of the realm or hiring bands of professional soldiers with whom there had been no prior contact. And, in any case, given that the kingdom-wide military community was comparatively small and settled at that time, it is likely that some at least of the newly engaged men would be familiar to the old hands in the retinue. Even if the regional origins of an off-the-peg company acquired in this way suggests a certain mismatch with the predominant character of the host retinue, the bonds of comradeship within the company would at least contribute to the strength of the whole contingent. Thus, when Sir Thomas Ughtred joined Warwick's retinue in 1345 he brought with him a company of Yorkshiremen, some of whom can be shown to have been military companions of long standing. Many of the others may well have been too, since they came from those areas of the East Riding and the neighbourhood of York where Ughtred's principal landholdings lay.[54]

---

[53] Ayton, 'The English army at Crécy', pp. 212–15.
[54] TNA C 81/1741, nos 10 (1346) and 21 (1345). Ayton, 'Sir Thomas Ughtred', pp. 122–5.

Change in the form of the continual renewal of manpower was a functional characteristic of even the most settled retinues in the early to mid fourteenth century. What this meant in practice was that a regularly serving captain's war retinue had a collective state more complex and dynamic than is suggested by the standard model of a stable nucleus surrounded by 'less stable elements'. Of course, the 'captain's war retinue' considered here was in reality a sequence of separately recruited contingents, each raised for a specific campaign and disbanded at the end of it. Comparison of one such contingent with those that had preceded it serves to distinguish newcomers from men who were returning to the fold, and it also highlights those who, for whatever reason, had not returned. Newcomers joined a group of men who, while having in common a bond with the captain and perhaps also their regional origins, were at different stages of their careers, both in general and under this particular banner. Consequently, the nature and strength of relationships within a retinue, and, indeed, within its constituent companies, were constantly evolving. As men disappeared from the scene, the bonds of shared experience between those who remained strengthened and were extended to those among the new arrivals who returned in the future. Thus, in the army retinues of the early to mid fourteenth century, the continual renewal of retinue manpower co-existed with a high level of continuity from campaign to campaign, a collective state to which the term 'dynamic stability' may be applied.

The mechanics of retinue formation and the dynamic collective state that resulted from them should be regarded as universal features of fourteenth-century armies. But the particular character of that collective state, which in the early to mid fourteenth century tended towards stability, was by no means a constant. We shall examine shortly how the agencies of change that could result in greater instability, indeed volatility, in retinue-based manpower were in fact varied in both their origins and the nature and severity of their effects. First, it is necessary, briefly, to return to the retinue-level prosopographical data in order to highlight a shift in the character of English armies that occurred during the second half of the fourteenth century. As we have seen, during the first half of the century moderate to high retinue-level stability of personnel was commonplace. After that point the evidence suggests a less stable world, in which moderate to poor reservice rates were more common and may, indeed, have become the norm.[55] This should perhaps occasion no surprise. We need only recall, for example, what Simon Walker wrote of John of Gaunt's retinue: that 'the overall rate of re-service under [his] command, during the period of his heaviest military commitments, was never very high'. 'Nor ... were his bannerets able to keep their men together with any success.'[56] The evidence of other comital

[55] This conclusion, it should be noted, is based upon a sample of retinues rather than a comprehensive survey of the mountain of available evidence for the last three decades of the century.

[56] Walker, *Lancastrian Affinity*, pp. 50–51; cf. pp. 40–41. Somewhat exceptional is the re-service of men known to have served with Gaunt in 1367: half were still with him in 1369

retinues suggests that Gaunt's was not a special case. What we know of the new earl of Warwick's retinue in the 1370s tends to agree with what has been found for Gaunt, though the evidence, drawn in part from enrolled protections, is rather patchy.[57] Fortunately, greater availability of retinue rolls and muster records for late-fourteenth-century armies (and, consequently, less reliance on enrolled protections) enables us to bring real precision to the problem. For example, a comparison of the earl of Arundel's retinues in 1387 and 1388 reveals that 19 per cent of his manpower for the second expedition had returned to his banner from the first.[58]

Turning to sub-comital captains, we find a similar pattern. Take, for example, the retinues raised by Guy, Lord Brian, for a sequence of naval expeditions during the 1370s.[59]

Number of men (% of whom returning from the preceding campaign)

	1370	1371	1372	1378
Men-at-arms	100	250 (8%)	45 (33%)	50 (24%)
Archers	198	230 (3%)	50 (20%)	60 (10%)

Compared with Brian's retinue in 1370, the very low rates of return among personnel serving in 1371 are no doubt to be explained in part by reference to the exceptionally large numbers raised in that year; but it is striking how few of them re-enlisted under Brian's banner in 1372. Of the men serving in 1370, 23 per cent of the men-at-arms and 5 per cent of the archers (11 per cent overall) returned for at least one of the later expeditions. Viewing matters from the other end of the sequence of campaigns, about a quarter of the men-at-arms who were with Brian in 1372 and 1378 were returning from earlier occasions. For the period, even that may well have represented a high rate of reservice. Comparison of a lengthy muster roll of Sir Walter Hewett's retinue,[60] probably drawn up for the French campaign of 1373, with records of that captain's contingents in the

and a third in 1370 and 1373. The problem here is that while it is not clear what proportion of Gaunt's manpower in 1367 can be identified by name, we do know that in this respect the retinues from 1369, 1370 and 1373 are unusually well documented. The unevenness of the prosopographical data for Gaunt's war retinue does illustrate rather nicely the methodological problems that bedevil efforts to establish reliable rates of re-service.

[57] Nine out of 24 of the earl's men in 1372, whose identity is known through enrolled protections, can be found on a roll of his retinue for the 1373 expedition. The earl's retinue doubled in size for the second of these campaigns. TNA C 76/55; E 101/32/39, mm. 3, 3d. I am pleased to acknowledge that the documentation cited here and in footnotes 58 and 59 below was consulted via The Soldier in Later Medieval England database.

[58] The rate of return for knights (35%) was higher than those for esquires (23%) and archers (13%). TNA E 101/40/33, E 101/40/34 (1387); E 101/41/5 (1388).

[59] Based on rolls of Brian's retinues for 1370 (TNA E 101/30/21, mm. 1, 2), 1371 (E 101/31/11, no. 2), 1372 (E 101/32/16, m. 1) and 1378 (E 101/36/32, m. 2).

[60] TNA E 101/35/2, no. 8.

1360s and in 1370 yields practically no common names. How such retinue-level instability could affect a whole army is nicely illustrated by the exceptionally well-documented expeditions of 1387 and 1388, as studied in detail by Adrian Bell. Focusing on the fourteen captains who contributed retinues to both armies, it can be seen that only 10 per cent of the esquires and archers serving in these retinues in 1388 had returned to them from the previous year's campaign.[61]

During the second half of the fourteenth century, what emerged from the mechanics of retinue formation was a collective state that was generally less settled than had been usual in earlier decades. According to this criterion the armies of the late fourteenth century appear less stable and cohesive than those of the recent past. That we can glimpse this shift in the character of English royal armies is only possible through the prosopographical reconstruction of individual military careers within the context of retinue-based service. But in order to understand how and why change had occurred, it is necessary to look beyond the data that illuminate the military lives of thousands of individuals and turn the spotlight on the circumstances and forces that caused those individuals to serve under particular captains, and on the personal relationships that underpinned that service. In short, we need to focus on, and conceptualise, the dynamics of recruitment.

*

The dynamics of recruitment may be defined as the circumstances and forces that drove, accompanied or were generated by the recruiting process: that process whereby captains drew upon or attracted the manpower resources of the various military communities within their recruiting reach, engaging with the shared identities of those military communities and exploiting their social networks. While the mechanics of retinue formation created the fundamental structures within an army, the atomic world of companies and individuals from which each retinue's dynamic collective state would emerge, it was the dynamics of recruitment, operating at all levels, that shaped the character of an army, from the form and number of its larger structures to the social identities of their rank and file manpower. And it was the dynamics of recruitment that moulded military service as a social and cultural phenomenon: they explain the incidence of military service – who served, when, where and with whom – and thus the accumulation of actual experience that fuelled fortunes and mentalities, individual and collective.

Clearly, much depended on the captains' status, as measured by wealth and social authority, political influence or martial experience, and on their relationships with the various military communities that lay within their reach. These

---

[61] Bell, *War and the Soldier*, pp. 56, 65–6, 96–101. Thirty of 78 returning archers were serving in one retinue. While over half of the retinue captains in 1388 had served in 1387, only 4 per cent of the army's esquires were serving under the same captain as in the previous year (Bell, *War and the Soldier*, pp. 65, 96, 98–9).

characteristics determined the size of their campaign retinues and how they were composed. With regard to the latter, what will concern us in particular is how far captains were able, individually and collectively, to rely upon settled recruiting networks – that is, upon men with whom personal relationships existed (among whom the well-connected local middlemen who could supply sub-retinues or smaller companies were particularly valued); and how far they needed to turn to men with whom they had no long-standing ties, including freelance soldiers.

If grasping the nature and extent of the recruiting reach of captains is crucial to an understanding of the dynamics of recruitment, we must recognise too the influential role played by the forces of supply and demand: by, on the one hand, the supply of available manpower, as determined by the size, social composition and mental outlook of the military communities that were accessible to captains; and, on the other, the scale of demand, which we may view either as the manpower requirements of polities or other employers, or – from the soldier's point of view – as military service opportunities. The dynamics of recruitment prevailing *at any particular moment* were, therefore, the result of the interaction of these three 'elements'. The demand for manpower from the English crown and also from other potential paymasters was satisfied by military communities through the mediation of captains whose personal circumstances, as individuals and collectively, strongly influenced the resulting patterns of recruitment. These are the basic components of a dynamics of recruitment model, but what brings it to life is the role played by change. What is important here is not simply that the dynamics of recruitment cannot be conceived of as static because our three interacting elements were all subject to various forms of change: it is that change is crucial to an understanding of how it was that the dynamics of recruitment influenced both the character of armies and the shaping of military service as a socio-cultural phenomenon.

The dynamics of recruitment could be affected by various agencies of change, of which five broad types are distinguishable. The first concerns the captains, the men upon whose shoulders the burden of recruitment was carried. The line-up of such men available to the crown or other paymasters was ever in a state of flux. On the one hand, there might be withdrawals from the military arena, through death, retirement, redeployment to other responsibilities or political exclusion. On the other, new or rising captains, emerging through inheritance, maturity or ability, would need to build retinues from scratch or at least expand them. A second form of change that could affect the dynamics of recruitment was associated with strategy and war management. In general terms, such change can be characterised as a major adjustment to the focus or purpose of military effort. In practice it might involve a shift in the predominant geographical focus of campaigning, as occurred at the outset of Edward III's French war, or a change in the nature of service required, as would accompany a switch in strategic emphasis from *chevauchées* involving short-service field armies to the long-term garrisoning of fortresses. Changes such as these would close down service opportunities for some specialist military communities and open them up for others. Much might depend upon whether their preoccupations were with warfare on their immediate doorstep or with military service of a particular kind. Captains might choose to be redeployed and yet, depending on where they were serving, draw upon different constituencies of manpower. A third form of change that could affect the dynamics of recruitment was connected with the way armies were raised and organised. Institutional or structural change would be likely to affect the recruiting task facing captains. In this respect, of particular significance in the mid Edwardian period was the emergence of the 'mixed retinue', a development that required captains at all levels of the military hierarchy to recruit archers (usually mounted) as well as men-at-arms. The fourth and fifth agencies of change took the form of influences which, while being apparently less directly connected with the dynamics of recruitment than the first three, could nevertheless have profound effects, though in complex ways. The fourth concerned developments within the multi-faceted military environment in continental Europe, developments that had consequences for the scale and nature of demand for English military manpower, while the fifth agency of change, and the most elusive of precise characterisation, involved the evolution of socio-economic and cultural conditions in England and the effects that such evolutionary processes had on the supply of men who were able and willing to fight.

Classifying the ways in which the dynamics of recruitment could be affected by change is but the first step towards understanding the real nature of change and the consequences that it could have. The classification carries with it the advantage of clarity but also the hazard of reductionism. To separate out the agencies of change in this way runs the risk of distorting and misrepresenting a complex reality, in which the various agencies intertwined and interacted and in which cause and effect may be unclear. Moreover, during periods of sustained campaigning there seems to have been a tendency, in tension with the various causes and forms of change, for our three elements – the captains' collective recruiting reach and the forces of supply and demand – to become coordinated in such a way that an equilibrium was established between them and the dynamics of recruitment took on the form of a settled 'system'. In assessing how the various agencies of change affected such a settled system, an important distinction can be made between two forms of change that had very different effects. Endogenous forms of change, which operated within the system, resulted in no more than adjustments to the prevailing dynamics of recruitment. Exogenous forms of change, originating outside the system, could have major destabilising effects on the dynamics of recruitment and ultimately bring about the establishment of a new equilibrium.

*

In what ways were the dynamics of recruitment in fourteenth-century England affected by the various agencies of change that we have identified, and what consequences did this have for the character of the armies raised and the composition and outlook of the military communities that provided manpower for them? Although complex, the story of what happened can be summarised concisely, the advantage of doing so here being to provide a narrative arc to accompany the more detailed thematic discussion that follows. In the early to mid fourteenth century, a period that witnessed protracted and at times intensive warfare in northern Britain and then France, the coordination of elements at work within the dynamics of recruitment resulted in what was essentially a settled system. However, during the second half of the century, as a consequence of pressure from exogenous forms of change, the prevailing balance of elements was upset and a new equilibrium established, based upon a different relationship between captains' recruiting reach and the demand for and supply of manpower. The major adjustments to the dynamics of recruitment that had been prompted by exogenous pressures had profound effects on the character of armies and military communities. There was now a greater reliance on 'professional' soldiers whose service (where, when and with whom) was no longer determined by the functioning of traditional recruiting networks over which leading captains exerted a powerful influence. These, sketched in barest outline, were the most important developments to have affected the dynamics of recruitment during the fourteenth century. We shall now turn our attention to the roles played in bringing about these developments by the various forms of endogenous and exogenous change.

The early to mid fourteenth century is conventionally presented as a time of great change for English armies, and in some ways this is indeed a valid view to take. But with regard to the dynamics of recruitment it would be more appropriate to depict this as a period of relative stability, or at least of only gradual and limited change. It is true that seeds were already sown that would yield greater change in the late fourteenth century; the shift in the crown's focus from Scotland to France and the emergence of armies built around the principle of mixed retinues – developments exogenous to the recruiting system – were to have significant implications for the dynamics of recruitment in later decades. But until at least the middle of the century, the agencies of change were predominantly endogenous; indeed, they should be viewed as a natural part of the functioning of the system.

Notable in this respect were changes to the line-up of captains. That these could be quantitatively significant and yet have comparatively little effect on the equilibrium of the dynamics of recruitment is nicely illustrated by the circumstances of the 1330s and 1340s. As we have seen, this was a time in which, because recruitment relied heavily on established social networks within a fairly settled manpower pool, an experienced captain might expect to secure for his retinue the repeated service of a stable group of men. Yet this was also a period in which a number of heavyweight captains disappeared from the military scene, while others, who were to acquire as much or more recruiting clout, emerged to take their place. The first decade of Edward III's reign witnessed the death or retirement of the earls of Kent, March, Lancaster, Norfolk, Hereford and Essex,

Cornwall and Warenne.[62] The comital community suffered further losses in the 1340s,[63] but in March 1337 the king had redressed the balance by elevating six bannerets to earldoms, with (where necessary) supporting endowments.[64] Then, in 1346, Edward, prince of Wales, emerged fully formed as a super heavyweight among recruiting captains.[65]

It is undeniable that the loss of front-rank, militarily active magnates would temporarily disrupt the smooth operation of established recruiting networks, which in turn could impose limits on the king's capacity to raise armies of appropriate size and weight. Naturally, the course of individual military careers would also be affected when a captain left the stage, as would, to some extent, the bonds of comradeship that had thrived under his banner. It is equally clear that the elevation of trusted and capable men to earldoms in 1337 and in later years addressed these issues by restoring recruiting capacity, which in some cases meant reviving lordship networks that had ceased to function.[66] If the line-up of captains changed from one campaign to the next, the character of an army that could be raised would be affected to some degree. But, in truth, the impact of such change, endogenous in character, on the settled system that was the essence of the prevailing dynamics of recruitment is unlikely to have been acute, and would certainly not be chronic. It could be accommodated without disruption to the equilibrium that had been established between the *collective* recruiting reach of captains and the forces of supply and demand.

Two features of the context within which the prevailing dynamics of recruitment operated at this time should be borne in mind: the first is that the system was essentially 'closed', with supply and demand relatively settled and constant; the second that the disappearance or rise of individual captains took place amidst a sea of stability. The break-up of an established retinue did not entail total fragmentation and dispersion, nor would the creation or expansion of a new one be achieved by the assembly from scratch of a crowd of individuals who were wholly unknown to one another. What occurred was the movement of men and, in particular, whole companies within a closed system. We have seen how important sub-retinues and companies were to a large retinue's stability and cohesion. An emerging captain would seek to engage such 'off-the-peg' contingents as were accessible to him. To forge a team with real *esprit de corps* founded upon shared experience and mutual trust would take time. But, given the regional context within which much recruiting occurred and, indeed, the small-world character

---

[62] A. Ayton, 'Edward III and the English Aristocracy at the Beginning of the Hundred Years War', in *Armies, Chivalry and Warfare in Medieval Britain and France*, ed. M. Strickland (Stamford, 1998), pp. 173–206 (188)

[63] Salisbury in 1344 and Gloucester in 1347.

[64] Ayton, 'Edward III and the English Aristocracy', pp. 188–9.

[65] Ayton, 'The English Army at Crécy', pp. 170–71, 214–15.

[66] Ayton, 'Edward III and the English Aristocracy', pp. 188–94; Ayton, 'The English Army at Crécy', pp. 169–71.

of the mid-Edwardian military community, there would probably be, from the outset, bonds of familiarity between some at least of the company leaders and among their men.[67] Moreover, within the wider context of retinues raised at any particular moment, movement of companies and individuals of the kind discussed here was probably more the exception than the rule. Alongside newly formed retinues, established ones, while perhaps fluctuating in size, remained essentially stable in composition. The repeat service of knights with their companies ensured that retinue-level stability was built up brick by brick, the bricks individually robust in composition and the whole retinue well bonded together. In the field, these two types of retinue are to be found fighting side by side, as we see, for example, in the vanguard 'battle' at Crécy. Here the retinue of the prince of Wales stood alongside those of the earls of Warwick and Northampton, and the elder Sir Bartholomew Burgherssh. All four were packed with experienced soldiers, but, while the prince's was a freshly assembled composite, those of Warwick, Northampton and Burgherssh were altogether more settled as fighting teams.[68]

For the historian of the Edwardian military scene, and of the dynamics of recruitment in particular, endogenous forms of change are of interest principally because they have consequences that illuminate how recruiting mechanisms worked in practice. Indeed, they remind us that adjustment to change of this kind was a necessary part of how a settled system functioned. But what of the other agencies of change that might affect the dynamics of recruitment? Much of this was exogenous change, which originated from outside the system and might well affect the equilibrium of the existing dynamics of recruitment. Let us first consider the impact of changes to military institutions and organisational structures. Neither the abandonment of the feudal summons nor the rise of military contracts in themselves had any direct effect on the dynamics of recruitment. David Simpkin's recent work has shown that the same recruitment networks were drawn upon irrespective of whether, from the crown's point of view, a soldier was part of a feudal quota or a paid company.[69] Seen from the perspective of the social realities of military service, the transition from 'feudal host' to early contract army involved little change.

From the viewpoint of the dynamics of recruitment, it was structural rather than administrative change that was important, and, in particular, the rise of the mixed retinue in the middle decades of the century, whereby archers – now mounted – were raised by captains for service alongside men-at-arms. This development has become a familiar feature of recent writing on Edwardian military organisation, as have the qualifications that generally accompany discussions of it: namely, that commissions of array did not disappear overnight nor indeed

[67] Ayton, 'Sir Thomas Ughtred', pp. 124–5.
[68] Ayton, 'The English Army at Crécy', pp. 205–15.
[69] Simpkin, *The English Aristocracy at War*, Ch. 5.

altogether, and that array-style procedures were sometimes used by magnates to raise archers for their retinues.[70] It took several decades for structurally hybrid armies, to which arrayed companies made a predominant numerical contribution, to be superseded, but the direction of change is unmistakable. The army raised for the summer campaign of 1335 was very much a hybrid host. About a third of the fighting men were serving in retinues, with (if the pay rolls are to be believed) only a proportion of those contingents being of mixed composition.[71] But in 1346 mixed retinues accounted for about 40 per cent of the army manpower, and, by 1359, it was over 80 per cent.[72] Less often commented upon than the rise of the mixed retinue is the consolidation of manpower in a smaller number of units, a process spearheaded by the emergence of what might be termed 'super mixed retinues'. A degree of consolidation is already observable in the 1340s,[73] but it is during the second half of the century that the trend becomes clear. In 1359 the combined strength of the mixed retinues of only three captains, the prince of Wales (1,500 men), the duke of Lancaster (1,100) and the earl of March (500), was 3,100 men, or over 30 per cent of the army's manpower.[74] Super mixed retinues became a particularly striking feature of English military organisation after the resumption of the French war in 1369. The expeditionary force that sailed for Brittany in 1375, in all 4,000 men, was composed of only four retinues, while the earl of Buckingham's super-sized personal contingent in 1380, over 2,500 men, contributed nearly half of his army's manpower.[75] This is not, of course, to suggest that moderate-sized separately accounting retinues disappeared from the armies of this period.[76] Nor, indeed, is the intention here to obscure the fact that much grass-roots recruiting continued to involve men joining small companies, which were then brought together as the building blocks of larger retinues. What had changed was that the mixed retinues that were built in this way were now generally larger than before, with the largest acquiring the proportions and characteristics of compact armies.

What impact did these developments have on the dynamics of recruitment? In itself, transferring the burden of recruiting and equipping mounted archers from commissioners of array and shire communities to the leaders of mixed retinues was not insignificant. The normal ratio of one archer to one man-at-arms

---

[70] Ayton, *Knights and Warhorses*, pp. 10–15; Ayton, 'Armies and Military Communities', pp. 218–19.

[71] R. Nicholson, *Edward III and the Scots* (Oxford, 1965), pp. 198–200, 248–55.

[72] For 1346, see Ayton, 'The English Army at Crécy', p. 189. For 1359–60, see Ayton, 'Armies and Military Communities', p. 219 n. 8 and sources cited there.

[73] Ayton, 'The English Army at Crécy', pp. 227–8.

[74] TNA E 101/393/11, fos 79r–79v. In the cases of the Prince and the duke, the figures have been rounded to the nearest hundred.

[75] Sherborne, 'Indentured Retinues', pp. 13–15.

[76] The army that the earl of Cambridge led to Portugal in 1381 consisted of ten retinues ranging in size from 1,000 men to 40. TNA C 47/2/49, no. 2.

meant, of course, a doubling of the combatants that a captain had to find. For many of them, the most obvious ready source of manpower was the tenantry of their estates, and there is plenty of evidence that this was, indeed, the pool of potential recruits that captains initially turned to.[77] In other words, it would often be possible for them to meet their new recruiting responsibility by recourse to traditional sources of manpower, similar to those that had long been exploited to raise men-at-arms. With regard to the dynamics of recruitment, the really important development that forced change in the second half of the fourteenth century was the appearance of enlarged mixed retinues, especially the super-sized ones, and the associated concentration of recruiting responsibility at the highest levels in the hands of a smaller number of captains, not all whom were magnates. To raise a super mixed retinue, it would be necessary for a captain to look beyond established recruiting networks based on landholdings and social connections, and to place greater reliance on sub-contractors with whom he had no previous close ties and, indeed, on the general pool of unattached recruits, including true freelance soldiers. In these circumstances, adventurers such as Jankyn Nowell, who contracted to serve with a company of four men-at-arms and five archers in Sir Hugh Hastings's retinue in 1380, provided an important service.[78] The likely – indeed perhaps unavoidable – consequence of this change to the way the dynamics of recruitment operated would be reduced retinue-level stability of personnel, which, as was seen earlier, is exactly what can be observed in later-fourteenth-century armies.

Some at least of the newly hired contractors would have been able to call upon settled companies, which would result in more 'modules' of cohesion within a super-sized retinue than there might appear to be at first glance. This, it will be recalled, is what happened in the early and mid fourteenth century when retinues were built from scratch or significantly expanded. But, later in the century, the emergence of larger retinues meant that recruiting beyond established, 'personal' networks was now more pervasive. It was something that proportionately more captains had to do, including those contributing sub-retinues to the super-sized contingents in an army; and it accounted for the recruitment of a larger propor-tion of manpower at retinue level. In the late fourteenth century captains were raising retinues of a size that earlier would have been considered beyond what was sustainable by their wealth, social authority and connections. This was a predicament shared by leading magnates and middle-ranking knights alike.[79] As

---

[77] Morgan, *War and Society in Medieval Cheshire*, pp. 48, 75–6. Six of the earl of Huntingdon's archers in 1346 were tenants from his manor of Worfield, near Bridgnorth in Shropshire: TNA SC 1/39, no. 190.

[78] Goodman, 'The Military Subcontracts of Sir Hugh Hastings', pp. 116–17. For Nowell's career, see K. Fowler, *Medieval Mercenaries. 1: The Great Companies* (Oxford, 2001), pp. 20–21.

[79] For example, even John of Gaunt, who could draw on the extended resources of a large affinity as well as commissions of array, had need of large companies raised by independent subcontractors 'upon whose loyalty he had no special call'. Walker, *Lancastrian Affinity*, pp.

a result of it, kingdom-wide, the service of a greater proportion of men-at-arms and archers, and in particular under whose banner they served, was determined not by any pre-existing ties that they might have to a captain but by a careerist mentality and the contractual terms that had been agreed.

Emblematic of the trend towards military service that was disengaged from established social networks, and powerfully illustrative of the implications of it, are the retinues raised by a new breed of captains whose social origins were certainly sub-noble and sometimes, like Sir Robert Knolles's, positively obscure.[80] Footloose professionals such as Jankyn Nowell were surely indispensable for a captain like Sir John Minsterworth, who lacked extensive recruiting networks in England based on landholdings and social connections, and yet contracted to raise 200 men-at-arms and 300 archers for the army of 1370.[81] And it is small wonder that there is so little evidence of stability in the war retinues raised by another of these 'professional' captains, Sir Walter Hewitt. In 1370, like Minsterworth, Hewitt contracted to raise a mixed contingent of 500 men.[82] That, fewer than twenty-five years earlier, the only retinue larger than this in the English host at Crécy had been led by the prince of Wales offers some indication of the extent to which army structural change had occurred in the interim and, indeed, how far that change had been accompanied by a transformation in the social foundations of military service.

The advent of much enlarged mixed retinues had a multi-faceted impact on the dynamics of recruitment. Not only was the recruiting reach (individual and collective) of captains affected, but also, inevitably, were those other elements that contributed to the equilibrium of a settled system. Changes in the pattern of demand arising from captains' altered recruiting requirements were accompanied by changes in the character of the manpower supplied. Admittedly, it is difficult here to distinguish cause and effect. One interpretation of what happened to the dynamics of recruitment in the late fourteenth century might be to identify a form of symbiotic relationship between army structural change and the growing numbers of careerist – or simply opportunist – men-at-arms and archers within the pool of available manpower. What we may be certain of is that these developments should not be interpreted as though they occurred in isolation, for this was a period in which the elements of demand and supply that contributed to

46–50. Lacking any form of personal military following, the bishop of Norwich in 1383 was wholly dependent on a group of careerist captains, including Sir Hugh Calveley and Sir William Elmham, to raise the 5,000 men whom he had contracted to lead to Flanders: J. Magee, 'Sir William Elmham and the Recruitment for Henry Despenser's Crusade of 1383', *Medieval Prosopography* 20 (1999), pp. 181–90.

[80] M. Jones, 'Knolles, Sir Robert (d. 1407)', *ODNB*, May 2009.

[81] TNA E 101/30/25. Minsterworth's origins are obscure. For his limited landholdings in Gloucestershire, worth about £15 per annum, see *Calendar of Inquisitions Miscellaneous*, 7 vols (London, 1916–69), III, no. 885.

[82] F. Devon, ed., *Issue Roll of Thomas de Brantingham* (London, 1835), pp. 119–20.

the dynamics of recruitment were affected by other exogenous influences: firstly, by developments within the wider – and very complex – military environment of continental Europe, which led to changes in the demand for English manpower; and, secondly, by social, economic and cultural developments in England. The latter, in part connected with the impact, from mid century, of successive plague visitations and in part with the longer-term evolution of social groups, their mentalities and non-military roles, affected the supply (numbers, social identities) of men available for military service as men-at-arms and archers. Through their operation and interaction, these exogenous influences did much to shape the social context from which emerged responses to the new recruiting demands generated by army structural change. A good deal more basic research is needed if we are to understand what happened in detail. For the moment, we can but offer a sketch which is necessarily general rather than precise, and tentative in its conclusions.

To begin with demand: during the second half of the fourteenth century, enterprising Englishmen could take advantage of an increased range and intensity of martial opportunities. From 1369, the English king's war in France was intensively fought. The armies that were sent to the continent were not uncommonly large, but so regularly were these campaigns mounted that, cumulatively, and combined with the permanent garrisons there, they created a deep well of martial opportunity, not least for careerist soldiers. And this war was extensively fought too, a multi-dimensional struggle with, on occasion, foci of conflict as distant from one another as Portugal and Scotland. It also created plentiful opportunities for freelance soldiering in France, which spilled over into the Italian and Iberian peninsulas, and from there, it seems, around the Mediterranean as far as the Balkans, Anatolia and Egypt.[83] There were, moreover, further openings for the restless warrior in the remotest corners of Europe: witness the many Englishmen who travelled to Prussia to fight in the Teutonic Order's protracted conflict with the pagan (or formerly so) duchy of Lithuania, or the English archers who can be glimpsed serving in a Hungarian garrison in southern Transylvania.[84]

In short, we might say that martial opportunities abounded in a late medieval landscape of warfare in which military activity, often inter-related, took many forms and was in some regions endemic. What is striking about the pattern of response to these opportunities is that while there were careerist soldiers, indeed communities of them, who specialised (for example, in one region of France on

---

[83] On the range of opportunities that existed at this time, see Fowler, *Medieval Mercenaries*; W. Caferro, *John Hawkwood: An English Mercenary in Fourteenth-Century Italy* (Baltimore, 2006); A. Luttrell, 'Chaucer's Knight and the Mediterranean', *Library of Mediterranean History* I (1994), pp. 127–60; C. Tyerman, *England and the Crusades, 1095–1588* (Chicago and London, 1988), Ch. 10.

[84] Johannes de Thurocz, *Chronica Hungarorum*, vol. I: *Textus*, ed. E. Galántai and Gy. Kristó, Bibliotheca scriptorum medii recentisque aevorum, Series nova, vol. 7 (Budapest, 1985), p. 182.

the manning of garrisons),[85] the evidence points to a plenitude, and perhaps preponderance, of generalists who pursued 'mixed' careers. This is not altogether surprising. Expert contemporary commentators such as Geoffroi de Charny saw no incompatibility between mercenary service and crusading: they were merely different facets of the martial calling.[86] With regard to motivation, 'salvation, honour, wealth and a good fight were complementary incentives, not mutually exclusive.'[87] While the extraordinarily diverse career that Chaucer assigned to his Knight in the General Prologue of the Canterbury Tales may well have had no parallel among contemporary warriors,[88] the military lives of such men as Nicholas Sabraham, an obscure northern esquire, demonstrate how it was indeed possible for one man to embrace many of the varied martial opportunities that were available in later-fourteenth-century Europe.[89]

What effect did this diverse and enriched menu of martial opportunities have on the dynamics of recruitment in England? Most obviously, what a career such as Sabraham's suggests is that, from the English crown's point of view, there was potential for serious competition from other employers, which might disrupt the functioning of domestic recruitment networks and, in general, deplete the pool of manpower available to the king. The crown's periodic refusal to issue licences to men wishing to go on crusade should be read in this light; and it is certainly the case that English engagement with crusading flourished most during periods of truce in the king's wars.[90] However, it is unlikely that other forms of non-royal service could be so easily regulated by the crown. For example, the movement of English freelances to the Italian peninsula, where they operated collectively as parasites or in the service of fiercely competitive city states, was also encouraged by periods of truce in the French war, notably during the 1360s. But, compared with participants in a Prussian *Reise*, these mercenaries were less likely to return to England promptly. Moreover, if the wider range of martial opportunities is to be seen *in itself* as a disturber of the 'settled system' at the heart of the dynamics of recruitment, then it must be remembered that a good deal of that diversity arose as a consequence of the pursuit of English royal interests. As noted earlier, major shifts in – or diversification of – the focus of royal campaigning should be counted among the exogenous agents of change that could affect the dynamics of recruitment. Already in the late 1330s, with the French war beginning while

---

[85] Morgan, *War and Society in Medieval Cheshire*, Ch. 3.

[86] *The Book of Chivalry of Geoffroi de Charny*, ed. R. Kaeuper and E. Kennedy (Philadelphia, 1996).

[87] Tyerman, *England and the Crusades*, p .289.

[88] M. Keen, 'Chaucer's Knight, the English Aristocracy and the Crusade', in M. Keen, *Nobles, Knights and Men-at-arms in the Middle Ages* (London and Rio Grande, 1996), pp. 101–19. But see now: S. Vander Elst, '"Tu es pélerin en la sainte cite": Chaucer's Knight and Philippe de Mézières', *Studies in Philology* 106 (2009), pp. 379–401.

[89] *The Scrope and Grosvenor Controversy*, ed. N.H. Nicolas, 2 vols (London, 1832) I, pp. 124–5.

[90] Tyerman, *England and the Crusades*, pp. 266, 268, 277, 278–9, 289–90, 294.

an actively defensive stance was maintained towards Scotland, a captain with interests in the north but who was also required to serve with a strong retinue on the continent would find the manpower resources to which he had ready access stretched and divided. Later in the century, when enterprising soldiers were faced by a wider range of martial options and quite possibly influenced by an evolving recruiting culture that resulted in looser bonds within enlarged retinues, we should not be surprised to find markedly less retinue-level loyalty and stability than had been evident in earlier decades.

*

If the military communities that were exposed to the varied martial opportunities of the late fourteenth century had remained essentially unchanged in size and composition, the available manpower would have been, to a greater or lesser degree, shuffled or spread more thinly, according to the particular demands of the moment. But it is evident that what actually happened was far more complex: that increased and diversified demand for English men-at-arms and archers was accompanied by changes in the character of England's military communities. While it is certain that, in some respects at least, the supply of manpower changed during this period, for the moment it is impossible to be precise about the extent and nature of the changes that occurred. Late-fourteenth-century military service has begun to receive systematic attention only recently. As yet, all we can do is pose the necessary questions and reflect upon possible answers. Had England's military communities – the overall pool of warrior manpower and its constituent parts – expanded or contracted during the second half of the century? To what extent and in what ways had the social composition and, indeed, social identities of the men who fought changed?

Some indication of the number of men available for recruitment at a single moment is provided by the size and composition of the largest armies raised during this period. In 1359 Edward III's kingdom supplied in the region of 3,000 men-at-arms and over 6,000 archers for what was to be his last expedition to France.[91] Those numbers were exceeded in 1385, when an army composed of 4,500 men-at-arms and over 9,000 archers accompanied Richard II to Scotland.[92] A simple comparison with the armies raised during the first half of the century, right up to the pre-plague recruitment peak achieved for the siege of Calais (1346–7), highlights two areas of change within England's military communities during the second half of the century. On the one hand, it would seem that there were now more individuals willing and able to serve as men-at-arms. The figure for 1385 is particularly significant, not least because it was achieved while also maintaining garrisons at Calais, Berwick and elsewhere. Indeed, it is unlikely

[91] Ayton, 'Armies and military communities', p. 219 n. 8.
[92] N.B. Lewis, 'The Last Medieval Summons of the English Feudal Levy, 13 June 1385', *EHR* 73 (1958), pp. 1–26 (5–6).

that the English crown had ever before had so many home-grown men-at-arms simultaneously on the pay roll. On the other hand, although the crown now had need of fewer archers than earlier in the century, those who were employed were mostly mounted and serving in mixed retinues. There is no way of knowing how fully the largest armies of the period had exploited the pool of available manpower, but they are nevertheless of value as indicators of the *minimum* size of the kingdom's overall military community, or rather of the various sub-sets of potential recruits within it.

Further light is cast on the size and character of these sub-sets of manpower when the documentation that illuminates the personnel of royal armies is approached comparatively. Take, for example, the complete muster rolls that have survived for the expeditionary forces with which the earl of Arundel campaigned on the French coast in 1387 and 1388. These rolls enable us to compare the composition of two armies raised in quick succession, and such a comparison is indeed revealing. Only 19 per cent of the 2,497 men who enlisted in 1387 returned in 1388. Still more striking is the fact that, of a total of 5,616 identifiable men who served in these armies, only 473 (8%) did so on both occasions.[93] Two points should be highlighted here. First, it can be seen that the low level of retinue-level stability from the first campaign to the second that we noted earlier was not the consequence of the widespread transfer of allegiance. Men did not switch between retinues; they stayed away altogether from the second muster. As far as the crown and Arundel were concerned, that did not matter, because what these figures make clear is that there was in England at this time no shortage of men willing to serve as men-at-arms and archers. The regular mounting of continental expeditions did not depend upon securing a high rate of repeat service.

A second, related point that arises from comparison of the personnel of these two armies is that it provides further evidence that the pool of manpower, at least with regard to potential men-at-arms, was larger than it had been in the early to mid fourteenth century. When it is recognised that of a total of 2,294 individual sub-knightly men-at-arms who served on either or both of these expeditions, fewer than 7 per cent did so on both occasions,[94] it is difficult to avoid the conclusion that these 2,300 or so men represented only a fraction of the overall pool of manpower within the kingdom: a conclusion that, as we have seen, is reinforced by the exceptionally large number of men-at-arms who had served in the great royal army of 1385. With regard to the men who were available for recruitment as archers, it is less easy to arrive at such conclusions because the service context of this type of soldier had changed so much during the course of the century. What we can say is that the pool of men who served as *mounted* archers had probably grown; and that, as a consequence of various inter-related developments, this group, together with the expanded community

93 Bell, *War and the Soldier*, pp. 56, 64–5, 133 n. 109, 221.
94 Bell, *War and the Soldier*, pp. 56, 64–5, 98.

of potential men-at-arms, had become more volatile and restless than before. We have seen already how the emergence of enlarged, mixed retinues as the predominant recruiting context in England, when combined with changes in the demand for and supply of manpower across Europe, encouraged the disengagement of recruitment from traditional social networks. What gave particular impetus to these developments were the peculiar social and economic conditions that followed in the wake of the Black Death's arrival in Europe in 1347–8.

To conceive of a military community that, at least in some of its constituent parts, had expanded during the second half of the fourteenth century may seem counter-intuitive, given the demographic context within which these developments occurred. We might expect that the dramatic collapse in England's population that was caused by a series of plague visitations, and the economic and social consequences of that collapse, would have had a depressive effect on the manpower available for military service. Compared with the early years of the century, the number of adult males had halved.[95] If those who could be described as surplus to economic requirements had been prominent among the rank and file soldiery earlier in the century, their numbers were now much diminished. And, accompanying a general rise in living standards, there were improved domestic opportunities for the bulk of the surviving rural population.[96] Indeed, it may well be that the crown's abandonment of the massed recruitment of the rural peasantry by means of commissions of array was prompted, in part at least, by the demographic and economic realities of the time.[97] But in other respects both the demand for and supply of military manpower remained buoyant. In wartorn and plague-ravaged France there was an abundance of freelance soldiering opportunities and there appear to have been no shortage of Englishmen attracted by them, including 'new men' from outside the traditional socio-military elite: the ambitious, restless, 'unknown youths from different regions of England' of whom Sir Thomas Gray wrote.[98] The emergence of such opportunities merely added to the pressures on the social networks that both regulated and animated society: the system of bonds and conduits that had already been damaged directly by catastrophic population losses and indirectly by the social and economic consequences of those losses. It is notable that, of the young men who went to France 'in astonishing numbers', Gray added that 'all of them [did so] on their own account without any leader'.[99] If within rural society there was a 'weakening and

---

[95] 'Between the onset of the Great European Famine in 1315 and the end of the fourth plague outbreak in 1375, the population was halved'. B.M.S. Campbell, 'The Land', in *A Social History of England, 1200–1500*, ed. R. Horrox and W.M. Ormrod (Cambridge, 2006), p. 234.

[96] See, for example, Campbell, 'The Land', pp. 207, 217–18.

[97] It is notable that the last time foot archers were raised in large numbers in the shires was for the Crécy–Calais campaign, on the eve of the first plague visitation.

[98] Sir Thomas Gray, *Scalacronica, 1272–1363*, ed. A. King, Surtees Society 209 (Woodbridge, 2005), pp. 156–7.

[99] King, *Scalacronica*, pp. 152–3.

contraction of kin networks as access to holdings no longer depended upon inheritance and the maintenance of family ties',[100] so we might also expect to find an attenuation of traditional recruiting networks as new opportunities for careerist soldiering were opening up in continental Europe, whether in the free-lance sphere or in the enlarged mixed retinues that had now become the norm in royal armies.

Identifying, albeit in general terms, the forces and circumstances that contributed to the reshaping of the English military community during the second half of the fourteenth century is fundamentally important. It enhances our understanding of the men who were recruited and fought during that period, which in turn informs interpretations of (among other things) the performance of armies and the place of the soldier in society. There is, however, much about the late-Edwardian and Ricardian military community that has yet to be researched in any detail. As noted at the outset of this essay, a conceptual grasp of the dynamics of recruitment should be combined with a prosopographical approach to military service data. And yet it remains to be seen whether, given the difficulties that attend the linkage of military service records with 'life data' of other kinds, a prosopographical approach can provide the key to unlocking the complex and dynamic social identities of the various overlapping sub-sets within the military community.

In this respect, the mounted archers who from the 1350s became numerically predominant within the military community present the greatest problems.[101] Who were these men? The cost of horse and harness has prompted some historians to suggest that, in contrast with the poorly equipped conscripted foot soldiers of Edward I's reign, who were of 'villein status', 'the mounted archers are likely to have been drawn from the elite of village society': they were men 'of yeoman standing'.[102] There is congruence here with the image of the yeoman archer that we find in literature and popular 'rymes' from the late fourteenth and fifteenth centuries.[103] Moreover, it was precisely such men who, from the time of

---

100 J. Hatcher and M. Bailey, *Modelling the Middle Ages. The History and Theory of England's Economic Development* (Oxford, 2001), p. 30, which draws on Z. Razi, 'The Myth of the Immutable English Family', *Past and Present* 40 (1993), pp. 22–44.

101 Predominant that is in English royal armies. With regard to mercenary service, it has been pointed out that English archers were not especially numerous or influential in late-fourteenth-century Italy. Caferro, *John Hawkwood*, pp. 20, 50, 356 n. 49.

102 M. Prestwich, *Armies and Warfare in the Middle Ages. The English Experience* (London, 1996), p. 143; Ayton, *Knights and Warhorses*, pp. 15–16, and references cited there. See also Ayton and Preston, *The Battle of Crécy*, pp. 215–24.

103 Note, however, that both Chaucer's Knight's Yeoman and Robin Hood are presented as yeomen of a particular kind: foresters. K.J. Thompson, 'Chaucer's Warrior Bowman: The Roles and Equipment of the Knight's Yeoman', *The Chaucer Review* 40 (2006), pp. 386–415; A. Ayton, 'Military Service and the Development of the Robin Hood Legend in the Fourteenth Century', *Nottingham Medieval Studies* 36 (1992), pp. 126–47; A.J. Pollard, *Imagining Robin Hood* (Abingdon, 2004).

the mounted archer's first emergence as a distinguishable type of combatant, the crown expected to serve in this capacity. Thus, the experimental military assessment of the mid 1340s specified that a landowner whose property was worth £5 *per annum* was to be, or to provide, a mounted archer.[104] These do indeed look like the 'minor landholders, not gentry, but a cut above the ordinary peasant husbandman',[105] who later would be known as yeomen; and, in spite of the heavy loss of potential manpower to the plague, growing prosperity within rural society ensured that their ranks were replenished during the second half of the century. This was a significant development, in that the military potential of a prosperous stratum of society, which earlier in the century had largely escaped the attention of commissioners of array,[106] could now be exploited.

However, we should be wary of locating mounted archers too exclusively within any single social stratum, not least because the circumstances of their recruitment suggest more heterogeneous origins.[107] Much would depend on whether the archer or his family provided his horse and equipment, or whether these were supplied by his retinue captain or sponsor. The mounting of archers by their captains is occasionally mentioned in the records,[108] and if this was indeed a regular practice it would make more likely a continuing military role for the less prosperous sections of the rural population. So, while as a broad brush-stroke generalisation there is something to be said for the view that the emergence of the mounted archer, combined with that of the mixed, mounted retinue, brought about 'the retreat of military service into a narrower social spectrum below the nobility',[109] in practice it is likely that the recruitment net would need to be cast more widely. Indeed, in some regions this may well have been the only way in which the high number of mounted bowmen evident in late-fourteenth-century armies could be raised.

With regard to the reshaping of England's military community, there is another way of characterising the importance of the mounted archer: namely, that he bridged the chasm that had earlier divided the peasant foot-soldier from the genteel man-at-arms. This had consequences for the social identities – and, indeed, the numbers – of men who were willing and able to serve as archers and men-at-arms. From the outset, the mounted archer was a more inclusive category of combatant, and one from which individuals might launch a bid for military

---

[104] A landowner with £10 *per annum* owed a hobelar, while £25 equated with the provision of a man-at-arms. M. Powicke, *Military Obligation in Medieval England* (Oxford, 1962), pp. 195–8.

[105] M. Keen, *The Outlaws of Medieval Legend*, revised paperback edn (London, 1987), p. xvii.

[106] For the probable social composition of the companies raised by the commissioners of array, see Ayton and Preston, *The Battle of Crécy*, pp. 220–21.

[107] Ayton, 'Military Service and the Development of the Robin Hood Legend', pp. 136ff.

[108] J.M.W. Bean, *From Lord to Patron. Lordship in Medieval England* (Manchester, 1989), p. 239. See also Ayton and Preston, *The Battle of Crécy*, p. 221.

[109] Morgan, *War and Society in Medieval Cheshire*, p. 39.

and social advancement. Thus, while there were younger sons from the lesser gentry who served as mounted bowmen because their families were unable to furnish the arms, armour and horses required for a man-at-arms, so there were yeomen, artisans and husbandmen who, while starting out as archers, aspired to be men-at-arms. By 'reinvesting their earnings in horses and armour' they 'were able to rise slowly through the ranks'.[110] Indeed, according to Sir Thomas Gray, in France during the 1350s and 1360s that rise could be rapid. Many 'unknown youths' who began as archers became knights.[111] Notable among those who succeeded in this way, to the extent of becoming wealthy and armigerous, were Sir Robert Knolles, who sprang from burgess or yeoman roots in Cheshire,[112] and Sir John Hawkwood, who was a younger son of a 'rising' but still sub-genteel landholding family in Essex.[113] Although hard evidence for their early careers in arms is lacking, we can surmise that both men began as mounted archers, serving as members of mixed retinues led by 'local' knights of their acquaintance.[114] While the heights achieved by Knolles and Hawkwood were exceptional, the early stages of their careers illustrate rather well how a social group that would later become known as the 'middling sort' was now making an important military contribution. Often enterprising and upwardly mobile, its members had a participatory role that helps to explain the large numbers of men-at-arms as well as archers available for recruitment in late-fourteenth-century England.

If one of the challenges facing future prosopographical research will be to establish just how influential these 'new men' were in the expanded pool of men-at-arms, in terms of overall numbers and their place in the command hierarchy, another, equally important, concerns the role played by the traditional martial elite, the nobility and gentry. Did this continue much as before or did it change in any significant respect? By the early decades of the fifteenth century there is evidence of demilitarisation within certain sections of the lay landholding community.[115] Indeed, some historians have argued that a declining enthusiasm for active participation in war is already detectable during the later decades of the fourteenth.[116] The problem with this interpretation as it stands is that, in the absence of systematically obtained prosopographical data, it is necessarily reliant

---

[110] M. Bennett, *Community, Class and Careerism: Cheshire and Lancashire Society in the Age of Sir Gawain and the Green Knight* (Cambridge, 1983), pp. 162, 182 (for examples from the north-west of England). For further examples, see Fowler, *Medieval Mercenaries*, pp. 11–12.

[111] King, *Scalacronica*, pp. 152–3, 156–7.

[112] Jones, 'Knolles, Sir Robert (d. 1407)', *ODNB*.

[113] Caferro, *John Hawkwood*, pp. 32–7. On the poll tax roll of 1381, Hawkwood's elder brother was listed as a franklin, on which social gradation see P. Coss, 'An Age of Deference', in *A Social History of England, 1200–1500*, ed. R. Horrox and W.M. Ormrod (Cambridge, 2006).

[114] Jones, 'Knolles, Sir Robert (d. 1407)', *ODNB*; Caferro, *John Hawkwood*, pp. 38–41.

[115] M. Keen, *Origins of the English Gentleman* (Stroud, 2002), pp. 88–91; A. Goodman, 'Responses to Requests in Yorkshire for Military Service under Henry V', *Northern History* 17 (1981), pp. 240–52.

[116] Walker, *Lancastrian Affinity*, pp. 45, 80.

upon a combination of less robust methods and patchy evidence. For example,
the most recent outing for this interpretation rests upon an isolated county-level
study and the colourful testimony of a chronicler,[117] the argument supported
by an assessment of the *likely* impact of such issues as the deteriorating terms
(and profitability) of service in English armies and the perceived shift to a more
protracted, attritional style of warfare in France.[118] The case is advocated with
such skill that the reader may not realise that its evidential base is so insubstan-
tial. Be that as it may, according to this viewpoint, for knights and esquires with
landholding interests in England, war service was now a less appealing prospect
than it had been during the heyday of the great *chevauchées*.

What complicates any assessment of the gentry's involvement in war at this
time is the as yet imperfectly understood dynamic social and cultural context
within which this involvement occurred. The gentry, whose 'crystallisation' as a
social formation has been convincingly traced to the first half of the fourteenth
century, continued to evolve during the second: an evolution involving the recognition of status gradations within the gentry and the movement of individuals
and families between those social strata.[119] But although we may be aware of these
changes, it is difficult to quantify them or to judge how they and their effects
should be interpreted, given the turbulent demographic context within which
they occurred: the backdrop of population collapse with its wider economic
and social implications. Of the various gradations of gentility, the knights are
easier to identify, individually and collectively, than their sub-knightly comrades
in arms, but assessing their martial role is by no means straightforward. Thus,
while in terms of the numbers serving and as a proportion of all men-at-arms,
the contribution that knights made to late-fourteenth-century royal armies was
undoubtedly smaller than it had been in earlier decades,[120] it is not at all clear
how this should be interpreted. Was it the consequence of the progressive disengagement of knights from the king's wars, perhaps for the reasons mentioned
above? Or was there at this time a growing disinclination among men of suitable
standing to take up knighthood?[121] Indeed, was the most important reason for

---

[117] J. Sumption, *Hundred Years War III: Divided Houses* (London, 2009), p. 777 and n. 4
(942), which relies on N. Saul, *Knights and Esquires: The Gloucestershire Gentry in the Fourteenth Century* (Oxford, 1981), pp. 288–92 (but cf. pp. 51–3) and *The St Albans Chronicle. The
Chronica maiora of Thomas Walsingham I (1376–1394)*, ed. and trans. J. Taylor, W.R. Childs
and L. Watkiss (Oxford, 2003), pp. 809–11 (Arundel's expedition of 1387).

[118] Sumption, *Divided Houses*, pp. 733–7, 740–43.

[119] P. Coss, *The Origins of the Gentry* (Cambridge, 2003), especially Chs 9 and 10.

[120] Ayton, *Knights and Warhorses*, pp. 228–9 and works cited there; Bell, *War and the Soldier*,
pp. 56, 64–5.

[121] In the absence of a quantitative investigation of knights active in the mid- to late fourteenth century, evidence for a decline in numbers has been sought in the records of 1436,
which were first analysed by H.L. Gray: 'Incomes from land in England', *EHR* 44 (1934),
pp. 607–39. The most recent discussion links the smaller numbers evident in early- to
mid-fifteenth-century England to 'increasing selectivity in assuming knighthood', which is

the reduced number of knights in late-fourteenth-century armies quite simply that their ranks, like those of the rest of the population, had been substantially pruned by successive plague visitations?

If what the knights brought to the English armies of the early to mid four-teenth century was leadership, in the recruiting sphere and by example with the sword, it was the lower, sub-knightly levels of the pyramid of gentility that contributed the bulk of the rank and file men-at-arms to those armies. For every serving knight there were three or four sergeants or 'esquires' (*scutiferi, armigeri*), many of whom were scions of lesser gentry families. But to what extent was such heavy martial participation maintained by the sub-knightly strata of the gentry during the later decades of the century? Were the men who had taken the place of knights in the king's armies of essentially the same socio-economic and military standing: that is, wealthy esquires who had eschewed knighthood? Looking beyond that small group to the social origins of the 80 to 90 per cent of men-at-arms in a late-fourteenth-century army who were not knights: to what extent had the men of gentle blood whose families had traditionally served in this capacity already, by the closing decades of the century, been replaced by careerists of obscure or humble origins?

The issue is not as simple as it seems. While a prosopographical approach would no doubt allow us to distinguish between sons of long-established gentry families and the 'newest' among the *parvenu* men-at-arms, the social reality of the military community as a whole was less tidy and had always been so. There was constant mobility and consequent refreshment of the ranks of the gentry. For every 'new man', there would be another who had just achieved social respect-ability through public service. Moreover, such mobility was occurring within a society in which, for the modern historian, the status gradations of the gentry and the threshold into its lowest levels are difficult to define or characterise with precision, not least with regard to what form of military responsibility was expected of particular rungs of the social ladder. Take, for example, the occu-pants of the social rung – in reality a broad category – who, during the middle third of the century, acquired distinctiveness through the designation 'esquire'.[122] At a time when £40 *per annum* was deemed sufficient income to support knight-hood, the tariff of wealth-determined martial roles that informed the Crown's attempted re-assessment of military obligation in the mid 1340s stipulated that a landholder with an annual income of £25 was required to serve as, or equip, a man-at-arms.[123] It is tempting (and, by and large, may well be valid) to relate this level of prosperity and, thus, military obligation to the newly recognised esquires. But we should not forget that 'esquire' was a social gradation which

explained in terms of diminished 'military inducements' and the heavy cost of maintaining the necessary equipment and trappings. G. Harriss, *Shaping the Nation: England 1360–1461* (Oxford, 2005), p. 139.

[122]   Coss, *Origins of the Gentry*, pp. 18, 236–7.

[123]   Powicke, *Military Obligation*, pp. 195–8.

did not necessarily equate with a particular level of income. As the sumptuary legislation of 1363 made clear, there were wealthy esquires, who together with knights were regarded very differently from poorer esquires and 'toutes maneres de gentils gentz'.[124]

With regard to this second group, which was less prosperous but undoubtedly part of the gentry, it is particularly difficult to generalise about their military role. Their landed income would have located many of them, according to the 1340s military assessment tariff, within the substantial gap between the level at which a man-at-arms was owed (£25 *per annum*) and that at which a hobelar was demanded (£10). Collectively to such men, and particularly to those at the lower end of that wealth spectrum, for whom, certainly by the mid 1380s, the social designation 'gentleman' could be employed,[125] modern scholarship has applied the rather apt term 'parish gentry'. This was the broad base of the pyramid of gentility, consisting of perhaps three-quarters of the 10,000 or so families that could be considered gentry at this time.[126] Perhaps in terms of mental outlook and how they, and others, perceived their social standing, the parish gentry had much in common with the knights and wealthier esquires of the shires, but to what extent they actually contributed to the pool of genteel men-at-arms is not at all clear. The crown's equation of an annual income of £25 with service as a man-at-arms suggests that many in the parish gentry would have struggled to acquire and maintain the horseflesh and equipment required for such service, unless they received assistance from a wealthier patron.[127] It may well be that the sub-knightly men-at-arms of the 1340s were drawn predominantly from the ranks of the more prosperous esquires and that, as a group, their 'military participation ratio' was a good deal higher than that of the gentry as a whole. This would add weight to Maurice Keen's suggestion that it was the esquire's outstanding martial contribution that ensured his admission into 'the charmed world of the armigerous', his social distinctiveness thereby reinforced by the adoption of his own heraldic identity.[128] As with the knights, what complicates our assessment

---

[124] *Statutes of the Realm, 1101–1713*, ed. A. Luders et al., 11 vols (London, 1810–28), I, pp. 380–82. The graded poll tax of 1379 distinguished two categories of lesser esquire (with and without land) from those whose estate indicated that they should be knights. Coss, *Origins of the Gentry*, pp. 228–9.

[125] On the gentleman, see Keen, *Origins of the English Gentleman*, Ch. 7, especially pp. 101, 109–11, for some important observations about social status and wealth.

[126] C. Given-Wilson, *The English Nobility in the Late Middle Ages* (London, 1987), pp. 69–73. Cf. Campbell, 'The Land', p. 202 (Table 7.1), 205, where it is suggested that 'at the start of the fourteenth century individuals corresponding in status to the later esquires and gentlemen probably enjoyed incomes of about £12'.

[127] An impression that is reinforced by the re-enacted statute of Winchester of December 1334, which had set the income threshold for possession of equipment and horseflesh appropriate for service as a man-at-arms at £20 (*Foedera, conventiones, litterae et cujuscunque generis acta publica*, ed. T. Rymer, revised edn, 4 vols in 7 parts (London, 1816–69), II, ii, pp. 900–901).

[128] M. Keen, 'Heraldry and Hierarchy: Esquires and Gentlemen', in *Orders and Hierarchies*

of the military contribution of esquires and gentlemen is that we cannot be sure how it was affected by the Black Death. We would expect their numbers to have fallen with a trajectory similar to that followed by the decline of the population as a whole, and it is possible to interpret the kingdom-wide data that can be compiled by extrapolation from the income tax returns of 1436 as indicating that such shrinkage had in fact occurred.[129] Even more uncertain is whether, on balance, the socio-economic conditions of post-plague England, combined with the perceived character of overseas warfare, encouraged or discouraged military service among the squirearchy and parish gentry: whether, as a consequence, a social group traditionally associated with the sword held its own or lost ground within the expanded 'pool' of men-at-arms in late-fourteenth-century England.

*

It remains to be seen whether the knotty problem of how the evolving gentry of fourteenth-century England responded to the responsibilities, challenges and opportunities presented by war, particularly during the later decades of the century, can be unravelled through comprehensive prosopographical investigation. In the meantime, an alternative perspective on the problem is offered by the evidence that is to be found in the records from that arena of socio-cultural exclusivity, the Court of Chivalry, and specifically the witnesses' statements from the two great armorial disputes of the mid 1380s.[130] By focusing on what many of the witnesses revealed of themselves and their military experience it is possible to recover skeletal career profiles for scores of men who saw service with the sword during the previous half century and more. For many of them, the sketch can be supplemented with information from other sources, though that is perhaps less important than the fact that their own testimony has provided core life profiles that are unaffected by the central methodological issues facing the prosopographer of military service: namely, how, using sources of varied provenance, character and reliability, to identify and isolate individuals and to apply consistent criteria to the task of piecing together their lives.

In many ways it is both valid and instructive to regard the witnesses' statements from the two well-documented armorial disputes of the 1380s as a single body of evidence. The issues at the heart of these disputes were similar, as were

---

in *Late Medieval and Renaissance Europe*, ed. J. Denton (Basingstoke and London, 1999), pp. 94–108 (98–100); Keen, *Origins of the English Gentleman*, Ch. 5. Cf. Coss, *Origins of the Gentry*, pp. 243–8.

[129] By comparison with the early fourteenth century, the number of gentry households in 1436 may have fallen by a third. See Harriss, *Shaping the Nation*, p. 138.

[130] *The Scrope and Grosvenor Controversy*, ed. N.H. Nicolas, 2 vols (London, 1832). Lovel v. Morley: TNA, C 47/6/1; PRO 30/26/69. For analyses of these records, see A. Ayton, 'Knights, Esquires and Military Service: The Evidence of the Armorial Cases before the Court of Chivalry', in *The Medieval Military Revolution: State, Society and Military Change in Medieval and Early Modern Europe*, ed. A. Ayton and J.L. Price (London and New York, 1995), pp. 81–104; Keen, *Origins of the English Gentleman*, Chs 3 and 4.

the bureaucratic processes that generated the written testimony. The evidence for both cases was gathered during the same short period, in 1386–7, and there is little overlap between the two lists of witnesses, at least in the incomplete state that they have come down to us.[131] However, because the evidence yielded by the surviving records is neither complete nor altogether consistent with regard to focus, emphasis and precision, it is not always appropriate to treat the witnesses' testimony as though it constitutes a uniform body of information. For some purposes it is most effectively analysed in self-defining subsets rather than as a whole. A subset that is particularly useful for our present purpose consists of those witnesses who spoke in support of Thomas, Lord Morley's claim in his armorial dispute with John, Lord Lovel. The records, in the form that they have come down to us, include testimony from 160 individuals, of whom 102 were laymen.[132] Immediately evident is that most of these laymen (82 per cent) claimed some experience of the 'voiages, guerres et batailles' of the king of England or other lords, with many of them boasting lengthy and eventful careers in the saddle.[133] Setting aside the old soldiers who, it seems, had already hung up their swords for good before the resumption of the French war at the end of the 1360s, we are left with fifty-two witnesses who testified to campaigning at least once during the years from 1369 until 1385. In addition to the extent and nature of that service (to which we shall return shortly), what is important for the present investigation is that only one in five of the young and middle-aged witnesses who spoke on Morley's behalf gave no indication of service with the sword during this period.[134]

However we might choose to characterise the Morleys' extended social circle, it could hardly be said to be demilitarised. But to what extent can this group be taken as broadly representative of the late-fourteenth-century gentry? It is generally assumed that the very selection of the witnesses for their experience and knowledge has distorted the sample,[135] though that suspicion appears to be based upon the further assumption that the pattern of military service revealed cannot have been typical. We need to remember that, in assembling his witnesses, Morley turned not simply to the most experienced soldiers in England but rather to men who could speak convincingly about the legitimacy of his family's heraldic identity, particularly as it had been publicly demonstrated over

[131] All told, testimony survives from about 500 laymen. Only nine witnesses, all knights, appear in the records of both cases; eight of them testified on behalf of Scrope and Morley.
[132] There are 177 depositions, but 17 men gave evidence on two separate occasions. Fifty-eight churchmen spoke in support of Morley's cause. TNA C 47/6/1; Ayton, 'Knights, Esquires and Military Service', p. 86.
[133] Of 102 lay witnesses, only 18 offered no evidence of martial experience. For general analysis of the military testimony, see Ayton, 'Knights, Esquires and Military Service', pp. 88–97.
[134] Of the under-fifties, 8 gave non-martial testimony whereas 32 spoke in general or specific terms of personal military experience. The vast majority of middle-aged witnesses had fought at least once.
[135] Keen, Origins of the English Gentleman, p. 60.

time on campaign. As it happened, in 1386–7 it was neither difficult for Morley to find militarily experienced gentlemen to testify on his behalf nor necessary for him to rely primarily upon those who could speak only of heraldic trappings, artworks and monuments located in domestic or ecclesiastical settings. 'Fighting' witnesses also turned out in large numbers in support of Richard, Lord Scrope's armorial claim against Sir Robert Grosvenor, but what is apparent about that group is the prominence among them of members of John of Gaunt's extensive military affinity.[136] By contrast, Morley's supporters cannot be characterised as atypical occupants of a 'belligerent enclave'.[137] For sure, his support had a regional basis, just as had Sir Robert Grosvenor's. The Morley family's landholding stronghold was in Norfolk and the witnesses who spoke on his behalf were predominantly drawn from East Anglia and neighbouring areas.[138] But, as the witnesses make clear, this wide tract of territory was a recruiting ground for a variety of magnates of the front rank, as well as for captains of purely regional significance.

The social composition of this group of witnesses is another of the distinctive characteristics which, taken together, make it an ideal sample for our present purposes. Within the group there were representatives from all levels of the pyramid of gentility, from the earl of Salisbury at the top to a handful of self-styled 'gentils hommes' at the bottom. On the more heavily populated intermediate levels, for every knight there were two esquires. Thus, whereas three-quarters of Scrope's lay witnesses were knights, among Morley's supporters it was the sub-knightly gentry who were numerically dominant. And yet, if the esquires' knowledge and experience were being exploited in the Court of Chivalry at something approaching a level proportionate to the military contribution that they had been making, we are left wondering whether those occupying the broad base of the pyramid of gentility were less well represented among witnesses speaking in support of Morley's cause, and if so, why. It is notable that the three witnesses who stated simply that they were 'de gentil sanc' were all old soldiers of considerable experience.[139] But equally striking is that none of the five who styled himself 'gentil homme' was able to provide any 'military' testimony.[140] We should be wary of drawing conclusions of wide application from so small a sample, especially with regard to the significance of the *gentils hommes*' testimony. However, if a tentative conclusion were to be offered at this stage it would be that Morley's supporters should be viewed as broadly representative of the militarily active (mainly upper and middle) levels of the gentry, rather than of the gentry as a whole.

---

136   Keen, *Origins of the English Gentleman*, p. 65.
137   A term coined by Sumption, *Divided Houses*, pp. 776–7.
138   Ayton, 'Knights, Esquires and Military Service', p. 85 and n. 27.
139   William Sutton, Philip Warenner and, most notably, Henry Hoo, whose career stretched from the battle of Halidon Hill (1333) to the campaign of 1369. TNA C 47/6/1, nos 5, 10, 11.
140   TNA C 47/6/1, nos 78, 168, 170, 175, 177.

What does the individual and collective experience of our sample-group of Morley supporters – and especially the fifty-two witnesses who mentioned service with the sword from 1369 to 1385 – reveal about the extent and nature of the late-fourteenth-century gentry's involvement in war? As it stands, the testimony focuses in the main on royal expeditions to France, though nineteen men also noted that, in 1385, they had served with Richard II's army in Scotland, which had been the occasion of the initial flare-up of the Lovel v. Morley armorial dispute. We need to be aware of the limitations of the information at our disposal, particularly of the distortion that has resulted from the Court of Chivalry's predominant concern with gathering evidence on the occasions when the contestant families bore the disputed arms. No fewer than twenty-seven men recalled that they had seen Sir William Morley serving in France in 1369, but the expeditions of the next decade and a half appear more intermittently in our witnesses' statements.[141] While we would expect service in unusually large royal armies, such as those raised in 1359–60 – recalled by nearly half (forty-one) of Morley's witnesses – and 1385, to figure prominently in the testimony, it is difficult to believe that only one of our witnesses was among the 3,000 or so men-at-arms who participated in John of Gaunt's *chevauchée* of 1373,[142] and that none of them had fought with Bishop Despenser in Flanders in 1383. In fact, other sources of evidence for the personnel of these two armies suggest that at least another seven of Morley's witnesses had actually been serving on Gaunt's expedition in 1373, and that seven of them were also probably involved in the Flanders 'crusade' ten years later.[143] Here, therefore, by drawing on enrolled letters of protection and the many retinue rolls that have survived from this period, we have a means of supplementing and enriching the core evidence of the Court of Chivalry depositions.[144] The problems, principally connected with nominal record linkage, which perennially attend prosopographical exercises such as this, while not disappearing altogether, will have diminished considerably. Rather than having to imagine military careers from scratch, with the linking of each fragment of evidence all too often accompanied by a measure of speculation, we have an opportunity to anchor these fragments to an existing chronological framework that is already well endowed with personal information concerning age, spells of service and associated captains. The essential reliability of these

[141] 1375 (5 witnesses), 1378 (9), 1380 (6). Cf. the rather more plentiful evidence for the 1370s that can be extracted from the records of the Grey v. Hastings case of 1408–10: M. Keen, 'Military Experience and the Court of Chivalry: The Case of Grey v. Hastings', in M. Keen, *Nobles, Knights and Men-at-arms*, pp. 167–85 (182).

[142] Ralph Bocking (C 47/6/1, no. 101).

[143] Here and below, in compiling these statistics I have made use of The Soldier in Later Medieval England database. Witnesses who are likely to have served in 1373 are: TNA C 47/6/1, nos 3, 37, 40, 42, 62, 69 and 102. 1383: C 47/6/1, nos 24, 40, 48, 51, 53, 62, 10.

[144] We can also draw on a little of the Scrope v. Grosvenor evidence, since 5 of our sample group of 52 witnesses spoke on behalf of Scrope as well. Nicolas, *Scrope v. Grosvenor*, I, pp. 63, 162–3, 173–4, 201–2, 208–9.

existing career profiles is not in doubt. Lapses in memory there may occasionally have been, but when the Court of Chivalry testimony can be checked against the 'military-administrative' records, as can sometimes be done with the Morley depositions, the recollections of our witnesses are consistently confirmed.

The extensive coverage of the late-fourteenth-century military-administrative records means that the supplementation and enrichment of the Morley witnesses' career profiles affects not only such headline campaigns as Gaunt's 'great' *chevauchée* of 1373, but also the generality of less well-known expeditions, including the naval and amphibious operations that were so notable a feature of this phase of the French war, and garrison service in fortresses held by the English Crown.[145] As a consequence, some witnesses can be shown to have led military lives that were altogether busier than their Court of Chivalry testimony would suggest.[146] It is possible to extend the careers of some of them beyond 1385. Overall, evidence from other records approximately doubles the number of occasions on which members of our sample-group can be shown to have gone to war during the period 1369–85.[147] However, what we should not forget is that although in some respects more revealing than their counterparts for earlier decades of the century, the surviving military-administrative records for the period from 1369 are neither complete nor uniform in coverage.[148] Some indication of this is discernible with those witnesses – about twenty of them – whose testimony cannot be supplemented in any way by searching other sources:[149] what these men revealed before the Court of Chivalry is all that can be known about their careers with the sword. In general, what this means is that if we are to regard the collective military experience of our sample as in some sense representative of that of the wider pool of militarily active gentry, perhaps as a guide to the intensity of their service, the incompleteness of the military-prosopographical data does need to be recognised and compensated for.

The martial experiences of individuals as recalled in their Court of Chivalry testimony and what those recollections might reveal about patterns of military

---

145 We find, for example, that Thomas Lampete, esquire (TNA C 47/6/1, no. 67) was a specialist in naval expeditions during the 1370s, something that was not revealed in his testimony.

146 E.g. Sir William Elmham (TNA C 47/6/1, no. 62), who admitted only to serving in Scotland in 1385. Cf. TNA E 101/31/11, no. 2, m. 1 (1371); C 76/56, m. 14 (1373); C 76/64, m. 16 (1379–80); C 76/67, mm. 8, 16 (1383); C 76/69, m. 28 (1384); E 101/40/39, m. 1 (naval, 1385). See also Magee, 'Sir William Elmham and the Recruitment for Henry Despenser's Crusade of 1383'.

147 Uncertain linkages are excluded from this calculation. Evidence for knights is more plentiful than it is for esquires.

148 The completeness of the retinue rolls for the 1387 and 1388 campaigns is exceptional, and it is hardly surprising that about a dozen of the men in our sample appear to have served on one or both of these occasions.

149 In four of these cases, the military-administrative records verify what we know of particular periods of service, but add no new information.

service in fourteenth-century England have received a good deal of attention from historians.[150] But in addition to lacking systematic access to the military-administrative records, these studies have not focused explicitly on the period from the resumption of the French war in 1369 until the Scottish campaign of 1385 and beyond, which is our particular concern.[151] The fifty-two witnesses who comprise our sample were a heterogeneous group. Their ages in 1386–7 ranged from 19 to 70 and their experiences of the French war were correspondingly varied.[152] For a dozen of those who had first taken up arms during the 1330s, 1340s and 1350s, the campaign of 1369 was to be their last.[153] Hugh Coursoun of Careleton, who had first fought in Aquitaine in 1345, stated that he had not borne arms during the 'time' of Thomas, Lord Morley 'par cause des diverses maladies'.[154] Others, including three veterans of Halidon Hill (1333), may simply have been feeling their age.[155] Yet we should not imagine that the army of 1369, nor even the Peace of Brétigny, marked a clear watershed – an end and a beginning – as far as army personnel were concerned. In our sample, for every fighter from the first ten to fifteen years of the French war who retired from the fray for good after 1369, there was another who continued to enlist into the 1370s and, in some cases, the 1380s, thereby maintaining in the armies of that period a significant thread of continuity from the era of English military successes.[156]

The greybeards who were already veterans when the French war resumed in 1369 form a distinguishable subset within our sample-group. A second consists of twenty-one younger men for whom the experience of war had begun in 1369 or, as in most cases, during the 1370s and 1380s. A few of them appear to have served only once or twice, though – as noted above – this may be an impression created by uneven documentary survival. So frequent were the opportunities for campaigning during the two decades preceding the truce of Leulinghem (1389) that it was possible to acquire considerable experience at this time, and a core group – at least a third of the twenty-one – certainly did so.[157] The intermingling of experience and new blood, of continuity and renewal, which we find within the genteel military community is neatly illustrated by what our sample-group

[150] Ayton, 'Knights, Esquires and Military Service', pp. 88–97; Keen, *Origins of the English Gentlemen*, Ch. 4.

[151] For a brief but useful summary, see Keen, 'Military Experience and the Court of Chivalry: The Case of Grey v. Hastings', p. 182.

[152] On the issue of 'Age in the Sources', see R. Gorski, *The Fourteenth-Century Sheriff. English Local Administration in the Late Middle Ages* (Woodbridge, 2003), pp. 130–35.

[153] TNA C 47/6/1, nos 8, 10, 14, 22, 29, 30, 31, 36, 38, 92, 99, 104.

[154] TNA C 47/6/1, no. 99.

[155] TNA C 47/6/1, nos 10, 29, 92.

[156] Continuity from the Reims campaign of 1359–60 is particularly striking. Of Morley's 41 witnesses in 1386–7 who recalled that campaign, over a dozen (perhaps as many as 16) continued to serve into the 1370s and often into the 1380s.

[157] Eight witnesses served on at least three occasions during the period 1369–1385: TNA C 47/6/1, nos 40, 47, 48, 53, 62, 67, 68, 93.

reveals about the composition of the army that accompanied Richard II to Scotland in 1385. Of the twenty witnesses who recalled this campaign,[158] three appear to be first-timers, eight had fought once or twice before and nine, nearly half, had served on at least three previous occasions. That some of these men could recall the Reims campaign is perhaps unremarkable. More worthy of note is the experiential reach of those that stretched back to the battles 'despaynolx sur le mer' (1350) or Mauron (1352).[159]

If our sample-group indicates that repeat-serving knights, esquires and gentlemen were as common as 'occasional' soldiers in the late fourteenth century, and probably more so, it would mean, too, that, in terms of accumulation of experience within the military community, nothing had changed since the first half of the century. What we might expect to have changed is the connection, evident earlier in the century, between repeated service and loyalty to a single captain. As we have seen, moderate to high retinue-level stability of personnel had been commonplace during the first half of the century, while during the last third the proportion of men who returned repeatedly to the same captain was generally smaller. Exogenous forces had destabilised the dynamics of recruitment that had prevailed during the early to mid fourteenth century and the new equilibrium established between the captains' collective recruiting reach and the forces of supply and demand was less likely to foster retinue-level stability of manpower over time.

In relation to this issue, the regular identification of captains in both the Morley witnesses' testimony and the military-administrative records provides evidence that is instructive. It is certainly true that a man like the esquire Oliver Mendham, who served under the Morleys on five successive occasions from 1369 to 1385, stands out as exceptional.[160] While in the 1330s and 1340s William Thweyt, esquire, a younger son from the parish gentry of Norfolk, served repeatedly under the banners of Sir John Norwich or members of the Ufford family, influential captains within the recruiting networks of that region,[161] the initial impression given by the service records of our sample-group of fifty-two witnesses is one of inconstancy. But a closer look reveals underlying patterns

---

[158]   One of the 20, Sir John Breux (or Brewes), did not mention the 1385 campaign in his testimony in support of Morley's cause, but did imply that he had participated in it in his deposition in support of Richard, Lord Scrope: TNA C 47/6/1, no. 102; Nicolas, *Scrope and Grosvenor*, I, p. 63.

[159]   Espaynolx sur le mer: Edmund Breton, esquire (TNA C 47/6/1, no. 44), Sir John Breux (C 47/6/1, no. 102) and Sir John Burgh (C 47/6/1, no. 37). Mauron: Sir John Breux (Nicolas, *Scrope and Grosvenor*, I, p. 63) and Sir John Lakyngheth (Nicolas, *Scrope and Grosvenor*, I, pp. 208–9).

[160]   TNA C 47/6/1, no. 26. He was a feed servant of Thomas, Lord Morley.

[161]   TNA C 47/6/1, no. 92; A. Ayton, 'William de Thweyt, Esquire: Deputy Constable of Corfe Castle in the 1340s', *Notes and Queries for Somerset and Dorset*, 32 (1989), pp. 731–8, which includes much additional material from the military-administrative records of the period.

of loyalty not unlike those that are abundantly visible in the early to mid fourteenth century. The problem is that these patterns are sometimes obscured by
the consequences of such endogenous forces for change as the death or retirement of captains. The thirteen witnesses who had served under Humphrey de
Bohun, earl of Hereford, in the campaigns of 1369, 1371 or 1372 were obliged
to look elsewhere after his untimely death in 1373.[162] Several of them turned
to the duke of Gloucester.[163] The death of the elderly earl of Suffolk in 1369
appears to have had similar consequences, though at least three of the seven
witnesses who had served with him in 1356 or 1359 were able to continue this
association under his son's banner, where they were joined by four more.[164] These
threads of continuity are instructive, indicating that the instability of retinue
manpower in the late fourteenth century was not simply the consequence of a
general change in the behaviour of all potential men-at-arms. Within the context
of powerful exogenous forces, it was the large number of military professionals
in the expanded pool of men-at-arms, including many of sub-genteel origin, that
appears to have been the principal cause of this shift to instability. The Court of
Chivalry was not concerned with such men, at least not until they had become
socially respectable. Not for nothing was each of the Morley witnesses asked
whether he was 'un home de jentil sanc ou non', and at the heart of what many
of the younger men among them revealed was an engagement with traditional,
socially rooted recruiting networks that was not so very different from the experience of their elderly peers.

The testimony of the Court of Chivalry focused primarily on major field
campaigns in France or Scotland, only occasionally on crusading and rarely on
freelance soldiering. In general, a witness's recollections of 'non-royal' service
would be deemed relevant only if one of the armorial contestants, or a relative, had been seen engaging in such service. It is in this light that the almost
complete silence of Morley's witnesses on these matters should be viewed. Sir
John Breux mentions that he had fought in 'Pruce' and 'outre la grande mier'
only in order to emphasise that he had seen Sir John Lovel in these locations
in arms different from those claimed in 1386.[165] On the other hand, Richard,
Lord Scrope's witnesses revealed more about their own travels to the frontiers
of Christendom because the Scropes themselves 'had a crusading record beside

---

[162]   The depositions of the 13 (TNA C 47/61, nos 21, 25, 37, 38, 44, 47, 52, 55, 56, 58, 61, 67,
102) are significantly enriched by the military-administrative records. Sir John Burgh (no. 37)
was in receipt of a 40-mark annuity from the earl, and Sir Thomas Mandeville (no. 47) had
been granted the manor of Great Leighs by him: Holmes, *The Estates of the Higher Nobility*,
p. 70 and n. 9.

[163]   TNA C 47/6/1, nos 44, 47, 67.

[164]   TNA C 47/6/1, nos 14, 23, 31, 34, 36, 37, 42, 48, 52, 53, 101.

[165]   TNA C 47/6/1, no. 102. One of a group of more elaborate depositions that survive from
the hearing at the Austin friars, Norwich, on 5 April 1386.

which those of Morley [and] Lovel ... pale into insignificance'.[166] Some of these witnesses also offer fleeting glimpses of the world of freelance soldiering. John Charnels, esquire, recalled an incident in 'les veillez guerrez' in France, when he and forty companions had been operating from a castle called 'Quarranteau', while Sir John Godard spoke of service further afield, in the company of the 'duke of Duras beyond Venice'.[167] In each of these cases a Scrope had been in attendance; but in a couple of other instances the witnesses admitted to this style of military life only in order to make clear to the Court the limits of their knowledge. Thus, when Sir Hugh Browe stated that he had served 'en garnisouns & en les compaignez en France', but never in 'grauntz viagez', he did so in order to distance himself from the mainstream military context that had preoccupied the Scropes, the point being that Browe was not a supporter of their claim to the disputed arms.[168] However, the evidence of the military-administrative records suggests a service record with a rather different focus and trajectory: a career in which the distinctive military life that Browe claimed for himself was intermingled with conventional service in the king's armies.[169]

The most that can be said of what the testimony of Court of Chivalry witnesses reveals of 'non-royal' service would be that, quantitatively speaking, it is patchy. We are probably seeing no more than the tip of the iceberg of the witnesses' crusading, and not even that for their freelance soldiering.[170] It may well be that we should turn the research spotlight on the lacunae in our witnesses' declared military records, for these apparent breaks from active service were sometimes lengthy and otherwise inexplicable. When a soldier-esquire such as William Thweyt, who had fought for the English Crown with professional regularity from 1333 to 1347, disappears from royal service for over twenty years, only to return to the king's army in 1369, we are bound to wonder whether in the interim he had been exploiting freelance opportunities in France and perhaps Italy.[171] With regard to tracing particular fighting men in the 'garrisons and companies' in France, the royal military-administrative records will be of little use, because – as was highlighted by Sir Walter Bentley's report from Brittany in 1352 – freelance companies based in local strongholds, who 'guerroient pur lur singuler profit',

166 Keen, 'Chaucer's Knight, the English Aristocracy and the Crusade', p. 108.

167 Nicolas, *Scrope and Grosvenor*, I, pp. 171–2, 211–12. The 'duke of Duras' is probably Charles of Durazzo, who invaded Dalmatia and marched on Buda in 1385.

168 Nicolas, *Scrope and Grosvenor*, I, p. 82; cf. his deposition in support of Grosvenor's claim, I, pp. 256–7. Note also John Neulande, who remarked that he 'estoit en garnison en Normandie, en Bretaigne, en Burgoigne & en les grauntez compaignies': Nicolas, *Scrope and Grosvenor*, I, p. 138.

169 *The House of Commons 1386–1421*, ed. J.S. Roskell, L. Clark and C. Rawcliffe, 4 vols (Stroud, 1992), vol. ii, pp. 384–6; Bell, *War and the Soldier*, pp. 101–4.

170 For English involvement in the Baltic crusades, see Werner Paravicini, *Die Preussenreisen des europäischen Adels*, 2 vols (Sigmaringen, 1989–95), I, pp. 115–35: all participants known by name are listed there in Table 9 (pp. 123–7).

171 TNA C 47/6/1, no. 92; Ayton, 'William de Thweyt, Esquire'.

were neither paid nor systematically recorded by the English Crown.[172] Elsewhere, however, and most notably in the Italian peninsula, Englishmen serving
as mercenaries will have left a mark in the records. Although the historian of
the English military community lacks a convenient work of reference comparable
with Karl-Heinrich Schäfer's monumental volumes on the German knights and
squires who served in Italy,[173] recent research in the Italian archives suggests that
it will be possible to add a mercenary dimension to more than a few military
careers that otherwise we would assume to have been exclusively focused on the
king of England's wars in France or Scotland.[174] Indeed, it seems that a spell of
service under Sir John Hawkwood's command can even be added to the extraordinarily adventurous career that Nicholas Sabraham outlined before the Court
of Chivalry.[175] Therefore, if it would be necessary to scale-up any prosopographi-
cally based assessment of the gentry's martial role in order to compensate for
our incomplete knowledge of service performed in royal armies and garrisons,
additional adjustment would be needed to take account of the still less visible
service undertaken in the freelance sphere.

    To the problem of how many gentlemen soldiers from England were actively
engaged in freelance or company-based mercenary service, we can as yet bring
only informed guesswork to bear. What we can be sure of is that there were
constituencies of manpower within – or, rather, on the margins of – the gentry
to whom such opportunities would have appealed. Knowing 'no other calling but
arms', and brought up to consider that calling honourable, these were men 'who
by the custom of the land have little or no portion in the inheritance of their
fathers and who by poverty are often constrained to follow wars that are unjust
and tyrannical so as to sustain their estate of *noblesse*'.[176] Philippe de Mézières's
words sum up the plight of younger or illegitimate sons, and also more generally
that of the menfolk of families perched precariously on the fringes of gentility at
a time of economic and social upheaval. Indeed, this was an all too often experi-

---

[172] *Oeuvres de Froissart*, ed. Kervyn de Lettenhove, 25 vols (Brussells, 1867–77), xviii, pp.
339–43; K. Fowler, 'Les finances et la discipline dans les armées anglaises en France au xiv^e
siècle', *Les Cahiers Vernonnais* 4 (1964), pp. 55–84 (77–8). Cf. Fowler, *Medieval Mercenaries*,
pp. 8–9.

[173] Karl-Heinrich Schäfer, *Deutsche Ritter und Edelknechte in Italien*, 4 vols (Paderborn,
1911–40). See also Stephan Selzer, *Deutsche Söldner im Italien des Trecento* (Tübingen, 2001).

[174] See, for example, A.R. Bell, 'The Fourteenth-Century Soldier – more Chaucer's Knight
or Medieval Career?', in *Mercenaries and Paid Men. The Mercenary Identity in the Middle Ages*,
ed. J. France (Leiden and Boston, 2008), pp. 301–15 (309–10, Table 3), drawing on the archival
research of William Caferro.

[175] Nicolas, *Scrope and Grosvenor*, I, pp. 124–5; Caferro, *John Hawkwood*, pp. 200–201. This
assumes that the man called 'Sabraam' in Archivio di Stato di Mantova, Archivio Gonzaga,
busta 2388, no. 284 is one and the same as the Court of Chivalry deponent. I am grateful to
Professor Caferro for sending me a copy of this document.

[176] M. Keen, 'War, Peace and Chivalry', in M. Keen, *Nobles, Knights and Men-at-Arms*, pp.
1–20 (14).

enced predicament among the petty nobilities of Europe and, as a consequence, the down-at-heel English gentleman seeking employment for his sword could expect to rub shoulders with his social counterparts from France, Germany, Hungary or Italy in what could be a cosmopolitan community of military professionals.[177] He would also find himself serving alongside those 'unknown youths' of sub-genteel origin, who, as we have seen, were equally attracted to the lifestyle associated with professional soldiering. This world of social and cultural heterogeneity, of shared adventure and hardship, 'blurred societal markers and distinctions and forced soldiers into the unique position of re-creating themselves'.[178] For the historian seeking to reconstruct and quantify the English gentry's martial role at this time, men who 're-created' themselves in this way, achieving wealth, reputation and social elevation through professional soldiering, complicate the investigation but also serve as a timely reminder that the 'gentry' was a dynamic social formation, its ranks constantly refreshed, the relative status of its members changing. That the aforementioned veteran Sir Hugh Browe had been required by both parties in the Scrope v. Grosvenor dispute to give evidence before the Court of Chivalry offers some indication of how a yeoman's son could, as a result of prolonged and distinguished service with the sword, earn social acceptance from the gentle born and admittance to their ranks.[179]

*

Reflection upon our Court of Chivalry witnesses and their testimony, on who they were, what they recalled and also what they omitted to mention, prompts two general observations. The first, quite simply, is that we should not underestimate the contribution made by the gentry to the enlarged pool of active men-at-arms during the last third of the fourteenth century. That only nine knights and none at all of the sub-knightly witnesses were called upon to give evidence in both of the armorial cases of the mid-1380s surely offers some indication of just how many active and retired men-at-arms there were within the gentry at that time. The age and career profiles of our fifty-two witnesses indicate that there had been a steady take-up of new recruits since the 1360s and that willingness to return to the fray continued well into mid-life. Indeed, viewed as a proportion of available genteel combatants, those who served repeatedly appear

[177] For the social backgrounds of mercenary captains and their subordinates, both English and continental, see Fowler, *Medieval Mercenaries*, pp. 10–23; Caferro, *John Hawkwood*, pp. 69, 334–5.

[178] Caferro, *John Hawkwood*, p. 334.

[179] Bennett, *Community, Class and Careerism*, pp. 175, 182. With reference to Browe's social acceptance, it may be significant that 'his line's principal seat' was established not in his native Cheshire, but at Teigh in Rutland, for which county he served as justice of the peace and member of parliament. Bennett, *Community, Class and Careerism*, pp. 188–9; *The House of Commons 1386–1421*, vol. ii, pp. 384–6.

to have been just as numerous in the 1370s and 1380s as they had been back in the 1330s and 1340s; and, as we have seen, the service of at least a proportion of fighting knights and esquires continued to be closely related to established recruitment networks and their exploitation by the king's captains. This is not to suggest that their military role was unaffected by the powerful exogenous forces that had been at work on the dynamics of recruitment, and in particular by the emergence of enlarged, mixed retinues which forced captains to reach beyond established networks based on locality, landholdings and social connections. But a more influential role in bringing about the greater instability of personnel that is evident in the retinues of late-fourteenth-century armies appears to have been played by socially disengaged military professionals, many of them of sub-genteel origin.

Whether the various levels of the pyramid of gentility were making proportionate contributions to the pool of active men-at-arms (in terms of numbers of individuals and intensity of service) is not altogether clear. Our sample of fifty-two witnesses does tend to support the idea that the militarily active section of the gentry was populated predominantly by knights and esquires, with less intensive participation by the 'gentlemen' occupying the broad base of the pyramid of gentility. But the modest representation of the 'parish' gentry in our sample may have other explanations. There might have been a certain reluctance to call as witnesses those who themselves had not yet been admitted to the 'charmed world of the armigerous'. Moreover, it was also precisely such men who were likely to migrate from the margins of domestic gentility into the continental world of professional soldiering, and that would have resulted in long-term absences from England. However, in an assessment of the role of the gentry, what was happening at the margins of gentility is perhaps less important than the deeds and preoccupations of those at its centre, particularly with regard to engagement with the mainstream of royal expeditions. In this respect the thrust of the evidence is clear. If, as some historians have argued, the English gentry was progressively disengaging from war during the last three decades of the fourteenth century, this can only have become a significant trend after 1389, when opportunities for major continental expeditions ceased. Prior to the Truce of Leulinghem the decline in active participation appears more marked than it really was partly because the pool of manpower able and willing to serve as men-at-arms had grown and partly because a proportion of gentleman fighters, having adopted a careerist style of military life that could take them well away from France, were often unavailable for recruitment into royal armies. The professional soldiers of sub-genteel origin were not replacing the traditional 'military class' but supplementing it and, in the case of the fortunate ones, mingling with it.

The second general observation that arises from this contextualised analysis of Court of Chivalry testimony concerns how the mid- to late-fourteenth-century military community as a whole should be characterised, and how its constituent sub-groups, including the gentry, should be situated within that characterisation.

Clearly the difference between the contribution and outlook of the gentleman warrior whose service was rooted in traditional values and social structures and those of the socially disengaged professional soldier of sub-genteel origin is important, but it represents only part of the story. To view the military community in that way would be, in effect, to tell a tale of two military classes, the 'old' and the 'new', whereas we need also to take account of a third group composed of genteel military careerists. But how should we characterise their role? Was theirs really a discrete third group, or should it be seen as forming a socio-cultural bridge between the two sharply contrasted camps, with a foot planted very firmly in both? Indeed, was their role at the very heart of the evolutionary processes that shaped the distinctive character of England's military community in the late fourteenth and early fifteenth centuries, contributing on the one hand to the rise and socio-military integration of the professional soldier and on the other to processes whereby the traditional values, self-image and behaviour of the 'old' military class were scrutinised, re-evaluated and, in some respects, modified? Addressing these questions in the depth that their implications demand must be postponed to a later occasion. For the moment, a summary of issues, which may also serve as a general conclusion for this essay, must suffice.

The gentleman military careerist who is clearly visible in the mid to late fourteenth century pursuing the life of the roving routier or the more sedentarily employed mercenary, either exclusively or intermingled with spells of royal service, was a phenomenon with identifiable origins. There had always been career openings that offered regular or long-term service to men willing and able to engage in specialist forms of soldiering (for example, garrison service) or to be flexible during periods of intensive warfare. And there had always been scions of established gentry families to whom, usually for reasons of delayed or inadequate inheritance, such opportunities might appeal. The matching of demand and supply in this way had certainly occurred during the reigns of Edward I and Edward II, but what appears to have been of foundational importance for the development of the gentleman military professional in England was the decade and a half of intensively waged, large-scale warfare that commenced in 1332–3. This was a period in which permanent garrisons were maintained in Scotland and then France, and which saw the raising of a series of major field armies to which the gentry were required to make a substantial contribution.[180] In creating a much increased and sustained demand for manpower, this intensive period of warfare put a strain on established recruitment networks and encouraged careerism in a recognisable form, as service opportunities requiring professional specialisation and commitment became readily available in a variety of contexts. Although the agencies of change affecting the dynamics of recruitment were initially predominantly endogenous in nature, the enlistment of a proportion of army and garrison personnel had already become disengaged from

---

180 Ayton, 'Edward III and the English Aristocracy', pp. 196–206.

traditional social networks. During the second half of the century the primacy of powerful exogenous forces accelerated the process to the point of reconfiguring the dynamics of recruitment, changing the structure and character of armies and ensuring the ubiquity of the military professional.

For some careerist soldiers, the liberating military experiences of these years, located as they were amidst conditions of economic and political upheaval in continental Europe, led them naturally into the world of mercenary service: a world in which employment was 'socially unembedded', evidently self-interested and wholly indifferent to political concerns.[181] To reside permanently in this world (as we see with Sir John Hawkwood) represents one end of the spectrum of military professionalism. Rather different, and more likely to influence martial culture in England, were those men for whom service with the sword never (or only occasionally) became wholly detached from the social and political context of their birth. Among gentleman careerists, such men as this were probably in the majority.[182] Is it possible that by deed and association they influenced genteel martial culture 'from within' in a mildly subversive way? They actively pursued careers that broke away from the gentleman warrior's traditional focus on 'socially embedded' service under the banner of a regional lord or supra-regional magnate. They also associated freely with sub-genteel professionals and in all likelihood helped the more successful among them to secure a measure of social acceptability within the ranks of the gentle born. From his detached viewpoint, the historian will ponder the likely effects of this transfusion of vigorous new blood on the health of the gentry. But that might be to focus upon physical well-being at the expense of mental state. For it would have been difficult for contemporaries wholly to disassociate the gentleman careerist and his barely respectable comrades in arms from that more unsettling phenomenon: the recently emergent, socially amorphous form of military community in which experienced professionals mingled with opportunists, criminals and social misfits. It is more than likely that the rampant individualism of these ubiquitous military enterprisers played a part in the disintegration of traditional recruiting networks. Discouraged thereby from participating in war directly, the gentry's identification with the martial calling would lessen and ultimately it would become demilitarised as a social group. However, that outcome, influenced by a variety of forces, was reached only gradually. From the vantage point of the mid 1380s, as provided by the records of the Court of Chivalry, we can plainly see that there was still at that time a significant constituency within the gentry who were prepared to enlist for

---

[181] For a definition of the mercenary within a broader typological analysis of military service, see S. Morillo, 'Mercenaries, mamluks and militia: towards a cross-cultural typology of military service', in *Mercenaries and Paid Men. The Mercenary Identity in the Middle Ages*, ed. J. France (Leiden and Boston, 2008), pp. 244–60.

[182] A good example from the group of Morley witnesses would be Sir William Elmham. See Magee, 'Sir William Elmham and the Recruitment for Henry Despenser's Crusade of 1383'.

war when the opportunity arose and in doing so utilise traditional avenues to recruitment: a form of military service that harmonises well with the evidence that can be pieced together for the knights and esquires who had fought at Crécy under the earl of Warwick's banner forty years earlier.

2

Total War in the Middle Ages?
The Contribution of English Landed Society
to the Wars of Edward I and Edward II

David Simpkin

The association between landholding, wealth and military obligation in the Middle Ages has been a much studied subject.[1] It is axiomatic that in an age before the rise of professional, standing armies the successful recruitment of large numbers of soldiers, both mounted and foot, depended, in the main, on the exploitation of essentially private resources, both material and human. In other words, warfare in the Middle Ages was a collective private enterprise that could, through the muster process and (at least from the later fourteenth century) the issuing of military ordinances be made into a centrally controlled public enterprise for the duration of a campaign, usually a few weeks or months.[2] It is one thing, however,

---

[1]   The most relevant studies are: H.M. Chew, *The English Ecclesiastical Tenants-in-Chief and Knight Service, especially in the Thirteenth and Fourteenth Centuries* (London, 1932); E.G. Kimball, *Serjeanty Tenure in Medieval England* (London, 1936); M.R. Powicke, 'The General Obligation to Cavalry Service under Edward I', *Speculum* 28 (1953), pp. 814–33; M.R. Powicke, 'Edward II and Military Obligation', *Speculum* 31 (1956), pp. 92–119; I.J. Sanders, *Feudal Military Service in England: A Study of the Constitutional and Military Powers of the Barones in Medieval England* (Oxford, 1956); B.D. Lyon, *From Fief to Indenture: The Transition from Feudal to Non-Feudal Contract in Western Europe* (Cambridge, Mass., 1957); M.R. Powicke, *Military Obligation in Medieval England: A Study in Liberty and Duty* (Oxford, 1962); M. Prestwich, 'Cavalry Service in Early Fourteenth-Century England', in *War and Government in the Middle Ages: Essays in Honour of J.O. Prestwich*, ed. J. Gillingham and J.C. Holt (Woodbridge, 1984), pp. 147–58.
[2]   A. Ayton, 'Armies and Military Communities in Fourteenth-Century England', in *Soldiers, Nobles and Gentlemen: Essays in Honour of Maurice Keen*, ed. P. Coss and C. Tyerman (Woodbridge, 2009), pp. 215–39. The debt that this paper owes to Dr Ayton's work and to this article in particular will be clear to those who are familiar with them. For discussion of later medieval ordinances of war, see M. Keen, 'Richard II's Ordinances of War of 1385', in *Rulers and Ruled in Late Medieval England: Essays presented to Gerald Harriss*, ed. R.E. Archer and S. Walker (London, 1995), pp. 33–48; A. Curry, 'The Military Ordinances of Henry V:

to know *that* the mounted arm of medieval armies comprised large numbers of privately assembled companies (military retinues) brought together from the localities, but quite another to know *how* these retinues were assembled and the nature of the social and landholding ties that underpinned them. In order to analyse more closely the influence that local, regional and landholding ties had on retinue composition it is necessary to have access both to detailed sources that shed light on the identities of landholders within a kingdom, on the one hand, and to sources that record the names of large numbers of soldiers serving in the armies of the same realm, on the other. In England, these conditions are met for the first time in the late thirteenth century during the reign of Edward I, a king renowned almost as much for his inquests into local government and landholding as for his pursuit of an English hegemony within the British Isles. This paper will explore the potential benefits of an integrated study of the land-holding sources and military service records for the reigns of Edwards I and II via an analysis of the evidence relating to just two counties, Cambridgeshire and Nottinghamshire.

Of course, a study that seeks to combine two distinct bodies of evidence into an integrated analysis must first acknowledge the limitations of the sources as well as the scholarly work already carried out on them. This paper seeks to build, in particular, on a growing body of research into the personnel and composi-tion of English armies of the later Middle Ages; that is, on an approach that focuses attention on the 'military community', or 'multiple military communities',[3] from which soldiers were drawn. As the concept of 'community' suggests,[4] this is a methodology that concentrates primarily (though by no means exclusively) on the roots of military service in later medieval England rather than on the conduct and activities of armies once they had mustered. What the 'roots' of military service actually means might, of course, vary from historian to histo-rian, but there does seem to be general consensus that, somewhere along the line, a consideration of where soldiers came from – specifically, where they held their lands – must play a part. For example, Philip Morgan, an early advocate of the concept of an Edwardian military community, chose to centre his atten-tion on one particular county, Cheshire, and on the social, lordship and tenurial networks within it.[5] Nor is it surprising that historians conducting a whole range

Texts and Contexts', in *War, Government and Aristocracy in the British Isles, c.1150–1500: Essays in Honour of Michael Prestwich*, ed. C. Given-Wilson, A. Kettle and L. Scales (Woodbridge, 2008), pp. 214–49.

[3] Ayton, 'Armies and Military Communities', p. 216. In French historiography the equivalent term is perhaps Philippe Contamine's 'société militaire'; P. Contamine, *Guerre, état et société à la fin du Moyen Age. Etudes sur les armées des rois de France, 1337–1494* (Paris, 1972), p. 542.

[4] Use of the word 'community' in this sense is not to everybody's taste. See, for example, C. Carpenter, 'Gentry and Community in Medieval England', *Journal of British Studies* 33 (1994), pp. 340–80.

[5] P. Morgan, *War and Society in Medieval Cheshire, 1277–1403* (Manchester, 1987), especially p. 150.

of studies on the gentry of later medieval England have used the county as their main focus of analysis, a method that implies a strong link between regional landholding, on the one hand, and a whole range of public activities, including soldiering, on the other.[6] Even historians working on the campaigning experiences of soldiers more generally, and at a national level, have often had recourse to trace their men back to the regions and localities from whence they came.[7] The basic premise upon which this paper is built is not, therefore, a new or original one. However, it will be shown that it is possible to investigate the influence of landholding on the composition of military retinues more comprehensively and thoroughly than has hitherto been attempted, at least when the sources allow, as they do for the reigns of Edward I and his son. From the outset it should be stressed that this paper does not seek to support the models of regional, county or local communities; rather, the aim is to see what the landholding sources can add to our understanding of military and social networks more generally.

This brings us, then, to the sources to be utilised in this paper. Thankfully, there is now a much healthier understanding of the potential, and pitfalls, of the sources for Edwardian armies than there used to be. This is due in no small part to the painstaking work carried out by Andrew Ayton on the sources for English armies dating from the fourteenth century, but especially for the reign of Edward III. In his monograph *Knights and Warhorses*, Ayton produced a much-needed and discerning guide for scholars working with a whole range of informative but potentially hazardous and misleading sources, including horse inventories (or horse-valuation rolls), letters of protection and of attorney, *vadia guerre* accounts

---

6   Examples are: A.R.J. Juřica, 'The Knights of Edward I: An Investigation of the Social Significance of Knightly Rank in the Period 1272–1307 Based on a Study of the Knights of Somerset', PhD thesis, University of Birmingham, 1976; G.G. Astill, 'The Medieval Gentry: A Study in Leicestershire Society, 1350–1399', PhD thesis, University of Birmingham, 1977; N. Saul, *Knights and Esquires: The Gloucestershire Gentry in the Fourteenth Century* (Oxford, 1981); M.J. Bennett, *Community, Class and Careerism: Cheshire and Lancashire Society in the Age of* Sir Gawain and the Green Knight (Cambridge, 1983); N. Saul, *Scenes from Provincial Life: Knightly Families in Sussex 1280–1400* (Oxford, 1986); S.J.P. Howarth, 'King, Government and Community in Cumberland and Westmorland c.1200–c.1400', PhD thesis, University of Liverpool, 1988; J.C. Ward, *The Essex Gentry and the County Community in the Fourteenth Century* (Chelmsford, 1991); C. Carpenter, *Locality and Polity. A Study of Warwickshire Landed Society, 1401–1499* (Cambridge, 1992); A. King, 'War, Politics and Landed Society in Northumberland, c.1296–c.1408', PhD thesis, University of Durham, 2001. See also P. Coss, 'Identity and the Gentry, c.1200–c.1340', *Thirteenth Century England VI*, ed. M. Prestwich, R.H. Britnell and R. Frame (Woodbridge, 1997), pp. 49–60. More recently, some attention has been given to the role of liberties as potential foci of communal interests and social networks. See, for example, M.L. Holford, 'War, Lordship and Community in the Liberty of Norhamshire', in *Liberties and Identities in the Medieval British Isles*, ed. M. Prestwich (Woodbridge, 2008), pp. 77–97.

7   A.R. Bell, *War and the Soldier in the Fourteenth Century* (Woodbridge, 2004), pp. 159–62; A. Ayton, 'The English Army at Crécy', in A. Ayton and P. Preston, *The Battle of Crécy, 1346* (Woodbridge, 2005), p. 213; D. Simpkin, *The English Aristocracy at War: From the Welsh Wars of Edward I to the Battle of Bannockburn* (Woodbridge, 2008), pp. 98–9, 147–8.

(or pay-rolls), proffer rolls and letters of pardon. These sources are, as Ayton described, 'the principal source materials for the names of serving men-at-arms in the fourteenth century';[8] and his study was all the more important for the reason that many of these sources also exist for the reigns of Edward I and Edward II. Perhaps the most significant finding on the armies of the later thirteenth and early fourteenth centuries, however, was made by Michael Prestwich when he observed that the armies of this period were a mixture of 'paid', 'feudal' and 'voluntary unpaid' elements.[9] In essence (and importantly for this study), this means that often the names of only a third or a half of the mounted, armoured warriors in the armies of Edward I and Edward II are known. Sometimes the proportion of surviving names is even smaller, as for the especially poorly documented campaign of Edward II to Scotland in 1314 that culminated in the battle of Bannockburn.[10] The names of hardly any of the thousands of arrayed foot soldiers serving in English armies during this stage of the wars are known, but this is not of great significance to this particular investigation as such men as these did not tend to be landholders.[11] Nevertheless, the incompleteness of the records for military service (as demonstrated by Ayton), combined with the fact that only a relatively small proportion of men-at-arms in early Edwardian armies received pay from the Crown and therefore appear in the surviving records (as shown by Prestwich), means that there is a large grey area of unknowing when it comes to reconstructing the service of English soldiers in this period. Whenever it seems, therefore, that a particular individual from a particular locality did not perform military service or that he did so on only a few occasions, it must be remembered that this only *seems* to be the case, and that the reality might have been different.

Having explained some of the limitations of the records for military service of the reigns of Edward I and Edward II, it nevertheless remains to draw attention to their considerable potential. Few of these records – the horse inventories, the letters of protection, the proffer rolls and so on – have been published,[12] which means that for most historians they remain difficult to access and daunting in scale and scope. The present study would, therefore, be impossible were it not for the fact that, as part of my previous research, I transcribed and computerised the majority of these sources for the years 1270 to 1314, including effectively all of the ones that name the men-at-arms serving in English armies of the period. In total,

---

[8] A. Ayton, *Knights and Warhorses: Military Service and the English Aristocracy under Edward III* (Woodbridge, 1994), p. 156.

[9] M. Prestwich, *War, Politics and Finance under Edward I* (London, 1972), pp. 69, 91.

[10] J.E. Morris, *Bannockburn* (Cambridge, 1914), p. 24.

[11] For the identities of the men involved in leading these arrayed troops on campaign, however, see the article in this volume by D.S. Bachrach.

[12] The campaign of 1298 is the most obvious exception as most of the documents for the English army in that year have been published for some time: *Scotland in 1298: Documents relating to the Campaign of Edward I in that Year*, ed. H. Gough (London, 1888).

these sources yield some 38,000 names relating to the performance of military service and an additional 10,000 or so names of men-at-arms engaged in the mobilisation process in some way, such as in lists of men summoned to muster.[13] Identifying specific individuals from this morass of data is a most difficult task, not least because one of the most voluminous bodies of evidence – letters of protection, of attorney and of respite of debts – does not, as a rule, give information on military status: whether the men in question were knights or sergeants (*scutiferi, servientes, armigeri* or *valetti*). Nevertheless, a tentative count based on this imperfect evidence reveals the names of some 1,350 knights and 4,900 sergeants who were militarily active in the years from 1270 up to and including the battle of Bannockburn.[14] Moreover, there are many additional named soldiers whose military (and social) status is simply not known. By drawing on this rich pool of evidence it has already been possible to demonstrate the extent to which the English gentry were involved in the wars of Edward I and Edward II. Some 84 per cent of the knights bachelor named on the Parliamentary roll of arms of *c.*1312, for example, gave military service at some point, and it was common for knights to serve on five or more campaigns during their lifetimes.[15] These were years, then, of intensive and extensive soldiering among the landholding community.

The next step is to build up the profiles of these knights and sergeants and trace them back to their local and regional communities, thereby revealing more about the social networks underpinning their military service. Fortunately, the landholding sources utilised in this paper are less problematic and varied in format and coverage than the records for military service. There are a number of different types of source that could be used to trace soldiers to a particular locality, some of which – like the Hundred rolls[16] – concern the possession of landed estates, and others of which – like the lay subsidy returns[17] – do not.

---

[13]　Simpkin, *The English Aristocracy at War*, p. 68, n. 1.

[14]　Simpkin, *The English Aristocracy at War*, p. 68.

[15]　Simpkin, *The English Aristocracy at War*, pp. 22–3, 89.

[16]　*Rotuli Hundredorum temp. Hen. III. and Edw. I. in Turr' Lond' et in Curia Receptae Scaccarii Westm. asservati*, 2 vols, ed. W. Illingworth and J. Caley (Record Commission, 1812–18). For work carried out on these returns, see H.M. Cam, 'Studies in the Hundred Rolls: Some Aspects of Thirteenth-Century Administration', in *Oxford Studies in Social and Legal History*, ed. P. Vinogradoff, vi (Oxford, 1921); H.M. Cam, *The Hundred and the Hundred Rolls: An Outline of Local Government in Medieval England* (London, 1930); S. Raban, *A Second Domesday? The Hundred Rolls of 1279–80* (Oxford, 2004).

[17]　J.F. Willard, *Parliamentary Taxes on Personal Property 1290 to 1334: A Study in Mediaeval English Financial Administration* (Cambridge, Mass., 1934), pp. 162–70. Some of the returns are in print for particular counties, but a large proportion of them remain in manuscript form in The National Archives E 179 series. The ones in print include: *Yorkshire Lay Subsidy being a Ninth, collected 25 Edward I (1297)*, ed. W. Brown, Yorkshire Archaeological Society Record Series 16 (1894); *Yorkshire Lay Subsidy being a Fifteenth, collected 30 Edward I (1301)*, ed. W. Brown, Yorkshire Archaeological Society Record Series 21 (1897); *The Tax Roll for Devon 31 Edward I*, ed. T.M. Whale, *Transactions of the Devonshire Association for the Advancement*

But in this paper it has been deemed most suitable to focus on three printed surveys that record the names of holders of knights' fees, or at least portions of knights' fees, in the English shires, or, in the case of the survey of 1316, the names of the main landholders in the vills.[18] The first, chronologically, is known as *Kirkby's Quest*. This survey dates from the twelfth and thirteenth years of the reign of Edward I (1284–5). Its main purpose was to inquire into debts owed to the Crown, but the inclusion of additional information relating to the holders of knights' fees suggests that it might also have been 'designed to facilitate the collection of the scutage of 10 Edward I'.[19] Whatever the precise purpose of the survey, the information presented in it – the names of landholders in a multitude of counties, hundreds, wapentakes and vills – is similar to that recorded in a survey of 1303 undertaken in pursuit of an aid towards the marriage of the king's eldest daughter, Eleanor, to Alfonso III of Aragon.[20] Once again, in this survey of 1303, we find the information divided into counties, wapentakes, hundreds and vills, with the names of the holders of fees, or parts of fees, given for each vill. A typical entry, taken from the returns for the wapentake of Bingham in Nottinghamshire, reads: 'Robert Bardolf and John Bozon hold the eight part of one fee in Screveton' (*Robertus Bardolf et Johannes Boxon tenent viii. partem j. f. in Screveton*).[21] Finally, the survey of 1316, known as *Nomina Villarum* (or 'names of vills') 'was ordered in consequence of a grant of the parliament of Lincoln, made on 20 February 1316, of one man-at-arms for each *Villa* not being a city, a borough, or part of the royal demesne'.[22] Though not concerned with feudal tenure, the data contained in these returns for 1316 – the names of the main landholders within the vills – are essentially similar to the data presented in the returns of 1284–5 and 1303.

Between them, these three sets of returns yield the names of thousands of individual landholders in England in the late thirteenth and early fourteenth centuries. Precisely how many landholders are named remains to be worked out, as the great majority of these returns have not yet been computerised. Some idea as to the scope of the surveys and the richness of the evidence within can,

of Science, Literature and Art 31 (1899), pp. 376–429; *The Northumberland Lay Subsidy Roll of 1296*, ed. C.M. Fraser (Newcastle upon Tyne, 1968); *The Dorset Lay Subsidy Roll of 1327*, ed. A.R. Rumble, Dorset Record Society 6 (1980); P. Franklin, *The Taxpayers of Medieval Gloucestershire. An Analysis of the 1327 Lay Subsidy Roll with a New Edition of its Text* (Stroud, 1993). Various other returns are printed, mainly in local record series.

[18] All three surveys can be found in *Inquisitions and Assessments Relating to Feudal Aids, 1284–1431*, 6 vols (London, 1899–1920).

[19] *Feudal Aids*, i, p. xiv.

[20] *Feudal Aids*, i, p. xxii.

[21] *Feudal Aids*, iv, p. 101.

[22] *Feudal Aids*, i, pp. xxiii–xxiv. Some questions about the purpose of this survey are, however, raised in R.B. Pugh, 'England's Earliest Gazetteer?', *Bulletin of the Institute of Historical Research* 51 (1978), pp. 113–23. For additional comment on the survey, see Saul, *Knights and Esquires*, pp. 4–5, 224–7.

however, be gauged from the fact that the six surveys for the counties of Notting-hamshire and Cambridgeshire (the only counties for which the data have been computerised) produce a combined total of 1,115 names, including duplicates. It seems likely, therefore, that the computerisation of the data for all counties covered by these surveys might yield in excess of 20,000 or 30,000 records. The value of these surveys lies not only in the quantity of data, however. Almost as significant is the fact that they cover the whole period of the wars of Edward I and Edward II and can therefore be matched to the names of men-at-arms engaged in different stages of the wars. *Kirkby's Quest*, for example, was carried out just a year or two after the end of the second Welsh war, of 1282–3; the survey of 1303 into the aid for the marrying of the king's eldest daughter came at the height of the wars in Scotland at a time when Edward I was just embarking on what he hoped would be his last major push in the north; and the *Nomina Villarum* of 1316 dates from just two years after the crushing English defeat at Bannockburn. This convenient chronological spread means that it is possible, by comparing them one with another as well as with the records for military service, to gain insights into how the men of particular vills engaged in the Crown's wars from generation to generation, and not only at a specific moment in time. In other words, an integrated analysis of these surveys with the records for military service holds the potential for a more detailed insight into the military commu-nities of early Edwardian England.

Not surprisingly, these landholding surveys are not without drawbacks of their own, but these are mainly to do with the incompleteness of the surveys as they have come down to us rather than any major methodological complexi-ties in their use. There are, for example, no extant returns at all for the counties of the far north of England; that is, north of Lancashire in the west and the North Riding of Yorkshire in the east. This is particularly to be regretted as the wars in Scotland constituted the most difficult and draining conflict of the period and are known to have engaged large numbers of gentry from the far north of England in particular.[23] For other counties it is sometimes the case that only one or two surveys are intact. Even counties for which all three surveys have survived suffer from gaps in the evidence, for often there are only frag-ments covering just a few hundreds or wapentakes rather than the whole county. These problems explain, in large part, why the counties of Nottinghamshire and Cambridgeshire have been selected for this pilot study, for all three surveys are extant for these counties, even though the returns for 1284–5, in particular, are incomplete,[24] and for Cambridgeshire the returns of 1316 are known to omit

[23] See, in particular, A. King, '"Pur Salvation du Roiaume": Military Service and Obligation in Fourteenth-Century Northumberland', *Fourteenth Century England II*, ed. C. Given-Wilson (Woodbridge, 2002), pp. 13–31.

[24] For Nottinghamshire the extant returns for 1284–5 contain only very few entries for the wapentakes of Newark and Ruschliffe and more substantial returns for Bingham and Broxtow only, missing out Bassetlaw and Thurgarton completely. The returns for that year from

some lords of vills.[25] There are additional reasons, however, why these counties might be seen as a good choice for such a pilot study. Firstly, both shires are similar in size and of fairly average size for the kingdom as a whole.[26] This means that comparisons between the two counties are likely to be meaningful and that they can, perhaps, be held as reasonably representative of most counties in the realm (unlike, for example, the much larger counties of Yorkshire, Lincolnshire and Northumberland). A second point is that neither county lies especially close to any of the major Edwardian theatres of war – though Nottinghamshire was usually grouped, for the purposes of military organisation, with the counties of the north.[27] This means that patterns of soldiering found there are more likely to be representative of trends within the kingdom as a whole than are patterns of military service in border counties like Shropshire.[28] Thirdly, the counties of Nottinghamshire and Cambridgeshire can with some justification be described as gentry-orientated rather than magnate-orientated.[29] Although Thomas, earl of Lancaster, held extensive estates in the wapentake of Bassetlaw in northern Nottinghamshire as well as a few scattered estates elsewhere in the county,[30] it cannot really be said that he dominated the county. Likewise, none of the three earls with significant landed interests in Cambridgeshire – Jean de Bretagne, earl of Richmond, Aymer de Valence, earl of Pembroke, and Robert de Vere, earl of Oxford – came close to monopolising the landholding in the county, nor

Cambridgeshire, meanwhile, contain barely any information on the hundreds of Armingford and Longstow, and no details at all for Cambridge borough, the Isle of Ely, Radfield, Thriplow and Wisbech. There are also a few missing entries from the other two sets of returns, but these are, on the whole, far more complete.

[25] Pugh, 'England's Earliest Gazetteer?', p. 118.

[26] A list of the historic counties of England by area, according to the Arrowsmith map of 1815–16, shows that Cambridgeshire contained 858 square miles and Nottinghamshire 837 square miles. Of the 40 counties of England listed (including Monmouthshire), 13 (33%) were smaller in size and 25 (63%) were larger in size than these two counties.

[27] For example, in the summons to the twenty-librate holders in 1297, the men of Nottinghamshire and Derbyshire were ordered to serve with the earl Warenne in Scotland rather than with the king in Flanders; *Parliamentary Writs and Writs of Military Summons*, ed. F. Palgrave, 2 vols in 4 parts (London, 1827–34), i, pp. 286–8.

[28] In this and other counties along the Welsh border there was a long tradition of military service that created a large group of experienced soldiers. See, for example, F.C. Suppe, *Military Institutions on the Welsh Marches: Shropshire, AD 1066–1300* (Woodbridge, 1994), especially p. 33.

[29] That Cambridgeshire had a gentry community who identified with the county is suggested by the fact that 162 suitors attended a session of the county court in the mid-thirteenth century; J.R. Maddicott, 'The County Community and the Making of Public Opinion in Fourteenth-Century England', *TRHS* 5th series 28 (1978), pp. 29–30. For Nottinghamshire, albeit for a slightly later period, see S. Payling, *Political Society in Lancastrian England: The Greater Gentry of Nottinghamshire* (Oxford, 1991), pp. 4–18.

[30] *Feudal Aids*, iv, pp. 107–10; J.R. Maddicott, *Thomas of Lancaster 1307–1322: A Study in the Reign of Edward II* (Oxford, 1970), pp. 10–11.

did they do so even when their estates are combined.[31] These considerations are important given that this paper is primarily concerned with the recruitment for military service of the gentry. For their part, the magnates are interesting less because of their military service (which was customary for the nobility) than because of their role as recruiters.

As a final preliminary to the main section of this paper, a little more attention must be given to the administrative divisions of, and landholding patterns within, the counties of Nottinghamshire and Cambridgeshire, if only in order to facilitate a better understanding of the following analysis. Nottinghamshire was divided into six smaller administrative units known as wapentakes (as opposed to the more usual hundreds: a sign of the former Danish influence on the area). These wapentakes were: Bassetlaw (covering the whole of the north of the county); Broxtow, Thurgarton and Newark across the centre of the county, going from west to east; and Bingham and Rushcliffe in the south.[32] There were significant gentry residences in each wapentake, while Sherwood Forest spread primarily across the wapentakes of Bassetlaw and Broxton in the north and west of the county.[33] Among the major gentry families holding lands in the shire (though in several cases with more significant interests elsewhere) were the Annesleys, Bardolfs, Cressys, Cromwells, Deincourts, Everinghams, Furnivalls, Morteyns, Orrebys, Pierpoints, Stotevilles and Strelleys, to name just a few.[34] The county of Cambridgeshire, meanwhile, was split into nineteen hundreds, including Cambridge borough, Cheveley, Ely, Thriplow, Flendish, Northstow, Papworth, Staploe and Wisbech.[35] Here there was a major distinction between the sparsely populated north of the county, where the fens dominated, and the much more densely populated south and west.[36] Gentry families with lands in this county included: the Avenels, Bassingbournes, Burdeleys, Cheynys, Colvilles, Crekes, Engaines, Frivilles, Fraunceys, Manners, Muschets, Saint Georges, Scales and

---

[31] Bretagne possessed estates in Bassingbourn, Armingford hundred, Swavesey, Papworth hundred, Dry Drayton with Childerley, Chesterton hundred, Oakington, Northstow hundred, Babraham, Chilford hundred, and Stow cum Quy, Staine hundred; *Feudal Aids*, ii, pp. 145, 150, 152, 153, 155, 156. Valence held lands in Ickleton, Whittlesford hundred, Caxton, Longstow hundred, Trumpington, Thriplow hundred, and Great Shelford, Thriplow hundred; *Feudal Aids*, ii, pp. 144, 154, 155, 157. Vere's interests lay in Great Abington, Chilford hundred, Camps, Chilford hundred, Hildersham, Chilford hundred, Ditton Valens, Cheveley hundred, and Little Wilbraham, Staine hundred; *Feudal Aids*, ii, pp. 140, 145, 154, 155.

[32] Payling, *Political Society*, p. xiii, fig. 1.

[33] Payling, *Political Society*, p. xiii, fig. 1.

[34] These families have been identified from *Feudal Aids*, iv, pp. 91–111.

[35] *The Victoria History of the County of Cambridgeshire and the Isle of Ely*, ed. L.F. Salzman, 10 vols (London, 1938–2002), i, pp. 340–41.

[36] C. Taylor, *The Cambridgeshire Landscape: Cambridgeshire and the Southern Fens* (London, 1973), map of settlements, inside front and back covers.

Trumpetons.[37] All in all, these were typical English counties, where a magnate influence coexisted alongside a majority gentry presence, and where armigerous families and individuals renowned for their public service resided near to many more obscure small landholders.

This brings us, then, to the main part of this paper and to an integrated analysis of the landholding and military service records for these two counties. Before assessing the influence that landholding and locality had on the composition of military retinues, however, let us briefly consider the issue of military recruitment more generally. What can we learn, by digging down into the wapentakes, hundreds and vills of Nottinghamshire and Cambridgeshire, about the proportion of gentry from these two counties who served in the Crown's wars? A number of additional questions can be asked of the data, both for the counties internally as well as in relation to one another. Is it possible, for example, to detect significant variations in the commitment to military service among the gentry of these counties, both generational (that is, from one landholding survey to the next) and in terms of internal geography (from one hundred, wapentake or vill to another)? Moreover, were there different patterns of service depending on the theatre of war? Did the men of the more northerly county of Nottinghamshire show a greater commitment to the wars in Scotland than their counterparts in Cambridgeshire; and, if so, were these roles reversed in France?

These and many similar, related questions can be answered accurately only by drawing on the full range of records relating to military service and by using them in conjunction with the relevant landholding records: a difficult process.[38] Thankfully, however, an attempt has already been made to gauge the commitment to military service among the men of these two counties. This has been done by matching the names of knights bachelor listed by county on the Parliamentary roll of arms (c.1312) against the names of men-at-arms recorded in the records of military service for the reigns of the first two Edwards, up to and including the battle of Bannockburn (1314). Although the Parliamentary roll relates only to knights and not to the many members of the landholding community of England who did not take up knighthood,[39] the results provide a convenient starting points for this analysis. They show that of the twenty-nine bachelors listed on the armorial under Cambridgeshire, a minimum of twenty (69 per cent) served in the Crown's wars. Unfortunately, the knights of Nottinghamshire are listed with the knights of the neighbouring county of Derbyshire; but, of the twenty-two men listed under these two shires, at least nineteen (86 per cent) are known to have given military service in Wales, France or Scotland. To put

---

37 Some of these families are identified in *VCH Cambridgeshire*, ii, p. 398, while others have been identified from the landholding returns in *Feudal Aids*, ii, pp. 135–57.

38 This is the kind of large-scale approach that, as Christine Carpenter has pointed out, is possible only through use of the computer: Carpenter, 'Gentry and Community', pp. 368–9.

39 M. Keen, 'Heraldry and Hierarchy: Esquires and Gentlemen', in *Orders and Hierarchies in Late Medieval and Renaissance Europe*, ed. J. Denton (London, 1999), p. 97.

these figures into perspective, the national average for the proportion of militarily active knights was, as we have seen, 84 per cent,[40] which means that the knights of Nottinghamshire seem to have been slightly more bellicose than many of their contemporaries in other counties, but the knights of Cambridgeshire somewhat less so. This is as one might expect given the greater proximity of Nottinghamshire to Scotland and the fact that Scotland was, for most of this period, the main theatre of war. But these statistics should not be taken too literally because of the incompleteness of the records relating to military service. Even in Cambridgeshire the proportion of militarily active knights was high, especially as these are all minimum figures.

These, then, are very useful raw statistics for the commitment to military service among the upper gentry of each county. One of the advantages of drawing on the more detailed landholding records, however, is that they enable us to go beyond the rather static impression of social networks provided by the county towards an understanding of these networks that is more multi-dimensional and, consequently, realistic. This is because these landholding surveys provide data not only at the level of the county, but also, as we have seen, at the level of the wapentake, hundred and vill, areas and units that might well have correlated more closely to the circles in which the gentry moved. As Andrew Ayton has observed, too much focus on the county can be misleading because, 'for the secular landholding estate, the geographical and social background to their involvement in war was usually at once more local and yet more expansive.'[41] Later we shall have cause to observe how, for some men, recruitment into a military retinue did bring them into contact with retinue leaders and men-at-arms from other parts of the country. For now, however, we are concerned primarily with more general observations about their military service, including how patterns of recruitment varied between localities and generations.

Let us continue, then, by looking at the big picture. The number of individual gentry (not including duplicates) named in the three landholding surveys for the counties of Nottinghamshire and Cambridgeshire combined, minus earls, females, clergy and men who were inquisitors only, is 568. Of these, 281 (49 per cent) appear in the extant records for military service from the years 1270 (the beginning of the Lord Edward's crusade) to 1327 (the year of the Weardale campaign in the first year of the reign of Edward III).[42] This does not include an additional thirty-eight men from both counties who were summoned to perform military service but for whom no actual evidence of service survives. Thus, from the two counties combined it can be said that a minimum of a half of all gentry served in the Crown's wars under the first two Edwards. The respective figures

[40] Simpkin, *The English Aristocracy at War*, pp. 22–3.
[41] Ayton, 'Armies and Military Communities', pp. 220–21. See also M. Prestwich, *English Politics in the Thirteenth Century* (London, 1990), p. 59.
[42] I am grateful to Andrew Ayton for the data on the armies of 1314, 1319, 1322, 1324–5 and 1327.

for the two counties are: 217 men named in the surveys for Nottinghamshire, of whom 115 (53 per cent) are known to have performed military service; and 362 men named in the surveys for Cambridgeshire, of whom 166 (46 per cent) are known to have served in war. These figures are lower than those extracted from an analysis of the Parliamentary roll of arms (even though the higher levels of militarisation in Nottinghamshire are reflected in both analyses), but this is to be expected for a number of reasons. Firstly, the Parliamentary roll of arms contains information on a relatively small pool of gentry, many, if not all, of whom might have been included on the armorial precisely because of their commitment to arms.[43] Secondly, and related to the first point, knights tend to be over-represented in the records for military service in relation to their sub-knightly counterparts, not least because they were more likely to obtain letters of protection, of attorney and of respite of debts, sources on which we are heavily reliant.[44] And, of course, it must be remembered – and this is a point worth re-stressing – that the records for military service are incomplete, for some campaigns quite dramatically so. As such, it seems reasonable to conclude that both of these counties were fairly heavily militarised, with a majority of the gentry in both counties apparently having some experience of military service (the extent of this experience is set out in more detail below). This is despite the fact that, as we have seen, neither county was particularly close to any of the major Edwardian theatres of war. Moreover, it must be remembered that these figures relate only to service given by *landed* gentry. Large numbers of landless younger sons and eldest sons awaiting their inheritances also served in the mounted arm of Edwardian armies,[45] meaning that the contribution of the gentry in its widest sense was significantly greater than these figures show.

Keeping the analysis at the level of the county for the moment, it is possible, through a series of charts and graphs, to show how the commitment to military service of the gentry of Nottinghamshire and Cambridgeshire varied from theatre of war to theatre of war and from generation to generation. The four main theatres of war during the late thirteenth and early fourteenth centuries were, as we have seen, Wales, Gascony, Flanders and Scotland. The wars in Wales occupied the first two-thirds of the reign of Edward I but were limited, in essence, to four campaigns: 1277, 1282–3, 1287 and 1294–5. These wars were discontinuous but nevertheless involved the mobilisation of large numbers of men, especially in 1282 and 1294.[46] The main period of warfare on the continent came between 1294 and 1298 following the confiscation of the duchy of Gascony by Philip IV of France. Most of the action took place in the south-west of France, with two main expeditionary forces of relatively small size being sent to that region between

[43] Simpkin, *The English Aristocracy at War*, p. 25.

[44] Ayton, *Knights and Warhorses*, p. 162.

[45] See, for example, Morgan, *War and Society*, p. 22.

[46] J.E. Morris, *The Welsh Wars of Edward I* (2nd edn, Stroud, 1996), pp. 160, 247–8; M. Prestwich, *Edward I* (London, 1988), pp. 190, 197–8, 221.

1294 and 1297.[47] However, Edward I also led an army to the Low Countries in person in 1297 in an attempt to relieve the pressure on Gascony and bring the war to an end.[48] There was one other major conflict in France during this period with the so-called War of Saint-Sardos, again over disputed rights in Gascony, during 1324–5.[49] Yet the most intense and demanding series of wars were the ones fought in Scotland, which stretched almost continuously in one form or another from 1296 to 1328,[50] though major expeditions to the north became less common under Edward II than they had been during the reign of his father. In addition to these theatres of war, the Lord Edward also led a crusade to the Holy Land in 1270 and the names of some of the men-at-arms who joined him in the east are known.[51]

The data for the gentry's involvement in these theatres of war are best represented in the form of three pie charts: one for the counties of Nottinghamshire and Cambridgeshire combined and then one for each county. These charts also provide information on the number of gentry from these shires known to have

---

47 The main events of these campaigns are discussed in M.W. Labarge, *Gascony, England's First Colony 1204–1453* (London, 1980), pp. 63–72; M.G.A. Vale, 'The Gascon Nobility and the Anglo-French War, 1294–98', in *War and Government in the Middle Ages: Essays in Honour of J.O. Prestwich*, ed. J. Gillingham and J.C. Holt (Woodbridge, 1984), pp. 134–46; M.G.A. Vale, *The Origins of the Hundred Years War: The Angevin Legacy 1250–1340* (Oxford, 2004 reprint), pp. 200–215. Vale has observed that 'almost 60 per cent [of annual expenditure on the war in Gascony] was spent on wages to Gascon cavalry and infantry, while English troops accounted for only 10 per cent of the budget': Vale, *Origins of the Hundred Years War*, p. 206. Through careful scrutiny of the letters of protection, of attorney and of respite of debts, the only substantial source for the names of men-at-arms going to Gascony, R.P. Lawton has identified 238 men-at-arms setting out with Jean de Bretagne and Sir John de St John in 1294 (estimated upwards through consultation of other sources to 301 men-at-arms), and 229 men-at-arms setting out with the earls of Lancaster and Lincoln in January 1296; R.P. Lawton, 'Henry de Lacy, Earl of Lincoln (1272–1311) as *locum tenens et capitaneus* in the duchy of Aquitaine', PhD thesis, University of London, 1974, pp. 127, 141, 154. It does not appear, therefore, that especially large numbers of English men-at-arms served in Gascony during the mid-1290s.

48 This was another campaign on which relatively few gentry served. The army reached a peak of 895 men-at-arms, most of whom were connected in one way or another to the royal household; N.B. Lewis, 'The English Forces in Flanders, August–November 1297', in *Studies in Medieval History presented to F.M. Powicke*, ed. R.W. Hunt, W.A. Pantin and R.W. Southern (Oxford, 1948), pp. 312–14. The reasons for this low turnout are discussed most pointedly in *Documents Illustrating the Crisis of 1297–8 in England*, ed. M. Prestwich, Camden Society, 4th series 24 (1980), pp. 1–37, and A. Spencer, 'The Lay Opposition to Edward I in 1297: Its Composition and Character', *Thirteenth Century England XII*, ed. J. Burton, P. Schofield and B. Weiler (Woodbridge, 2009), pp. 91–106.

49 Vale, *Origins of the Hundred Years War*, pp. 227–44.

50 For recent narratives of the main events of these wars and campaigns, see M. Brown, *The Wars of Scotland 1214–1371* (Edinburgh, 2004), pp. 179–231; and M. Prestwich, *Plantagenet England 1225–1360* (Oxford, 2005), pp. 230–44.

51 B. Beebe, 'The English Baronage and the Crusade of 1270', *BIHR* 48 (1975), pp. 127–48; S. Lloyd, *English Society and the Crusade 1216–1307* (Oxford, 1988), appendix 4.

served in more than one theatre of war, whether that was in two, three or all
four theatres.

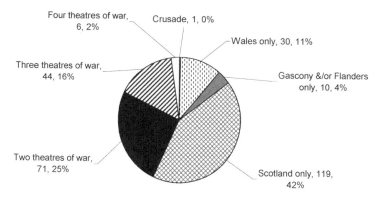

Theatres of war served in by male, lay landholders from
Cambs & Notts, 1270 to 1327

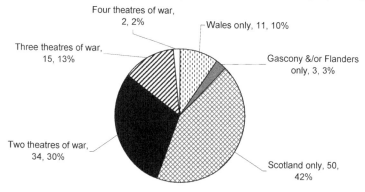

Theatres of war served in by male, lay landholders from Notts, 1270 to 1327

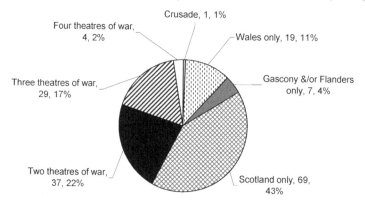

Theatres of war served in by male, lay landholders from Cambs, 1270 to 1327

When looking at these three pie charts, a number of observations immediately come to mind. It is not at all surprising to find from the first chart – relating to the data for the two counties combined – that of the gentry known to have served in only one theatre of war, the largest proportion (42 per cent) campaigned in Scotland, followed by 11 per cent who seem to have served only in Wales and 4 per cent who seem to have served only on the continent. This reflects the fact that the war in Scotland was more continuous and manpower-intensive than either of the other two conflicts. Where one might expect to find greater variation is in the data as presented for the two counties separately; but, in fact, the proportions of gentry from the two counties serving in the different theatres of war are almost identical. This might suggest that in counties located in the heart of England, the gentry were not especially drawn on for service in any particular theatre of war but simply followed general patterns of recruitment throughout the country when major expeditions were launched. It would be interesting to see whether the variation is much greater in counties lying at the extremities of the realm: in the far north, far south and on the Welsh border. Another interesting point arising from all three charts is the proportion of militarily active gentry from Nottinghamshire and Cambridgeshire known to have served in more than one theatre of war: 45.2 per cent for Nottinghamshire, 41 per cent for Cambridgeshire, and 43.2 per cent for the two counties combined. This is a valuable additional indicator of the levels of militarisation within the two counties, as almost half of militarily active gentry can be shown to have taken part in at least two separate conflicts, with almost a fifth known to have served in three or all four main theatres of war. To add a human dimension to all this, Sir Thomas Paynel, a landholder in the vill of Melbourn, south Cambridgeshire (as well as elsewhere), is one of six individuals from this sample known to have served in all four theatres of war. This is explained by his regular service in the military retinue of Sir John de St John, a household banneret of Edward I. Altogether he is known to have served in Wales in 1282–3, Gascony in 1294, Flanders in 1297 and Scotland in 1300, 1301, 1303–4 and 1306.[52]

Before moving on to look at the wapentakes and hundreds of these counties and the patterns of military recruitment within them, let us briefly consider one additional way in which the data can be presented at county level. Having said a little about variations of service between the major theatres of war, it remains to be seen what an integrated study of the landholding and military service records reveals about patterns of military service over time. This can be done by matching the names that appear in each landholding survey in turn – those of 1284–5, 1303 and 1316 – against the names that appear in the records for military service, in the first instance generally, and then for each of the major campaigns

---

[52] 1282 (*Parl. Writs*, i, p. 231); 1294 (*Rôles Gascons 1242–1307*, ed. F. Michel, C. Bémont and Y. Renouard, 5 vols (Paris, 1885–1962), iii, no. 2874; 1297 (TNA E 101/6/37, m. 2); 1300 (TNA C 67/14, m. 14d); 1301 (TNA C 67/14, m. 4); 1303–4 (TNA C 67/15, m. 7d); 1306 (TNA E 101/612/15, m. 1).

of the period. The results of this analysis can be seen in Table 1 and in the three related line graphs set out below.

Table 1: Male, lay landholders giving military service, by year of survey

	Number of landholders named		Number of landholders serving	
	Cambs.	Notts.	Cambs.	Notts.
1284–6	94	39	44 (47%)	22 (56%)
1302–3	208	131	93 (45%)	67 (51%)
1316	117	105	66 (56%)	58 (55%)

Distribution of service across campaigns by Cambs & Notts gentry named in 1284–6 survey

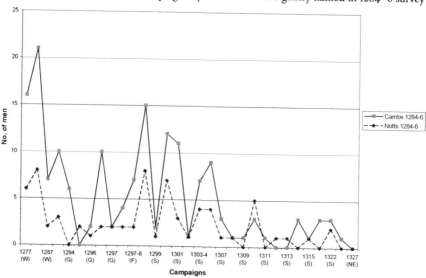

Turning first to Table 1, we can see that, for Nottinghamshire, the proportion of militarily active gentry appears roughly similar across all three surveys, but, for Cambridgeshire, the proportion increases considerably in the survey for 1316. One might expect the kind of rise seen in the figures for Cambridgeshire as the wars in Scotland witnessed the mobilisation of ever greater numbers of gentry; but, in fact, the figures for Nottinghamshire seem to indicate that the gentry of that county were not much more militarised in the 1300s and 1310s than they had been during the 1280s. These data are, however, more complex, and perhaps misleading, than they appear. For one thing, the survey of 1284–5 was carried out only just over a decade before the outbreak of the Scottish wars and only thirty years before the last of the surveys in the series, which means

Distribution of service across campaigns by Cambs & Notts gentry named in 1302–3 survey

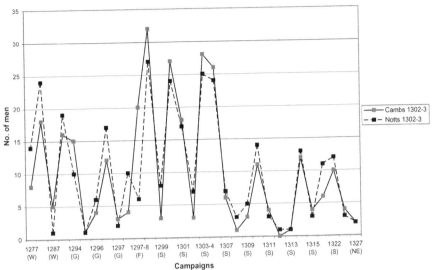

Distribution of service across campaigns by Cambs & Notts gentry named in 1316 survey

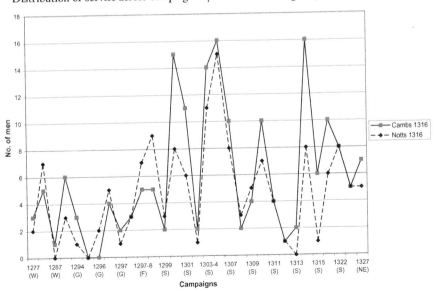

that some similarity of experience between the gentry named in the first survey and the gentry named in the other two surveys is to be expected. Indeed, often the same individual is named as a landholder in two and sometimes even in all three of the surveys.[53] However, even more problematic when attempting to interpret these figures is the fact that the data from the surveys are uneven. The landholding survey for Nottinghamshire in the mid 1280s, in particular, is incomplete, which means that the relatively high levels of militarisation among the gentry in that year may well be misleading. Nevertheless, we should bear in mind that the Welsh wars themselves led to the militarisation of large numbers of gentry within medieval England,[54] even if this process was accelerated during the Scottish wars.[55] What these data seem to indicate, therefore, is that a large proportion of the gentry who served in the Scottish wars had, in fact, already obtained military experience from the wars in Wales.[56] Indeed, this would accord with the phenomenon, noted above, of large numbers of gentry serving in more than just one theatre of war.

The three line graphs allow us to consider these phenomena in greater detail. What we can see from the first graph, for the survey of 1284–5, is that the second Welsh war of 1282–3 did indeed witness high levels of mobilisation, with a minimum of twenty-one (22 per cent) of the ninety-four gentry recorded in the survey for Cambridgeshire serving in Wales in that year. This might not seem like a particularly large proportion of the landholding community. However, given the incompleteness of the records for military service relating to this campaign,[57] the fact that almost one in four gentry from Cambridgeshire – a county not

[53] Of the 39 men appearing in the survey for Nottinghamshire in 1284–5, 19 (49%) are also named in at least one of the two later surveys.

[54] Morris, *Welsh Wars of Edward I*, pp. 65, 72–4; Powicke, *Military Obligation in Medieval England*, pp. 103–10; Simpkin, *The English Aristocracy at War*, pp. 11–12, 24, 86; Prestwich, *Plantagenet England*, p. 157.

[55] A. Ayton, 'Sir Thomas Ughtred and the Edwardian Military Revolution', in *The Age of Edward III*, ed. J. Bothwell (Woodbridge, 2001), pp. 111–14; Simpkin, *The English Aristocracy at War*, pp. 84–91; Ayton, 'Armies and Military Communities', pp. 221–2; D. Simpkin, 'The Galloway Roll (1300): Its Content, Composition and Value to Military History', *Historical Research* 82 (2009), pp. 626–32.

[56] Cf. Simpkin, *The English Aristocracy at War*, pp. 85–6, 96, 101.

[57] This is, actually, one of the better-documented campaigns for the service of men-at-arms, with horse inventories, pay rolls, proffer roll and letters of protection all extant (Horse inventories: TNA C 47/2/21, m. 29; TNA C 47/2/5, TNA C 47/2/6; TNA C 47/2/7; TNA C 47/2/8. Pay rolls: TNA C 47/2/3; TNA E 101/4/1. Proffer roll: *Parl. Writs*, i, pp. 228–5. Letters of protection: TNA C 67/8). However, comparison of the proffer roll with the scutage rolls indicates that the former is incomplete, with perhaps the names of some 250 proffered men-at-arms missing; and not all the leaders named on the pay roll appear with appraised horses; Simpkin, *The English Aristocracy at War*, pp. 61, 160. See also Morris, *Welsh Wars*, p. 45. Moreover, there is the usual problem of service given gratuitously, the implications of which have been worked out for forces of men-at-arms raised during the Scottish wars, but less so for the Welsh wars.

near to Wales – are known to have served does suggest a healthy turnout (the figures for Nottinghamshire are, as we have seen, imperfect). Not surprisingly, the war of 1282–3 seems to have witnessed the highest levels of mobilisation among the gentry named in this particular survey. However, a look at the data presented in all three line graphs shows that the real peaks of recruitment came during the height of the Scottish wars of Edward I, between 1298 and 1304. In all three graphs the levels of recruitment for these campaigns from the counties of Nottinghamshire and Cambridgeshire are relatively high;[58] and it is during these years that we see the gentry of Nottinghamshire almost match the gentry of Cambridgeshire in terms of numbers serving, despite the fact that there were fewer of them named in the surveys. For example, the second graph shows that, for the Falkirk campaign of 1298, at least twenty-seven gentry from Nottinghamshire (21 per cent of the men in the survey for 1303) served, compared with thirty-two gentry from Cambridgeshire (15 per cent of the men in the survey). This suggests that at this stage of the wars the gentry of Nottinghamshire were becoming slightly more militarised than their counterparts in Cambridgeshire, as one might expect given that this was the more northerly of the two shires. However, the third graph shows that this disparity was not sustained, and it is the gentry of Cambridgeshire rather than the gentry of Nottinghamshire who appear to have made the greater contribution to the Bannockburn campaign. This suggests that the geographical location of a county was not necessarily the only, or even main, stimulus behind the military service of the gentry in a particular theatre of war. The main consideration might well have been the identities of the retinue leaders serving on a specific campaign and the location of their recruiting grounds.[59] This is significant because of the fact that the majority of the household retainers of Edward I and Edward II were drawn from the southern counties of England,[60] and, of course, the household retinues of both kings played a significant role in their campaigns.[61]

    This leads us neatly into a consideration of the recruitment processes taking place within the hundreds and wapentakes of these counties. Within the limitations of the remainder of this paper attention will be focused, in particular, on

---

58 Again, variations in the patterns of source survival do need to be taken into account when comparing the figures from campaign to campaign, but some of the largest forces of men-at-arms were raised during these years, with the armies of 1298 and 1303–4 each containing in the region of 3,000 mounted, armoured warriors; Prestwich, *Edward I*, p. 479; M. Haskell, 'Breaking the Stalemate: The Scottish Campaign of Edward I, 1303–1304', *Thirteenth Century England VII*, ed. M. Prestwich, R. Britnell and R. Frame (Woodbridge, 1999), p. 229.

59 Cf. Morgan, *War and Society*, p. 56; Ayton, 'Armies and Military Communities', pp. 225–6.

60 R.L. Ingamells, 'The Household Knights of Edward I', 2 vols, PhD thesis, University of Durham, 1992, i., p. 57.

61 Morris, *Welsh Wars*, pp. 84–5; Prestwich, *War, Politics and Finance*, pp. 42–57; Ingamells, 'The Household Knights of Edward I', i, p. 79, though the comments are qualified at pp. 82–3; A. Tebbit, 'Household Knights and Military Service under the Direction of Edward II', in *The Reign of Edward II: New Perspectives*, ed. G. Dodd and A. Musson (York, 2006), pp. 76–96.

Table 2: Proportion of gentry within the wapentakes of Nottinghamshire known to have performed military service, 1270–1327

Wapentake	Number of named men	Number who served
Bassetlaw	44	27 (61%)
Bingham	49	34 (69%)
Broxtow	46	23 (50%)
Newark	34	23 (68%)
Rushcliffe	21	11 (52%)
Thurgarton	58	33 (57%)

Table 3: Proportion of gentry within the hundreds of Cambridgeshire known to have performed military service, 1270–1327

Hundred	Number of named men	Number who served
Armingford	58	25 (43%)
Cambridge borough	4	0 (0%)
Chesterton	18	9 (50%)
Cheveley	16	7 (44%)
Chilford	51	28 (55%)
Ely (isle of)[a]	15	7 (47%)
Flendish	16	5 (31%)
Longstow	26	10 (38%)
Northstow	21	15 (71%)
Papworth	23	12 (52%)
Radfield	11	5 (45%)
Staine	27	10 (37%)
Staploe	23	14 (61%)
Thriplow	18	11 (61%)
Wetherley	60	34 (57%)
Whittlesford	24	14 (58%)
Wisbech	10	6 (60%)

[a] Apparently includes the returns for the hundreds of North Witchford and South Witchford

two related areas of analysis: the identities of the military recruiters (the retinue leaders) active in these localities; and the degree to which the gentry holding land in these localities did, or did not, serve under the same retinue leaders repeatedly. In short, the focus will be on retinue-level recruitment and the existence or otherwise of stable networks.

It is not possible in this present study to consider the evidence for all the wapentakes and hundreds in Nottinghamshire and Cambridgeshire respectively. Consequently, it makes sense to focus only on those administrative units for which the evidence is likely to be most revealing: in this instance, this means the wapentakes and hundreds where the levels of militarisation were highest. Tables 2 and 3 reveal the proportion of known militarily active gentry in each hundred and wapentake.

Tables 2 and 3 show that levels of militarisation varied not only from one county to another but also between the various localities within a county. This is particularly evident in the data for Cambridgeshire, where in four of the seventeen hundreds less than 40 per cent of gentry are known to have performed military service, while, at the opposite extreme, in another four of the hundreds the proportion of militarily active gentry was over 60 per cent. The question is why do these variations occur? Of course, it is always necessary to bear in mind the incompleteness of the records for military service and the impact that this might have on the evidence, but it is unlikely that significant differences in the levels of militarisation can be accounted for in this way. If this were the case, one would expect to find similar variations in the data for the wapentakes of Nottinghamshire, but there the proportions of militarily active gentry are fairly similar across all parts of the county. One possible explanation for the differing levels of militarisation is that traditions of military service had developed more strongly in some regions of the county than in others, for example in the north more than in the south or in the east more than in the west. However, this idea does not really hold up in the case of Cambridgeshire. A pattern can possibly be discerned in the fact that three of the hundreds where levels of militarisation were lowest lie in relatively central positions within the county (Cambridge borough, Flendish and Staine) whereas three of the hundreds with the highest proportions of militarily active gentry lie at the periphery of the county (Wisbech in the far north, Staploe in the east, and Thriplow in the south). But such an explanation would be far more convincing if the hundreds with the highest levels of militarisation lay in close proximity to one another, which they do not. Therefore, perhaps a more plausible explanation of these variations is that the realm's military recruiters – the retinue leaders in the armies – were more active in, and had stronger links to, some localities than others. For this explanation to hold true it is necessary to show that some retinue leaders were indeed repeatedly returning to the same localities and drawing on the same men for service in their retinues. It now remains to be seen whether or not this was in fact the case, both in the wapentakes of Nottinghamshire and in the hundreds of Cambridgeshire.

For this purpose, let us take the localities where the proportions of militarily active gentry were highest, namely the wapentake of Bingham in the south-east of Nottinghamshire and the hundred of Northstow in central Cambridgeshire, lying just to the north of Cambridge. Forty-nine individuals are named in the various surveys for Bingham, of whom thirty-four (69 per cent) are known to have performed military service at some point between 1270 and 1327. From the hundred of Northstow there are twenty-one named individuals, of whom fifteen (71 per cent) are known to have served. However, the fact that these men held lands in the same area and served in the kings' armies does not necessarily mean that their experiences of war were similar. What we really need to know in order to assess the nature of the recruitment networks in these localities are: the campaigns on which these gentry served; the regularity with which they served; and, perhaps most importantly of all, the names of the retinue leaders under whom they served. This information is presented in Tables 4 and 5 for each of the two localities respectively. It is worth reiterating that some of the gentry listed in these tables did not reside in Bingham or Northstow but merely held lands there: Thomas Chaworth, for example, was from the Welsh March, while the Bardolfs were primarily a Norfolk family. Such men as these have been included in the tables, however, owing to the fact that their estates in Nottinghamshire and Cambridgeshire might have been significant in the context of their military recruitment and service. There is, indeed, no easy way of overcoming the complexity of medieval landholding in an analysis such as this. Ideally it would be possible to create a more accurate picture by drawing on the full range of landholding sources from across England.

In Tables 4 and 5, bold type is used to highlight the cases where links between a member of the gentry and a particular retinue leader can be shown to have lasted for more than one campaign. Even a cursory glance through the tables reveals that this was a common phenomenon in these two localities. In the wapentake of Bingham, for example, of the seventeen gentry known to have served in a military retinue (not including as leader) in more than one army, eleven (65 per cent) can be shown to have been recruited by the same man on at least two separate occasions. The figures for the hundred of Northstow are: eight men serving in a retinue in more than one army, of whom at least four (50 per cent) served under the same leader at least twice. These relatively high levels of repeated service within the same military retinue (they are certainly high compared with levels of continuity in the later fourteenth century)[62] reflect the high rates of retinue-level continuity throughout the armies of Edward I and Edward II.[63] Of greater relevance to this paper, however, is what these figures also reveal about the way that some retinue leaders were repeatedly returning to the same localities to recruit soldiers; or, put another way, the way that the gentry with lands in these areas often knew in advance of a campaign under whom they were likely to be serving. The stability in these relationships gives meaning to the concept of military communities in Edwardian England, for, were it not for the element of continuity in the gentry's military recruitment reflected in Tables 4 and 5, we might simply be looking at a hotchpotch of soldiers and retinue leaders who incoherently bungled their way from one military campaign to the next. The growing body of research in this field shows that this was far from being the

---

[62] As the AHRC project 'The Soldier in Later Medieval England, 1369–1453' is currently in the process of showing.

[63] Simpkin, *The English Aristocracy at War*, pp. 119–41; A. Spencer, 'The Comital Military Retinue in the Reign of Edward I', *Historical Research* 83 (2010), pp. 46–59.

Table 4: Military service given by gentry in Bingham hundred, Nottinghamshire

Name	Survey	Campaigns	Retinue leader
Aslacton, Reginald	1284–5	–	–
Aslacton, Walter	1284–5	–	–
Astley, James	1302–3	Wales 1282	**Segrave, Nicholas**
		Wales 1294	Birmingham, William
		Scotland 1301	**Segrave, John**
		Scotland 1302	**Segrave, John**
		Scotland 1303	Independent (Berwick)
Bardolf, Hugh	1302–3	Gascony 1294	Lincoln, Henry, earl of
		Gascony 1297	Retinue leader
		Scotland 1300	Retinue leader
		Scotland 1301	Retinue leader
		Scotland 1303	Retinue leader
Bardolf, Robert	1302–3	Wales 1282	Independent
		Scotland 1296	Carrick, Robert, earl of
Bardolf, Thomas	1316	Scotland 1303	Bardolf, Hugh
		Scotland 1306	Retinue leader
Bardolf, William	1284–5	Wales 1277	Independent
		Wales 1282	Independent
Barry, John	1316	Scotland 1312	Caunton, Will. (Berwick)
		Scotland 1322	Plukenet, William (P)
Barry, Ralph	1302–3	Crusade 1270–2?	Independent
Barry, Richard	1284–5	–	–
Basset, Ralph	1302–3	Scotland 1300	**Despenser, Hugh le**
	1316	Scotland 1301	**Despenser, Hugh le**
		Scotland 1306	Retinue leader
		Scotland 1309	Cromwell, John
		Scotland 1310	Retinue leader
		Scotland 1314	**Grey, Richard**
		Scotland 1315	**Grey, Richard**
		Scotland 1319	Norfolk, Thomas, earl of
		Scotland 1322	**Despenser, Hugh le**
		N. England 1327	Independent
Bingham, Richard	1284–5	–	–
	1302–3		
Boteler, William	1284–5	–	–
	1316		
Bozon, John	1302–3	–	–
Brabazon, Roger	1302–3	–	–
	1316		
Bret, Amanieu de la	1302–3	Wales 1282	Independent
		Scotland 1300	Retinue leader
		Scotland 1301	Retinue leader

Bret, Roger	1284–5	Wales 1277	**Deincourt, Edmund (P)**
		Wales 1282	**Deincourt, Edmund (P)**
		Flanders 1297	Scales, Robert
		Scotland 1300	Beauchamp, Robert
		Scotland 1306	**Courtenay, Philip**
		Scotland 1307	**Courtenay, Philip**
Chaworth, Thomas	1302–3	Wales 1282	Independent
Clifton, Gervase	1302–3	–	–
	1316		
Deincourt, Edmund	1284–5	Wales 1277	Independent
	1302–3	Wales 1282	Independent
	1316	Wales 1294–5	Retinue leader
		Gascony 1295	**Lancaster, Edm., earl of**
		Gascony 1296	**Lancaster, Edm., earl of**
		Scotland 1298	Retinue leader
		Scotland 1300	Retinue leader
		Scotland 1303	Retinue leader
Deincourt, John	1302–3	Gascony 1295	**Deincourt, Edmund**
		Gascony 1296	**Deincourt, Edmund**
		Scotland 1300	**Deincourt, Edmund**
		Scotland 1303	Grey, Reginald
		Scotland 1322	**Deincourt, Edmund (P)**
Everingham, Adam	1302–3	Scotland 1296	Durham, bishop of
	1316	Scotland 1306	Independent
		Scotland 1310	Cornwall, Piers, earl of
		Scotland 1314	Independent
		Scotland 1319	Lancaster, Thomas, earl of
Everingham, Robert	1284–5	Wales 1282	Independent
Fitz William, Robert	1302–3	Wales 1282	Latimer, William
		Scotland 1303	Fitz William, Ralph
		Scotland 1310	Percy, Henry
Flintham, William	1284–5	Scotland 1298	Botetourt, John
Furnivall, Thomas	1316	Scotland 1296	Norfolk, Roger, earl of
		Scotland 1297	Warenne, John, earl
		Scotland 1298	Retinue leader
		Scotland 1300	Retinue leader
		Scotland 1303	Retinue leader
		Scotland 1306	Independent
		Scotland 1307	Despenser, Hugh le
		Scotland 1322	Independent
		Gascony 1294–5	Retinue leader
Goushill, Walter	1284–5	–	–
	1316		
Grant, William	1284–5	Crusade 1270–2?	Independent
Grey, Henry	1284–5	Scotland 1301	**Grey, Reginald**
	1302–3	Scotland 1303	**Grey, Reginald**
		Scotland 1306	Valence, Aymer
		Scotland 1322	Retinue leader
Grey, Richard I	1284–5	Wales 1282	Independent

Grey, Richard II	1316	Scotland 1303	Grey, Reginald
		Scotland 1306	Independent
		Scotland 1307	Retinue leader
		Scotland 1311	Grey, Robert
		Scotland 1314	Retinue leader
		Scotland 1315	Sub leader
		Scotland 1319	Norfolk, Thomas, earl of
		Scotland 1322	Retinue leader
		Gascony 1324–5	Retinue leader
		N. England 1327	Retinue leader
Huse, Hugh	1302–3	–	–
Huse, John	1284–5	Wales 1287	Lestrange, John
		Wales 1294–5	**Lovel, John**
		Scotland 1298	Fitz Payn, Robert
		Scotland 1300	Independent
		Scotland 1303	**Lovel, John**
		Scotland 1306	**Lovel, John**
		Scotland 1310	Gloucester, Gilbert, earl of
Lutterel, Geoffrey	1316	Scotland 1299	Warenne, John, earl
		Scotland 1306	Retinue leader
Newmarch, Thomas	1302–3	Scotland 1297	**Clifford, Robert**
	1316	Scotland 1298	**Clifford, Robert**
		Scotland 1299	**Clifford, Robert**
		Scotland 1303	Lovel, John
		Scotland 1319	Beaumont, Henry
		Gascony 1324–5	Furnivall, Thomas
Outhorpe, John	1284–5	–	–
	1302–3		
Outhorpe, Ralph	1316	–	–
Pierpoint, Henry	1284–5	–	–
Radcliff, Thomas	1302–3	–	–
Radcliff, William	1284–5	Scotland 1298	Warenne, John, earl
Ros, Nicholas	1316	–	–
Ros, Robert	1284–5	–	–
Staunton, Ralph	1284–5	Scotland 1303	**Warde, Robert de la**
		Scotland 1306	**Warde, Robert de la**
Staunton, Robert	1302–3	Wales 1294–5	Hastings, John
		Scotland 1296	Fraunceys, Richard le
		Flanders 1297	Independent
		Scotland 1298	Gloucester, Ralph, earl of
		Scotland 1300	**Warde, Robert de la**
		Scotland 1303	**Warde, Robert de la**
		Scotland 1306	**Warde, Robert de la**
		Scotland 1310	Independent
		Scotland 1314	Independent
		Scotland 1319	Independent
Strelley, Robert	1284–5	–	–

Tibetot, Payn	1302–3	Scotland 1300	Independent
		Scotland 1301	Retinue leader
		Scotland 1303	Sub (**Prince Edward**)
		Scotland 1306	Sub (**Prince Edward**)
		Scotland 1307	Retinue leader
		Scotland 1309	Retinue leader
		Scotland 1310	Retinue leader
		Scotland 1314	Retinue leader
Vere, Thomas	1316	Scotland 1300	Retinue leader
		Scotland 1301	Retinue leader
		Scotland 1303	Retinue leader
		Scotland 1306	Retinue leader
		Scotland 1314	Independent
		N. England 1327	Retinue leader
Villers, John, I	1284–5	Scotland 1298	Leyburn, William
	1302–3	Scotland 1299	Independent (Edinburgh)
		Scotland 1301	Independent (Lochmaben)
		Scotland 1302	Independent (Linlithgow)
		Scotland 1306	Independent
		Scotland 1307	Independent (Carlisle)
		Scotland 1314	Huwys, Thomas
Villers, Payn	1316	–	–

(P) = making proffer at feudal muster

case,[64] and the evidence presented here serves to confirm the underlying robustness of these armies.[65]

It is one thing, however, to show that the men from a particular locality
repeatedly served in the military retinues of the same leaders, but quite another
to know what impact the locality itself had on the patterns, or, as it has been put,
the 'dynamics', of recruitment.[66] In other words, did local landholding networks
have any part to play in giving extra stability to the armies of Edward I and
Edward II, or is it the case that ties of service between retinue leaders and their
men existed regardless of where they happened to hold their lands?[67] To answer
this question conclusively it would be necessary to draw on a much wider body

[64] See, in particular, the preceding footnote and Ayton, 'The English Army at Crécy', pp.
197–215.
[65] Some historians have expressed more negative views about the armies of this period, but
these tend to be based on the perceived weaknesses in organisation and drilling of these
armies rather than on any assessment of the social relationships underpinning them: e.g. M.
Prestwich, 'Miles in Armis Strenuus: The Knight at War', *TRHS* 6th series 5 (1995), p. 214.
[66] See the paper in this volume by A. Ayton.
[67] Work carried out to date indicates that ties between lordship, landholding and military
service were strongest at the extremities of the realm, along the Welsh March and in the
far north of England; R.R. Davies, *Lordship and Society in the March of Wales, 1282–1400*
(Oxford, 1978), pp. 66–77; M. Hicks, *Bastard Feudalism* (London, 1995), pp. 81–2. However,
the greater complexity of estates in the midlands and southern counties of England possibly
obscures similar ties elsewhere.

Table 5: Military service given by gentry in Northstow hundred, Cambridgeshire

Name	Surveys	Campaigns	Retinue Leader
Baldock, William	1302–3	–	–
Beke, Anthony	1302–3	–	–
Bray, Hugh	1284–6	–	–
Burdeleys, Geoff.	1284–6, 1302–3, 1316	Flanders 1297	Retinue leader
		Scotland 1298	Mouncy, Walter
		Scotland 1301	Scales, Robert
		Scotland 1306	Vere, Hugh de
Chamberlain, Henry	1302–3, 1316	Scotland 1298	**Warwick, Guy, earl of**
		Scotland 1300	**Warwick, Guy, earl of**
Chavent, John	1316	Wales, 1294–5	Independent
		Flanders 1297	Retinue leader
		Scotland 1298	Retinue leader
		Scotland 1300	Retinue leader
		Scotland 1303	Retinue leader
		Scotland 1306	Independent
		Scotland 1307	Retinue leader
Chavent, Peter	1284–6, 1302–3	Wales 1282–3	Retinue leader
		Wales 1294–5	Retinue leader
		Scotland 1296	Retinue leader
		Flanders 1297	Independent
		Scotland 1298	Retinue leader
Cheyny, Henry	1284–6	–	–
Cheyny, John	1316	Scotland 1303	Hauville, Thomas
		Scotland 1310	Filing, William (Berwick)
Cheyny, Nicholas	1302–3, 1316	Wales 1282–3	Bek, Antony
		Flanders 1297	Retinue leader
		Scotland 1301	Edward, prince of Wales
Colville, Philip	1284–6, 1302–3	Wales 1277	**Gloucester, Gilb., earl of**
		Wales 1282	Independent
		Wales 1287	**Gloucester, Gilb., earl of**
		Scotland 1296	Independent
Dulay, John	1284–6, 1302–3	Scotland 1306	Wolrington, John (P)
Fitz Walter, Robert	1316	Wales 1277	Retinue leader
		Wales 1282	Retinue leader
		Wales 1294–5	Retinue leader
		Gascony 1297	Retinue leader
		Scotland 1298	Retinue leader
		Scotland 1299	Sub leader (earl Warenne)
		Scotland 1300	Retinue leader
		Scotland 1301	Retinue leader
		Scotland 1303	Retinue leader
		Scotland 1306	Lincoln, Henry, earl of
		Scotland 1307	Retinue leader
Giffard, Roger	1284–6	Scotland 1296	Independent
Grancete, John	1302–3	–	–

Lestrange, John I	1284–6	Wales 1277	Independent
	1302–3	Wales 1282	Independent
		Wales 1287	Retinue leader
		Gascony 1294	Retinue leader
		Scotland 1298	Retinue leader
		Scotland 1300	Retinue leader
		Scotland 1301	Independent
		Scotland 1303	Retinue leader
		Scotland 1306	Independent
		Scotland 1307	Independent
		Scotland 1308	Independent
Lestrange, John II	1316	Scotland 1310	Retinue leader
		Scotland 1319	Retinue leader
Lisle, Warin	1284–6	Wales 1294–5	**Segrave junior, Nicholas**
		Scotland 1298	**Hereford, Hump., earl of**
		Scotland 1299	Independent
		Scotland 1300	**Segrave, Nic., (Hereford)**
		Scotland 1303	**Segrave, Nicholas**
		Scotland 1306	Tyes, Henry
		Scotland 1310	Cornwall, Piers, earl of
Tony, Ralph	1284–6	Wales 1277	Independent
		Wales 1282	Retinue leader
		Wales 1287	Retinue leader
		Gascony 1294	Retinue leader
Trumpeton, Giles	1302–3	Gascony 1294	**Lincoln, Henry, earl of**
	1316	Gascony 1295	**Lincoln, Henry, earl of**
		Scotland 1298	**Lincoln, Henry, earl of**
		Scotland 1300	**Lincoln, Henry, earl of**
		Scotland 1303	**Lincoln, Henry, earl of**
		Scotland 1306	**Lincoln, Henry, earl of**
Waudenheye, Philip	1302–3	–	–

(P) = making proffer at feudal muster

of evidence than is considered here, not least because many members of the better-off gentry, and a large number of retinue leaders, held land in more than one locality and often in more than one county.[68] Nevertheless, the highly mili-

---

[68] See, for example, C. Carpenter, 'Who Ruled the Midlands in the Later Middle Ages?', *Midland History* 19 (1994), p. 4. Philip Morgan was right to point out that the gentry, in contrast to the nobility, 'remained rooted in the locality, in a series of particular regional and local communities'; P. Morgan, 'Making the English Gentry', *Thirteenth Century England V*, ed. P.R. Coss and S.D. Lloyd (Woodbridge, 1995), p. 21. Nigel Saul has also commented how 'Overall the impression remains that gentle society in the fourteenth century was still very localised': Saul, *Knights and Esquires*, p. 82. However, in terms of military recruitment the difference between, on the one hand, gentry whose landed interests were regional, and, on the other, those who estates were restricted to a specific vill, is significant, as is the fact that the very process of recruitment to a retinue brought men into contact with individuals from other parts of the country, thereby broadening their horizons to some degree. See also P. Coss, *Lordship, Knighthood and Locality: A Study in English Society c.1180–c.1280* (Cambridge,

tarised wapentake of Bingham and hundred of Northstow provide as good a starting point as any for such an investigation.

Turning once more, then, to Tables 4 and 5, one thing is immediately apparent: in these localities at least, no one single retinue leader was able to monopolise control of the recruitment pools. This should not, however, occasion surprise, as there was little direct influence from any of the realm's super-magnates, the earls, in Bingham or Northstow. Indeed, not one earl is named in any of the three extant surveys for Bingham, while only in the returns for 1316 do any earls appear under the heading of Northstow: Guy, earl of Warwick, in Long Stanton; Humphrey, earl of Hereford, in Waterbeach; and Jean, earl of Richmond, in Oakington.[69] It is little wonder, then, that no single earl was able to gain a strong, direct military following among the gentry of Bingham and Northstow. Collectively they did, however, have some influence; and it is interesting to find, for example, that a Henry Chamberlain served in the retinue of Guy, earl of Warwick, on at least two occasions: in Scotland in 1298, for the Falkirk campaign, and 1300.[70] It is likely that this was the Henry Chamberlain who held lands in Landbeach,[71] lying about six miles east of Long Stanton, where the earl later had landed interests. In total throughout the period, thirteen earls recruited men from Bingham or Northstow for service in their military retinues: eleven in Bingham and six in Northstow (four drew men from both areas). The thoroughness and depth of the earls' recruiting activities in these localities appears limited, with in Bingham only the earls of Lancaster, Norfolk and Surrey, and in Northstow the earl of Lincoln, drawing on the services of more than one man residing there. However, it would be a mistake to suggest that the earls were not making much headway into these particular recruitment pools, for instead of drawing on the local gentry directly, they seem to have been content to call on the services of men who had stronger ties to the men of the area and who were able to act on their behalf as sub-recruiters.

It is when we get down to the level of these sub-leaders, and, indeed, of retinue leaders of sub-comital status more generally, that the links between locality and military recruitment begin to look a little stronger. First of all, we can see from Tables 4 and 5 that the type of men recruited by the earls were not usually the lowest level of gentry – the parish gentry – who held land in one or two vills in Bingham or Northstow and nowhere else in the country; rather, they were members of the baronage and country gentry, men with additional landed interests elsewhere, with diverse social networks, and who in many cases acted as retinue leaders in their own right on several occasions. A good example of this is the recruitment by Edmund, earl of Lancaster, of Sir Edmund Deincourt,

---

1991), pp. 307–8; J.C. Ward, *The Essex Gentry and the County Community in the Fourteenth Century* (Chelmsford, 1991), p. 20; C. Carpenter, *Locality and Polity*, p. 290.

[69] *Feudal Aids*, ii, p. 152.

[70] TNA C 67/13, m. 6; TNA C 67/14, m. 11.

[71] *Feudal Aids*, ii, pp. 148, 152.

banneret, for his retinue in Gascony in 1295 and 1296.[72] Although Deincourt held
lands in the vill of Granby in the wapentake of Bingham,[73] his landed interests
went further than this, both within Nottinghamshire itself (where he held lands
in Newark wapentake) and in the counties of Derbyshire and Lincolnshire.[74]
By recruiting Deincourt, the earl of Lancaster was aware that he might therefore gain access to recruitment pools that would otherwise have escaped him.[75]
Deincourt had already drawn on men from Bingham for service in his retinue,
having proffered Roger Bret – who held land in Wiverton,[76] just a few miles west
of Granby – at the feudal musters in Wales in 1277 and 1282.[77] In 1295 we know
that Deincourt took at least one man from the wapentake of Bingham into the
retinue of the earl of Lancaster for service in Gascony: his kinsman John, who
held land in the vill of Aslockton, just to the north of Granby.[78] And, given the
incompleteness of the evidence for this particular campaign, there may have been
others besides. This is, of course, only one example of how a magnate might
employ a sub-recruiter to activate recruitment pools on a relatively small scale
within a particular locality; nor is this evidence, presented in isolation, conclu-
sive. However, it can easily be imagined how by drawing on a much wider corpus
of evidence it might be possible to understand much more fully how the different
levels of recruitment worked in practice.

What seems to be emerging, then, is a hierarchy in which magnates (with
lands in various shires), sub-recruiters among the baronage and country gentry
(possessing estates in two or three shires, or at least in several parts of one
shire) and the parish gentry (with lands restricted to a specific locality) operated at different levels of the military community or military communities. It is
the interaction between these layers that makes the recruitment to Edwardian
armies appear so complex and that accounts, in large part, for the fact that military retinues, though essentially stable in composition, seldom look exactly the
same from one campaign to the next. It should also be clear that it is precisely
because these different levels of recruitment existed, with the magnates and
country gentry functioning above and beyond any specific locality, that any study
focusing on just one area, or indeed one county, can only ever uncover part of the
picture, one piece of the jigsaw. That said, it should also be evident that there is
one group within the military community whose recruitment to the armies can
best be studied at the level of the wapentake, hundred and vill, and that this

---

[72] *Rôles Gascons*, iii, nos 2421, 3913 (at p. 297).

[73] *Feudal Aids*, iv, pp. 91, 101, 104.

[74] *Feudal Aids*, iv, p. 100; *Calendar of Inquisitions Post Mortem and other Analogous Documents*,
23 vols (London, 1904–2004), vi, no. 746.

[75] Cf. Ayton, *Knights and Warhorses*, p. 234; Ayton, 'Armies and Military Communities',
p. 226.

[76] *Feudal Aids*, iv, p. 93.

[77] *Parl. Writs*, i, pp. 204, 230. Bret mustered on both occasions as a *serviens*.

[78] *Rôles Gascons*, iii, nos 2422, 3913 (at p. 297); *Feudal Aids*, iv, p. 101.

is the group whose interests, or at least landed interests, were mainly confined to these areas: the parish gentry. It remains, then, to consider what the data presented in Tables 4 and 5 reveal about the recruitment of this group.

There are perhaps two main ways of approaching the evidence in this regard: one is by focusing on the recruitment of these parish gentry to serve in particular retinues, with the emphasis being on the leaders of these retinues; and the other is to look at the data through the lens of a particular military campaign. Immediately, however, one is confronted with some problems. Firstly, it is not always immediately clear whether a particular individual belongs to the parish gentry or country gentry: not surprisingly given that, in the words of Peter Coss, the term "'gentry" as employed by historians is a construct'.[79] Not only were the boundaries between these two groups blurred, but there is also the more fundamental problem of accurately identifying individuals and ascertaining the extent of their landed interests. This problem is not, of course, helped by the fact that the present study is concerned with only a fraction of the total available evidence on landholders and their estates. An additional difficulty arises from the fact that the parish gentry – men of relatively limited wealth and social connections – are precisely the kind of men less likely to appear in the extant records for military service.[80] Therefore, even when one is able to identify a member of the parish gentry successfully, there is no guarantee that one will be able accurately to trace all, or even any, aspects of their military service. Thus, many of the most likely candidates for the status of parish gentry in Tables 4 and 5 – Reginald Aslacton, Richard Bingham and John Outhorpe from Bingham, and William Baldock, John Grancete and Philip Waudenheye from Northstow – are also the men for whom no evidence of military service survives, even though some of these men probably did serve as they received individual summons.[81] Such are the frustrations involved in military service prosopography; but at least we can accept that these problems are thrown up by gaps in the sources and are not necessarily reflective of reality.

There are, however, a couple of men from Tables 4 and 5 who can, from toponymic evidence, be described with some confidence as parish gentry and for whom some evidence of military service survives. These are William Flinntam of Woodborough, Thurgarton wapentake, who in the returns for 1284–5 is incorrectly included in the returns for Bingham (but whose surname probably derives

---

79 P. Coss, *The Origins of the English Gentry* (Cambridge, 2003), p. 7. On the issue of terminology, see also, for example, D. Crouch, *The Image of Aristocracy in Britain, 1000–1300* (London, 1992), p. 27.

80 Ayton, *Knights and Warhorses*, p. 185.

81 For example, Richard Bingham, who actually held lands in the vill of Bingham in the wapentake of the same name, was summoned to serve in Scotland in 1297 and 1298; *Feudal Aids*, iv, pp. 91, 93, 102; *Parl. Writs*, i, pp. 287, 309, 310. In the summons for 1297 he is described as a justice of gaol delivery and was summoned from the counties of Nottinghamshire and Derbyshire. He might well have been one of the approximately 1,500 men-at-arms in the army in that year who did not serve for crown pay.

from the vill of Flintham in Bingham wapentake),[82] and William Radeclyve of
Radcliffe-on-Trent in Bingham wapentake (also included in the survey of 1284–
5).[83] The only known military service of both Flinntam and Radeclyve is for the
army that campaigned in Scotland in 1298. As this was the largest army of the
reign, their involvement suggests that some individuals who perhaps did not
give military service on any other occasion were being drawn into the host in
1298. If so, the Falkirk campaign certainly represented a baptism of fire for such
men as these. Flinntam (or 'Flintham' as he is described in the sources for the
army) is listed on the household horse inventory as a *valletus* – a sub-knightly
man-at-arms – in the retinue of Sir John Botetourt, a household banneret. His
horse was appraised at the sum of 6 marks.[84] William Radeclyve, meanwhile,
appears (if the identification is correct) with a letter of protection dated 7 April
1298 for service in the retinue of the earl Warenne.[85] How either of these men
ended up in the retinues that they did is not immediately obvious, as neither
Botetourt nor the earl Warenne held any estates in Nottinghamshire, let alone
in Bingham wapentake. However, this perhaps proves Andrew Ayton's point
about the networks of many soldiers – even those of modest status – extending
beyond the county.[86] Indeed, it seems that William Radeclyve was not the only
Nottinghamshire man in Warenne's retinue in 1298, for the retinue also included
a William Cressy, possibly the man of that name who held land in the vill of
Hodsock in Bassetlaw wapentake.[87] William Cressy also made plans to serve
with Warenne in Scotland in 1299.[88] Unfortunately, it is not at all clear that he
was responsible for Radeclyve's presence in the retinue, as the two men obtained
their letters of protection in 1298 on separate dates. Overall, then, the reasons
why Flinntam and Radecylve served with the leaders they did in Scotland in 1298
remain rather obscure.

Such obscurity is, of course, both a symptom of the fact that much still
remains to be understood about the gentry's military service as well as further
proof of the need to draw on as large a corpus of data as possible when trying to
get to grips with these complex problems. There were, nevertheless, landholders
in both Bingham and Northstow whose recruitment into military retinues can,
perhaps, be explained by social networks arising within the locality. Take, for
example, Sir James Astley, Sir Thomas Newmarch and Sir Geoffrey Burdeleys.

---

[82] *Feudal Aids*, iv, p. 93.
[83] *Feudal Aids*, iv, p. 92.
[84] *Scotland in 1298*, p. 167.
[85] TNA C 67/13, m. 2.
[86] Ayton, 'Armies and Military Communities', pp. 220–21.
[87] TNA C 67/13, m. 8; *Feudal Aids*, iv, p. 97. In 1294 a man of this name made a life indenture
with a certain William Doylly in which 'he promised the latter a robe … in return for service
in the Gascon campaign of that year': J.M.W. Bean, *From Lord to Patron: Lordship in Late
Medieval England* (Manchester, 1989), pp. 47–8.
[88] TNA C 67/14, m. 15.

All three of these men were, as their knightly status suggests, a cut above the men already discussed and ought to be considered – if, for sake of convenience, we continue to use these terms – as country gentry rather than parish gentry. Indeed, Newmarch and Burdeleys appear among the knights listed on the Parliamentary roll of arms under the headings Nottinghamshire and Cambridgeshire respectively.[89] That said, these men held their lands primarily in one county and are likely, therefore, to have spent most of their time, and felt most at ease, in the company of the local gentry. As such, it is interesting to find that all three men found repeated service in the retinues of bannerets who had more wide-ranging interests and connections than their own but who also happened to possess estates in Nottinghamshire and Cambridgeshire. Astley served in the retinue of the Segrave family on three occasions, at first as a *valletus* in Wales in 1282–3 but later, by 1302, probably as a knight.[90] His lands in Cropwell Butler, Bingham wapentake, lay in fairly close proximity to the vill of Thorp in Glebes, in the neighbouring wapentake of Rushcliffe, which Sir John Segrave held in 1303.[91] Sir Thomas Newmarch held one-and-a-half knights' fees in Whatton, Bingham wapentake, which lies just a few miles south of Shelton, in Newark wapentake, where Sir Robert Clifford held the third part of a fee in 1303.[92] This local connection might well account for Newmarch's service in Clifford's retinues in Scotland between 1297 and 1299, when he had still not been knighted.[93] Clifford tended to recruit most of his men from his main powerbase in the far north-west of England.[94] Sir Geoffrey Burdeleys, meanwhile, held several estates in and around Cambridge, not only in the vill of Madingley in Northstow hundred, but also a little to the north in Cottenham, Chesterton hundred, and to the south in Comberton, Wetherley hundred.[95] Table 5 shows that Burdeleys served in the retinues of at least two different bannerets during the Scottish wars, both of whom – Sir Robert Scales and Sir Hugh Vere[96] – possessed estates in Cambridgeshire even though their main landed interests lay elsewhere. Vere held a fee in the hundred of Cheveley in the east of the county,[97] while Scales held quarter of a fee in the vill of Haslingfield,[98] which lies just three

[89] *Parl. Writs*, i, p. 415.

[90] 1282 (TNA C 47/2/7, m. 8); 1301 (TNA C 67/14, m. 5); 1302 (TNA C 67/15, m. 15). The reason for thinking that he was a knight by 1302 is that he appears as a knight in the garrison of Berwick during 1303–4; TNA E 101/12/18, fol. 1r.

[91] *Feudal Aids*, iv, pp. 101, 102.

[92] *Feudal Aids*, iv, pp. 100, 102.

[93] TNA E 101/6/30; *Scotland in 1298*, p. 197; TNA C 67/14, m. 15.

[94] Simpkin, *The English Aristocracy at War*, p. 99.

[95] *Feudal Aids*, ii, pp. 138, 146, 148, 153.

[96] TNA E 101/9/24, m. 2 (service with Scales, 1301); TNA C 67/16, m. 8 (service with Vere, 1306).

[97] *Feudal Aids*, ii, p. 142.

[98] *Feudal Aids*, ii, p. 146.

miles south of Burdeleys' lands in Comberton. Thus, for all three men, it seems
likely that the military retinues in which they served owed something to where
they held their estates, or, more precisely, to the fact that they held their estates
in close proximity to those of men who served as major recruiters for the army.[99]

One final significant point that can be drawn from Tables 4 and 5 is that there
is very little evidence of gentry from the same hundred or wapentake serving in
the same retinue on campaign.[100] In other words, in the military sphere at least,
there is no indication that local or county identity played a major part in recruitment; any impact that landholding did have on recruitment seems to have been
'vertical' (between the retinue leader and one or two landholders nearby) rather
than 'horizontal' (between several gentry of similar status) in nature. One thing
that is clear, therefore, is that the concept of county communities is too simplistic
and rigid to allow for the diverse social relations enjoyed by most members of
landholding society in Edwardian England. The way forward is through the
study of social networks in a broader sense.

In conclusion, then, this paper has sought to demonstrate some of the potential benefits of an integrated analysis of the landholding and military service
records of the reigns of Edward I and Edward II. In particular, it has aimed to
do so as part of a growing body of research into the military communities of
later medieval England and with the express aim of moving this body of research
forward. It might, of course, be argued that the ideas put forward in this paper –
about the influence that social networks had on military recruitment, and about
the increased militarisation brought about by the wars of the period – are not
new. However, it is not so much the novelty of the ideas as the novelty of the
approach that concerns us here, for while it is one thing to make observations
based on a limited body of evidence relating to the gentry of one county or
one region, it is quite another to bring to bear the full range of landholding
and military service records in a study that is both more broad and yet more
detailed than those that have been conducted before. Indeed, such a painstaking
and comprehensive approach to the sources is essential if we are to capitalise
fully on the recent advances made in the study of Edwardian armies and the
social landscapes that underpinned them. Although this paper has been able to
do little more than make some preliminary observations relating to the gentry
of two counties and two smaller administrative units within those counties, it is
hoped that it has at least served the purpose of drawing attention to what might
be made possible if such a study were extended to incorporate the landholding
community of the greater part of the realm.

[99]   Cf., for example, S. Walker, *The Lancastrian Affinity 1361–1399* (Oxford, 1990), pp. 26–7;
Ward, *The Essex Gentry*, p. 18.
[100]   I would like to thank the reviewer of an earlier draft of this paper for drawing my attention to this point.

3

A Warlike People? Gentry Enthusiasm for Edward I's Scottish Campaigns, 1296–1307

Andrew Spencer

One of Edward I's defining characteristics is his single-mindedness, and his conduct of war in the last decade of his reign is one of the most conspicuous examples of this. Edward had clear objectives in mind: from 1294 to 1297, the recovery of Gascony, and from 1298 onwards the subjection of Scotland; and he was not going to allow anyone or anything to stand in his way if he could possibly help it. This article examines how willing the English gentry were to aid their king in his struggles.[1]

Edward is generally recognised as having created a harmony of interests between Crown and gentry in his domestic governance of England but, as the political tension of the years between 1297 and 1301 demonstrate, the domestic harmony Edward had created in the first two decades of his reign was fractured somewhat by the almost constant warfare between 1294 and 1307.[2] Opposition to the king's policies, led by the earl of Norfolk and the archbishop of Canterbury, played to the concerns of the gentry rather than the nobility: taxation, the royal forest, the prise, the attack on franchises, and the extension of the king's military demands to those of relatively modest means.[3] To what extent did the gentry vote with their feet during these years?

---

[1] There is, of course, a great deal of controversy about the use of the word gentry to describe those landholders below the rank of baron and it has been argued by Peter Coss that in Edward I's reign one can only talk of 'proto-gentry'. See particularly P.R. Coss, 'The Formation of the English Gentry', *Past and Present* 147 (1995), pp. 38–64; P.R. Coss, *The Origins of the English Gentry* (Cambridge, 2003). While appreciating the force of his arguments, this author believes that 'gentry' still has utility. In this article it is generally applied to those landholders with more than one manor in any given county.

[2] J.R. Maddicott, 'Edward I and the Lessons of Baronial Reform: Local Government, 1258–80', *Thirteenth Century England I* (Woodbridge, 1986), pp. 1–30.

[3] The standard view of what happened in 1297 is set out in M.C. Prestwich, *War, Politics and Finance Under Edward I* (London, 1972), pp. 247–61; M.C. Prestwich, *Edward I*, 2nd edn (New Haven and London, 1997), pp. 401–35; *Documents Illustrating the Crisis of 1297–98 in*

To try and answer this question lists of landholders have been drawn together from three different sources and then compared to the extensive, if incomplete, sources we have for the campaigns after 1294. The first source is a series of six royal summonses for military service from eight counties: Devon, Lincolnshire, Norfolk and Suffolk, Northamptonshire, Surrey and Sussex, and Yorkshire.[4] The second source is the *Victoria County History* for North Yorkshire, Cambridgeshire and Huntingdonshire, and five of the six rapes in Sussex.[5] Using the parish histories in these, a list was compiled of each family which held two or more manors in the county. Although their choice was largely dictated by the vagaries of completion rates by *VCH* historians, these three areas provide interesting geographical and tenurial contrasts.

Sussex was split into six vertical and self-contained rapes, each of was held by a single tenant-in-chief who controlled by far the largest number of manors. Beneath him there was usually at least one major religious house in each rape and three or four major knightly tenants of the lord who usually held around four manors each, and below them a number of families holding one or two manors. In all, forty families held at least two manors.

The low-lying fens and arable lands of Cambridgeshire and Huntingdonshire were dominated above all by the great ecclesiastical institutions of Ely and Ramsey. The latter held thirty-one manors across the two counties, while the bishop and cathedral priory of Ely held twenty-three and fourteen manors respectively. Several great secular lords held lands in the counties, but no earl held more than three manors and no lay lord held more than six.[6] The rest of the land was held by a plethora of gentry families possessing between one and three manors each. A total of fifty-one families had at least two manors.

England, ed. M.C. Prestwich, Camden Society, 4th series, 24 (1980), introduction; M. Morris, *A Great and Terrible King: Edward I and the Forging of Britain* (London, 2008), pp. 290–300. For an alternative view, which emphasises the importance of the gentry and the constitutional considerations, see A.M. Spencer, 'The Lay Opposition to Edward I in 1297: Its Composition and Character', *Thirteenth Century England XII* (Woodbridge, 2009), pp. 91–106.

[4] *Parliamentary Writs and Writs of Military Summons*, ed. F. Palgrave, 2 vols (London, 1827–34), i, pp. 331–3 (Yorkshire), pp. 293–4 (Surrey and Sussex), pp. 288–9 (Northants), pp. 351 (Devon), pp. 354 (Norfolk and Suffolk), pp. 333–4 (Lincolnshire).

[5] *A History of the County of York North Riding*, ed. W. Page, 2 vols (Victoria County History, 1914–23); *A History of the County of Cambridge and the Isle of Ely*, ed. L.F. Salzman et al., 10 vols (Victoria County History, 1938–2002); *A History of the County of Huntingdon*, ed. William Page, Granville Proby and S. Inskip Ladds, 3 vols (Victoria County History, 1932–4); *A History of the County of Sussex*, ed. W. Page, L.F. Salzman et al., 9 vols (Victoria County History, 1905–1997). The five rapes were Chichester (incomplete), Arundel, Bramber, Lewes, and Hastings.

[6] The earls holding manors in the counties were the earls of Lancaster (Lancaster in Barton, Cambs. and Godmanchester, Hunts.); the earls of Hereford and Essex (Earl's in Waresley, Cambs.; Kimbolton and Swineshead, Hunts.); the earls of Oxford (Great Abington and Great Camps, Cambs.; Swaffham Bulbeck, Hunts.). The three lay landholding families with the most manors were d'Engayne and Lisle, with six manors each, and Bassingbourn with five.

The great moorlands of the North Riding of Yorkshire, by contrast, were home to a large number of secular magnates. There were the two great comital honours of Richmond, held by the eponymous earls, and Pickering, owned by the earls of Lancaster, as well as the great abbeys of St Mary's York, Rievaulx, Jervaulx, Fountains, Whitby and the rest; but considerable tracts of the riding were held by magnates beneath the rank of earl. No fewer than sixteen barons held six or more manors in the riding, with eight holding nine or more.[7] In an area the size of the North Riding, of course, one would expect to find large numbers of gentry and there are indeed considerable numbers of families holding two or three manors and even more single-manor families. No fewer than ninety-one families meet the criterion for consideration.

The final source chosen for study are the knights of the shire elected for each parliament between 1295 and 1307, a total of 376 men.[8] These three sources, then, bring together those whom the king thought important, those whom the county communities chose to represent them, and those whom historians know were significant landholders.

Before going further, it is interesting to note that there is some discrepancy between the evidence from the *VCH* and that of the royal summonses. Of the ninety-one families identified as holding two or more manors in North Yorkshire, members of only thirty-six appear in the royal summonses of £40 landholders in Yorkshire from 1300. Among the missing names there are some surprising omissions, including Henry Percy, who held seven manors in the North Riding, and Henry le Scrope, who held five manors.[9] Of the forty families from Sussex, only eighteen appear in the list of £20 landholders summoned from Surrey and Sussex in 1297. Among the prominent missing names is that of William de Braose, lord of the rape of Bramber. That the lists the sheriffs drew up are so incomplete indicates that the information the king was receiving was seriously flawed: either because the sheriffs were unable to procure the information the king wanted or because they were unwilling to do so. Both possibilities are intriguing ones and Edward's unhappiness with the performance of his sheriffs in 1297, when the summons for all £20 landholders to do military service was issued, may be the reason why he changed eighteen out of twenty-eight, four of them twice, in 1297 and 1298.[10]

---

7 These were the families of Fitz Hugh of Ravensworth, Latimer, Cleasby, Meynill, Fitz Alan of Bedale, Tateshall, Fitz William, Marmion, Wake, Nevill, Stapleton, Percy, two Colvills, Mauley and Walton. The first eight all held nine or more manors.

8 *Return of Members of Parliament, Part 1 1213–1702* (London, 1878), pp. 3–26.

9 The Percies held Topcliffe Castle and manor, Gristhwaite (Birdforth Wapentake); Throxenby, Seamer, East Ayton, Irton (Pickering Lythe Wapentake). The Scrope family had not yet reached the power it was to attain in the fourteenth century but in Edward I's reign Henry le Scrope held the manors of Bolton, Low Bolton (Hang West Wapentake); Fleetham, Great Fencote (Hang East Wapentake); Yarnwick (Hallikeld Wapentake).

10 Evidence is taken from *List of Sheriffs for England and Wales from the Earliest Times to A.D. 1831*, List and Index Society 9 (New York, 1963).

Figure 1. Percentage in military service from counties
with royal summonses, 1295–1307

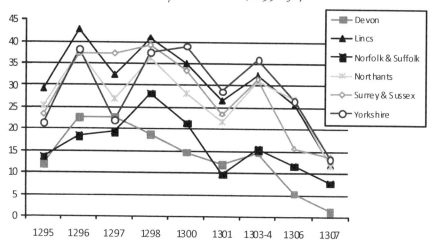

There are two chief sources in Edward I's reign for what Andrew Ayton has termed 'military service prosopography'.[11] The first are letters of protection, mainly enrolled in TNA C 67 but also to be found elsewhere in the printed and unprinted sources of The National Archives.[12] These provide evidence of a man's intention to go on campaign, although he did not always subsequently do so. Although this source provides by far the largest number of names, they are by no means complete. A better, but rarer, source are the horse-valuation rolls, which provide us with the names of people who definitely went on campaign and provide a more complete picture of retinues, but only for those who were willing to accept the king's pay.[13] The sources available are far from complete and findings should therefore be treated with caution, but they do provide some interesting results nonetheless.

[11] A. Ayton, 'The English Army at Crécy', in A. Ayton and P. Preston, *The Battle of Crécy* (Woodbridge, 2005), p. 160.

[12] Letters of protection and respite from debts can be found in numerous sources but especially TNA C 67/8–16; CPR 1272–1281, 1281–1292, 1292–1301, 1301–1307; *Rotuli Scotiae, 1291–1377* (London, 1814); *Calendar of Documents Relating to Scotland*, ed. J. Bain, 4 vols (Edinburgh, 1881–8), ii; 'Calendar of Welsh Rolls' in *Calendar of Chancery Rolls Various, 1277–1326* (London, 1912); *Scotland in 1298: documents relating to the campaign of Edward I in that year and especially to the battle of Falkirk*, ed. H. Gough (Paisley, 1888); *Rôles Gascon*, ed. C. Bémont, 3 vols (Paris, 1896–1906), iii. Requests by magnates for protections or respites for men in their retinues can be found in TNA C 81 and TNA SC 1: for example, C 81/1728, fol. 55, and SC 1/27/183.

[13] There are numerous horse-valuation rolls for the reign of Edward I to be found in TNA E 101, especially E 101/5/23, 6/19, 6/28, 6/37, 8/23, 8/26, 9/23, 9/24 and 13/7; *Scotland in 1298*, pp. 161–237. For general information on these types of source, see A. Ayton, *Knights and Warhorses: military service and the English aristocracy under Edward III* (Woodbridge, 1994), pp. 156–9.

Taking first those in receipt of a royal summons for service (Figure 1[14]), a clear pattern emerges across all eight counties. Participation picked up from under 30 per cent in 1295 to just below 40 per cent between 1296 and 1298 in the more northerly counties of Yorkshire, Lincolnshire and Northamptonshire as well as Surrey and Sussex and from under 15 per cent to around 20 per cent in Devon, Norfolk and Suffolk. There was a dip in 1297, which reflects the political situation in that year, and in most counties participation peaks in the 1298 Falkirk campaign. This is not surprising given that Falkirk is the best documented and best attended campaign in this period.[15] After Falkirk, however, there was a steady decline across the board, with an increase in the 1303–4 campaign which saw Edward finally complete his second conquest of Scotland. The campaigns in 1300 and 1301 took place during intense and fractious parliamentary negotiations over Magna Carta and the royal forest and so it is to be expected that military participation was down.[16] The 1303–4 campaign took place after the domestic political disputes had been seemingly resolved by royal concessions and was the product of an intense effort by Edward to subdue the Scots. The declining participation in 1306 and 1307 is probably the reflection of a number of factors: Edward's own declining health and non-participation in 1306, his reneging on the promises made in 1301, and a sense that Edward had trapped his realm in an unending circle of rebellions and military expeditions north of the border.

It is significant that in only one county, Lincolnshire, did more than 40 per cent of those summoned participate in any single campaign. Although these are, of course, only the minimum possible figures, they are not hugely encouraging for gentry participation, especially when one considers that they include the participation of many of baronial, rather than gentry, status and that the king, having summoned these men, would have wanted, if perhaps not expected, 100 per cent turnout.

Turning to the groups of landholders in North Yorkshire, Cambridge and Huntingdon and Sussex (Figure 2), a similar pattern and similar figures emerge compared to that of the royal summonses. Again, the peak year was 1298, with participation dropping in the years of political tension, 1297, 1300 and 1301, and increasing in 1303–4. Participation levels across these three counties were broadly similar to each other, with the most southerly, Sussex, not surprisingly having

---

[14] The figures for 1295 are those for the Welsh campaign of 1294–5. A large number of letters of protection were issued for service in Gascony in 1294 but these have not been included in these figures because the main expedition was cancelled and it is not possible to tell with ease how many went in the advance guard to Gascony. The figures for 1296 include those serving in Scotland and those on Edmund of Lancaster's expedition to Gascony. The figures for 1297 include those serving in Flanders with the king, those in Scotland with Earl Warenne, and those who went to Gascony with Edmund of Lancaster in 1296 and who are not known to have returned before the earl of Lincoln in 1298.

[15] The Falkirk campaign record is deficient only in lacking a pay record for cavalry which we have for 1300, 1301 and 1303–4.

[16] Prestwich, *Edward I*, pp. 522–8; Morris, *Great and Terrible King*, pp. 321–3, 327–30.

Figure 2. Percentage in military service in North Yorkshire, Sussex, Cambridgeshire and Huntingdonshire

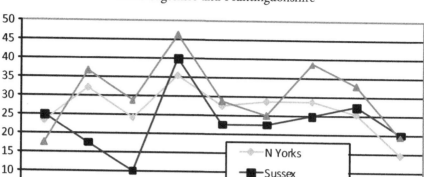

Figure 3. Percentage in Military service in North Yorkshire, Sussex, Cambridgeshire and Huntingdonshire excluding the nobility

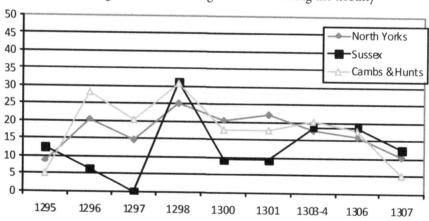

the lowest level of participation and, more intriguingly, with participation from Cambridgeshire and Huntingdonshire usually slightly above that from North Yorkshire.

These figures, however, like those of the royal summonses, include participation from among the nobility as well as the gentry. When the nobility is removed from the figures, leaving only the gentry (Figure 3), there is a significant drop in participation levels of roughly 10 per cent in each county in each campaigning year. The shape of the graph remains approximately the same, except for a flat-lining of gentry participation after 1298 of around 20 per cent, before a decline to c.10 per cent in 1307. It is a similar story when one looks at participation by the parliamentary knights of the shire (Figure 4). Only in 1298 was participation

Figure 4. Percentage of parliamentary knights of the shire
in military service, 1295–1307

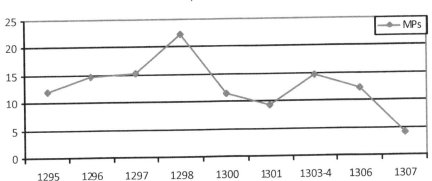

ever as high as 20 per cent and there is a terminal decline after that year, with only a temporary increase in 1303–4.

These, then, are the figures for participation from year to year, which fluctuated for many reasons, but what about absolute participation? What percentage of people from the three sources is it possible to know for certain went on at least one campaign? Looking again at the royal summonses (Figure 5), there is diversity across the counties. A little under half of those summoned from Norfolk and Suffolk and Devon served at least once, while the remaining counties varied between 62 per cent in Northamptonshire and 70 per cent in Lincolnshire. These are minimum figures, of course, and it is impressive that on average around two-thirds of people summoned by the king did make the arduous journey to Scotland, Wales, Gascony or Flanders and were prepared potentially to put their lives on the line at considerable expense and for little prospect of reward. Consistent service, however, which was, after all, probably more useful to Edward, was much rarer. Just 12 per cent of those summoned from Devon served on four or more occasions. On the other hand, 36 per cent of those from Lincolnshire served four or more times. For the other counties, the percentages are mostly in the low twenties.

It is interesting that Figure 6 shows that the percentage of MPs who served at least once is considerably lower than that for the other three columns, at 47.3 per cent. The disparity in the military experience between the shires as a whole and those they chose to represent them in parliament is significant and would not have made Edward's task in persuading MPs of the urgency of his military and financial needs any easier. It is particularly striking that, when one considers the three most difficult parliaments of these years, 1297, 1300 and 1301, the percentage of knights of the shire with previous military experience since 1294 is lower still: just a quarter in 1297, 36.5 per cent in 1300 and 45.5 per cent in 1301. Before leaving the detailed statistics and turning to the context, it is worth emphasising once again the difference in service levels between the nobility and greater gentry (those with at least four manors in a single county) and those of lesser means.

Figure 5. Number of campaigns udertaken by those in receipt of a royal summons

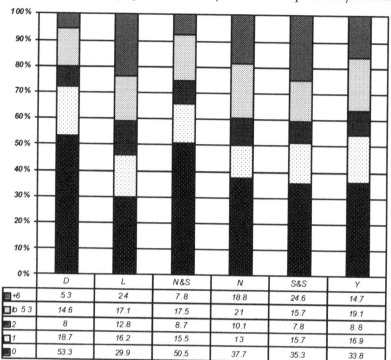

	D	L	N&S	N	S&S	Y
+6	5.3	24	7.8	18.8	24.6	14.7
b 5 3	14.6	17.1	17.5	21	15.7	19.1
2	8	12.8	8.7	10.1	7.8	8.8
1	18.7	16.2	15.5	13	15.7	16.9
0	53.3	29.9	50.5	37.7	35.3	33.8

Figure 6. Number of campaigns undertaken by major landholders from North Yorkshire, Sussex, Cambridge and Huntingdonshire and knights of the shire

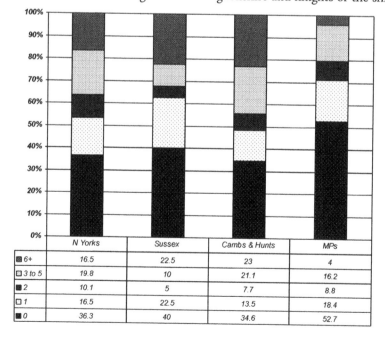

	N Yorks	Sussex	Cambs & Hunts	MPs
6+	16.5	22.5	23	4
3 to 5	19.8	10	21.1	16.2
2	10.1	5	7.7	8.8
1	16.5	22.5	13.5	18.4
0	36.3	40	34.6	52.7

Figure 7. Number of campaigns undertaken by North Yorkshire landholders

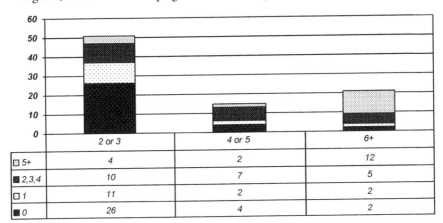

	2 or 3	4 or 5	6+
▨ 5+	4	2	12
▩ 2,3,4	10	7	5
☐ 1	11	2	2
▪ 0	26	4	2

Figure 7 demonstrates that in North Yorkshire, just under half of those with only two or three manors served at least once. Eleven of fifteen with four or five manors served at least once, and only two of twenty-one with six or more manors failed to go on campaign during this period. Among this last group, no fewer than twelve can be shown to have served at least five times: it was the nobility and the royal household who were providing the backbone of Edward's cavalry, serving year after year, and onto whose retinues the lesser gentry might attach themselves when they stirred themselves to do military service. This is particularly illustrated by David Simpkin's finding that thirty-nine of a sample of 140 knights at Falkirk served on at least seven campaigns between 1270 and 1314: there was a hard core of men who came back year after year and around whom Edward built his armies.[17] It is worth noting that many of the lesser or middling gentry who did serve regularly were, like Sir Edward Charles in North Yorkshire, royal household knights or, like Sir Giles de Trumpington in Cambridgeshire, close associates of great magnates: in his case the earl of Lincoln.[18]

Thus far this article has produced plenty of statistics, but statistics of this kind are of little use if an effort is not made to place them within the context of the politics of the last decade of Edward I's reign. Only then it is possible to interpret a set of figures which could easily be presented either optimistically or pessimistically. It is necessary to lift one's eyes from the trees and try to make out the shape of the wood.

17   D. Simpkin, 'The English Aristocracy at War, 1272–1314', PhD thesis, University of Hull, 2006, p. 108.
18   For Charles, see C. Moor, *The Knights of Edward I*, 5 vols (Leeds, 1929–32), i, p. 193; for Trumpington's military service and association with the earl of Lincoln, see A.M. Spencer, 'The Earls in the Reign of Edward I (1272–1307)', PhD thesis, University of Cambridge, 2009, p. 268.

The evidence from the last thirteen years of Edward I's reign suggests that, from the king's perspective, the glass was half empty. Edward was consistently demanding more, particularly in military service, than his subjects were prepared to offer. His attempts to extend military service further down the social scale, to all £20 landholders in 1297 and to £40 landholders in 1300, were both deeply unpopular and spectacularly unsuccessful.[19] His plan in 1301 of summoning 935 men individually seems to have had little more success and this experimentation in the way of summoning lesser landholders is probably evidence of frustration on Edward's part at not finding a successful formula; he eventually returned in 1303 and 1306 to the formal feudal summons, which was much harder to ignore or complain about.[20]

His success in obtaining overseas service was negligible compared to the monarchs of the Hundred Years War. The most famous example of opposition comes, of course, from the magnates (and principally Roger Bigod, earl of Norfolk) at the Salisbury Parliament of February 1297, memorably recorded and embellished by Walter of Guisborough; but, by opposing Edward's demands for service in Gascony, the earl was catching up to where many of the gentry had been three years previously.[21] The abbot of Ramsey cajoled, pleaded and distrained his tenants to perform their feudal service in Gascony in 1294, all to no avail.[22] Yet this was a campaign which the earls of Norfolk and Hereford, the leaders of the opposition in 1297, were prepared, even eager, to attend.[23] Of those who refused to go to Gascony in 1295, incurring the king's wrath and foreclosure on their debts, only two, the earl of Arundel and Edmund Mortimer, were of the front rank of nobles.[24] The rest were minor barons and gentry.[25] In 1297, even when Edward I made concessions by offering pay to try to obtain more support for his expedition to Flanders, it appears that only sixty-three extra people agreed to go.[26]

In Scotland, too, it was not easy to recruit gentry, particularly for winter campaigns. In the winter of 1297–8 four earls and Henry Percy contracted with the regency government to raise 450 men-at-arms to recover the English posi-

[19]   Prestwich, *War, Politics and Finance*, pp. 84–9.
[20]   Prestwich, *War, Politics and Finance*, p. 89.
[21]   Walter of Guisborough, *The Chronicle of Walter of Guisborough*, ed. H. Rothwell (Camden 3rd series, 89, 1957), pp. 289–90.
[22]   Morris, *Great and Terrible King*, p. 273.
[23]   M. Morris, *The Bigod Earls of Norfolk in the Thirteenth Century* (Woodbridge, 2005), p. 155; *CPR 1292–1301*, p. 84.
[24]   E.B. Fryde, 'Magnate Debts to Edward I and Edward III: A Study of Common Problems and Contrasting Royal Reactions to Them', *The National Library of Wales Journal*, 27 (1992), pp. 262–5.
[25]   Walter de Huntercombe, Roger de Mohaut, William Martin, William de Vescy, Philip Kyme, William Mortimer and Robert Fitz Roger.
[26]   Prestwich, *Edward I*, p. 424.

tion in Scotland after the disaster of Stirling Bridge.[27] Only seventy-eight men
took out letters of protection with these five lords, including just nine of the
ninety the earl of Hereford promised.[28] This may be merely further evidence of
the incompleteness of the sources, but there is probably more at work here than
just that.

Edward's planned winter campaign of 1299, intended to relieve the strate-
gically vital Stirling Castle, failed utterly and humiliatingly for the king when
he turned up at Newcastle and then Berwick, but virtually no cavalry joined
him.[29] The campaign never got started, Stirling fell and it took Edward five years
to recapture it. There was a growing suspicion of Edward's military demands
in these years, particularly in the north, and a stubborn desire to ensure that
his demands did not exceed his rights. In both 1297 and 1300 the gentry of
Westmorland and Cumberland, when faced with demands to serve in Scotland
beyond the regular campaigning season, obtained letters from their commander
and the king that such service would not be taken as precedent.[30] In the spring of
1300 the gentry of County Durham claimed that, as 'St Cuthbert's Folk', they did
not owe military service beyond the Tyne and Tees. This was nonsense, but their
deployment of the argument suggests a growing disenchantment with Edward's
seemingly unending demands for service in Scotland.[31] In Yorkshire around the
same time, a council for many of the county's lords was called to discuss the
extent of military service due from the county.[32]

In 1300 Edward was clearly expecting problems with recruitment, unsur-
prisingly given the acrimonious end of the parliament just a few weeks before
he made his summons of £40 landholders in April. Those appointed to raise
knights for service were told to place the names of those who refused in the
royal wardrobe.[33] All the same, Edward must have been shocked when in Yorkshire in early June knights from across the country came to tell the king that
they owed no service in Scotland.[34] Edward was able to disprove this notion
with relative ease by referring to history, but that he had to do so demonstrates
the distinct lack of enthusiasm being shown by the gentry towards the idea of
military service in Scotland in 1300.

The Feast of the Swans in 1306 was clearly an attempt by Edward I to rally the
new generation around the idea of destroying the nascent Bruce rebellion and
confirming English control over Scotland, but, as has been shown, recruitment of

27   *Scotland in 1298*, pp. 64–5.
28   *Scotland in 1298*, pp. 12–23.
29   Morris, *Great and Terrible King*, p. 321.
30   *Documents Illustrative of the History of Scotland*, ed. J. Stevenson, 2 vols (Edinburgh, 1870),
ii, no. 443; *Parl. Writs*, i, p. 345.
31   Morris, *Great and Terrible King*, pp. 323–4.
32   *Parl. Writs*, i, pp. 86–7.
33   *Parl. Writs*, i, 342.
34   Morris, *Great and Terrible King*, p. 324.

cavalry for the 1306 campaign was relatively low and by the autumn of that year even the prince of Wales himself appears to have lost interest in the campaign, disappearing to a tournament overseas along with twenty-two knights.[35]

Instances of opposition or inertia in the face of the king's demands are numerous, therefore, and do not speak of any great enthusiasm for participation in their king's wars among most of the gentry. The question needs to be asked: what might induce people to go on campaign and what might make them wish to stay at home? On the positive side of the ledger can be placed simple patriotism and obligation to their king or to their lord. The defeat at Stirling Bridge in 1297 momentarily dissolved the political tension of that summer and the desire to put the Scots in their place and extract revenge for Wallace's invasion of northern England undoubtedly helped to swell the ranks of English cavalry at Falkirk. Edward played heavily on the theme of the realm in danger, an argument which was probably more effective in the years of active warfare against the French than when England faced Scotland alone.

There was the inducement of pay for those willing to take it, but many of the gentry seem, like their noble captains, to have served without pay.[36] Anyhow, even for those taking pay, the expense of equipping oneself and going on campaign must have outweighed the wages. The most expensive item was, of course, their warhorse, and for those of the VCH sample whose horses were valued in 1298, the mean value was just under £16, a considerable sum of money.[37] The warhorse was, however, just the start. As well as his warhorse, a knight would have had one or two palfreys and his armour, and would have had to pay for his food as well as the maintenance of his attendants. The cost of war, therefore, must be placed on the negative side of the ledger.

Rewards might induce a man to go, but Scotland was a poor prospect for rewards for the knights, unless they were particularly attached to one of the nobles who received land grants at various times, and even then prospects were not great.[38] Edward's mishandling of land grants in the wake of the victory at Falkirk and his constant desire to proffer the hand of lordship to those Scots willing to take it meant that he was criticised at the time, perhaps unfairly, for not being generous enough. Aside from lands, ransoms were rare and the prospects for plunder limited. The promise of gain, therefore, was unlikely to have lured men to Scotland in the same way it did ambitious young men to France from the 1340s onwards.

---

[35] Prestwich, *Edward I*, pp. 509–10.

[36] Prestwich, *War, Politics and Finance*, pp. 69–74. It is possible that gentry serving with magnates expected to be paid by their captain, but there is no clear evidence that this was so.

[37] *Scotland in 1298*, pp. 161–237.

[38] Around 40 barons obtained grants of land in Scotland. D.A. Barrie, 'The *Maiores Barones* in the Second Half of the Reign of Edward I, 1290–1307', PhD thesis, University of St Andrews, 1991, p. 298.

A powerful negative factor in recruitment may have been fear of crime. The absence of the king and nobility on campaign for so long seriously disturbed the peace of England and it is clear that people took advantage of this to raid the properties of those who had gone on campaign. There were 186 commissions of *oyer* and *terminer* issued in the last ten years of the reign for trespasses in the private parks of the nobility and gentry, compared to 118 in the previous ten, and barely a year went by without Earl Warenne having to obtain a new commission for yet another break into his parks.[39] For a great earl like him such occurrences were undoubtedly extremely irksome, but would not affect him too adversely; but for a middling or lesser member of the gentry such an event in a park or his manor would be infinitely more damaging and he would also find it much harder to obtain redress.

In the face of such negative inducements, it is commendable that as many gentry turned out as did. That they did so is, in large part, testimony to the extraordinary and magnetic will of Edward I himself. His achievements in Scotland, achieved as much in the face of his own subjects as with their backing, are remarkable and there is something magnificent in his raging against the dying of the light in 1306 and 1307 as he drove his subordinates on to try and achieve what his ailing body could no longer accomplish itself. The political costs of such achievements, however, were grave. Edward had skilfully outmanoeuvred his domestic opponents in the last years of his reign and had successfully won the active support of the new generation of nobility for his Scottish ventures, but his military demands had alienated the gentry and provoked powerful opposition from them on occasion. Having used the military class to achieve what he hoped was final victory in Scotland in 1304, Edward quickly sought to dismantle the concessions he had been forced to make at the parliaments of 1300 and 1301. Edward was leaving a volatile inheritance to his heir: the disaffected gentry were without a leader following the retirement of Norfolk in 1302 and Archbishop Winchelsey's suspension in 1305, but their demands remained unsatisfied and unchanged and there was now an unfinished war as well. It is notable how similar the Statute of Stamford in 1309 is to the *Articuli super cartas* of 1300: seven of its eleven clauses are taken directly or indirectly from the *Articuli*.[40] The legacy of Edward's Scottish wars, therefore, and the means he had used to prosecute them would have taxed the wit of a greater mind than that of Edward II: even the latter's passion for ditch-digging could not get him out of the hole in which his father had left him.

---

39   These figures are taken from an examination of *oyer* and *terminer* commissions from the patent rolls. Earl Warenne obtained seven commissions for park breaking between 1297 and 1304. *CPR 1292–1301*, pp. 317, 472, 552, 629; *CPR 1301–1307*, pp. 94–5, 278.

40   J.R. Maddicott, *Thomas of Lancaster, 1307–1322: a study in the reign of Edward II* (Oxford, 1970), pp. 97–8. For the text of the articles, see *Select Documents of English Constitutional History, 1307–1485*, ed. S.B. Chrimes and A.L. Brown (London, 1961), no. 5.

4

Edward I's Centurions: Professional Soldiers in an Era of Militia Armies

DAVID BACHRACH

Introduction

In the thirteenth and early fourteenth centuries, a wide range of occupations in England were characterised by a high degree of professionalisation.[1] In the military sphere, this type of professionalisation has received considerable attention with regard to engineers, and particularly those employed in the construction of siege engines of various types.[2] Similarly, the men who constructed the king's crossbows and fabricated his crossbow quarrels have garnered significant attention from scholars.[3] With respect to military personnel, professional army chap-

[1] Regarding the details of professionalisation in the building trades, including wage rates and ranks within the professions, see L.F. Salzman, *Building in England down to 1540: A Documentary History*, rev. edn (Oxford, 1967); D. Knoop and G.P. Jones, *The Medieval Mason*, 3rd edn (Manchester, 1967); *Building Accounts of King Henry III*, ed. Howard M. Colvin (Oxford, 1971); M. de Boüard, *Manuel d'archéologie médiévale de la fouille à l'histoire* (Paris, 1975); and Paul Latimer, 'Wages in Late Twelfth-and Early Thirteenth-Century England', *Haskins Society Journal* 9 (1997), pp. 185–205.

[2] See, in this regard, A.Z. Freeman, 'Wall-breakers and River-bridgers: Military Engineers in the Scottish Wars of Edward I', *Journal of British Studies* 10 (1971), pp. 1–16; A.J. Taylor, 'Master Bertram, Ingeniator Regis', in *Studies in Medieval History Presented to R. Allen Brown* (Woodbridge, 1989), pp. 289–315; David S. Bachrach, 'The Military Administration of England (1216–1272): The Royal Artillery', *Journal of Military History* 68 (2004), pp. 1083–104; David S. Bachrach, 'The Royal Arms Makers of England 1199–1216: A Prosopographical Survey', *Medieval Prosopography* 25 (2004, appearing 2008), pp. 49–75; and David S. Bachrach, 'English Artillery 1189–1307: The Implications of Terminology', *EHR* 121 (2006), pp. 1408–30.

[3] Concerning the professionals who built crossbows and made crossbow bolts, see Alf Webb, 'John Malemort – King's Quarreler: The King's "Great Arsenal, St. Briavels and the Royal Forest of Dean', *Society of Archer Antiquaries* 31 (1988), pp. 40–46; David S. Bachrach, 'The Crossbow Makers of England, 1204–1272', *Nottingham Medieval Studies* 47 (2003), pp. 168–97; David S. Bachrach, 'The Origins of the English Crossbow Industry', *Journal of Medieval Military History* 2 (2003), pp. 73–87; David S. Bachrach, 'Crossbows for the King:

lains have been identified as serving in considerable numbers in the armies of
Edward I.[4] Members of the military households of English kings also have been
recognised by scholars to have developed noteworthy professional expertise in a
wide array of military affairs, including logistics, recruitment and commanding
mounted forces in the field.[5]

Absent from discussions of professionalisation up to this point, however, have
been lower ranking officers, particularly those who commanded units of foot
soldiers. The burden of this paper, therefore, is to shed light on the large number
of men who commanded infantry forces in Edward I's wars in Wales and Scotland. In this context, I use the term professional to designate men whose primary
occupation over a significant period of time was as soldiers.

In setting out to address this problem, the student of Edward I's reign is blessed
with a vast corpus of administrative records that shed light on foot soldiers who
served in royal armies, and on the officers who led them. These records include:
memoranda detailing the transfer of supplies; garrison rolls; horse-valuation
lists; memoranda for the replacement of horses; and, most important of all, pay
records. The clerks who drew up these records, whether serving in garrisons or
in the field with the troops, or in the more leisurely setting of the Chancery,
Exchequer or Wardrobe, tended to use standardised terminology to describe
military matters, including particular types of equipment as well as types of
fighting men.[6]

This habit of standardisation and, indeed, of terminological precision is
important as it allows the modern scholar to identify when new military classifications appear in the records, as well as to differentiate among the various
classifications used by royal clerks to describe fighting men in the king's service.
The current study relies on my investigation of a *corpus* of about 2,000 documents dealing with Edward's campaigns, principally in Scotland during the last
decade of his reign. Many times this number of documents remain to be read

Some Observations on the Development of the Crossbow during the Reigns of King John
and Henry III of England, 1204–72', *Technology and Culture* 45 (2004), pp. 102–19; and David
S. Bachrach, 'Crossbows for the King Part Two: The Crossbow during the Reign of Edward
I of England (1272–1307)', *Technology and Culture* 47 (2006), pp. 81–90.

[4]   David S. Bachrach, 'The Organisation of Military Religion in the Armies of Edward I of
England (1272–1307)', *Journal of Medieval History* 29 (2003), pp. 265–86.

[5]   Regarding the military household, see Norman Lewis, 'The English Forces in Flanders,
August–November 1297', in *Studies in Medieval History Presented to Frederick Maurice
Powicke*, ed. R.W. Hunt, W.A. Pantin and R.W. Southern (Oxford, 1948), pp. 310–18;
C. Warren Hollister, *The Military Organization of Norman England* (Oxford, 1965), pp. 171–6;
J.O. Prestwich, 'The Military Household of the Norman kings', in *Anglo-Norman Warfare*, ed.
Matthew Strickland (Woodbridge, 1992), pp. 93–128; and Michael Prestwich, *War, Politics
and Finance under Edward I* (Totowa, New Jersey, 1972), pp. 41–66.

[6]   Regarding this tendency toward standardisation and precision in administrative vocabulary,
see Bachrach, 'English Artillery 1189–1307', pp. 1408–30; and Bachrach, 'Crossbows for the
King Part Two', pp. 81–90.

and analysed, so that the conclusions reached here must be considered tentative, but likely to be borne out by further research, at least for the ten years that are the focus of this study.

Professional Officers

Welsh troops in royal service, men of the shire levies and men mobilised directly by their lords served, as is well-known, in groups of twenty commanded by *vintenarii*. Generally, five such units were then organised in groups of a hundred men commanded by *centenarii*, also denoted in royal administrative records by the synonym *constabularii*.[7] English *centenarii* serving in Edward's Scottish wars, who are the primary focus of this study, were usually equipped with an armoured war horse; that is, their mounts were *cooperti*. In a handful of cases, however, English *centenarii* can be identified as being equipped with non-armoured horses; that is, their mounts were *discooperti*.[8] Those *centenarii* who possessed an armoured horse received a pay rate of one shilling per day. Officers who had an unarmoured horse received just half this rate – six pence per day.

Given the considerable expense involved in owning a warhorse, it is likely that the majority of the men who served as *centenarii* were of that economic stratum, below the knightly class, to whom King Edward appealed quite frequently to provide the bulk of his heavy cavalry, on the basis of long-established requirements for military service.[9] Many of the 1,200 *centenarii* whom I have identified by name appear but a single time in the pay records examined thus far as leading infantry companies in a single campaign during Edward I's reign. However, a considerable number of these *centenarii* can be identified leading infantry companies year after year, and in some cases for more than a decade.[10] These men clearly chose a military career, and can be identified as professional soldiers. A few examples will serve to illustrate the careers of these officers.

Professional Centenarii

It would appear that there were, in fact, several career paths open to men who wished to serve as professional infantry officers in Edward I's armies. The first of

---

[7]   Prestwich, *War, Politics and Finance*, p. 106; and the earlier observation on this point, J.E. Morris, *The Welsh Wars of Edward I* (Oxford, 1901), pp. 95–6.

[8]   See, for example, TNA E 372/132 for Robert Dalton, who is a *centenarius disccoopertus* from Derbyshire.

[9]   See, for example, TNA E 101/6/30 and E 101/6/31 for the mobilisation orders for 1,270 men with *equi cooperti* from York, Surrey, Norfolk, Suffolk, Gloucestershire, Hertfordshire, Essex and Herfordshire in 1298. For a discussion of the mobilisation of mounted forces in 1298, see Prestwich, *War, Politics and Finance*, pp. 68–70.

[10]   These men are listed below in Appendix 1.

these is illuminated by the service of a man named Nicholas de Preston, whom I have first identified on campaign in early March 1298. He was present at the relief of the fortress of Berwick upon Tweed with his company of Lancashire foot archers, along with more than 2,600 men from that shire.[11] It is not clear whether Nicholas served in Scotland in 1299, but he was certainly back again through the summer and autumn of 1300 as a *centenarius* from Lancashire.[12] For at least part of this period, the Lancashire men were in the garrison at Berwick, which remained a major English magazine and fortress throughout Edward's Scottish wars.[13]

I have not yet found references to Nicholas de Preston's service in either 1302 or 1303, but he was back once more in Scotland in 1304 leading a *centena* of Lancashire foot archers as part of the garrison of Berwick,[14] and appears again in the garrison roll for Berwick in June 1305. At this time he assumed command of 101 Lancashire men who had been detached from the *centenae* commanded by two other Lancashire *centenarii* named Walter de Hoton and Adam Chernoke.[15] It appears that Nicholas departed from Berwick later in the summer, as the garrison roll for August notes that seventy-seven men from his *centena* were seconded for service with another *centenarius* named Thomas de Berwick.[16] Nicholas again went on campaign in 1307, when he commanded one of seven *centenae* of foot archers from Lancashire mustered by John de Segrave, one of Edward's chief lieutenants in Scotland.[17] At the beginning of the campaign Nicholas led a hundred foot archers but this number was reduced substantially to just sixty men after the troops arrived in Scotland.[18]

In sum, Nicholas de Preston led troops from Lancashire in at least five campaigns in Scotland over a period of nine years. The number of years in which he served may well be higher, as there are still many thousands of documents pertaining to these campaigns that I have not yet read. Nicholas' lengthy tours of duty over many years clearly indicate that he had taken on a career as a military officer who specialised in the command of foot soldiers.

A second career path that can be identified among Edward's professional infantry officers saw these men pass back and forth between leading infantry companies and serving as *soldarii*. The term *soldarius*, which had been used since at least the mid twelfth century by the authors of narrative sources to designate paid fighting men, appears to have been introduced into official use in England

---

[11] TNA E 101/7/2 9r.

[12] TNA E 101/612/25.

[13] On 3 August Nicholas commanded some 65 foot archers in the garrison at Berwick. See TNA E 101/8/20.

[14] TNA E 101/12/17.

[15] TNA E 101/11/15.

[16] TNA E 101/11/15.

[17] TNA E 39/4/3.

[18] TNA E 101/612/2.

by royal clerks in the context of Edward's campaign to Flanders in 1297.[19] I believe that this term was used to designate men who volunteered to serve as heavy cavalry in Edward's army, but who were not obligated to do so either because their income level was too low, or because the gentry from their shire had not been mobilised for service in a particular campaign.[20]

A useful example of this type of transition between *centenarius* and *soldarius* is provided by one of the most splendidly named of all of Edward's *centenarii*, John Bagepus. He first appears in royal pay records on 22 May 1295 leading a contingent of ninety-six Cheshire foot archers in Wales, as part of a force of eighteen infantry *centenae* from that shire.[21] The next piece of information regarding John's service that I have identified, thus far, comes from the administrative accounts produced in the course of the large-scale mobilisation of English troops in late 1297 to put down a major Scottish rebellion, led by, among others, William Wallace.[22] It was in the context of this campaign that Nicholas de Preston, discussed above, also first appears in the royal pay records.

John Bagepus commanded a *centena* of foot archers from Cheshire at Newcastle upon Tyne in mid December 1297 as part of a force of 1,800 men led by the earl of Surrey.[23] John's company took part in the relief of the fortress at Roxburgh in February 1298, and then briefly remained in the garrison there.[24] Sometime before the earl of Surrey's troops arrived at Roxburgh, however, John received promotion to the rank of *millenarius*, perhaps as a result of earlier campaign experience in Wales.[25] The rank of *millenarius* – that is, the commander of a thousand men – appears to have been a brevet rather than a permanent rank. John was one of thirteen *millenarii* present at Roxburgh from 2 to 14 February who led 146 *centenae* comprising 14,845 foot archers.[26] By no later than 3 March 1298 John, still holding the rank of *millenarius*, and his *centena* of foot archers had arrived at Berwick.[27] He remained there with his men throughout March and the remainder of the spring, as is indicated by a list of payments issued on

---

[19] The first use of this term that I have identified in English government records is in BL Additional MS 7965, which was edited by Bryce and Mary Lyon as *The Wardrobe Book of 1296–1297: A Financial and Logistical Record of Edward I's 1297 Autumn Campaign in Flanders Against Philip IV of France* (Brussels, 2004), p. 97. It should be noted that some of the *centenarii* who remained in service in Scotland after the departure of their troops for home were denoted as *valletti* rather than as *soldarii*. On this point, see *Liber quotidianus contrarotulatoris garderobae*, ed. John Topham (London, 1799), p. 256.

[20] I plan a focused study on the *soldarii* in the near future.

[21] TNA E 101/5/18, fol. 17r.

[22] Regarding the campaign of 1297–8 in Scotland, see the discussion by Prestwich, *Edward I* (Yale, 1997), pp. 476–83.

[23] TNA E 101/7/2, fol. 2v.

[24] TNA E 101/7/2, fol. 2v.

[25] TNA E 101/7/2, fol. 7v.

[26] TNA E 101/7/2, fol. 7v.

[27] TNA E 101/7/2, fol. 10r.

10 June to officers of foot, including Bagepus, by Richard Bremesgrave, the chief
logistics officer at Berwick.[28]

Bagepus also probably continued to serve in the garrison at Berwick
throughout the remainder of 1298 and the first half of 1299.[29] At some point,
however, his unit was demobilised and sent back to Cheshire. From late July
1299, at the latest, he served at Berwick as a *soldarius* rather than as an infantry
officer. Among the other forty-eight *soldarii* in the garrison at Berwick in the
summer of 1299 was a man named John le Balancer, who had also held the rank
of *millenarius* alongside John Bagepus in March 1298.[30] Bagepus continued to
serve for the next five years, apparently continuously, as a *soldarius* up through
the spring of 1304, in the garrisons at both Berwick and Edinburgh.[31] However,
at some point in 1304, John again assumed command of a *centena* of infantry, and
is identified as a *centenarius* in a 1304 pay roll for troops in Scotland.[32]

In considering John Bagepus's career, we see a man commanding infantry
units in at least three separate campaigns over a period of nine years. He was
sufficiently respected by his superiors that he was elevated to the brevet rank
of *millenarius* during the 1298 campaign in Scotland. Whether John's service
as *soldarius* during the period 1299–1304 also included periods in command of
infantry *centenae* must await further research. Other officers, however, certainly
did pass back and forth between service as *soldarii* and *centenarii*.

One man who followed this path was John de Herle, who first appears serving
in Scotland in 1300 as a *centenarius* leading a unit of foot archers from Northumberland.[33] In that same year John appears in the garrison roll at the fort of
Dumfries as a *soldarius*, alongside two other men, named John de Luken and
Robert de Herle, who also had served as Northumberland *centenarii*. The latter
was perhaps John's brother.[34] In 1301 John de Herle was again serving as an
infantry officer, leading 130 foot archers from Northumberland.[35] Once more
he appears alongside Robert de Herle, who also was in command of a *centena*
of Northumberland foot archers.[36] John was still serving in Scotland as a *centenarius* in February 1302, although his command had now been reduced to just
thirty-three men;[37] but in September 1302 he appeared in the garrison roll for
Bothwell as a *soldarius*.[38] I have not yet found records for John de Herle's service

---

[28] TNA E 101/7/2, fol. 12 v, and C 47/2/17, no. 4.
[29] TNA E 101/7/8, fol. 1 v.
[30] TNA E 101/7/2, fol. 10r.
[31] See TNA E 101/13/34, E 101/9/16, E 101/10/5 and E 101/11/1.
[32] TNA E 101/11/29, fol. 2r.
[33] TNA E 101/13/34.
[34] TNA E 101/13/34.
[35] BL Additional MS 7966A, fol. 108v.
[36] BL Additional MS 7966A, fol. 108v.
[37] TNA E 101/7/13.
[38] TNA E 101/10/5.

in 1303, but in April 1304 he received just under ten pounds – that is, approximately 200 days' wages – in arrears for his service as a *soldarius* at Linlithgow, permitting the inference that he had been there since 1303.[39] He was back in command of a *centena* of foot archers from Northumberland when he received pay in August 1304,[40] and in 1305 was back in the garrison at Linlithgow, again serving as a *soldarius*.[41]

This regular back and forth between service as a *soldarius* in various Scottish garrisons and as commander of infantry *centenae* from Northumberland gave John de Herle considerable experience leading shire troops. However, just as importantly, by staying in Scotland on an almost permanent basis, John was able to keep well informed, through personal experience, about the state of political and military affairs in the regions in which he led his men. Obviously, both of these types of experience were valuable to John's commanders in the field, and may well have given them confidence that officers such as John could effectively lead even semi-trained levies from the shires. Just as importantly, John de Herle's career is clearly indicative of his status as a professional officer.

Officers following a third career path also began by leading troops from the shire levies, but then took command of units of what appear to have been contract companies of professional foot archers. The men serving in these professional units, which I will discuss in more detail below, were designated as coming from *diversis comitibus* – that is, various shires – in contrast to *centenae*, whose members were all recruited from the same shire.[42] Thus, for example, an officer named Richard le Ronet is described in a royal pay account from 1307 as commanding 'foot soldiers from various parts of England, who have been retained for wages at the order of the king'.[43] These contract companies of foot archers can be seen to parallel the contract companies of mounted troops raised by numerous magnates at the direction and pay of the royal government during Edward I's reign.[44]

One typical officer, named Gilbert Mody, led a company of Northumberland foot archers in Scotland from December 1297 until March 1298, and took part in the relief of Roxburgh.[45] Gilbert was back in Scotland in command of

39 TNA E 101/11/16.

40 TNA E 101/12/16.

41 TNA E 101/12/38.

42 Prestwich, *War, Politics and Finance*, p. 106.

43 TNA E 101/373/15, fol. 13v: *pedites diversarum partium Anglie retentum ad vadi iuxta ordinacionem Regis*.

44 A considerable number of military contracts survive from the Scottish campaigns. See, for example, TNA E 101/9/15 for a contract with William of Durham for ten heavy cavalry, and E 101/681/1 for a list of military retainer agreements with Aymer de Valence, earl of Pembroke, Thomas de Berkeley and Robert Hastang. On the practice of writing up military contracts with magnates for the purpose of obtaining units of mounted forces, see Prestwich, *War, Politics and Finance*, pp. 61–4.

45 TNA C 47/2/20.

Northumberland troops in 1300, remaining there for at least four months.[46] The next year, however, he took on command of a *centena de diversis comitibus*, which served at Berwick from July through October 1301.[47] By the end of the year he had given up command of this *centena* and joined the garrison at Kirkintilloch as a *soldarius*, mirroring the transition between service as a *centenarius* and *soldarius* seen in the case of John de Herle.[48] By February 1302 Gilbert was back in command of a unit of foot archers when he received supplies of grain for his seventy-five men from Peter de Chichester, one of Edward I's household clerks, who was given responsibility for delivering provisions to troops stationed in Scotland.[49] No later than August, he had again given up command of his *centena* and re-entered the garrison at Kirkintilloch, where he served as a *soldarius* until December 1302.[50] I have not yet found information regarding his service in 1303, but in May 1304 he was back in Scotland in command of a contract *centena de diversis comitibus* numbering ninety-three men.[51] In August of that year his company had grown to 156 foot archers.[52] Whether he served in Scotland in 1305 remains unclear, but he was back for at least five months in 1306, from May to September, again in command of a *centena* of foot archers numbering ninety-five men.[53]

As was true of the other officers noted earlier, Gilbert Mody gained enormous experience leading troops in Scotland, serving there during at least six years between 1298 and 1306. Whether in garrison or in the field, this type of experience was invaluable for maintaining discipline and tactical control over troops, including both men of the shire levies and the professional soldiers of the contract companies. Moreover, as is true of the other officers discussed thus far, Gilbert Mody's career is clearly that of a professional officer.

The three career paths considered thus far concern the command of companies of foot archers. The final group of professional officers, by contrast, commanded crossbowmen (*balistarii*). For the most part, crossbowmen served in units of just twenty soldiers, and their officers, correspondingly, were *vintenarii* rather than *centenarii*. Moreover, the officers of crossbow units tended not to be mounted and earned only half as much as their mounted contemporaries – that is, six pence a day, rather than a shilling. Another important difference is that virtually

---

[46] For the command of Northumberland troops, see TNA E 101/13/34. For his receipt of just over six and half pounds for his service to date, see TNA E 101/684/46. At a shilling per day, this amounts to 130 days' service.

[47] BL Additional MS 7966A, fols 109r, 110v, 111v, 113v, and 114r; and TNA E 101/8/28.

[48] TNA E 101/9/16.

[49] TNA E 101/7/13. Regarding Peter of Chichester's service under King Edward, see Prestwich, *Edward I*, p. 158.

[50] TNA E 101/10/5 and E 101/11/1.

[51] TNA E 101/12/17.

[52] TNA E 101/12/16.

[53] TNA E 101/13/16.

all of the crossbowmen whom they commanded, particularly in Edward's Scottish wars, were professionals rather than men of the shire levies.[54]

Robert Lankerdaunce, for example, appears to have begun his military career during Edward I's campaign in Wales in 1295, leading a small unit of just nine *balistarii* in May and June of that year.[55] The pay records indicate that, at this early date, Robert's men all came from Cheshire since they are listed with the *centenae* of foot archers from that shire rather than separately under the rubric of *balistarii*. During the Scottish wars royal clerks separated out crossbowmen from other foot soldiers and listed them under the rubric of *balistarii* in both pay records and garrison rolls.[56] In 1298 Robert joined the garrison at Berwick as a *vintenarius* in command of nineteen *balistarii*.[57] He remained in Scotland more or less continuously up through May 1301, commanding his unit of crossbowmen at both Berwick castle and at the *castrum* of Lochmaben.[58] I have not yet found information regarding Robert's service in 1302 or 1303, but no later than August 1304 he was back in the garrison at Berwick, again commanding a unit of crossbowmen as their *vintenarius*.[59]

William de Gascony, another *vintenarius* of crossbowman, had a similar career in Scotland. He first appears in 1300, receiving supplies of grain and wine for his nineteen men at Perth on the river Tay in central Scotland.[60] It is not clear whether William served in Scotland in 1301, but in 1302 and 1303 he commanded his unit of crossbowmen in the garrison at Berwick before being transferred to Roxburgh.[61] In 1304 William's unit was back at Berwick.[62] I have not found information regarding William's service in 1305, but he was in command of a unit of crossbowmen at the fortress at Tibbers (Dumfries) no later than February 1306.[63]

As is clear from this brief account, Robert and William gave their superiors the benefit of years of experience of service in Scotland in much the same manner as the *centenarii*, discussed earlier, who commanded *centenae* of foot archers. It

---

[54] I have found no information regarding the mobilisation of crossbowmen from the shire levies for the wars in Scotland. By contrast, at least one summons of troops from Hampshire, Dorset and Wiltshire in 1295 called for both foot archers and crossbowmen to serve in Gascony. See *CPR, 1292–1301*, p. 151.

[55] TNA E 101/516 and E 101/5/18.

[56] For administrative purposes, the separation of crossbowmen from foot archers was useful because the men were paid different wages and required different types of supplies.

[57] TNA E 101/7/8; and C 47/2/17, which records Robert's receipt of a barrel of wine for his men.

[58] TNA E 101/7/20; E 101/684/46; E 101/13/34; and BL Additional MS 7966A, fol. 64v.

[59] TNA E 101/11/15.

[60] TNA E 101/13/36 no. 219.

[61] For Berwick, see TNA E 101/9/14; E 101/11/1; and E 101/9/4. For Roxburgh, see TNA E 101/10/26.

[62] TNA E 101/11/15 and E 101/11/16 nos 38, 43, 60 and 61.

[63] TNA E 101/13/16, fol. 17v.

should be emphasised, however, that, unlike the officers of foot archers, the *vintenarii* of the crossbow units appear to have served almost exclusively in garrisons rather than in the field.[64]

Professional Soldiers

The luxury of having large numbers of officers with years of command experience may well have been one of the reasons King Edward chose year after year to mobilise many thousands of men from the shire levies for military service, both in Wales and in Scotland. But he might also have been influenced in this decision by his knowledge that these shire levies would benefit from the presence of substantial numbers of professional soldiers both in garrison and in the field. The 'stiffening' effect of a core of professional soldiers had long been recognised in the medieval West from Charlemagne onward. To cite but one example, Harold Godwinson's housecarls appear to have done an admirable job of maintaining the resolve of the militia forces at Senlac until Harold's unfortunate meeting with a Norman arrow. I alluded above to two categories of professional foot soldiers in Edward's armies, the crossbowmen and the foot archers *de diversis comitibus*. I will now describe these in greater depth.

In both 1277 and 1287 King Edward deployed urban militia units equipped with crossbows for his invasions of Wales. In July 1277, for example, ninety-eight London crossbowmen under two officers (*constabularii*) reported to Chester for service in Wales.[65] Similarly, a unit of crossbowmen from the Oxford militia served in Chester in that year.[66] Units of London crossbowmen and Bristol crossbowmen were also mobilised for service in Wales in 1287.[67] The practice of deploying urban militiamen armed with crossbows continued in a limited way even during the latter part of Edward's reign. In 1296, for example, a unit of London crossbowmen was dispatched to help guard the Isle of Wight.[68]

---

[64] There are very good tactical reasons for deploying crossbowmen in fortifications. The most important of these is that crossbows could be aimed at individual targets while the crossbowman took cover in the defenses offered by the fortifications that Edward garrisoned throughout Scotland and Wales. In addition, a major liability of the crossbow is the considerable length of time required to load the weapon. Crossbowmen deployed in the field require more protection from other soldiers while they are loading their weapons than is the case with archers equipped with self bows.

[65] TNA E 101/3/11; C 62/56, fol. 9r.

[66] TNA E 372/121, fol. 11v.

[67] TNA E 101/4/20; E 372/132, fol. 22r; C 62/64, fol. 4r; and E 372/133, fol. 29r. For a detailed examination of the deployment of urban militias by both Henry III and Edward I, see David S. Bachrach, 'Urban Military Forces of England and Germany c.1240–c.1315: A Comparison', in *Mercenaries and Paid Fighting Men: The Mercenary Identity in the Middle Ages*, ed. John France (Turnhout, 2008), pp. 231–42.

[68] TNA E 101/5/27.

Edward II also made use of urban militia forces, deploying a unit of cross-bowmen from York to serve at Berwick in 1315.[69]

Early in his reign Edward I supplemented these militia units of crossbowmen with large numbers of professional *balistarii* from Gascony, particularly during the Welsh war of 1282–4.[70] During the final third of his reign, however, Edward appears to have relied on domestic companies of professional crossbowmen. These domestic contract companies may have numbered, in aggregate, as many as 800 soldiers, particularly during periods of substantial mobilisation. In this context, I have been able to identify by name more than seventy *vintenarii* of crossbowmen who served in Scotland between 1298 and 1307.[71] Of these officers, at least twenty led companies in 1304. In July of that year more than 450 crossbowmen served together in the garrison at Berwick alone.[72]

The detailed pay records for the Scottish wars, and especially documents that record payments of wages in arrears, make clear that the individual crossbowmen in these contract companies also served for long periods of time, often stretching on for years. On 12 May 1304, for example, a *balistarius* named Roger de Sutton from the unit of Jordan of Oxford received his back-pay at Berwick.[73] The memo-randum noted that Roger had spent the entire year in 1303 and the first four and a half months of 1304 in service at Berwick under Jordan's command. Other *balistarii* stationed in Scotland for long terms of service were seconded from unit to unit. A crossbowman named John le Archer, for example, served under the *vintenarius* John Dansard at Berwick for part of 1303.[74] He then transferred to Jordan of Oxford later in the year and remained with his new commander well into 1304.[75] It is not yet clear whether the individual crossbowmen were free to join a new company when their contracted period of service ended, or if the deci-sion about seconding men from unit to unit rested with the officers themselves.

The substantial numbers of crossbowmen on what appears to have been long-term service in Scotland led Edward's government to station specialists in crossbow production and repair in many of the fortresses there, including Berwick, Jedburgh, Lochmaben, Dumfries, Edinburgh, Linlithgow and Kirkin-tilloch.[76] In addition, specially trained artisans employed by the royal government

---

[69] TNA E 101/14/33.

[70] See TNA E 101/3/27 for a total of 85 mounted and 876 foot crossbowmen from Gascony serving in Wales. Also see the discussion by Prestwich in *War, Politics and Finance*, p. 108, where he identifies a total of 10 mounted crossbowmen and 1,313 Gascon crossbowmen serving on foot.

[71] See Appendix 2 for the list of crossbow officers whom I have identified thus far.

[72] TNA E 101/12/17 and E 101/13/16.

[73] TNA E 101/11/16 no. 45.

[74] TNA E 101/10/26.

[75] TNA E 101/10/26 and E 101/11/20.

[76] See TNA E 101/7/10; C 47/22/9 no. 71; E 39/93/18; E 101/9/9; E 101/10/6; E 101/11/1; E 101/12/10; E 101/68/1; E 101/8/27; E 101/12/18.

produced enormous quantities of crossbow quarrels for use in Scotland. Production and repair facilities for quarrels were organised at Newcastle upon Tyne, Berwick, Roxburgh and Dumfries.[77] In addition, the government purchased considerable quantities of crossbow ammunition, ordering, for example, 104,000 crossbow bolts in 1298.[78] All in all, Edward's government devoted considerable resources to ensuring that a sizeable contingent of professional crossbowmen was deployed in Scotland on a regular basis. However, this effort was dwarfed by the costs associated with maintaining large numbers of professional foot archers there throughout the period 1298–1307. It is to this group that I now turn.

As Michael Prestwich has noted, royal clerks generally grouped together all foot soldiers in the pay records and garrison rolls according to the shire from which they came.[79] The two major exceptions to this practice, especially in the context of Edward's Scottish wars, were the *balistarii*, noted above, and the *centenae de diversis comitibus*. Early in Edward's reign royal clerks used the phrase *de diversis comitibus* to denote that a particular pay-master was conducting units of infantry from several shires: for example, ten *centenae* of foot soldiers from Cheshire and eight *centenae* of foot soldiers from Shropshire.[80] By 1295, however, royal clerks had altered their practice so that the phrase *de diversis comitibus* now meant that the men in a particular *centena* were drawn from several shires. A memorandum regarding soldiers' wages in Wales in May 1295, for example, identifies infantry companies from Lancashire, Cheshire, Shropshire and also *de diversis comitibus*.[81] Royal clerks continued to draw this distinction between men of the shire levies and men serving in the companies *de diversis comitibus* through the entire period 1297–1307.[82]

It remains unclear precisely how these units were recruited. However, it seems likely that the men in these *centenae* were drawn from the pool of soldiers who had previous experience serving in the levies, particularly those from the northern shires. Many of the commanders of these companies, including men such as Henry Benteley of Northumberland, Henry de Manefeld of Cumberland, John Bristol of York, Philip de Montgomery from York and Richard de Ludlowe from Northumberland, originally hailed from the north.[83] All these

---

[77] TNA C 62/74, fol. 5r; E 101/8/24; E 101/9/30, no. 25; and E 101/14/1.
[78] TNA C 62/74, fol. 6r.
[79] Prestwich, *War, Politics and Finance*, p. 106.
[80] See TNA E 101/3/11 for the use of the phrase in this manner in 1277; and E 101/3/30 for the use of the phrase in this manner in 1282.
[81] TNA E 101/5/16.
[82] See, for example, TNA E 101/7/8; E 101/13/36; E 101/13/34; BL Additional MS 7966A; TNA E 101/7/13; E 101/11/1; E 101/12/17; and E 101/373/15.
[83] For Henry Benteley, see BL Additional MS 7966A; TNA E 101/8/20; E 101/13/34; E 101/9/16; E 101/9/9; and E 101/12/16. For Henry de Manefeld, see TNA E 101/8/18; E 101/3/9; E 101/13/36; E 101/13/34; E 101/7/13; E 101/11/1; E 101/11/15; and E 101/11/29. For John Bristol, see TNA E 101/8/20; E 101/13/34; BL Additional MS 7966A; TNA E 101/7/13; E 101/12/16; and E 101/12/17. For Philip de Montgomery, see TNA E 101/11/15; E 101/11/29;

officers had led units of foot archers from their home shires and thereby had a large number of contacts on which to draw when recruiting men to serve in their professional companies on a long-term basis. The *centenae de diversis comitibus* in aggregate numbered many thousands of men, and they played a substantial role in several campaigns. During the course of 1304, for example, no fewer than forty-nine *centenae de diversis comitibus* served in Scotland.[84] In July of that year, forty-three *centenarii* commanding units *de diversis comitibus* had a total of 3,923 foot archers under their command.[85]

In order to ensure that the men of the contract companies, and perhaps some of the shire units as well, were equipped for military operations, the royal government devoted considerable resources to stockpiling arrows in Scottish fortresses. The substantial efforts to supply the army at the siege of Stirling in 1304 with both arrows and bows are well known.[86] However, it should also be noted that every garrison in Scotland had on staff both a smith and a carpenter, usually with an assistant.[87] These craftsmen could turn out arrow-shafts and, potentially, arrow-heads if the smiths had received training in this skill. In addition, at least four garrisons – Newcastle upon Tyne, Berwick, Roxburgh and Dumfries – had fletchers on staff.[88] The royal government regularly obtained supplies of glue and feathers for the use of these fletchers to make arrows as well as for the fletchers who attached feathers to crossbow bolts.[89]

The bulk of Edward I's troops in the period 1296–1307 were militiamen from the shire levies. It seems, in addition, that many and perhaps a majority of the officers who led them also should be classified as militia. Nevertheless, noteworthy numbers of *centenarii* who commanded units of foot archers, and virtually all of the *vintenarii* who commanded crossbowmen in Scotland, were professionals. This cadre of officers provided the king with a wealth of leadership experience and tactical knowledge regarding the peculiar realities of warfare in Scotland. In addition, the thousands of soldiers serving in contract units of foot archers and crossbowmen had the potential to impart an important element of continuity and *esprit de corps*, as well as practical experience, to their more numerous but less well-trained comrades in arms from the shire levies.

and E 101/13/34. For Richard de Ludlowe, see TNA E 101/13/34; BL Additional MS 7966A; TNA E 101/7/13; and E 101/12/16.

[84] See TNA E 101/11/15; E 101/11/29; E 101/12/16; and E 101/12/17.

[85] TNA E 101/12/17.

[86] See TNA E 101/12/12. Prestwich, in *War, Politics and Finance*, discusses the supply of bows and arrows to the besiegers at Stirling, but does not identify the efforts of the royal government to supply these arms on other occasions.

[87] See, for example, the list of garrisons in TNA E 101/13/34.

[88] TNA C 62/74, fol. 5r; E 101/8/24; E 101/9/30 no. 25; and E 101/14/1.

[89] TNA C 47/22/4; E 372/139, fol. 6r; E 372/145, fol. 19v; C 62/74, fol. 5r; and C 62/76, fol. 2r.

Appendix One:
Centenarii who can be identified serving in three or more campaigns

These men are organised alphabetically by shire (all references are to TNA unless otherwise stated).

Cheshire
John Bagepus: E 101/5/18 (1295); C 47/2/17 (1297–1298); E 101/7/2 (1298); E 101/7/8 (1298–1299); E 101/13/34 (1300); E 101/9/16 (1301); E 101/10/5 (1302); E 101/11/1 (1302–3); E 101/11/15 (1303–4); E 101/12/18 (1303–4); E 101/11/29 (1304)

Cumberland
Adam Talon: E 101/13/34 (1300); E 101/11/15 (1303–4); E 101/11/29 (1304)
Henry de Manefeld: E 101/8/18 (1300); E 101/13/34 (1300); E 101/13/36 (1300); E 101/7/13 (1302); E 101/11/15 (1303–4); E 101/11/29 (1304); E 101/3/9 (1306)
Hugh de Norton: BL Additional MS 7966A (1300–1301); E 101/7/13 (1302); E 101/11/1 (1302–3); E 101/11/1 (1302–3); E 101/11/15 (1303–4); E 101/12/16 (1304)
Jordan Kendale: E 101/8/20 (1300); E 101/13/34 (1300); BL Additional MS 7966A (1300–1301); E 101/11/15 (1303–4)
Richard le Bret: E 101/612/25 (1300); E 101/8/20 (1300); E 101/11/15 (1303–4); E 101/11/29 (1304)

Gloucestershire
Nicholas le Lung: BL Additional MS 7966A (1300–1301); E 101/9/17 (1301); E 101/12/16 (1304)
Richard de London: BL Additional MS 7966A (1300–1301); E 101/9/17 (1301); E 101/12/16 (1304)

Herefordshire
Dominus Milo Pichard: E 101/13/34 (1300); BL Additional MS 7966A (1300–1301); E 101/12/16 (1304)
Thomas Pichard: E 101/13/34 (1300); BL Additional MS 7966A (1300–1301); E 101/12/16 (1304)
William Deverois: C 47/2/17 (1297–1298); E 101/13/34 (1300); E 101/9/17 (1301); BL Additional MS 7966A (1300–1301); E 101/12/16 (1304)
William Warin: E 101/13/34 (1300); E 101/9/17 (1301); BL Additional MS 7966A (1300–1301); E 101/12/16 (1304)

Lancashire
Adam Clou: E 101/6/1 (1296–1297); E 101/8/20 (1300); E 101/12/17 (1304)
John de Noteshaw: E 101/5/16 (1295); E 101/7/2 (1298); E 101/12/17 (1304)
Nicholas de Preston: E 101/7/2 (1298); E 101/13/34 (1300); E 101/612/25 (1300); E 101/8/20 (1300); E 101/11/15 (1303–4); E 39/4/3 (1307); E 101/612/2 (1307)
Peter le Taillour de Preston: E 101/612/25 (1300); E 101/12/17 (1304); E 39/4/3 (1307)

Robert Whetele: E 101/13/34 (1300); E 101/7/13 (1302); E101/11/15 (1303–4); E101/11/29 (1304); E 101/11/15 (1303–4)

William de Worthington: E 101/8/20 (1300); E 101/9/14 (1300–1303); E 101/11/1 (1302–3)

Northumberland

Gilbert Mody: C 47/2/20 (1298); E 101/13/34 (1300); E 101/684/46 (1300); BL Additional MS 7966A (1300–1301); E 101/9/16 (1301); E 101/8/28 (1301); E 101/7/13 (1302); E 101/10/5 (1302); E 101/11/1 (1302–3); E 101/11/15 (1303–4); E 101/12/16 (1304); E 101/12/17 (1304); E 101/13/16 (1305–1307)

Henry Benteley: E 101/8/20 (1300); E 101/13/34 (1300); BL Additional MS 7966A (1300–1301); E 101/9/16 (1301); E 101/9/9 (1301); E 101/7/13 (1302); E 101/10/5 (1302); E 101/11/1 (1302–3); E 101/12/16 (1304)

John Herle: E 101/13/34 (1300); BL Additional MS 7966A (1300–1301); E 101/7/13 (1302); E 101/12/16 (1304)

Richard de Bilton: E 101/8/20 (1300); E 101/13/34 (1300); E 101/684/52 (1300); BL Additional MS 7966A (1300–1301); E 101/9/16 (1301); E 101/10/5 (1302); E 101/11/1 (1302–3); E 101/11/15 (1303–4)

Richard de Ludlowe: E 101/13/34 (1300); BL Additional MS 7966A (1300–1301); E 101/7/13 (1302)

Robert de Bilton: E 101/9/16 (1301); E 101/10/5 (1302); E 101/11/15 (1303–4)

Robert Herle: E 101/13/34 (1300); BL Additional MS 7966A (1300–1301); E 101/7/13 (1302); E 101/11/16 (1303–1304); E 101/12/16 (1304); E 101/373/15 (1306)

William de Aspele: E 101/13/34 (1300); BL Additional MS 7966A (1300–1301); E 101/12/16 (1304)

William de Dalton: E 101/684/52 (1300); E 101/10/5 (1302); E 101/11/1 (1302–3); E 101/11/15 (1303–4)

William le Grant: E 101/8/20 (1300); E 101/13/34 (1300); BL Additional MS 7966A (1300–1301); E 101/12/16 (1304)

William de Hedon: BL Additional MS 7966A (1300–1301); E 101/7/13 (1302); E 101/12/16 (1304)

Nottinghamshire

Adam Carbonel: E 101/13/34 (1300); E 101/13/36 (1300); E 101/8/20 (1300); E 101/10/5 (1302); E 101/11/15 (1303–4); E 101/11/29 (1304); E 101/12/17 (1304)

Hugh de Clover: E 101/13/34 (1300); BL Additional MS 7966A (1300–1301); E 101/11/15 (1303–4)

Hugh de Oconner: E 101/8/20 (1300); E 101/13/34 (1300); E 101/13/36 (1300); BL Additional MS 7966A (1300–1301); E 101/7/13 (1302); E 101/11/15 (1303–4)

Shropshire and Staffordshire

Clement de Casterton: E 101/13/34 (1300); BL Additional MS 7966A (1300–1301); E 101/7/13 (1302); E 101/11/15 (1303–4); E 101/11/29 (1304); E 101/12/16 (1304)

Egidius de Staundon: E 101/13/34 (1300); BL Additional MS 7966A (1300–1301); E101/7/13 (1302); E101/12/16 (1304)

John de Charleton: C 47/2/17 (1297–1298); C 47/2/20 (1298); E 101/13/34 (1300); BL Additional MS 7966A (1300–1301); E 101/12/16 (1304)

John Langele: E 101/13/34 (1300); BL Additional MS 7966A (1300–1301); E 101/12/16 (1304)

John de Spreham: E 101/13/34 (1300); BL Additional MS 7966A (1300–1301); E 101/12/16 (1304); E 101/12/17 (1304)

John de Stirchester: C 47/2/20 (1298); E 101/8/20 (1300); E 101/12/17 (1304)

Robert Dalton: E 101/7/2 (1298); E 101/684/52 (1300); E 101/684/46 (1300); E 101/13/34 (1300); BL Additional MS 7966A (1300–1301); E 101/9/16 (1301); E 101/10/5 (1302); E 101/11/1 (1302–3); E 101/11/15 (1303–4); E 101/12/18 (1303–4); E 101/11/29 (1304)

Stephen de Acton: E 101/5/16 (1295); E 101/5/18 (1295); E 101/13/34 (1300); BL Additional MS 7966A (1300–1301); E 101/7/13 (1302); E 101/12/16 (1304)

Dominus Theobald miles de Neyville: E 101/13/34 (1300); BL Additional MS 7966A (1300–1301); E101/12/16 (1304)

William de Brideshale: E 101/5/16 (1295); E 101/5/18 (1295); E 101/7/2 (1298); E 101/12/17 (1304)

William Griffin: E 101/13/34 (1300); BL Additional MS 7966A (1300–1301); E 101/12/16 (1304); E 101/12/17 (1304)

Yorkshire

Henry de Manfeld: E 101/612/25 (1300); E 101/8/20 (1300); BL Additional MS 7966A (1300–1301); E 101/12/16 (1304)

Hugh de Baskerville: E 101/13/34 (1300); BL Additional MS 7966A (1300–1301); E 101/7/13 (1302); E 101/12/16 (1304)

John de Bristol: E 101/8/20 (1300); E 101/13/34 (1300); BL Additional MS 7966A (1300–1301); E 101/7/13 (1302); E 101/12/16 (1304); E 101/12/17 (1304)

John de Langton: E 101/13/34 (1300); E 101/684/52 (1300); E 101/9/16 (1301); E 101/10/5 (1302); E 101/11/1 (1302–3); E 101/11/15 (1303–4); E 101/11/29 (1304)

John de Upsale: E 101/13/34 (1300); BL Additional MS 7966A (1300–1301); E 101/7/13 (1302); E 101/11/1 (1302–3); E 101/11/15 (1303–4); E 101/11/16 (1303–1304); E 101/12/16 (1304)

Paul Ketell: E 101/612/25 (1300); E 101/8/20 (1300); E 101/13/34 (1300); E 101/11/15 (1303–4); E 101/13/16 (1305–1307)

Richard de Middelham: E 101/13/34 (1300); BL Additional MS 7966A (1300–1301); E 101/12/16 (1304)

Richard filius Henry de Wakefield: E 101/612/25 (1300); E 101/8/20 (1300); BL Additional MS 7966A (1300–1301); E 101/12/16 (1304)

Robert Pothou: E 101/13/34 (1300); BL Additional MS 7966A (1300–1301); E 101/12/16 (1304)

Thomas de Arches: E 101/13/34 (1300); BL Additional MS 7966A (1300–1301); E 101/7/13 (1302)

William de Alta Ripa: E 101/13/34 (1300); BL Additional MS 7966A (1300–1301); E 101/11/15 (1303–4); E 101/12/16 (1304)

William de Bateley: E 101/8/20 (1300); E 101/13/34 (1300); BL Additional MS 7966A (1300–1301); E 101/11/15 (1303–4); E 101/12/16 (1304)

William de Den: E 101/13/34 (1300); BL Additional MS 7966A (1300–1301); E101/12/16 (1304)

Westmorland
Henry de Burgo: E 101/8/20 (1300); E 101/11/1 (1302–3); E 101/11/15 (1303–4)

Shire not yet identified
Adam Prendergast: E 101/7/8 (1298–1299); E 101/13/34 (1300); E 101/11/1 (1302–3); E 101/12/17 (1304)
Henry Normant: E 101/13/34 (1300); BL Additional MS 7966A (1300–1301); E 101/12/16 (1304)
Ingeram Scrope: C 47/2/17 (1297–1298); E 101/7/8 (1298–1299); E 101/12/17 (1304)
John de Hibernia: BL Additional MS 7966A; C 47/2/20 (1298); E 101/13/34 (1300); E 101/7/13 (1302); E 101/11/1 (1302–3); E 101/12/28 (1303); E 101/12/18 (1303–4); E 101/11/16 (1303–1304); E 101/12/20 (1304); E 101/12/16 (1304)
John de Pimberton: E 101/684/52 (1300); E 101/13/34 (1300); E 101/11/1 (1302–3); E 101/11/15 (1303–4)
John de Shropham: E 101/13/34 (1300); E 101/11/1 (1302–3); E 101/12/18 (1303–4)
John Uthank: E 101/9/16 (1301); E 101/10/5 (1302); E 101/12/18 (1303–4)
John Vigrous: E 101/11/1 (1302–3); E 101/11/20 (1303); E 101/12/18 (1303–4)
Madoc le Waleys: E 101/684/46 (1300); E 101/13/34 (1300); E 101/13/34 (1300); E 101/7/13 (1302); E 101/10/5 (1302); E 101/11/1 (1302–3); E 101/11/15 (1303–4)
Marmaduke de Bilton: E 101/9/16 (1301); E 101/10/5 (1302); E 101/11/1 (1302–3)
Meredith Waleys: E 101/9/16 (1301); E 101/10/5 (1302); E 101/11/1 (1302–3)
Nicholas de Arderne: E 101/10/5 (1302); E 101/11/1 (1302–3); E 101/12/18 (1303–4)
Nicholas de Denlaco: E 101/10/5 (1302); E 101/11/1 (1302–3); E 101/12/18 (1303–4)
Patrick le Sauser: E 101/10/5 (1302); E 101/11/1 (1302–3); E 101/12/18 (1303–4); E 101/11/16 (1303–1304)
Peter de Leyberton: E 101/9/16 (1301); E 101/10/5 (1302); E 101/11/1 (1302–3)
Philip Morteyn: E 101/10/5 (1302); E 101/11/1 (1302–3); E 101/12/18 (1303–4)
Philip Northbridge: E 101/7/8 (1298–1299); E 101/9/16 (1301); E 101/10/5 (1302); E 101/11/1 (1302–3); E 101/11/15 (1303–4); E 101/11/16 (1303–1304)
Ralph de Benton: E 101/10/5 (1302); E 101/11/1 (1302–3); E 101/11/16 (1303–1304); E 101/12/18 (1303–4)
Richard de Dalton: E 101/13/34 (1300); E 101/11/1 (1302–3); E 101/373/15 (1306)
Richard Galoun: E 101/9/16 (1301); E 101/10/5 (1302); E 101/11/1 (1302–3); E 101/12/18 (1303–4)
Robert Jolif: E 101/684/52 (1300); E 101/10/5 (1302); E 101/11/1 (1302–3); E 101/11/1 (1302–1303)
Robert de Wallingsford: E 101/9/16 (1301); E 101/11/1 (1302–3); E 101/12/18 (1303–4)
Roger de Ravensdale: E 101/7/8 (1298–1299); BL Additional MS 7966A (1300–1301); E 101/9/16 (1301); E 101/10/5 (1302); E 101/11/1 (1302–3); E 101/11/15 (1303–4); E 101/11/29 (1304); E 101/13/16 (1305–1307)
Roger de Sutton: E 101/9/16 (1301); E 101/10/5 (1302); E 101/11/1 (1302–3); E 101/12/18 (1303–4)
Sevan de Mare: E 101/9/16 (1301); E 101/10/5 (1302); E 101/11/1 (1302–3); E 101/11/15 (1303–1304); E 101/12/18 (1303–4)
Simon de Middenhale: E 101/684/52 (1300); E 101/13/34 (1300); E 101/684/46 (1300); E 101/11/1 (1302–3); E 101/11/15 (1303–4)

Stephen de Walton: E 101/7/8 (1298–1299); E 101/13/34 (1300); E 101/9/16 (1301);
    E 101/10/5 (1302); E 101/11/1 (1302–3)
Thomas de Bradford: E 101/684/52 (1300); E 101/13/34 (1300); E 101/9/16 (1301);
    E 101/10/5 (1302); E 101/11/1 (1302–3); E 101/11/15 (1303–4)
Thomas de Langton: E 101/684/46 (1300); E 101/11/15 (1303–4); E 101/11/29 (1304)
Thomas Ramsey: E 101/13/34 (1300); E 101/9/16 (1301); E 101/10/5 (1302); E 101/11/1
    (1302–3); E 101/11/15 (1303–4); E 101/12/18 (1303–4); E 101/12/38 (1305)
Thomas de Ravensdale: E 101/8/20 (1300); E 101/13/34 (1300); E 101/9/16 (1301);
    E 101/7/13 (1302); E 101/10/5 (1302); E 101/11/1 (1302–3); E 101/11/15 (1303–4);
    E 101/12/18 (1303–4)
Walter Aynhou: C 47/2/20 (1298); E 101/9/16 (1301); E 101/10/5 (1302); E 101/11/1
    (1302–3); E 101/12/18 (1303–4)
Walter de Chiltone: E 101/9/16 (1301); E 101/10/5 (1302); E 101/11/1 (1302–3);
    E 101/12/18 (1303–4)
Walter de Greneford: E 101/9/16 (1301); E 101/10/5 (1302); E 101/11/1 (1302–3) ;
    E 101/12/18 (1303–4)
William de Batel: E 101/13/34 (1300); E 101/7/13 (1302); E 101/11/15 (1303–4)
William de Corbridge: E 101/9/16 (1301); E 101/10/5 (1302); E 101/11/1 (1302–3);
    E 101/12/18 (1303–4)
William de la Mare: E 101/13/34 (1300); E 101/11/1 (1302–3); E 101/11/15 (1303–4);
    E 101/11/29 (1304)
William Menant: E 101/684/52 (1300); E 101/13/34 (1300); E 101/10/5 (1302);
    E 101/11/1 (1302–3); E 101/11/15 (1303–4)
William de Northbridge: E 101/9/16 (1301); E 101/10/5 (1302); E 101/11/1 (1302–3)
William de Skyeburn: E 101/684/52 (1300); E 101/10/5 (1302); E 101/11/1 (1302–3);
    E 101/11/16 (1303–1304)
William de Strother: E 101/7/2 (1298); E 101/9/16 (1301); E 101/10/5 (1302); E 101/11/1
    (1302–3); E 101/11/15 (1303–4); E 101/12/18 (1303–4)
William Usher: E 101/684/52 (1300); E 101/9/16 (1301); E 101/10/5 (1302)
William de Weston: E 101/7/8 (1298–1299); E 101/684/52 (1300); E 101/10/5 (1302);
    E 101/11/1 (1302–3); E 101/12/17 (1304)

Appendix Two: Crossbow officers organised alphabetically

Adam de Dimolin: C 47/2/3 (1282)
Adam Warin: E 101/12/17 (1304)
Alex Malton: E 101/684/52 (1300)
Galfrid de Sherewind: E 101/13/16 (1305–1307)
Henry de Cherlton: E 101/13/34 (1300); E101/11/15 (1303–4)
Henry de Greneford: E 101/5/10 (1295)
Henry le Taverner: E 101/13/34 (1300); E 101/11/15 (1303–4); E 101/11/16 (1303–1304)
Hugh de Norton: E 101/7/8 (1298–1299); C 47/2/17 (1297–1298)
Hugh Scarlet: E 101/7/2 (1298); E 101/12/17 (1304)
Ingeram de Oxford: E 101/13/34 (1300)
John de Alta Ripa: E 101/13/34 (1300); E 101/11/1 (1302–3); E 101/11/16 (1303–1304);
    E 101/12/18 (1303–4)

John Bachelor: E 101/13/34 (1300); E 101/11/1 (1302–3)

John Ballamer: E 101/7/2 (1298)

John de Cama: E 101/7/2 (1298)

John de Crandon: E 101/13/16 (1305–1307)

John Dansard: E 101/10/26 (1303)

John de Kenilworth: C 47/2/3 (1282)

John Latilletur: BL Additional MS 7966A (1300–1301)

John de March: E 101/13/34 (1300); BL Additional MS 7966A (1300–1301)

John de Oxford: E 101/13/34 (1300); E 101/10/26 (1303)

John Pragin: C 47/2/20 (1298)

John Scarlet: E 101/10/26 (1303)

John Shubode: E 101/13/16 (1305–1307)

John Tamour: E 101/13/16 (1305–1307)

John de Thornhull: E 101/7/2 (1298)

John Wymandeslan: E 101/13/16 (1305–1307)

Jordan Oxford: E 101/684/53 (1300); E 101/9/9 (1301); E 101/11/1 (1302–3); E 101/11/20 (1303); E 101/10/26 (1303); E 101/11/15 (1303–4); E 101/11/16 (1303–1304); E 101/12/18 (1303–4)

Meredith: E 101/9/9 (1301)

Nicholas Mewe: E 101/7/8 (1298–1299); E 101/12/17 (1304)

Nicholas de Leyster: C 47/2/3 (1282)

Peter de Leicester: E 101/11/15 (1303–4)

Peter de Malding: E 101/7/8 (1298–1299)

Peter le Porter: E 101/11/15 (1303–4)

Richard de Clavering: E 101/7/8 (1298–1299); C 47/2/17 (1297–1298)

Richard de Farnham: E 101/12/17 (1304)

Richard le Port: E 101/9/9 (1301)

Richard le Tailleur: E 101/11/15 (1303–4)

Richard Wyghton: BL Additional MS 7966A (1300–1301); E 101/11/15 (1303–4)

Robert Cole: E 101/7/2 (1298)

Robert Darkdamme: E 101/13/34 (1300)

Robert Fanlin: E 101/7/8 (1298–1299); E 101/9/9 (1301)

Robert de Heketon: E 101/12/17 (1304)

Robert Landerkdaunte: E 101/7/8 (1298–1299); C 47/2/17 (1297–1298); E 101/7/20 (1299); E 101/684/46 (1300); E 101/13/34 (1300); BL Additional MS 7966A (1300–1301); E 101/11/15 (1303–4)

Robert Lanerky: E 101/10/26 (1303)

Roger de Arwe: C 47/2/17 (1297–1298); E 101/7/8 (1298–1299)

Roger de Lam: E 101/11/1 (1302–3); E 101/12/18 (1303–4); E 101/13/16 (1305–1307)

Roger Lanham: E 101/13/34 (1300); E 101/11/20 (1303); E 101/11/16 (1303–1304)

Simon de London: E 101/12/17 (1304)

Simon le Tanner de London: E 101/7/2 (1298)

Thomas Foreys: E 101/13/16 (1305–1307)

Thomas Tegan: E 101/684/52 (1300); E 101/13/34 (1300); E 101/11/15 (1303–4); E 101/12/38 (1305); E 101/13/16 (1305–1307)

Thomas de la Valeye: C 47/2/3 (1282)

Walter Baret: E 101/7/2 (1298)

Walter Brom: E 101/12/17 (1304)

Walter Kanesham: BL Additional MS 7966A (1300–1301)

William Aurifaber: E 101/11/1 (1302–3)

William de Bere: E 101/7/8 (1298–1299)

William de Boston: E 101/9/9 (1301)

William de Corham: E 101/7/8 (1298–1299)

William de Cornbrill: E 101/11/15 (1303–4)

William de Dorking: C 47/2/3 (1282)

William of Gascony: E 101/13/36 (1300); E 101/9/14 (1300–1303); E 101/11/1 (1302–3);
    E 101/9/4 (1303); E 101/10/26 (1303); E 101/11/15 (1303–4); E 101/11/16 (1303–
    1304); E 101/13/16 (1305–1307)

William de Maltone: E 101/11/1 (1302–3)

William Newerk: E 101/11/1 (1302–3)

William de Northampton: E 101/11/1 (1302–3)

William Panetir: E 101/9/9 (1301); E 101/9/18 (1301)

William Porter: E 101/13/34 (1300); E 101/11/15 (1303–4)

William Roleston: E 101/13/16 (1305–1307)

William de Selkirk: E 101/11/1 (1302–3)

William de Stenwyk: E 101/10/26 (1303)

William le Tenturer: E 101/7/2 (1298)

William de Wakefield: E 101/7/8 (1298–1299); C 47/2/17 (1297–1298)

5

Who's Afraid of the Big Bad Bruce? Balliol Scots and 'English Scots' during the Second Scottish War of Independence

Iain A. MacInnes

During the Scottish Wars of Independence many Scots chose, or were forced to choose, the apparent security of English allegiance. In the years when, for example, Edward I appeared most likely to win his war with Scotland, many opted to enter the English king's peace in the hope of retaining their lands, rights and privileges under the new administrative order. This acknowledgement of the likelihood of an Edwardian victory prompted a practical response from most leading Scottish figures. The war in Scotland, as Edward I himself discovered, was not, however, simply a choice between Scottish independence and English overlordship. There was, bubbling under the surface, the ongoing civil conflict between the Balliol/Comyn and Bruce factions. The divisions that existed between the supporters of both parties became permanently fixed following Robert I's killing of John Comyn in 1306 and the rebellion that followed. Those individuals and families who had previously fought for Scotland's continued independence, but who were diametrically opposed to Bruce and his cause, now found themselves in need of English support as the only option if they were to defeat the Bruce seizure of the Scottish throne. Ultimately the opponents of Bruce, even with English assistance, lost their struggle and although some were able to enter into the new king's peace others were unable or unwilling to do so and instead entered exile in England. This was not, however, the end of the story. After Robert I's death, the question of the 'Disinherited', those nobles and other individuals who had been dispossessed of their ancestral lands or whose claims to inheritance had been ignored in favour of loyal Bruce supporters, raised its head. And although the English Disinherited became the more famous, leading the invasion of Scotland in 1332 with Edward Balliol as their nominal leader, a number of Scottish Disinherited too re-entered Scotland in the wake of Balliol's early campaigns.

There were also those within Scotland whose allegiance to the Bruce dynasty had been extorted through force or the threat of its use against those who were unwilling to accept wholeheartedly the idea that Scottish independence and Bruce leadership were indelibly linked. The Guardianships that ruled Scotland in the name of David II were, therefore, faced with the challenge of governing a notably disunited kingdom. They also had to do so in the face of an active and militarily aggressive alternative in the shape of Edward Balliol assisted by various English Disinherited and Edward III of England. Various studies have examined, directly or indirectly, the subject of Scottish allegiance during the fourteenth-century war years. Most of these, such as Geoffrey Barrow's article on Lothian and Bruce Webster's study of Dumfriesshire, and, more recently, Michael Brown's analysis of Teviotdale and Richard Oram's examination of Galloway, deal with specific geographical areas.[1] In other works, authors such as Amanda Beam, Michael Penman and Michael Brown have produced more detailed examinations of Scots whose allegiance was not pro-Bruce.[2] In spite of such studies, there has been little detailed analysis of the actual extent of support for the alternative Balliol regime. It is probable that a comprehensive search of existing materials would unearth the names of many more Scots who sided with the Balliol regime. This paper cannot, however, hope to provide full coverage of this subject. Instead it will present details of the careers of individuals whose prominence is reflected in the surviving record evidence, providing an alternative to the seemingly pervading view that Edward Balliol's invasion was doomed to failure through a general lack of Scottish support. His ceding of southern Scotland to Edward III and his increasingly marginalised position in Scotland,

---

[1]   G.W.S. Barrow, 'Lothian in the First War of Independence', *Scottish Historical Review* 55 (1976), pp. 151–71; M.H. Brown, 'War, Allegiance, and Community in the Anglo-Scottish Marches: Teviotdale in the Fourteenth Century', *Northern History* 41 (2004), pp. 219–38; R.D. Oram, 'Bruce, Balliol and the Lordship of Galloway: South-West Scotland and the Wars of Independence', *Transactions of the Dumfriesshire and Galloway Natural History and Antiquarian Society* 3rd ser. 67 (1992), pp. 29–47; B. Webster, 'The English Occupation of Dumfriesshire in the Fourteenth Century', *Transactions of the Dumfriesshire and Galloway Natural History and Antiquarian Society* 3rd ser. 35 (1956–7), pp. 64–80.

[2]   A. Beam, *The Balliol Dynasty, 1210–1364* (Edinburgh, 2008), pp. 209–34; M.A. Penman, '"A Fell Coniuracioun agayn Robert the douchty king": The Soules Conspiracy of 1318–20', *Innes Review* 50 (1999), pp. 25–57; M.H. Brown, '*Scoti Anglicati*: Scots in Plantagenet Allegiance during the Fourteenth Century', in *England and Scotland in the Fourteenth Century: New Perspectives*, ed. A. King and M.A. Penman (Woodbridge, 2007), pp. 94–115. See also R.C. Reid, 'Edward de Balliol', *Transactions of the Dumfriesshire and Galloway Natural History and Antiquarian Society* 3rd ser. 35 (1956–7), pp. 38–63; idem, 'Myrton Castle', *Transactions of the Dumfriesshire and Galloway Natural History and Antiquarian Society* 3rd ser. 21 (1936–8), pp. 384–91; A. Ross, 'Men for All Seasons? The Strathbogie Earls of Atholl and the Wars of Independence, c.1290–c.1335. Part I', *Northern Scotland* 20 (2000), pp. 1–30; 'Part II', *Northern Scotland* 21 (2001), pp. 1–15; B. Webster, 'Scotland without a King, 1329–1341', in *Medieval Scotland, Crown, Lordship and Community: Essays Presented to G.W.S. Barrow*, ed. A. Grant and K.J. Stringer (Edinburgh, 1998), pp. 223–38.

perceived generally as steps along the road to his eventual downfall, do not appear to have removed support for him completely in Scotland. And it is worth examining some of the more prominent examples of individuals and, perhaps more importantly, families who did continue to support his cause. Such groups can in themselves provide the basis of a wider study of allegiance and the way in which familial commitment, ties of lordship and even geographical proximity influenced the loyalty of some Scots during the Second War of Independence.

Balliol Scots and Disinherited Scots in the Second War of Independence

Loyalty and allegiance to the Bruce dynasty were not as absolute as later-fourteenth-century Scottish chroniclers suggested. Indeed, as Michael Penman has argued, lingering Balliol support had already manifested itself in Scotland in the plot to overthrow Robert I in 1320.[3] It should, therefore, come as little surprise that the return of a Balliol representative to Scotland in 1332 reawakened either latent support for Edward Balliol, or at least lasting resentment against the Bruce dynasty. Robert I had, after all, compelled many Scots to support him at the point of the sword and with the threat, or reality, of devastation and later forfeiture of territories as a means of enforcing obedience to his regime. Edward Balliol was certainly reported to have believed that a body of support for his return existed within Scotland, and that such men would come to his aid following his invasion. English chronicles name Donald, Earl of Mar, as the principal supporter of Balliol, notwithstanding that he was named Scottish Guardian in 1332 following the death of Thomas Randolph.[4] Indeed, it seems inconceivable that the Disinherited would have staked their lives and prospects on an invasion if they did not anticipate some sort of popular support for their actions. Forward planning surely anticipated the recruitment of local levies to augment the relatively small Disinherited force sufficiently to face the inevitable Bruce military response.

And such support does appear to have been forthcoming, either in response to the Disinherited invasion or to Balliol's victory at Dupplin Moor. The Disinherited landing at Kinghorn in Fife provoked an armed response by Bruce forces under the command of the earl of Fife, but the apparent ease with which the Bruce forces were defeated bought the invading forces several days of security. In this time they traversed Fife, including a trip to Dunfermline, and it is likely that during this time both financial and physical support was recruited from the earldom. Questions may already have been raised at this time about the loyalty of the earl of Fife, who was described by one English chronicler as 'so wonder sorry, and full evil shamed that so little company had him discomfited,

3   Penman, 'The Soules Conspiracy'.
4   *The Brut*, ed. F.W.D. Brie, Early English Text Society 1st ser. 131, 136, 2 vols (1906–8), i, p. 274; *The Chronicle of Lanercost, 1272–1346*, ed. H.E. Maxwell (Glasgow, 1913), p. 268.

and shamefully put him and all his company that was alive for to flee.[5] Fife's career and loyalty over the next few years would indicate his own indecision regarding his allegiance, and he shall be examined in more detail in due course. There appears to be an assumption in analyses of the war that much of the early support that Balliol and the Disinherited were able to attract was a short-term response to the shock of Balliol's arrival and early success.[6] Those who did throw their weight behind Balliol in the early days are perceived as being less committed supporters and more political opportunists who thought they saw the political wind blowing in Balliol's direction. As Amanda Beam has pointed out, however, Edward Balliol did enjoy ongoing support from, for example, prominent Galwegian families based within the Balliol family's ancestral territories in the region.[7] Indeed, it was Galwegian forces under Eustace Maxwell who were reported to have risen in support of Balliol when the Disinherited were besieged in Perth and who may have been responsible in part for the abandonment of the siege.[8] And record evidence of support for Balliol within the Galloway area is relatively abundant, mostly through English administrative sources.

Of highest social rank within the area was the Maxwell family. As already indicated, it was Eustace Maxwell, lord of Caerlaverock, who was described leading the region's pro-Balliol forces to relieve Perth.[9] Without such support the Disinherited invasion, despite its success at Dupplin Moor, could well have failed at a very early stage. This early example of pro-Balliol loyalty appears to have become a pro-English stance on 1 February 1334, when Maxwell entered Edward III's service for life. This was done in return for the king finding Maxwell his wife and his children a manor to the value of £40 a year, suggesting that by this time some of his own territories had been lost to the Bruce Scots.[10] Maxwell's allegiance to Edward III appears to have been substantive and he received English pay for service with Edward III during the Roxburgh campaign over the winter of 1334–5.[11] In the following months he received £20 for service with the king over Easter.[12]

Thereafter his service to the English crown involved guardianship of his own castle of Caerlaverock, as well as service 'in other parts of Scotland' until 5 September 1335.[13] Maxwell was also appointed English sheriff of Dumfriesshire,

5   *Brut*, ed. Brie i, pp. 275–6.
6   Beam, *Balliol Dynasty*, pp. 223, 233–4; Brown, 'War, Allegiance, and Community', pp. 227–9; M.A. Penman, *David II, 1329–71* (East Linton, 2004), pp. 48–9; Webster, 'Scotland without a King', pp. 229–32.
7   Beam, *Balliol Dynasty*, pp. 223–4.
8   *Lanercost*, ed. Maxwell, pp. 272–3.
9   For Maxwell, see Oram, 'Bruce, Balliol and Galloway', pp. 43–4.
10 CDS, iii, no. 1143.
11 BL Cotton MS Nero C.VIII, fols 239, 253.
12 CDS, iii, no. 1161.
13 BL Cotton MS Nero C.VIII, fol. 256.

an administrative role from which he could draw an income.[14] No doubt it was convenient for Edward III to have a loyal Scot, and a local lord of note, in charge of this territory. It is, however, tempting to see the hand of Edward Balliol in the appointment, securing the reward of a prominent supporter for his loyalty and his actions in the recent conflict. Maxwell also continued to serve Edward III in a military capacity and was given £50 in May 1336 for his wages and those of his men-at-arms and hobelars 'recently serving the king in the war in Scotland'.[15] This service to the English king was a logical course of action following Edward Balliol's ceding of southern Scotland, Maxwell's territories included, to Edward III in 1334. That this altered political reality was in effect does not mean, however, that Maxwell had 'gone English'. Adoption of English status may have occurred in 1347 when Eustace's son Herbert Maxwell submitted to the earl of Northampton and was recognised as 'an Englishman'.[16] For Eustace Maxwell, however, English service appears to have been less a declaration of overwhelming English loyalty and more an indication of his enduring pro-Balliol/anti-Bruce inclinations.

Similarly, the receipt of English pay should not be perceived as a declaration of wholehearted adoption of an English identity. Like the Comyns after 1306, support of the English was a means to an end, for it was the English who provided the best chance of placing Edward Balliol on the Scottish throne, as well as providing the financial backing for the conflict. Even those Scots who were not officially enrolled in English service were as likely to have been paid by the English exchequer; after all, much of the money Edward Balliol used to pay his own troops was subsidised by payments from Edward III. From a basic financial viewpoint, therefore, it may be argued that Balliol service and English service were in effect one and the same thing. And this is perhaps one of the reasons why the extent of Balliol support is unclear. The records of Balliol's administration are lost and with them the names of most of those who supported his regime. Meanwhile, many of those, such as Maxwell, who served Balliol by engaging in English service have been regarded in the past as 'Scots in English service' rather than 'Balliol Scots'. This distinction may be narrow, but in denying or ignoring the pro-Balliol nature of such individuals it minimises their importance in the Scottish civil conflict of this period. Men such as Eustace Maxwell were Balliol supporters living in Scotland. They were an integrated part of Scottish society and as such they are potential indicators of the extent of wider support for Balliol.

English administrative evidence provides significant details on other Scots

[14] Webster, 'English Occupation of Dumfriesshire', pp. 69–72; Oram, 'Bruce, Balliol and Galloway', pp. 44–5.
[15] TNA E 403/288, m. 7. Maxwell also received a cash gift from Edward III in November 1335 of £40; BL Cotton MS Nero C.VIII, fol. 273.
[16] *Rot. Scot.*, i, p. 704.

who were Balliol supporters.[17] One of the most obvious is another family from south-west Scotland, the McCullochs. Although discussed less than that other prominent south-west kindred, the MacDowells, the McCullochs' record of service was impressive.[18] As a Wigtownshire family with a history of Balliol/English allegiance and English military service they lost their lands in Scotland following the success of Robert I against his internal enemies.[19] Their return to Scotland appears to have been either in the company of Edward Balliol or in the aftermath of the Disinherited invasion. In the first years of conflict there are no mentions of the family at all in English service, suggesting either their return to Scotland in the months after the 1333 invasion or active military service with Balliol for which the records are now lost. English service appears to have been the next logical step, at least after 1334, and the family is first represented in English records by William McCulloch in 1336. He served in the army of Edward Balliol, albeit in the retinue of Henry Beaumont, on the march of the two Edwards to Perth in the summer campaign of that year.[20]

It was, however, Patrick McCulloch who appears to have enjoyed the greatest benefits of long-term Balliol loyalty and English military service. Patrick was in receipt of an English pension by March 1338 and remained loyal throughout the 1340s.[21] He served with two *armiger* men-at-arms in the garrison of Berwick from June 1340 to July 1341.[22] Between 1341 and 1342 he received three payments for 'his good and loyal service' and for 'remaining in the king's peace'.[23] And in April 1344 he was one of a group of Disinherited Scots who petitioned Edward III for arrears of money owed to them. In McCulloch's case this amounted to 100 marks as wages for himself and two 'vallets'.[24] Patrick McCulloch then appears to have utilised his record of English service on the Anglo-Scottish frontier to

[17] Eustace Maxwell abandoned his support for Balliol in 1337 and suffered as a result, as his lands were devastated by the English. Still, he had returned to Balliol's support once more by 1339. His son Herbert followed a similar path and entered English peace in September 1347, probably in the wake of the Balliol/English campaigns in south-west Scotland following Neville's Cross. He had, according to a letter written by the earl of Northampton, entered England under a safe conduct and submitted to Edward III as his king and to Northampton as his lord for Annandale, also surrendering Caerlaverock Castle into the earl's custody; CDS, iii, no. 1507.
[18] Oram, 'Bruce, Balliol and Galloway', pp. 43–7.
[19] Reid, 'Myrton Castle', pp. 384–91; Reid, 'Edward de Balliol', pp. 51–2; Oram, 'Bruce, Balliol and Galloway', pp. 37–8, 44–7.
[20] William McCulloch had his horse, valued at £10, appraised at Berwick on 16 May 1336; TNA E 101/19/36, m. 2.
[21] *Rot. Scot.*, i, p. 541; cf. Reid, 'Edward de Balliol', pp. 51–2; Oram, 'Bruce, Balliol and Galloway', p. 44. In May 1338 Patrick McCulloch received one tun of wine from the king's stores at Carlisle; CCR 1339–41, p. 81.
[22] TNA E 403/321, m. 7.
[23] TNA E 403/318, m. 8; E 403/321, m. 6; E 403/326, m. 13; cf. Reid, 'Edward de Balliol', pp. 51–2.
[24] CDS, iii, no. 1432.

gain access to the potential rewards of continental service, in this case in Brittany. Between 1343 and 1347 he served with English forces in the duchy for at least sixteen months, for which he and his two *armigers* received regular payment.[25] McCulloch's Breton service may even have been a response to a wider English recruitment of Scots to serve on the continent. In April 1345 the crown ordered that safe conducts should be issued to those *Scotis Anglicatis* who wished to cross the sea to serve the English king, although further investigation is required to ascertain how many Scots took advantage of this opportunity.[26]

Having returned to the Anglo-Scottish frontier, Patrick McCulloch remained in English pay and service in March 1354.[27] He continued to receive money from the English exchequer as late as 1362, when sums paid to him were apparently part of a grant of 100 marks a year he was given 'until the lands and tenements which are of his inheritance in Scotland should be restored to him'.[28] By this late stage English service appears to have become his principal source of income and any territories he had recovered in Scotland during the war years had been lost once more to the Bruce party. By 1362, therefore, it may be argued that McCulloch had in effect 'gone English'. He may even represent an early Scottish example of a developing professional soldier earning his living wherever the English were willing to employ him. And Patrick McCulloch was certainly not alone in embarking on such a career. Various Scots are recorded serving in France for English pay in the 1370s.[29] This later career was, however, the obvious response of a Balliol supporter who had lost everything in his own, and his family's, continued support for the Balliol party and continued rejection of the ultimately successful Bruce dynasty.

Patrick's ongoing service in English pay appears also to have acted as a stimulus for other members of the McCulloch kin network to follow his example, accounting for a possible seven members of the family present in English service over the period 1343–7. Thomas and Michael McCulloch petitioned Edward III at the same time as Patrick (25 April 1344) over arrears of their wages of 12d a day for military service already performed.[30] Gilbert McCulloch was in receipt of English wages of 12d a day in February 1343 and was still in English service in the border region in 1347.[31] And a compilation of the names of those Scots recorded serving the English crown in a military capacity in August 1341, June 1342 and 1347 also includes those of John, son of Gilbert McCulloch; possibly another John; Patrick, son of Patrick McCulloch; John, son of Patrick; and Michael

[25] TNA E 101/23/39.

[26] *Rot. Scot.*, i, p. 660.

[27] *Rot. Scot.*, i, p. 763.

[28] *Issue Roll of Thomas de Brantingham, Bishop of Exeter, Lord High Treasurer of England*, ed. F. Devon (London, 1835), p. 457; *CDS*, v, nos 831, 833.

[29] See, for example, *Issue Roll of Thomas de Brantingham*, ed. Devon, pp. 410–11.

[30] *CDS*, iii, no. 1432.

[31] *CDS*, iii, no. 1406; *Rot. Scot.*, i, 690.

McCulloch, perhaps the same individual who petitioned Edward III in 1344.[32]
This, then, would appear to represent the service of a major south-west Scottish
kindred, not simply individual members adopting Balliol/English allegiance. As
with Maxwell, the service of these named individuals was often accompanied by
various others – hobelars, *armigers* and valets – who were probably extended
family, supporters, followers or tenants. The names of these individuals are not
recorded. Military service such as this does, however, suggest a wider basis of
support for the Balliol/English cause, based on the extended kin and military
service networks at work throughout, in this case, south-west Scotland.

Evidence for this process repeating itself outwith the south-west is more
limited, but Alisdair Ross has demonstrated that the return of David Strathbogie to his ancestral estates in Atholl reawakened latent support in the region
from families with long-standing links to the comital family.[33] Loyalty to lords
who had been forfeited in the wake of the Bruce settlement of the kingdom
almost twenty years before confirms that some Scots welcomed the return of
Disinherited families with long connections to particular areas, a situation that
almost certainly required the return of a Balliol king to overturn the Bruce
settlement. English records are also useful in demonstrating the importance of
familial links in regards to service in English forces, an action which may in
some cases also be interpreted as an acknowledgement of support for the Balliol
cause in English-controlled southern Scotland. Among such groups are several
families from Lothian. Some examples are provided by the families of Dalmahoy,
Pontekin, Crichton and Napier. Alexander and Roger Dalmahoy served alongside each other in the garrison of Edinburgh Castle in 1335, Roger at least continuing his service in 1339–40, while Alexander was recorded serving with English
forces patrolling the border region in 1342.[34] There is also record of a William
Dalamahoy, who at Perth in July 1336 received a gift of £10 from Edward III that
was intended for Alexander Mowbray.[35] This association of a member of the
family with the Mowbrays, one of the major families involved in the Disinherited enterprise from the beginning, is reinforced by evidence from the previous
year. In October 1335 William Dalmahoy is included in a long list of Scottish
'gentlemen' who received pardons from Edward III, presumably as a result of
abandoning their Balliol/English allegiance in the aftermath of the Disinherited
collapse in 1334 and returning to their previous allegiance following the summer
campaigns of 1335.[36] The men named (who included two other members of the

---

[32] *Rot. Scot.*, i, pp. 611–12, 626–8, 690.

[33] Ross, 'Men for All Seasons? Part II', pp. 4–5.

[34] *CDS*, iii, p. 361, nos 1390, 1407; *Rot. Scot.*, i, pp. 626–8 (Alexander Dalmahoy); *CDS*, iii,
pp. 360, 363; no. 1323; TNA E 101/22/20, m. 3; E 101/23/1, m. 1 (Roger Dalmahoy).

[35] BL Cotton MS Nero C.VIII, fol. 278v.

[36] *CDS*, iii, no. 1184. The names of those listed were William Mowbray, Roger Mowbray,
Alexander Craigie senior, Alexander Craigie junior, John Dunbar, Phillip Glen, William
Dalmahoy, James Dundas, William Fairly, William Bartholomew, John Comyn, Roger Young,

Mowbray family) had entered Edward III's peace 'on the same conditions as Sir Alexander Mowbray'.[37] If there was indeed a connection between the Dalmahoys and the Mowbrays this would appear to represent an example of the type of extended military network already alluded to in relation to the south-west kindreds.

Not all of the men pardoned in this year were necessarily linked to the Mowbrays and in turn with the Dalmahoys, but it does appear that the various named individuals were all linked through their support of Edward Balliol. Some of those others mentioned in 1335 can be traced through quite long periods of English service. These include men of the family of Craigie, with both Alexander senior and Alexander junior included in the 1335 warrant. Both men served in the garrison at Edinburgh in 1335–6, and were joined in this service by Gilbert and William Craigie.[38] The younger Alexander Craigie had left the garrison by January 1340 at the latest, but Craigie senior, who had remained in Edinburgh throughout the 1330s, was still in English service until at least 1342.[39] The departure of the younger Craigie may indicate a break with his father and with his Balliol/English outlook, for Craigie junior would later receive his father's estates from the Scottish crown as an apparent reward for the son's adoption of the Bruce allegiance.[40] These lands included the manor of Craigie as well as other lands in Lothian, such as Halton in Edinburgh, all lying within that area of southern Scotland administered by the English in the 1330s.[41] Another Alexander Craigie, possibly Alexander senior but referred to as 'le cosyn', was in receipt of an English grant in 1343.[42] The long service of Alexander senior, which, similar to those families already discussed, is likely to have begun before the recorded resubmission to Edward III in 1335, may have been based on a familial history of similar service. In particular, the Craigies had past associations with

Roger de Aulton, Hugh Crawford, Geoffrey Mowbray, John Comyn, Alexander Latoft, Robert Scott, Duncan Bell, Adam French, Ellis Lythe, Robert Barber and Geoffrey Makelly.

[37] *CDS*, iii, no. 1184.

[38] *CDS*, iii, p. 361, no. 1186.

[39] TNA E 101/22/20, mm. 3, 3v; *CDS*, iii, no. 1186, and pp. 361, 363. Both men had left Edinburgh by the time of the next financial account, which began on 26 January 1340; TNA E 101/23/1, m. 5.

[40] *CDS*, iii, pp. 360, 362, nos 1186, 1280, 1292, 1296, 1323, 1351, 1388, 1392, 1404; *Registrum magni sigilli regum Scotorum*, ed. J.M. Thomson and J.B. Paul, 11 vols (Edinburgh, 1882–1914), i, app. 2, p. 907. Craigie junior received £26 13s 4d from the Scottish chamberlain, on the orders of David II, in 1342; *The Exchequer Rolls of Scotland*, ed. J. Stuart et al., 23 vols (Edinburgh, 1878–1908), i, 509.

[41] *Rot. Scot.*, i, p. 323. Margaret Craigie was confirmed of the 6 mark annual return from the land of Halton in the sheriffdom of Edinburgh in a charter of 1377; *Registrum magni sigilli*, ed. Thomson and Paul, i, pp. 239–40.

[42] *CDS*, iii, no. 1412.

Edinburgh Castle: an Alexander and a William Craigie are among the members of the English garrison of the castle in 1312.[43]

Interestingly, the garrison at Edinburgh appears during the 1330s to have been the base for many Scots in Balliol/English service. Alongside Craigie senior served a fellow knight, William Ramsay of Colluthie.[44] He too possessed territorial interests in Lothian, including properties in Edinburgh.[45] His service in Edinburgh appears to have been almost as consistent as Craigie's, his name appearing in the accounts for 1336–7 and 1339–40, while he also received financial assistance from the English crown as late as 1343.[46] It was in this year, however, that Ramsey apparently decided to alter his allegiance, and submitted to David II.[47] Below the level of these knightly figures, other local men also performed military service in the keeping of Edinburgh Castle. Alexander and John Crichton, Thomas, Adam and William Pontekin, and Duncan, Richard and John Napier all served in the garrison at some stage between 1335 and 1340.[48] Their names suggest that they were all local Lothian men.[49] Of these three families it is the Crichtons who appear to have had the longest history of English service. In 1312 a Nicholas Crichton served both in the garrison and as a juror on an English inquisition into the forfeiture of lands in Edinburgh sheriffdom from Bruce rebels. The Pontekins, meanwhile, extended the geographical scope

---

[43] CDS, iii, p. 409.

[44] Ramsay's service was of considerable duration, recorded on the payrolls of the Edinburgh garrison for 1336–7 and 1339–40: TNA E 101/22/20, mm. 3, 3v; CDS, iii, pp. 360, 362, and no. 1323. He continued to receive money from the English Exchequer until around 1343, when he appears to have returned to the Bruce allegiance: CDS, iii, nos 1351, 1367, 1368, 1388, 1392, 1409.

[45] Rot. Scot., i, p. 689.

[46] CDS, iii, nos 1292, 1294, 1323, 1409; pp. 360, 362.

[47] Penman, David II, pp. 91–2, 101, 104, 107–8, 110.

[48] TNA E 101/22/20, m. 3; CDS, iii, nos 1184, 1323; p. 362 (Alexander Crichton); CDS, iii, pp. 360, 362 (John Crichton); CDS, iii, pp. 360, 363, no. 1323; CDS, iii, nos 1186, 1323, p. 363; TNA E 101/22/20, m. 3; E 101/23/1, m. 1; cf. CDS, iii, nos 1390, 1406, 1534 (Pontekin).

[49] The town of Crichton lay within the sheriffdom of Edinburgh, and a William Crichton, who apparently did not enter English service, was forfeited two acres of land in the town in 1335–6 for his Bruce allegiance: CDS, iii, 334, 380. Dalmahoy lies within the city of Edinburgh, and Pontekin, although not now apparently in existence, was recorded in 1311–12 as lying within Mussleburgh: CDS, iii, no. 245. Duncan Napier received a grant from the Scottish crown of the lands of William Edinburgh, within the town itself, after the forfeiture and death of William. This grant was probably made in the 1340s, and confirms not only his return to Bruce allegiance but also his territorial interests within Edinburgh: TNA E 101/22/20, m. 3; CDS, iii, pp. 361–2, no. 1323. All three Napiers appear to have left the garrison by the beginning of 1340: TNA E 101/23/1, m. 1.

of their military service outside the walls of Edinburgh Castle, with Adam and Thomas Pontekin both serving in English border forces in 1341 and 1342.[50]

The Lothian and Edinburgh connections of these families suggest that there may have been a local element at work in their choice of allegiance, the proximity of a nearby English garrison possibly being a strong factor in their decision. The examples of previous familial service hints, however, at something perhaps a little deeper and such a propensity to enter English service suggests underlying and enduring opposition to the Bruce regime. The defection of some of these individuals already mentioned in the 1340s, when castles such as Stirling, Roxburgh and Edinburgh fell, may indicate a final realisation by some that the Bruce Scots were winning the war and that a Balliol resurgence looked increasingly unlikely.[51] Still there remained those who sustained their allegiance to Edward Balliol and/ or Edward III. The MacDowells and McCullochs, one or two submissions to the Bruce Scots aside, remained loyal, with both families recorded in Balliol's circle of supporters in the 1350s.[52] The McCullochs, as already indicated, also sought greater service in English forces as a means of financial support. Elsewhere in Scotland a similar picture of continued anti-Bruce activities is suggested. As Michael Brown has demonstrated for Roxburghshire, the Corbet family continued their anti-Bruce stance. They too were a family with a history of support for the English. As a result of their allegiance some of their lands were granted by Robert I to Archibald Douglas during the first conflict.[53] During the second phase of the war, Roger Corbet served in the local garrison of Roxburgh in 1336 and 1337, as did Thomas Corbet, and Roger was joined in Roxburgh in 1340–42 by Richard Corbet.[54] The English recapture of Roxburgh Castle after Neville's Cross was followed by a return of an English administration in the area, and by 1357–8 the Corbets were once more participating actively within that system, with William, Gilbert and Alan Corbet all appearing as jurors on English inquisitions.[55]

---

50 CDS, iii, nos 1186, 1323; p. 363; TNA E 101/22/20, m. 3; E 101/23/1, m. 1; cf. CDS, iii, nos 1390, 1406, 1534.

51 Michael Brown has argued that, in Teviotdale, allegiance was to an extent governed by whoever held Roxburgh Castle at any given time: 'War, Allegiance, and Community', pp. 227–9.

52 See, for example, Beam, *Balliol Dynasty*, p. 342.

53 *Registrum magni sigilli*, ed. Thomson and Paul, i, app. 2, no. 279. In 1309 Thomas Corbet, son and heir of Robert Corbet and his wife Matilda, swore homage and fealty to Edward II: CDS, iii, no. 99. In 1333 Edward III granted Marjory, widow of Roger Corbet, five quarters of wheat because her lands had been burned in the recent Scottish invasion: TNA E 101/19/27, m. 9; E 101/22/40; CDS, iii, nos 1240, 1382).

54 TNA E 101/19/27, m. 9; E 101/22/40; CDS, iii, nos 1240, 1382. A Thomas Corbet served in Edinburgh Castle in 1336–7: CDS, iii, 363; cf. TNA E 101/35/3, for a Thomas Corbet on English campaign service.

55 CDS, iii, nos 1636, 1641, 1670; Brown, 'War, Allegiance, and Community', pp. 221, 228.

One final individual worth considering in such a study of allegiance and support for the Balliol party is Duncan, Earl of Fife. He provides an interesting example of the behaviour and allegiance of one of Scotland's principal magnates. Fife's loyalty to either side during the Second War of Independence was never particularly consistent. Amanda Beam's suggestion that he was 'at best … a closet Balliol partisan' may be complemented by suggesting that at worst he was a self-interested and self-serving waverer who changed allegiance whenever one side appeared close to victory.[56] More probably, his many changes of allegiance were a desperate attempt to ensure the retention of his earldom and protect the rights of his daughter as his sole heir. His vacillating loyalty does, however, provide a useful case study of the way in which the allegiance of a lord had a direct effect on the allegiance of his retainers and perhaps other prominent local figures. As already indicated, there may have been doubts over Fife's loyalty as a result of his capitulation when faced by the invading Disinherited force at Kinghorn. He did, however, take his place among the Bruce Scots at Dupplin Moor, his capture recorded in chronicle accounts as occurring amidst a desperate last stand by his knights.[57] His behaviour after his capture is more damning, for not only did he submit to Edward Balliol but his submission was apparently regarded as meaningful enough to ensure that he was entrusted with the custody of the new king's capital at Perth.[58] He also performed his ancestral duties at Balliol's coronation by crowning the alternative king of Scots, significantly a duty he had failed to perform at David II's own coronation.[59] Fife's attendance at Balliol's coronation is also notable for his appearance there with thirteen knights of his retinue. This was presumably intended to demonstrate to the new regime not only Earl Duncan's submission but that of his extended entourage and by association the knightly elite of Fife itself.[60] The earldom was also well represented at Balliol's coronation by the appearance of several local religious figures, as well as the representatives of local burghs.[61] In light of the catastrophic defeat at Dupplin Moor and Earl Duncan's own experience of two defeats at the hands of the

---

[56] Beam, *Balliol Dynasty*, p. 225.

[57] *Chronica gentis Scotorum*, ed. William F. Skene, 2 vols (Edinburgh, 1871–2), ii, p. 347; *The Orygynale Cronykil of Scotland*, ed. D. Laing, 3 vols (Edinburgh, 1872–9), ii, p. 391; *Scotichronicon*, ed. D.E.R. Watt et al., 9 vols (Aberdeen/Edinburgh, 1987–98), vii, pp. 77–9.

[58] For Fife's potential pro-Balliol affiliation, see R. Tanner, 'Cowing the Community? Coercion and Falsification in Robert Bruce's Parliaments, 1309–1318', in *Parliament and Politics in Scotland, 1235–1560*, ed. K.M. Brown and R.J. Tanner (Edinburgh, 2004), pp. 50–73 (71); Beam, *Balliol Dynasty*, pp. 224–5; Penman, 'The Soules conspiracy', p. 44.

[59] *Chronica*, ed. Skene, ii, p. 347; *Cronykil*, ed. Laing, ii, p. 392; *Scotichronicon*, ed. Watt et al., vii, p. 81; *Lanercost*, ed. Maxwell, p. 272; R. Nicholson, *Edward III and the Scots: The Formative Years of a Military Career, 1327–1335* (Oxford, 1965), pp. 93–4; Beam, *Balliol Dynasty*, pp. 224–5; Penman, *David II*, pp. 48–9.

[60] *Lanercost*, ed. Maxwell, p. 272; Nicholson, *Edward III and the Scots*, p. 93; Beam, *Balliol Dynasty*, p. 313.

[61] Penman, *David II*, p. 48.

Disinherited, defection to Edward Balliol, even without latent support for the Balliol cause, was probably a logical move for him personally. While the Disinherited army remained in the area, submission on a general scale by the population of the earldom was also a sensible precaution to take. There is, however, a lingering suspicion over the loyalty of Earl Duncan, his men and indeed much of his earldom in the ensuing years that suggests that this area retained Balliol sympathies.

A closer look at those who accompanied Earl Duncan to Edward Balliol's coronation suggests that those who submitted at the same time as their lord were indeed the knighthood of Fife and the earl's personal retinue.[62] Three of those named individuals – David Wemyss, Michael Wemyss and Michael Scott – were witnesses to one of the earl's charters around 1330,[63] and at least six of those listed were recorded in the same division as the earl at the battle of Halidon Hill (David Wemyss, Michael Scott, William Fraser, William Cambo, John Laundel and Walter Lundie).[64] The earl of Fife's political affiliation over the years from 1332 to around 1336 appears very complex, with several changes of allegiance in this relatively short period of time. His career is probably worthy of greater investigation in itself. Of interest here, however, are the pieces of evidence that suggest that Fife's men followed a similar path to that of their lord. For example, John of Inchmartin appears to have been in the Disinherited allegiance in June 1334, when John Stirling, the prominent Disinherited leader and later sheriff of Edinburgh, witnessed a grant of his to the Blackfriars of Perth.[65] Even in 1336, the year in which Earl Duncan appears to have made a final decision to support the Bruce party, Michael Wemyss was the recipient of a grant of £40 (and possibly also a separate grant of victuals) from Edward III on 24 March.[66] Greater analysis of the actions of the Fife affinity, if the evidence exists, would be useful for exploring the ways in which the lord's allegiance, as well as his actions in support of one side or the other, was replicated by his followers. The evidence provided here, although brief, is certainly suggestive of the earl's retainers following the example of their lord. Whether this was as a result of lingering Balliol loyalty on their part or of following the political allegiance of the earl is less clear. There is

---

[62] The knights were named as David Graham, Michael Wemyss, David Wemyss, Michael Scott, Alexander Lamberton, John Dunmore, John Bonvile, William Fraser, William Cambo, Roger Morton, John Laundel, Walter Lundie and John of Inchmartin; *Lanercost*, ed. Maxwell, p. 272; Nicholson, *Edward III and the Scots*, p. 93; Beam, *Balliol Dynasty*, p. 313.

[63] NAS RH1/2/103; GD1/349/1.

[64] *The Anonimalle Chronicle, 1307 to 1334, from Brotherton Collection MS. 29*, ed. W.R. Childs and J. Taylor, Yorkshire Archaeological Society Record Series 147 (Leeds, 1991), pp. 165–7; *Brut*, ed. Brie, i, pp. 283–6. A possible seventh individual is Roger Mortimer (Morton?). A Duncan, son of Roger Mortimer, was a hostage for the earl's ransom in 1350 following his capture at Neville's Cross: TNA E 39/14/1; Penman, *David II*, p. 205.

[65] NAS GD79/1/6. For more on Inchmartin, see Penman, *David II*, p. 69n.

[66] *Foedera, Conventiones, Litterae et Cuiscunque Generis Acta Publica*, ed. T. Rymer (London, 1816–69), II, ii, p. 935; *Rot. Scot.*, i, p. 411.

at least an indication that the decision to support Balliol instead of Bruce was one made by more individuals than has been recognised to date. That the decision appears to have been relatively easy for some men to make suggests that support for Balliol remained in existence throughout different parts of Scotland, and for a notably long period of time.

Conclusion

As already indicated, this paper has not provided a comprehensive discussion of the extent of Balliol support in Scotland during the period of the Second War of Independence. Such an investigation requires much more in the way of research, to locate references to those families and their associates to whom may be assigned some level of pro-Balliol allegiance. What this paper has suggested, however, is that the level of support for Balliol, some of it over a quite prolonged period of time, was stronger than has been recognised. The Bruce Scots, in spite of various individuals submitting to the Balliol/English party on several occasions, were relatively secure in having a committed base of support. Submissions to the Balliol party by individuals with pro-Bruce inclinations were mostly the result of short-term considerations or assumptions over the way in which the war was proceeding. Some individuals also remained who were so definite in their support that they did not submit at all, although these were the minority. Still, why should it be assumed that those who began as Balliol supporters, or who demonstrated such an allegiance from an early stage in the conflict, were quicker to submit to the Bruce party when things began to turn against them? Those who supported Edward Balliol may be argued to have done so as a result of much deeper loyalty to his cause, or at least to the change in Scottish land-ownership that a Balliol victory would represent, allowing the return of families who had been disinherited by Robert I.

Those individuals and families who were Disinherited Scots, who followed Balliol north or who returned to Scotland following his early successes in the hope of recovering lost territories, are indeed worthy of study in themselves. How many families were involved? Where had they been in the intervening years? How effective was their return, if there was indeed a return at all? And, considering the apparent primacy of the English Disinherited to the entire enterprise, how important were the Scottish Disinherited to the Balliol cause during the years of conflict which followed? This paper has suggested that some families who returned were of key importance to both Balliol's attempts to govern Scotland and Edward III's attempts to control the southern part of it. And this has been proposed without any reference to the prominent families who were at the forefront of anti-Bruce attacks during the First War of Independence, such as the Comyns, the MacDougalls and the MacDowells, all of whom are represented in the names of those in English pay from the 1330s onwards. This paper has also suggested that there is the possibility for analysing in more detail the careers of those Scots who had not gone into exile, who had instead submitted to the Bruce dynasty but who returned to a Balliol/English allegiance after 1332 and who fought to re-establish the Balliol dynasty once more. The scattered references in chronicles and administrative documents can be drawn together much more easily when potential patterns of service and loyalty are examined in more detail. The case of the earl of Fife is suggestive of the lordly military retinue acting to bind cohesively the men of the earldom to the allegiance of an individual lord. When expanded to its logical conclusion (even if, for a man like Fife, the extent of true loyalty to Balliol is more difficult to ascertain), this is suggestive of at-times large-scale support for the Balliol cause that can only have assisted his attempts to defeat the Bruce party. And if such support was available to Edward Balliol, then it suggests the need for a re-evaluation of the reasons behind his ultimate failure to capture the Scottish crown, and the Bruce party's eventual victory.

6

Rebels, Uchelwyr *and* Parvenus: *Welsh Knights in the Fourteenth Century*

Adam Chapman

The role of the knight in the fourteenth century is well explored, his expectations of military service are well understood, and knighthood's place in chivalric expression as a cultural phenomenon is well known. The place of the Welsh in England's wars in this period is perhaps less comprehensively understood, though a cursory glance at the campaign accounts of the first half of the century in particular reveal it to be substantial and, at times, truly extraordinary. The Shires and the March of Wales, a combat zone in the thirteenth century, became a recruitment ground for foreign wars in the fourteenth. The lands of Wales, in consequence, enjoyed an almost unprecedented century of relative peace; its men, however, knew war better than those of almost any part of England. They were rarely warriors of high status but they appear to have been generally efficient, notably loyal and, in the way of such commonplace people, largely unremarkable. If foreigners thought of the Welsh at all, however, it was as soldiers.

It is advisable to review briefly the status of the Welsh as soldiers from the fall of Gwynedd in 1283. These men, regardless of their lords, fought together and were led by men familiar in their communities, drawn from either the native aristocracy or from the descendants of the Norman invaders of earlier centuries. It is from this class of men that these knights of fourteenth-century Wales emerged. The military retainers of the lords of the March are interesting in their own right, as Rees Davies and more recently – albeit for an earlier period – Brock Holden have shown. Similarly, those Welshmen of similar status who served the king of France with Owain of Wales (d. 1378), the last direct descendant of the pre-Conquest princes of Gwynedd, will not be discussed in detail, though they are interesting in their own right and have received recent attention.[1] It is those

---

[1] For the role of such men in post-Conquest Marcher society, see R.R. Davies, *Lordship and Society in the March of Wales* (Oxford, 1978), pp. 67–86; and, for the establishment of some of these families, B. Holden, *Lords of the Central Marches, English Aristocracy and Frontier Society, 1087–1265* (Oxford, 2008). For some biographical details of Welshmen in French

members of the Welsh elite who achieved the rank of knight and who prospered following Edward I's conquest of Gwynedd that are the subject of this paper.

The Welsh knights of the fourteenth century are all the more interesting because of the cultural boundary they straddle. The concept of knighthood, as a social position or a military rank, appears to have had no place in pre-conquest Welsh society; it is not mentioned in Welsh law and the usual Welsh translation of the term 'Marchog' underlines its alien status, since it refers to a rider, a horseman. This is not to say that a certain parity of status was foreign to Wales. The March had long supported foreign lords who maintained military retainers among their households – English, French and occasionally Welsh. In the Welsh princedoms that survived into the thirteenth century, Gwynedd, Deheubarth and Powys, the *Teuluoedd* of their princes were the equivalent to the *familia* of an English king or Marcher lord. The extensive literature addressing the development of knighthood in England has little if anything to say on the shires and the March of Wales.

The Welshmen who achieved knighthood in the fourteenth century constitute an exceptionally small group. Only Morgan ap Maredudd, Gruffudd Llwyd, Sir Rhys ap Gruffudd I, his son, Sir Rhys Gruffudd, Sir Hywel ap Gruffudd (Syr Hywel y Fywall) and Sir Gregory Sais managed to forge military careers of any significance.[2] Only Morgan was of direct princely descent, though even his success was directly attributable to his connections to and co-operation with English government. The conquest of Wales had left a vacuum at the top of Welsh society. After the failure of the rebellion of Rhys ap Maredudd in 1287, the only princely dynasty to retain some of its former dignity was that of Powys. By the second decade of the century, however, their lands had found their way through marriage into the hands of a Shropshire esquire, John Charlton.[3] Few of the alien landowners established in the new principality were resident,

service after 1370, see M.P. Siddons, 'Welshmen in the Service of France', *Bulletin of the Board of Celtic Studies* 36 (1989) pp. 161–84; and A.D. Carr, *Owen of Wales: The End of the House of Gwynedd* (Cardiff, 1991).

[2]   This list is not quite comprehensive: Sir David Hanmer, well known as the father in law of Owain Glyn Dŵr, made his career as a jurist, while the military careers of Sir Philip ap Rhys, Sir John d'Avene (of Afan, Glamorgan) and Sir Hywel y Pedolau ap Gruffudd (Sir Hywel of the horseshoes) were in the first two cases brief and in the claim to the rank of knight latter so poorly evidenced as to be almost mythical. For Sir Rhys, see J.B. Smith, 'Marcher Regality: *Quo Warranto* Proceedings Relating to Cantrefselyf in the Lordship of Brecon, 1349', *Bulletin of the Board of Celtic Studies* 28 (1979–80), pp. 267–88; and for Sir Hywel y Pedolau, see *The Dictionary of Welsh Biography down to 1940*, ed. J.E. Lloyd and R.T. Jenkins (Cardiff, 1959), pp. 403–4.

[3]   The fate of the family of 'de la Pole' – the descendants of Gruffudd ap Gwenwynwyn – is documented in R. Morgan, 'The Barony of Powys, 1275–1360', *Welsh History Review* 10 (1980–81) and in A.D. Carr, 'An Aristocracy in Decline: The Native Welsh Lords after the Edwardian Conquest', *Welsh History Review* 5 (1970), pp. 107–10.

and the greater administrators were outsiders. One avenue open to the class of Welsh gentry born into the post-conquest environment was military service and leadership. Those among this new gentry class who advanced to the rank of knighthood managed to combine administrative skills with military adventure. Most were descended from men prominent in the service of the Welsh princes and some were claimants to tenuous royal dignity in their own right. The most famous of the post-conquest *Uchelwyr* (lit: high men, singular *uchelwr*) line were the descendants of Ednyfed Fychan, who died in 1246, *Distain* (Steward) of Llywelyn ab Iorwerth. This turbulent tribe, through their fecundity, ubiquity and eventual ascent to the throne of England in the person of Henry Tudor, are relatively well known,[4] and a number of them will be encountered in this paper. The position of the *Wyrion Eden* – the grandsons or descendants of Ednyfed Fychan – was a conscious development of a feudal model by the princes of Gwynedd, one which unfortunately opened a competition of lordship which Edward I was in a better position to win.

The fate of the *Uchelwyr* of princely descent in fourteenth-century Wales was traced by A.D. Carr; his title, 'An Aristocracy in Decline', indicates their general trajectory. Though there is some overlap, this is not the story of the administrative elite, from whose ranks our knights generally emerge. Only one of the knights we will encounter could claim direct descent from the *Barwniaid* of Wales, the pre-conquest tenants-in-chief and descendants of princes. This tenure, known variously as *Tir Pennaeth*, or Latinised as *Pennaethium*, equated directly to the familiar English terms of the knight service of a royal tenant-in-chief. Those who managed to provide heirs to survive them prospered, barons by name yet descendants of Welsh kings and, in their own minds, the equivalent of Marcher lords. From this group emerged Owain Glyndŵr, but beyond the heirs of Gruffudd ap Gwenwynwyn, lord of Powys, all but extinct by 1310, none achieved the rank of knighthood.

Some of the descendants of Ednyfed Fychan retained lands by tenure explicitly derived from this status through Ednyfed's marriage to Gwenllian (d. 1236), a daughter of the Lord Rhys (d. 1197), who had been prince of Deheubarth, the kingdom of west Wales. The most successful of these was born in 1283, being therefore a child of the post-conquest era. Sir Rhys ap Gruffudd (d. 1356) was the great-great-grandson of Ednyfed Fychan (d. 1246). It is probable that Rhys ap Gruffudd was raised in the English court and found his way into the household of Edward of Caernarfon. Although he was *de facto* royal governor of the Cardiganshire and Carmarthenshire for the crown for forty years, Sir Rhys was unambiguously a military man. He served both Edward II and Edward III in Scotland and in France at Crécy and Calais at the head of enormous numbers of Welsh

---

4   For the various Anglesey descendants of Ednyfed Fychan, see G. Roberts, 'Wyrion Eden: The Anglesey Descendants of Ednyfed Fychan in the Fourteenth Century' and 'Teulu Penmynydd', in idem, *Aspects of Welsh History. Selected Papers of the Late Glyn Roberts* (Cardiff, 1969), pp. 179–214 and pp. 240–74 respectively.

troops.[5] His son, also called Rhys, adopted a family surname in the English style – Gruffudd. Sir Rhys Gruffudd fought at Poiters and his son, Thomas Gruffudd, in the wars against Owain Glyndŵr. Though Thomas described himself as a native of Staffordshire and held no offices in Wales his son, John, held a variety of offices in the mid fifteenth century and gained knighthood himself.[6] This was no decline except in relative terms; lands and prosperity were passed on, even if Sir Rhys ap Gruffudd I's personal qualities and dominance were not.

His total dominance of Cardiganshire and Carmarthenshire can be seen in the verse of Dafydd ap Gwilym, the most celebrated of the fourteenth-century Welsh poets. When Dafydd, who lived near Llanbadarn Fawr (Aberystwyth, Cardiganshire), wished his lover's husband drowned or killed abroad, Dafydd's rival served not with the king of England, but with Rhys. Rhys can only have been Rhys ap Gruffudd. The poets, praising these men and their families, did not need to itemise their lineage. Another poet, Iolo Gogh, remembered Rhys – 'pen Cymry' (the leader of the Welsh) – as a warrior whose death was a cause for great lament. Later in his elegy, Iolo remembered Rhys's service with the Black Prince at Crécy. He describes him in the most warlike terms as 'Gwae a'i gweles yng Nghresi' ('the inflictor of many wounds at Crécy'). Iolo also, perhaps surprisingly, composed praise to Edward III, but it was Rhys whom he compared to Arthur. This was praise far removed from the more prosaic or barbaric actions of less privileged Welsh soldiers at the same battle included in the chronicle of Froissart:

> Et lá entre ces Englés avoit pillars et ribaus gallois et cornillois, qui poursieuvoient gens d'armes et arciers, qui portoient grandes coutilles, et venoient entre leurs gens d'armes et leurs arciers qui leur faisoient voie, et trouvoient ces gens d'armes en ce dangier, contes, barons, chevaliers et escuires: si les occioient sans merci, commes grans sires qu'il fust.

> However, among the English there were pillagers and irregulars, Welsh and Cornishmen armed with long knives, who went out after the French (their own men-at-arms and archers making way for them) and, when they found any in difficulty, whether they were counts, barons, knights or squires, they killed them without mercy.[7]

[5] R.A. Griffiths, 'Gentlemen and Rebels in Later Medieval Cardiganshire', *Ceredigion: Journal of the Cardiganshire Antiquarian Society* 5 (1964–7), pp. 143–67 (143–7) (reprinted in his *Conquerors and Conquered in Medieval Wales* (Stroud, 1994), pp. 49–66 (54–5)); and idem, *The Principality of Wales in the Later Middle Ages. The Structure and Personnel of Government. I: South Wales, 1277–1535* (Cardiff, 1972), pp. 99–102.

[6] Sir Rhys Gruffydd is otherwise known, confusingly, as Sir Rhys ap Gruffudd II; see Griffiths, *Principality of Wales*, pp. 262–3; Sir John Gruffydd, Griffiths, *Principality of Wales*, pp. 145–6.

[7] *Oeuvres de Froissart, publiées avec les variantes des divers Manuscrits*, ed. K. de Lettenhove, 25 vols (Brussels, 1867–7), v, pp. 65–6. Translation from John Froissart, *Chronicles*, ed. G. Brereton (London, 1978), p. 93.

Sir Rhys's cousin, Sir Gruffudd Llwyd of Tregarnedd, Anglesey, was perhaps the most significant of the Welsh knights of the fourteenth century.[8] His uncle, Sir Hywel ap Gruffudd, had apparently also been knighted for his service to Edward I after his defection from Llywelyn's cause in 1277 and he died in Edward's service in 1282. The defection of Hywel ap Gruffudd had a great symbolic, as well as practical, significance. The descendants of Ednyfed Fychan had retained the office of *Distain* (steward of the prince's household), which, in the fratricidal politics of the later thirteenth century, appears to have made its holder leader of the *Teulu* or household of the princes of Gwynedd.[9] Gruffudd's own father, at the time of his death around 1284, was entrusted with the keeping of the county of Caernarfon.[10] Some of Gruffudd's earliest known military service was against the rebellion of 1294–5. By lineage and deeds, Gruffudd was the indisputable leader of the Welsh administrative class to emerge in the post-conquest period and was even after his death a figure remembered as a leader of his community.[11]

The relationship between Edward II and his Welsh knights could almost be described as one of dependence. This is especially apparent during Edward's conflicts with his marcher lords under the leadership of the Roger Mortimer of Chirk. On 15 November 1321 Sir Gruffudd Llwyd and Rhys ap Gruffudd were ordered to raise forces from the principality (both north and south Wales) for the king, and to lead attacks on the possessions of Edward's key Marcher opponents. Principally, these attacks were concentrated upon the possessions of the Mortimers and their allies, namely the castles of Clun, La Pole and, most significantly, Chirk.[12] These efforts were complemented by an army led by Edward crossing the Severn on 14 January 1322 and advancing north to Hereford and Shrewsbury, compelling the Mortimers' surrender by 22 January.

While Edward's gratitude was clearly expressed in terms of lands and offices, something of the importance of this relationship can be discerned following the death of Gruffudd Fychan ap Syr Gruffudd in Scotland later in 1322. The expenses for his burial in Newcastle upon Tyne were paid from the king's own purse, one of several favours bestowed on the Welshmen led by Sir Gruffudd in the course of a disastrous Scottish campaign.[13] Edward's survival in the face

---

[8] J G. Edwards, 'Sir Gruffydd Llwyd', *EHR* 30 (1915), pp. 589–601.

[9] D. Stephenson, *The Governance of Gwynedd* (Cardiff, 1984), pp. 11–20. For more complete assessments from the earliest times, see S. Davies, 'The *Teulu c.*633–1283', *Welsh History Review* 21 (2003), pp. 413–54; A.D. Carr, 'Teulu and Penteulu', in *The Welsh King and his Court*, ed. T.M. Charles Edwards, M.E. Owen and P. Russell (Cardiff, 2000), pp. 63–81.

[10] *Calendar of Ancient Petitions Relating to Wales*, ed. W. Rees (Cardiff, 1975), pp. 265–6.

[11] *Calendar of Ancient Correspondence Concerning Wales*, ed. J.G. Edwards (Cardiff, 1935), pp. 247–8.

[12] J.B. Smith, 'Edward II and the Allegiance of Wales', *Welsh History Review* 8 (1976–7), pp. 139–71 (159). Clun, though an Arundel lordship, had been taken into the hands of Mortimer of Wigmore in the previous year: Smith, 'Edward II and the Allegiance of Wales', n. 107.

[13] N. Fryde, 'Welsh Troops in the Scottish Campaign of 1322', *Bulletin of the Board of Celtic Studies* 26 (1974), pp. 82–9.

of the rebellion instigated by Thomas of Lancaster was, in large part, a result of the military defeat of the marcher lords by Edward's Welsh subjects led by Sir Gruffudd Llwyd and Sir Rhys ap Gruffudd. It is no coincidence that Sir Gruffudd Llwyd twice suffered imprisonment at the hands of Roger Mortimer, since his influence on North Wales was a significant threat to Mortimer's own power.[14] The retreat of Edward II into Glamorgan in 1326 is generally associated with his relationship with the younger Despenser, but once again it shows Edward II's dependence upon his resources in Wales. In the final days of Edward's liberty Rhys ap Gruffudd was commissioned to treat with Isabella and incurred staggering expenses of £259 2s 8d for eight days' wages for men-at-arms and infantry which he led towards Brecon prior to Edward's capture. [15] More remarkable is the attempt, apparently instigated by Rhys but allegedly suggested by English magnates and supported by Sir Gruffudd Llwyd, to spring Edward from his captivity in Berkeley Castle in August of 1327. It is not known how advanced the plan was before it was reported to Mortimer by William Shaldeford, Mortimer's lieutenant Justiciar in North Wales, in a letter of 7 September. Certainly, in Wales it was believed that Shaldeford's letter was the prompt needed to bring about Edward II's death. The belief that Shaldeford was thus responsible for the king's death caused Sir Gruffudd Llwyd, with Hywel ap Gruffudd, a cleric and another Anglesey descendant of Ednyfed Fychan, to bring an unsuccessful action against Shaldeford, *coram rege*, after the fall of Mortimer in 1331. Final retribution for the Welshmen loyal to Edward II's memory came only after Sir Gruffudd Llwyd's death. Henry Shaldeford, undoubtedly a relative, possibly the son, of William, was murdered while acting as lieutenant to an absent Justiciar on St Valentine's Day 1345 at the hands of Hywel and the leaders of the North Wales elite.[16] The failure of Rhys's conspiracy attempt forced him to flee, briefly, to Scotland and to contemplate further rebellion in 1330, only receiving full pardon after the fall of Mortimer. His recovery after these setbacks was swift. By 1335 he had acquired his knighthood, the office of deputy justiciar of West Wales, which he retained until 1340, and a marriage to an English heiress.[17]

The financial records of the English crown clearly demonstrate the scale of command that Rhys ap Gruffudd and Gruffudd Llwyd were entrusted with. While both were men of the court, they are routinely found leading the levies

[14] J.B. Smith, 'Gruffudd Llwyd and the Celtic Alliance, 1315–18', *Bulletin of the Board of Celtic Studies* 26 (1974–6), pp. 463–78 (466–7); and, for a contemporary Welsh perspective, M.T. Davies, 'The Rhetoric of Gwilym Ddu's *Awdlau* to Sir Gruffudd Llwyd', *Studia Celtica* 40 (2006), pp. 155–72.

[15] The sum was eventually honoured by Edward III: see *Welsh Entries in the Memoranda Rolls, 1282–1343*, ed. N. Fryde (Cardiff, 1974), no. 593, p. 70.

[16] T.F. Tout, 'The Captivity and Death of Edward of Carnarvon', *Bulletin of the John Rylands Library* 6 (1921–2), particularly app. i, pp. 108–13. For Shaldeford's death, see Roberts, 'Wyrion Eden', pp. 193–7.

[17] Griffiths, *Principality of Wales*, pp. 101–2.

of Wales, both from the shires and the March, into battle as a single, Welsh-speaking and Welsh-led, unit. Numbering many thousands, these armies were greater than any led by the Welsh princes.[18] The power of their leadership was, whether by accident or design, a significant counterbalance to the power of the English barons of the March, marshalling the military resources of the crown, namely the population of its shires in Wales, against the military and political ambitions of the barons of the March.

Sir Morgan ap Maredudd of Tredegar in the marcher lordship of Gwynllŵg (Newport, Monmouthshire) was a man with a largely unrecognised gift for detecting the changes in the direction of the political winds in the southern March of Wales. A descendent of the last native lords of Caerleon, he first comes to our attention as a deponent in Edward I's inquiry into the laws of Wales, having apparently been dispossessed during Edward's absence on crusade. His legal challenge against Gilbert de Clare, earl of Gloucester and lord of Glamorgan, proved unsuccessful and he seems to have found shelter both with Llywelyn ap Gruffudd in Gwynedd and in Edward I's court. By 1283 he was clearly with Dafydd ap Gruffudd, brother of Llywelyn, witnessing charters granted by Dafydd to his followers in west Wales. For the next decade he existed in anonymity until the Welsh rebellions of 1294, when he can be found leading the revolt against his old adversary, Gilbert de Clare, lord of Glamorgan. The revolt in Glamorgan was expressed – very deliberately – not against the king, but against its lord, the earl of Gloucester.[19] Morgan very sensibly (and to the earl's immense displeasure) came to peace with the king and, as Rees Davies put it, received 'favour as well as his pardon' from Edward I. Later in 1295 he survived being implicated in the treason of one of Glamorgan's minor lords, Thomas Turberville, who was captured in France in English service, and was sufficiently trusted during the crisis of 1297 to be appointed to a commission enquiring into the liberties of the men of the lordship of Brecon.[20] Far from acting only as a mere *agent provocateur*, his knighthood came at the feast of Swans (1306).[21] His military career was comparatively low key but comparable with many household knights of the period. He continued as a royal agent, however, receiving robes from Edward II,

---

[18] M. Prestwich, *War, Politics and Finance* (London, 1972), pp. 90–108; A.J. Chapman, 'Welshmen in the Armies of Edward I', in *The Impact of the Edwardian Castles in Wales*, ed. D. Williams and J. Kenyon (Oxford, 2009), pp. 175–82.

[19] See *Calendar of Ancient Petitions*, ed. Rees, p. 218. This petition is dated a couple of years after the end of the rebellion – before 3 July 1297 – and calls it 'the war against the earl'.

[20] R.R. Davies, *The Age of Conquest, Wales 1063–1415* (Oxford, 1991), p. 284; J.G. Edwards, 'The Treason of Thomas Turberville, 1295', in *Studies in Medieval History Presented to F.M. Powicke*, ed. R.N. Hunt, W.A. Pantin and R.W. Southern (Oxford, 1948), pp. 296–309; *CPR 1292–1301*, p. 293.

[21] C. Moor (ed.), *Knights of Edward I*, 5 vols, Harleian Society (1929–32), i, p. 13.

proclaiming his royal connections within his locality.[22] In December 1315, in the period of political instability which followed the military disaster at Bannock-burn, Morgan, with Sir Gruffudd Llwyd and Anian, bishop of Bangor, journeyed to the king at Clipstone, Nottinghamshire, 'pro negociis statum terre Wallie tangentibus'.[23] The influence of these negotiations can be seen in ordinances concerning the principality of north and south Wales issued at the parliament held at Lincoln on 7 February 1316. The preamble, which makes reference to the king's birth in Wales, also, significantly, refers to the loyalty of the Welsh.[24] A more unusual example of the loyalty of the Welshmen of the principality to their one-time prince is shown in Gruffudd Llwyd's response when summoned to represent Merioneth at the parliament of 1327.[25] Sir Gruffudd, then serving as sheriff of Merioneth, replied that he would attend 'if convenient': a polite refusal. As J.G. Edwards noted, Gruffudd 'was still, therefore, a consistent partisan: he could no longer help his fallen master, but at any rate he could and did refuse to be present in the parliament which was to witness the final triumph of the opposing faction'.[26]

Like Gruffudd Llwyd, on his death in 1331 Morgan left no male heir.[27] There was no great estate to hand down in any case, but among the children born to his daughter Angharad was Ifor Hael (the generous) of Gwernyclepa near Bassaleg. Ifor was a man whose ancestors included members of the one of the oldest princely lineages, that of Deheubarth (or south-west Wales) and he himself was also the chief patron of Dafydd ap Gwilym, the greatest of the Welsh bards of the later Middle Ages. Angharad's father, Ifor's grandfather, was remembered in Dafydd's verse and such a marriage could only enhance an already impeccable pedigree.[28] This was a family which looked to the present and future as well as the past. Ifor's nephew, Philip ap Morgan, spent the early part of his career in the service of Roger Mortimer, earl of March (d. 1398), serving on his council and as steward of the lordship of Usk. It has been suggested that Philip was the patron of Iolo Gogh who commissioned the elegy to the young earl shortly before his death in Ireland. Philip was made chancellor of the duchy of Normandy by Henry V at Bayeux in August 1418, which was just another step on the ladder for him. He subsequently held the bishoprics of, first, Worcester, from 1419, and,

---

[22] For example, robes were granted to Rhys ap Gruffudd and Gruffudd Llwyd as valets of the king's chamber at Westminster and Langley respectively in 1310: BL Cotton MS Nero C.VIII, fol. 83v.

[23] TNA E 101/376/7, fol. 12, cited in Smith, 'Edward II and the Allegiance of Wales', pp. 149–50.

[24] Smith, 'Edward II and the Allegiance of Wales', pp. 150–51.

[25] This was the second of only two parliamentary summons addressed to Wales before the reign of Henry VIII. The first was in 1322.

[26] Edwards, 'Sir Gruffydd Llwyd', pp. 595–6.

[27] Calendar of Inquisitions Post Mortem, vii, no. 329, p. 247.

[28] I Fam Ifor Hael (To the mother of Ifor Hael), edited text 167: www.dafyddapgwilym.net.

later, Ely, after 1426.[29] The careers of Sir Morgan ap Maredudd, his son in law, Ifor Hael and that of Philip ap Morgan serve as a microcosm of how the English and Welsh communities had established long-lasting and effective relationships without either party surrendering its cultural and other identities.[30]

In general, however, the achievements of this first generation of Welshmen after the conquest of Gwynedd were not to be matched by those that followed. Sir Gruffudd Llwyd and Sir Rhys ap Gruffudd had been dominant figures in the shires of the principality and in England's wars. The succeeding generation were no more than local figures, prominent in their estates and holders of significant offices. Sir Hywel y Fwyall (Sir Hywel of the Axe, d. 1381) and Sir Rhys ap Gruffudd II were important men but they did not exercise power on a national stage. Their contemporary, Sir Gregory Sais, was a career soldier who gained much in France and who subsequently lost almost all of it in the years after 1369, but the failure was not his own. Praise to Owain Glyndŵr lamented this paucity and suggested that knighting Owain would offset the balance. Carr suggests that this omission might have been an act of deliberate policy; more probably the majority of the Welsh gentry were too poor, enfeebled by being subject to Welsh laws of partible inheritance and without the motivation or resources to participate in war at a level which matched their dignity. Added to this was the shift in the political focus away from Wales; Welshmen were no longer fixtures in the English court of Edward III. Edward II, though he retained Welshmen in his household, did not rear the succeeding generation of the elite of Wales as his father had done. Welshmen all but disappear from the immediate circle of the crown until the reign of Richard II; Edward III was never Prince of Wales and even his son, the Black Prince, maintained very few Welshmen among his household on a regular basis.

Syr Hywel y Fwyall, otherwise known as Sir Hywel ap Gruffudd of Eifionydd in the county of Merioneth, was one of these few men in the Black Prince's household. Like Sir Rhys ap Gruffudd II, he was a veteran of Poitiers and, like Sir Rhys ap Gruffudd I, he was a recipient of praise from Iolo Gogh. Iolo describes him in his later years, in retirement from the French wars, as constable of the castle of Criccieth, Merioneth. This post, which also made him *de facto* mayor of the associated borough of Criccieth, was clearly occupied in person

---

[29] *Forty-First Annual Report of the Deputy Keeper of the Public Records*, pp. 710, 801; Davies, *Lordship and Society*, pp. 205–6, 417, and R.R. Davies, *The Revolt of Owain Glyn Dŵr* (Oxford, 1995), pp. 43–4. For the link to Iolo Gogh, see D.F. Evans, '"Talm o Wentoedd": The Welsh Language and Literature, *c*.1070–*c*.1530', in *Gwent County History. II: The Age of the Marcher Lords*, ed. R.A. Griffiths, A. Hopkins and R. Howell (Cardiff, 2009), pp. 280–308 (288). Philip ap Morgan served on the council of Earl Roger Mortimer at about the time of the latter's expedition to Ireland in 1398; TNA SC 6/1184/23 (account roll of the Mortimer lordship of Denbigh), cited in G.A. Holmes, *The Estates of the Higher Nobility in Fourteenth Century England* (Cambridge, 1957), p. 76n.

[30] R.R. Davies, 'Plague and Revolt', in *Gwent County History. II: The Age of the Marcher Lords*, ed. R.A. Griffiths, A. Hopkins and R. Howell (Cardiff, 2009), pp. 217–40 (220).

by 'this greying gentleman'. That the castle of Criccieth was one of those begun by Llywelyn Fawr (Llywelyn ab Iorwerth), prince of Gwynedd, but redeveloped for Edward I had a significance all of its own. In it Sir Hywel held his court, dispensed his generosity and flew his standard from its towers. His son, Gruffudd, however, left no heir and again, the line ended. Sir Hywel's legacy – or, at least, that of his famous battleaxe – falls into the realm of myth. Sir John Wynn, writing in the late sixteenth or early seventeenth century, recorded a story that the Black Prince gave the weapon a place of honour in the royal hall, ordering food to be served before it daily, which was later distributed as alms, a ceremony which ended only during the reign of Elizabeth I.[31]

Sir Gregory Sais, despite a name which translates as Sir Gregory the Englishman, was also a descendant of the brood of Ednyfed Fychan. Froissart mentioned him on several occasions and he was noted as 'a foreigner' in Knighton's chronicle. His career is closely analogous to those of many of his English contemporaries, men like Sir Hugh Calveley or Sir Matthew Gournay; Sir Gregory achieved knighthood in recognition of his talents, and that it is easier to equate him to English exemplars rather than Welsh goes some way to justifying his cognomen. He was a member of the free companies in the 1360s, a prominent captain in France, Spain and Scotland into the 1380s, and had a Poitevin wife, Radegonde Bechet. Given his share of the manor of Mostyn in Flintshire and property in London, he could pass for a fully paid-up member of the English military aristocracy. When the war turned sour for the English in the early 1370s he was well on his way to establishing himself in some style in Poitevin society, and his marriage was one of the most successful cross-Channel matches of the period. Unlike Marguerite Baucay, wife of Sir Simon Burley, or Hugh Calverley's Catalan wife, Radegonde Bechet, dame de Mortemer, followed Sir Gregory back to England following the loss of Poitou, and she continued to receive royal patronage even after Sir Gregory's death in 1390. As late as 1399 Henry IV confirmed grants made to the couple by Richard II, including 200 marks *per annum* for life, issues of the king's custom at Bordeaux and the manor of Frodsham in the Wirral.[32]

Although much of Sir Gregory's military career was spent in France or Spain, he also served in Wales, securing Pembrokeshire against possible invasion in 1377, and in Scotland, as captain of Berwick in 1384 and on Richard II's expedition in 1385. He clearly moved frequently and easily across the Channel. Towards the end of his life he returned to his native Flintshire, but he was not, it seems, embedded in the affairs of that county on a regular basis. The surviving musters

---

[31] J. Wynn, *The History of the Gwydir Family*, ed. J. Ballinger (Cardiff, 1927), p. 56.

[32] *CPR 1399–1401*, p. 22; Frodsham was kept in the king's hand until 1406; see A.D. Carr, 'A Welsh Knight in the Hundred Years War: Sir Gregory Sais', *Transactions of the Honourable Society of Cymmrodorion* (1977), pp. 40–53 (51); M.C.E. Jones, 'Brittany and Wales in the Middle Ages: Contacts and Comparisons', *Transactions of the Honourable Society of Cymmrodorion* (2004), pp. 19–49 (43–4).

for retinues under his leadership suggest a man heavily connected with the gentry of the earldom of Chester, though his reputation was extensive in north-east Wales; he counted Owain Glyndŵr among his esquires at Berwick in 1384. This may go some way to explaining his absence from the poetry of the period. In the surviving sources his only mention was in Gruffudd Llywd's praise for Owain Glyndŵr, which was probably composed in the second half of the 1380s, following Owain's return from Scotland.[33]

An interesting comparison might be made with the fortunes of Edward I's curial knights and their families. Many made their careers in the wars in Wales. Otto de Grandison led the army which was ambushed crossing the Menai Straits from Anglesey in 1282, an ambush which claimed the life of Sir Hywel ap Gruffudd, uncle of Sir Gruffudd Llwyd. Several others, including John de Bevillard and William de Monte Casino, died in the course of siege operations at Dryslwyn in 1287.[34] They were, admittedly, generally of a higher status, though since the majority never rose above the rank of knighthood, and faced similar difficulties as outsiders in England, the comparison is a valid one.[35] Where the foreigners differed, however, was in their freedom of opportunity, and in the absence of ties to a pre-existing community within the realm of England. Most of the Welsh knights married within their own communities or into those of the lords of the March. Rhys ap Gruffudd I was the exception, and his marriage to a Staffordshire heiress – with lands held independently by secure tenure in England – was the foundations of his son's later prosperity and the family's establishment among the English gentry. In each case it was talent, mixed with a degree of political expediency, that secured the advancement of Welshmen, and continental courtiers, to the rank of knighthood.

Similarly instructive comparisons from later in the century can be made with the Welshmen who took the side of the French having earlier served with the English or in the Free Companies. Though frequently described as 'men-at-arms' in the surviving French records, even the most prominent among them failed to receive the rewards of knighthood. Owain of Wales (*Yvain de Gales* to the French), the last male descendant of the house of Gwynedd, claimed the title 'Prince of Wales', and, as a prominent and successful captain under Charles V, was

33 *Gwaith Gruffudd Llwyd a'r Llygliwiaid*, ed. R. Ifans (Aberystwyth, 2000), pp. 149–50. Note that the bard Gruffudd Llwyd (*fl. c.*1380–1410) and the knight (d. 1335) are neither related nor the same individual. Sais is often referred to as 'Sir Degory' and other, more unlikely, variations. Since this poem, the only contemporary Welsh reference to him calls him 'Syr Grigor'; Sir Gregory is the preferred spelling. See also Carr, 'A Welsh Knight in the Hundred Years War', p. 40.

34 *Calendar of Ancient Petitions*, ed. Rees, pp. 265–6; A.J. Taylor, 'Who was "John Pennardd, leader of the men of Gwynedd"?', *EHR* 91 (1976); and J. E. Morris, *The Welsh Wars of Edward I* (Oxford, 1901), pp. 204–13.

35 M.G.I. Ray, 'Alien Knights in a Hostile Land: The Experience of Curial Knights in Thirteenth Century England and the Assimilation of their Families', *Historical Research* 79 (2006) pp. 451–76.

even supported in these claims. Despite these claims, however, which were taken seriously enough in England to warrant Owain's assassination in 1378, Owain never rose above the rank of esquire. Neither did his contemporary, and lieutenant, Ieuan Wyn, the *Poursuivant d'amour*, who was in English service before 1369. He seems to have been an important figure even then, possibly fighting on the English side in the celebrated 'fight of the Thirty' at Ploërmel in 1351 and, at the time of his defection, was captain of the castle of Beaufort in Champagne. He remained in French service until at least 1384. Possibly their foreign origins counted against them: on a list of the forty leading captains in the service of Charles V, Owain and Ieuan are the only non-Frenchmen.[36]

In short, these men were exceptional figures who rose above the ranks of the native squirearchy of fourteenth-century Wales to occupy positions of power and privilege confirmed and enhanced by military leadership and their royal connections. The armies taken from the Shires and the March of Wales would have been very much more difficult to recruit and to have led without the power and influence of Gruffudd Llwyd and Rhys ap Gruffudd. These men made very deliberate efforts to take upon themselves the mantle of the princes Edward I had ousted. Their importance is revealed in the cultural reaction among their own community, and in the case of Sir Gregory Sais, in the pages of Froissart. Though most managed to secure gentility for their families, only one, Sir Rhys ap Gruffudd I, had descendants whose achievements could compare with his own.

As knights of the English crown, however, their careers are representative; they appear on all of the major campaigns, at the major engagements and in the household of the crown and of princes of Wales. Their service was not confined by their ethnicity and nor were their rewards reduced by it. Where they produced descendants they were generally able to insulate themselves from the worst effects of Welsh laws of partible inheritance, but since we are considering only a handful of men the impact was unlikely to have ever been substantial. It is unlikely that this was an act of policy, but rather that a combination of factors – the changes in the organisation of war, the reduction in scale and increased standard of equipment required of infantry soldiers and the relative poverty of the Welsh squirearchy – limited opportunities. The one man who managed to secure his legacy through a direct heir, Sir Rhys ap Gruffudd I, demonstrates a record which bears comparison with that of any of the more famous English knightly dynasties of the fourteenth and fifteenth centuries. It is, perhaps, a shade of what might have been.

---

[36] M.P. Siddons, 'Welshmen in the Service of France', *Bulletin of the Board of Celtic Studies* 36 (1989), pp. 161–3, citing P. Contamine, *Guerre, État et Société à la fin du Moyen Age. Études sur les armées des rois de France, 1337–1494* (Paris, 1972), p. 152. For more on the service of Welshmen in Brittany, see Jones, 'Brittany and Wales in the Middle Ages', pp. 41–4.

7

Breton Soldiers from the Battle of the Thirty (26 March 1351) to Nicopolis (25 September 1396)

Michael Jones

In Thomas Hardy's *Tess of the d'Urbervilles*, towards the end of her tragic life the eponymous heroine enters for the first time the church in which her distant forbears were buried. They included 'Sir Pagan d'Urberville, that renowned knight who came from Normandy with William the Conqueror, as appears by the Battle Abbey Roll'. Contemplating the mournful sight of tombs 'canopied, altar-shaped, and plain; their carvings being defaced and broken; their brasses torn from the matrices, the rivet holes remaining like martin-holes in a sand-cliff', she was forcibly reminded 'that her people were socially extinct'.[1] In Roman Polanski's film *Tess* (1979), with the delectable Nastassja Kinski in the starring role, this scene is played out against a backdrop of the authentic fourteenth-century tombs of the famous Breton knightly dynasty of Beaumanoir in the abbey of St-Magloire de Léhon, just outside Dinan. Among them is that of the family's most celebrated warrior, Jean (IV) de Beaumanoir, captain of Josselin.[2] On 26 March 1351 he led thirty fellow countrymen to victory against a similar number of English, Breton and German knights and esquires in the Battle of the Thirty, a bloody chivalric episode which cost the lives of a quarter or more of the sixty-two who took part. Feeling thirsty during a brief pause in the fighting, Beaumanoir was famously advised by a companion, 'Boy ton sang, Beaumanoir; ta soiff te passera', 'Drink your blood, Beaumanoir, your thirst will pass', according to a near-contemporary poetic account that ensured this minor skirmish passed

[1] Quotations from Thomas Hardy, *Tess of the d'Urbervilles. A Pure Woman*, Macmillan's Pocket Hardy, The Wessex Novels, vol. 1 (London, 1922), pp. 4 and 469.

[2] H. Torchet, *Réformation des fouages de 1426. Diocèse ou évêché de Saint-Malo* (Paris, 2005), pp. 82–3, provides a useful recent summary genealogy of the family. I have followed this in numbering the captain of the Thirty, Jean IV de Beaumanoir, rather than the more usual Jean III.

quickly into enduring legend.[3] This was notably embroidered by nineteenth-century romantic historians following the erection in 1819 of a still-surviving pillar to the memory of those who fought that day. However, enough reliable evidence survives to identify all the Breton soldiers who took part with some certainty.[4] In most instances their later military careers can also be followed and their family and social context described. I propose to use this information to illustrate *in petto* more general features of the experience of Breton troops who are to be found in almost every theatre of war in Western Europe in the latter half of the fourteenth century.[5]

The circumstances of the encounter at Mi-Voie, halfway between Josselin and Ploërmel in the modern département of Morbihan, are well-known.[6] Since 1341 Brittany had been divided by civil war over the succession to the late duke, John III, who had left no direct heir, with Philip VI of France supporting his nephew, Charles de Blois, who was married to the late duke's niece, Jeanne de Penthièvre, and Edward III of England supporting John de Montfort, the late duke's half-brother. Within a couple of years these opposing forces had largely taken up positions that then remained fairly constant for the rest of the twenty-year struggle until John de Montfort, the son of one pretender, and his English allies were able to kill Charles de Blois, defeat his army and achieve final success in the struggle for the ducal throne at Auray on 29 September 1364.[7] Thus for almost two decades Anglo-Breton forces held most of the Breton coastline west

[3]   I have used the edition by H.R. Brush, 'La Bataille de Trente Anglois et de Trente Bretons', *Modern Philology* 9 (1911–12), pp. 511–44, and 10 (1912–13), pp. 82–136, where the two main manuscript versions are printed side by side (BnF MS Nouvelle acquisition française 4165, 8 folios, usually called the Didot MS after a nineteenth-century owner, Firmin Didot, and BnF MS français 1555 fols 50v–58v, normally called the Bigot MS after the seventeenth-century scholar and owner, Bigot); Brush, 'La Bataille', p. 108, line 421, and p. 109, line 443, for this famous retort. Y. Gicquel, *Le combat des Trente. Épopée au cœur de de la mémoire bretonne* (Spézet, 2004), is a wide-ranging and well-illustrated recent account; Jean-Christophe Cassard, '«Bois ton sang, Beaumanoir, la soif te passera !» Le devenir du sang des Trente', in *Le sang au Moyen Âge* (Montpellier, 1999), pp. 293–320, reprinted in his collection *La Guerre de Succession de Bretagne* (Spézet, 2006), pp. 160–82, is another interesting contribution.

[4]   Gicquel, *Le combat des Trente*, pp. 74–5, identifies the Breton party, though my investigations suggest some minor modifications in detail. The four Bretons who fought with the English (Raoulet d'Apremont, Ardaine de Saint-Georges, Perrot de Comenan and Guillon Le Gaillard) have not been treated in detail here, but see Gicquel, *Le combat des Trente*, p. 85 and Appendix II.

[5]   F. Morvan, 'Les hommes d'armes du duché de Bretagne de 1213 à 1381', thèse de doctorat, 5 vols, Université de Lille III, 2007, is the most recent detailed study, but the published version, *La Chevalerie bretonne et la formation de l'armée ducale 1260–1341* (Rennes, 2009), omits the period after 1341.

[6]   A. de La Borderie, *Histoire de Bretagne* (continué par B. Pocquet), 6 vols (Rennes and Paris, 1896–1914), iii, pp. 510–29, for the classic account.

[7]   M. Jones, *Ducal Brittany 1364–1399* (Oxford, 1970), pp. 1–21; idem, 'The Breton Civil War', in *Froissart: Historian*, ed. J.J.N. Palmer (Woodbridge, 1981), pp. 64–81 and 169–72, reprinted in M. Jones, *The Creation of Brittany* (London, 1988), pp. 197–218.

from Morlaix in northern Brittany round to the mouth of the Loire, together with several inland towns and fortresses, with Vannes their main centre of administration. As for Charles de Blois and his French allies (especially after Charles's capture at the battle of La Roche Derrien in 1347 and subsequent imprisonment in England until 1356), they held most of north-eastern Brittany, including Rennes and the patrimony of Jeanne de Penthièvre in the dioceses of St-Brieuc and Tréguier, as well as normally holding Nantes, a key to the Loire valley. But along the spine of the duchy, in the wooded and broken landscape of central Brittany, the division was not so clear-cut, nor so easily maintained. Much of this upland area provided ideal country for guerilla warfare; skirmishes, ambushes and petty sieges were the order of the day. Here individual soldiers, often acknowledging only a loose allegiance to their respective lords, seized the opportunity to occupy castles, establish small garrisons and tyrannize the local populace from enclaves deep within enemy territory. In the absence of regular pay, they largely supported themselves by exacting levies, ransoms, *patis*, in money and kind from a largely defenceless peasantry. Those living between the main Anglo-Breton or Franco-Breton zones of military control might be obliged to pay both sides in order to preserve a fragile immunity, an experience repeated in many other parts of France as the Anglo-French war progressed.[8]

After a decade of civil war and the coincident social and economic disloca-tion of the Black Death, the fate of non-combatants had, however, begun to arouse sympathy even among hard-bitten military men. In a now well-studied memorandum submitted to the royal council in 1353 Sir Walter Bentley, Edward III's lieutenant in Brittany, analysed the root causes of the mistreatment of the native population and proposed more effective means of controlling the free-booting captains and soldiers nominally under his authority, recognizing the damage they were inflicting on the Anglo-Breton cause.[9] The saintly Charles de Blois's personal empathy for his oppressed subjects was well-known among his counsellors; it even occasionally caused friction with military advisers over what strategy to pursue.[10] Although he proved a hardliner on other occasions, in 1351 Jean de Beaumanoir seemed partly touched by similar sentiments since one intention in challenging Robert de Bamborough, captain of Ploërmel, to meet him with thirty companions in a battle à outrance was to relieve the suffer-ings of those caught between their two garrisons. More time could obviously be

[8]   Jonathan Sumption, *The Hundred Years War*, 3 vols to date (London, 1990–), provides the fullest modern account of this, as of all other aspects of the war.

[9]   Published in *Œuvres de Froissart*, ed. J.M.B.C. Kervyn de Lettenhove, 28 vols (Brussels, 1867–77), xviii, pp. 393–43; for commentary see K.A. Fowler, 'Les finances et la discipline dans les armées anglaises en France au XIVe siècle', *Les Cahiers Vernonnais* 4 (1964), pp. 55–84 (77–8).

[10]   Cassard, *La Guerre de Succession*, pp. 107–17 and his *Charles de Blois (1319–1364), duc de Bretagne et bienheureux* (Brest, 1994), esp. pp. 35–46.

spent discussing his motivation and the course of the battle that ensued, but my central purpose here is to survey the Breton participants.

We do not know how long Beaumanoir had contemplated his challenge nor whether he had reinforced his company by summoning knights and esquires with established military reputations to join him at Josselin. It is usually assumed that most who fought alongside him were indeed members of the garrison in March 1351, and I have not found evidence to the contrary. Moreover, the author of the poem on the Battle of the Thirty specifically noted that no appeal was made to the greatest Breton noble families, something which centuries later apparently still rankled with the Rohans, who included shields displaying their arms in a depiction of the battle decorating one of their castles (albeit one in nineteenth-century Czechoslovakia).[11] What, then, can be said of the social make-up of the eleven knights and twenty esquires comprising Beaumanoir's company?

First, it can be stressed that most came from long-established families of *ancienne chevalerie*, even *ancienne noblesse*.[12] That is, the majority belonged to families which were already of knightly status around a hundred years earlier. Some were scions of noble families which had emerged before 1200 (Raguenel, Montauban) or very shortly thereafter (Gouyon, Rochefort), or are reputed to be cadet branches of such families (Keranrais, Lanloup and Du Parc, for instance, were respectively *ramages* of the more aristocratic families of Avaugour, Coëtmen and Du Faou).[13] The ancestry of Alain and Jean de Tinténiac, for example, can be securely traced back to the mid eleventh century. Given the lack of convincing documentary evidence for the ancestry of a large proportion of the Breton noblesse prior to the Civil War of 1341–65 it is notable that such a high percentage of Beaumanoir's company in 1351 can be shown to descend in this fashion. Whether typical or not of other garrisons fighting for Charles de Blois (we simply do not have the detailed information for other fortresses at this point), Beaumanoir's was certainly not made up of adventurers, unlike Bamborough's team. For only six of those who fought on the Breton side at Mi-Voie has it so far proved impossible to find convincing ancestry; and the likelihood is that their background was very similar to that of their companions. Yet even if they were *arrivistes* making their fortunes by military service, five out of the six certainly left descendants who retained noble status to 1500 or beyond, as did more than 50 per cent of those with more proven ancestry in 1351.

The evidence does not survive to allow sensible remarks about the economic wealth of the Thirty. Disparities there certainly were between leading figures such as Beaumanoir, Montauban, Raguenel, Rochefort and Tinténiac, and the more obscure esquires, some of whom elude us almost completely. But virtually

---

[11] Gicquel, *Le combat des Trente*, pp. 181–2.

[12] Some details on individual careers are summarised in Appendix I.

[13] Pol Potier de Courcy, *Nobiliaire et armorial de Bretagne*, 6th edn, 2 vols (reprinted Mayenne, 1986), is a valuable tool for identifying Breton noble families, although it must be used with caution, especially for the earliest phases of any family's history.

all the families of Bretons who fought at Mi-Voie both inherited and transmitted landed estates and enjoyed at the very least the privileges and status of lesser gentry.

Sufficient is also known to determine their broad geographical distribution within the duchy.[14] Given the disposition of the opposing sides by this stage of the civil war, perhaps not surprisingly, this shows a predominance of men from northern Brittany. Only one of Beaumanoir's men appears to have had distant non-Breton ancestry: the family of Hugues Catus came originally from Poitou, though Hugo himself inhabited Évran in the diocese of St-Malo where Beaumanoir was himself born.[15] Ten others also came from this diocese, most of them relatively close neighbours of Beaumanoir. Ties of kinship and friendship can be suspected in bringing them into his service. The diocese of St-Malo shortly afterwards became one of the main recruiting grounds for the greatest Breton soldier of the period, Bertrand du Guesclin. He was born at Broons, about fifteen kilometres distant from Évran as the crow flies; Robin Raguenel, father of Bertrand's first wife, Tiphaine, was one of the Thirty, his second, Jeanne de Tinténiac, the grand-daughter of another.[16]

The other main region represented in 1351 was the northern diocese of Tréguier, which furnished a contingent almost as large as that of St-Malo. Here the Penthièvre party held extensive estates and important fortresses such as La Roche Derrien and Guingamp. It was also a diocese, as evidence from after 1400 shows, where the noblesse formed a higher percentage of the population than in most other parts of the duchy.[17] Conversely, the diocese of St-Brieuc, almost as densely settled by the lesser noblesse, supplied on this occasion only four combatants, a low figure given that the caput of the county of Penthièvre was at Lamballe and some of Beaumanoir's own major estates, such as La Hardouinaye, lay there. It, too, would provide Du Guesclin with many of his lieutenants. None of the other six Breton dioceses was home to more than two soldiers on the Breton side on 26 March 1351, and there was no one at all from the western diocese of St-Pol-de-Léon, which was largely under Anglo-Breton control.

What military experience did Beaumanoir and his companions bring with them? Surprisingly little is known about most of them before 1351. Take Beaumanoir himself: reputedly born in 1316 and thus 35 years old in 1351, he almost certainly fought from the start of the Civil War but nothing is known until he

[14] Gicquel, *Le combat des Trente*, p. 83 for a map; cf. n. 59 below for a potential problem over Morice du Parc's diocese of origin.

[15] Potier de Courcy, *Nobiliaire*, i, 210 traces the line back to Maurice Catus, seneschal of La Garnache, dép. Vendée, in 1185.

[16] Torchet, *Saint-Malo*, pp. 113 and 175 for Robin (Robert III) Raguenel, vicomte de la Bellière, *jure uxoris*. For Tiphaine, see E. Dupont, 'Une astrologue bretonne au Mont-Saint-Michel (1365–1370)', *Revue de Bretagne* 43 (1910), pp. 254–78.

[17] M. Nassiet, 'Dictionnaire des feudataires de l'évêché de Tréguier en 1481', *Mémoires de la Société d'Émulation des Côtes d'Armor* 127 (1998), pp. 5–76.

was captured at La Roche Derrien in 1347.[18] Even Charruel, his near contemporary in age, is reported by Froissart as a defender of Rennes in 1342, though this may be a later embellishment.[19] Olivier Arel, 'yeoman' of Hervé, vicomte de Léon, is named in 1343.[20] Alain de Tinténiac was at the siege of Quimper in 1344.[21] Others were certainly in their thirties by 1351, perhaps a majority of the knights present since Breton evidence accords with that from elsewhere in showing that many did not achieve this rank until well set in their careers. Morice de Trésiguidy, an esquire in 1351, for instance, was not knighted until 1364,[22] though Geoffroy de La Roche was knighted during a lull in the fighting at Mi-Voie.[23] The rest, we may assume, were physically mature, strong and fit young men, mainly in their twenties. Collectively they had almost certainly seen considerable service but none of this is reflected in surviving written sources. Musters, including some with horse valuations, only begin to survive in numbers for Breton companies from the 1350s, exponentially increasing information on the careers of ordinary men-at-arms and archers that would justify a serious analytical prosopographical database.

For those who survived – on Beaumanoir's side there were at least three fatalities (Mellon, Poulard, Rousselot) – all this changed, partly because, as just noted, record evidence becomes more plentiful, partly because, like heroes from other walks of life (sporting analogies might be Don Bradman's 1948 Australians, Bobby Moore's 1966 England, and the Welsh Grand Slam teams of the 1970s), their reputations went before them and the remainder of their lives attracted interest. Froissart, for instance, famously recorded meeting the grizzled and scarred Even Charruel at a banquet at Charles V's court in the 1370s,[24] though

---

[18] Gicquel, *Le combat des Trente*, pp. 80–81, and Morvan, 'Les hommes d'armes du duché de Bretagne de 1213 à 1381', v, pp. 36–41 for a summary of Beaumanoir's career; Pierre Le Baud, the late fifteenth-century Breton historian, is the first to record the tradition of his capture at La Roche Derrien.

[19] *Chroniques de Jean Froissart*, ed. S. Luce et al., 15 vols (Paris, 1869–1975), iii, p. 31, where he is said to be present at Rennes in 1342 with Du Guesclin, though no firm proof for the latter's participation in this defence is known (cf. *Letters, Orders and Musters of Bertrand du Guesclin, 1357–1380*, ed. M. Jones (Woodbridge, 2004), p. xxiii and n. 44). Charruel was, however, present in court at Lesneven on 23 March 1339 (Dom P.H. Morice, *Mémoires pour servir de preuves à l'histoire ecclésiastique et civile de Bretagne*, 3 vols (Paris, 1742–6), i, cols 1393–4).

[20] *CPR 1340–1343*, p. 578.

[21] La Borderie, *Histoire de Bretagne*, iii, pp. 484–5 for the siege of Quimper, April–May 1344.

[22] He was still an esquire in July 1363 (Morice, *Mémoires*, i, col. 1560) but knighted by late 1364, perhaps before the battle of Cocherel? Vicomte du Breil de Pontbriand, 'Maurice de Trésiguidy', *Revue historique de l'Ouest* 15 (1899), pp. 344–78, is a good summary and publishes certain key texts, including his will.

[23] Brush, 'La Bataille', p. 102, lines 324–31, and p. 103, lines 349–56.

[24] *Chroniques*, ed. Luce et al., iv, pp. xlv and 341.

his information on other participants is sometimes unreliable.[25] In the immediate aftermath of the battle, the camaraderie engendered by shared experience
is partly reflected in the way in which five survivors (Geoffroy du Bois, Alain
de Keranrais, Louis Gouyon, Olivier Le Fontenay, Tristan de Pestivien) served
together under Beaumanoir during the rest of 1351 when he and his company
were at royal wages.[26] On 14 August 1352 at least six of them were again present
on the same battlefield, Mauron, where four (Guillaume La Marche, Guillaume
de Montauban, Robin Raguenel and Jean de Tinténiac) were killed, and where
Beaumanoir may have had others serving with him.[27]

Thereafter the slowly dwindling band largely went their own ways: some, like
Charruel, Morice du Parc and Morice de Trésiguidy, led their own companies
or took on the captaincy of towns or castles for Charles de Blois or the king of
France. Du Parc, for instance, held those of Quimper (1359–60), Nantes (1363),
Limoges (1371) and La Rochelle (1372–5), dying in office,[28] and Trésiguidy held
Hennebont (1376–9) and Paris (1381–92).[29] In 1352 Guy de Rochefort was captain
of Nantes and in royal service in 1357, homonymy perhaps obscuring still later
employment.[30] Others, such as Simon Richart, who had briefly held the captaincy
of Lesneven in 1351, continued as subordinates with former companions. In 1356
he was with Even Charruel, along with three presumed relatives, Arnaut, another
esquire, and Derien and Rolant Richart, archers.[31] Jean de Sérent was similarly in
royal pay in 1356.[32] Caro de Bodegat, esquire, with Jean V de Beaumanoir in 1370
at the siege of Thury-Harcourt, was probably son of Caro de Bodegat, chevalier,
who fought in 1351.[33]

---

[25] Following Jean Le Bel, he names the leader of the Breton party as Robert de Beaumanoir,
though he correctly names Morice de Trésiguidy as one of the Thirty on several occasions.

[26] Morice, *Mémoires*, i, col. 1469 (22 June 1351), cols 1472–3 (Aug.–Sept. and 10 Oct. 1351).

[27] Robertus de Avesbury, *De gestis mirabilibus regis Edwardi tertii*, ed. E. Maunde Thompson,
Rolls Series (London, 1889), pp. 416–17.

[28] Morice, *Mémoires*, i, col. 1534; G. Dupont-Ferrier, *Gallia Regia, ou État des officiers royaux
des bailliages et de sénéchaussées de 1328 à 1515*, 7 vols (Paris, 1942–65), nos 14043 and 20118; H.
and Y. Torchet, *Réformation des fouages de 1426. Diocèse ou évêché de Cornouaille* (Paris, 2001),
p. 224.

[29] Pontbriand, 'Maurice de Trésiguidy', pp. 368–9; cf. Morice, *Mémoires*, ii, cols 187, 193, 416.

[30] La Borderie, *Histoire de Bretagne*, iii, p. 547; Morice, *Mémoires*, i, cols 1515–16.

[31] Morice, *Mémoires*, i, p. 1503; Simon himself was serving as an esquire with a horse (*blanc
gris*) worth 60 l. He is usually identified with Symon Richart, who swore to uphold the
second treaty of Guérande at La Roche Derrien on 2 May 1381 (Morice, *Mémoires*, ii, col. 279).

[32] Morice, *Mémoires*, i, col. 1506. For letters of Charles de Blois granting Jean de Sérent,
knight, 80 écus *pour se monter* see Morice, *Mémoires*, i, col. 1512, and *Recueil des Actes de
Charles de Blois et Jeanne de Penthièvre, duc et duchesse de Bretagne (1341–1364)*, ed. M. Jones
(Rennes, 1996), no. 169.

[33] BnF Pièces originales 245, Beaumanoir no. 2, 22 September 1370. Morice, *Mémoires*, i, col.
1470, July 1350, for Caro serving as a man-at-arms with Thibaud de Rochefort, together with
two other members of the Thirty, Guy de Rochefort and Hugues Catus. The distinctive name

Many other sons, grandsons and yet later generations would continue their families' military traditions. The future Jean V de Beaumanoir, chevalier banneret, first appeared as an esquire under his father in 1356, for instance, and when leading his own company in Normandy in 1370 was accompanied by Geoffroy Charruel, esquire, possibly a son or nephew of Even Charruel as well as the younger Caro de Bodegat.[34] Guillaume de La Lande, seigneur du Vaurouaud, who ratified the second treaty of Guérande in 1381, is sometimes identified as one of the thirty, though he may have been a son.[35] His own son, Tristan, was Grand Maître of the ducal household, dying in 1431.[36] The descent from Tristan de Pestivien is uncertain but there is a strong probability that Guillaume de Pestivien, captain of Brest in 1397, was his son.[37] Jean de Sérent, esquire in 1351, knighted by 1356, was father of Jean, chevalier in 1396, probably to be identifed with 'Jehan de Serrat' or 'Senat' serving in the company of Olivier du Pont at Gimont in the Gers in October 1375 and then with his brother Thibaud du Pont at Bellac and Limoges later that year.[38] Both the Du Ponts had come to the fore in Du Guesclin's service.[39] Olivier (IV) Arel, grandson of Olivier (II), was taken prisoner by the English in 1404; yet later members of the family served in the ducal bodyguard, campaigned during the War of the Public Weal and fell on the field at St-Aubin-du-Cormier in 1488.[40] Similar family networks can be established for every known Breton company of the period and require little further demonstration here. The presence of several members of the same family in particular companies has long been recognised as characteristic not only of Breton but also of other provincial groups in later medieval French royal armies.[41]

Caro was borne by family members for at least 250 years (Morice, *Mémoires*, i, cols 960–61, April 1255; Archives départementales des Côtes d'Armor, E 745, August 1503).

[34] Morice, *Mémoires*, i, col. 1637. Charles de Blois is reported to have once upbraided a young and garrulous Jean V de Beaumanoir for disrespect when passing a church and cemetery in Poitou (*Monuments*, ed. Serent, pp. 85–6 below n. 59).

[35] Was he the Guillaume de la Lande still serving as an esquire with Du Guesclin in 1370–71 (*Letters*, ed. Jones, p. 356)? No evidence otherwise for his career between 1351 and 1381 (Morice, *Mémoires*, ii, col. 275) has been discovered.

[36] An early mention is of Tristan as an esquire with the duke in 1384 (Arch. dép. Loire-Atlantique, E 88 no. 7). Ducal chamberlain and governor of Nantes in 1409 (ibid., G 476), he was Grand maître from 1413 to 1431, when he was succeeded by his eldest son, Tristan.

[37] Cf. Torchet, *Cornouaille*, pp. 228–9.

[38] BnF Pièces originales, 2330, du Pont no. 13 (along with Nicolas de Serent, also esquire, with Olivier du Pont), and Pièces originales, 2330, du Pont nos 18 and 26 (with Thibaut); for an *aveu* presented by the younger Jean in 1396, see Arch. dép. Loire-Atlantique, B 1484.

[39] P. Contamine, *Guerre, état et société à la fin du Moyen Âge. Études sur les armées des rois de France 1337–1494* (Paris and The Hague, 1972), pp. 585–6, summarises the brothers' careers.

[40] Torchet, *Cornouaille*, pp. 161–2. John Hawley, the famous Dartmouth merchant-pirate, bought a half-share in Olivier IV's ransom (*Royal and Historical Letters during the Reign of Henry the Fourth*, ed. F.C. Hingeston, Rolls Series, 2 vols (London, 1860–1965), i, p. 271).

[41] Contamine, *Guerre, état et société*, is the standard account, while in 'Les compaignies d'aventure en France pendant la Guerre de Cent Ans', *Mélanges de l'École française de Rome*.

Among the Thirty fighting in major battles after Mauron, Morice de Trési-guidy seems to have had the widest experience. He was certainly present with Du Guesclin at Cocherel (May 1364), although he missed Auray through serving in eastern France with the duke of Burgundy in the autumn of 1364.[42] He accom-panied Du Guesclin to Spain in 1366 and was thus almost certainly present at Najerá (3 April 1367), and was also in the peninsula again in 1369 and hence at Montiel.[43] Very active in many campaigns in the 1370s, especially various sieges,[44] he was with Du Guesclin again at the battle of Eymet (1377).[45] By 1382 in consid-erable royal favour as captain of Paris, he was at West Roosebeke, supporting the Oriflamme,[46] campaigned again in Flanders in 1383,[47] accompanied the duke of Bourbon to al-Mahidya in Tunisia in 1390 and may well have fought at Nicopolis (1396).[48] Nor must we forget that in 1360–61, while still young but already a royal

Moyen Âge, Temps modernes 87 (1975), pp. 365–96 (reprinted in his collection La France au XIVe et XVe siècles. Hommes, mentalité, guerre et paix (London 1981), Ch. VII), he provides further evidence, including that of some Breton companies.

[42] Morice, Mémoires, i, cols 1582–3 (September 1364); by 27 October 1364 he was serving with Regnaut de Trie and Philippe de Villiers with a company of 80 glaives (BnF MS Nouv. acq. fr. 7414 f. 72r).

[43] K.A. Fowler, Medieval Mercenaries. 1: The Great Companies (Oxford, 2001), pp. 146 and 261. He was in Barcelona as Du Guesclin's proctor in October 1368 arranging terms for the invasion of Sardinia (Letters, ed. Jones, nos 252 and 259) and in February 1369 at Borja when Du Guesclin performed homage to Charles II of Navarre (Letters, ed. Jones, no. 267).

[44] J. Cabaret d'Orville, La chronique du bon duc Loys de Bourbon, ed. A.-M. Chazaud (Paris, 1876), p. 43, records that in (May) 1373 'messire Morice de Terriguedis, le plus vaillant chevalier de Bretaigne, car il fut l'ung des chiefs de la bataille de trente, et avec lui estoit son nepveu le sire de Prustallet' delivered Dinan to Louis de Bourbon who retained him for life with his nephew 'lesquels l'ont despuis honnorablement et bien servi toute leur vie, en tous les lieux ou fut le duc de Bourbon; et estoit messire Morice de Terriguiedis a pension du duc de Bourbon'. He also accompanied Bourbon to Paris that year and then to the siege of Brive (d'Orville, Chronique du bon duc Loys de Bourbon, pp. 49, 58).

[45] Chroniques, ed. Luce et al., ix, pp. xix, 4–5, for his presence at the siege of Bergerac in late August 1377, and at the siege of Mortagne-sur-Gironde after the battle of Eymet (Chroniques, ed. Luce et al., ix, pp. 26–7). He also held the captaincy of Hennebont, dép. Morbihan, from 1376 to 1379.

[46] Chroniques, ed. Luce et al., xi, 6; he had been named captain of Paris on 19 February 1381 (Morice, Mémoires, ii, col. 303).

[47] BnF MSS français 32510 f. 254r, muster at Arras with 6 esquires, 24 Aug. 1383, Clairambault 107 pièce 2 and Cabinet d'Hozier 324 cote 9017 no. 2, quittances of 31 Aug. and 6 Sept. 1383.

[48] Contamine, Guerre, état et société, p. 591 (Africa). The evidence for his presence at Nicopolis is indirect: before 11 Feb. 1397 he received 152 francs from Philip the Bold in recompense for what he loaned at Venice to the duke's clerk en route to negotiate with Bajazet over the release of the count of Nevers (Arch. dép. Côte d'Or, B 1511 f. 153 et seq., published in J. Delaville Le Roulx, La France en Orient au XIVe siècle. Expéditions du Maréchal Boucicaut, 2 vols (Paris, 1886), ii, pp. 26–32 (29 and 32)), suggesting that he too was on his way home from Hungary. This is also suggested by a clause in his will (see n. 70 below) but he does not appear in A.S. Atiyah's list of crusaders in 1396 (The Crusade in the Later Middle Ages (London, 1938), pp. 523–8) nor does he or any other Breton feature in the otherwise informative contributions to

sergent d'armes, he had led a company of freebooters in the Auvergne under the general command of the royal bastard, Thomas de la Marche.[49] Few were more worthy than Trésiguidy to carry one of Du Guesclin's banners at his ceremonial re-interment at St-Denis in May 1389.[50]

No one else could match his record: Charruel was at Cocherel and, most probably, at Auray.[51] Morice du Parc may, likewise, have been at Auray, possibly at Soubise (1372) and more certainly at Chizé (March 1373).[52] Beaumanoir had three known battle honours, La Roche Derrien (1347), Mauron (1352) and Auray (1364), possibly also Najerá (1367), and had played a leading part either as an attacker or as a defender in several important sieges, such as Ploërmel (1351), Rennes (1356–7), Dinan (1357) and Bécherel (1363). Charruel was at the taking of Mantes and Meulan in 1364;[53] Rochefort had lost and then regained Nantes (1352).

What of the misfortunes of war? Beaumanoir was captured and ransomed at least three times (after La Roche Derrien (1347) and Auray (1364), as well as being taken in an ambush in August 1355).[54] It is probable that Trésiguidy was ransomed after Najerá, but no other information about specific ransoms appears to have survived though it is highly likely that many of the Thirty were captured at some point. Given the length and variety of service of men like Morice du Parc and Even Charruel this is a matter of some interest. So too may be mortality rates arising from military activity. As we have already seen, at least three of Beaumanoir's companions were killed on or died from wounds shortly after 26 March 1351, and another four were killed eighteen months later at Mauron. Working on a conservative basis that the average age of those fighting at Mi-Voie was between 25 and 30, and from somewhat fragmentary prosopographic detail, my calculations suggest that around half of the combatants were probably dead

'Nicopolis, 1396–1996. Actes du Colloque international, Dijon 18 octobre 1996', ed. J. Paviot and M. Chauney-Bouillot, *Annales de Bourgogne* 68, part 3 (1997), of which Professeur Bertrand Schnerb kindly sent me a copy.

[49] M. Boudet, *Thomas de la Marche, Bâtard de France et ses aventures (1318–1361)* (Riom, 1900, reprinted Geneva, 1978), cols 151, 195, 206–9, 338–45. Among his companions was Olivier Poulard, perhaps brother of Geoffroy, one of the Thirty (Boudet, *Thomas de la Marche*, pp. 155, 209).

[50] Morice, *Mémoires*, ii, cols 549–81; *Letters*, ed. Jones, no. 943 and nn.

[51] Charles V granted a remission at the request of Even Charruel, chevalier, for services at the siege of Mantes which immediately preceded Du Guesclin's campaign culminating in the battle of Cocherel (Archives Nationales, Paris, JJ 94 f. 19v no. 50).

[52] Torchet, *Cornouaille*, p. 224; he had also suffered a defeat in the Pays de Retz in the service of Charles de Blois (*Monuments*, ed. Serent, p. 161 below n. 59).

[53] S. Luce, *Histoire de Bertrand du Guesclin et de son époque. La jeunesse de Bertrand (1320–1364)* (Paris, 1876), p. 427.

[54] Avesbury, *De gestis mirabilibus regis Edwardi tertii*, p. 427, for his capture in 1355; for some outstanding debts for his ransom owing to Robert Knolles after Auray see Morice, *Mémoires*, i, cols 1621–2.

by the age of 30. Of the remainder, six could have survived into their early 40s and four into their early 50s (including Beaumanoir and Morice du Parc, both still militarily active); Charruel probably attained 60 and Morice de Trésiguidy, the last known survivor, was almost certainly well into his 70s by the time of his death in 1402. Even if he was not in Hungary in 1396, he had certainly fought in his 60s in North Africa and had at least one pilgrimage to Jerusalem to his credit.[55]

In addition to their military service to Charles de Blois, several of the Thirty acted as trusted counsellors, diplomats and envoys in the years immediately after the battle. Beaumanoir, Charruel, Alain de Keranrais and Pestivien, for instance, were despatched to England, most on more than one occasion, usually in connection with negotiations over the release and ransom of their master.[56] In 1348 Guillaume La Marche, later killed at Mauron, had been sent by Jeanne de Penthièvre to Avignon to discuss various marriage plans also connected with the release of her husband.[57] Beaumanoir eventually represented Jeanne when the first treaty of Guérande was negotiated in April 1365, bringing the civil war to its official conclusion.[58] Morice du Parc was for many years a ducal chamberlain, as testimony given at the inquiry into the sanctity of Charles de Blois in 1371 confirms.[59] Geoffroy Poulard did not survive the battle, but Pierre Poulard, possibly a brother or uncle, was one of Charles de Blois's senior advisers, and

---

[55] Pontbriand, 'Maurice de Trésiguidy', p. 357, suggests he may have gone to Jerusalem as early as 1380; Torchet, *Cornouaille*, p. 252, cites a licence from 1395 for him obtaining the right to have the sacrament administered by a priest of his choice to his whole retinue when visiting holy places, possibly connected with the voyage which took him to Venice in 1396 when he may well have been *en route* to or from the Holy Land as much as to Hungary.

[56] *Recueil des Actes de Charles de Blois*, ed. Jones, index sub nom. Eugène Déprez, 'La querelle de Bretagne', *Mémoires de la Société d'Histoire et d'Archéologie de Bretagne* 7 (1926), pp. 25–60, is the fullest account of negotiations for the release of Charles de Blois.

[57] *Recueil des Actes de Charles de Blois*, ed. Jones, no. 97.

[58] Morice, *Mémoires*, i, cols 1587–8, cf. *Recueil des Actes de Charles de Blois*, ed. Jones, no. 302. He had been one of the hostages for the truce of Landes d'Evran (July 1363) and is reported to have tried to mediate before the battle of Auray, according to the fifteenth-century Breton chronicler Jean de St-Paul; he died shortly before 23 November 1366 (Nantes, Médiathèque, fonds Bizeul MS 1703 no. 4, partition of his goods between his widow and second wife, Marguerite de Rohan (later to marry Olivier V de Clisson, Constable of France) and his eldest son, Jean V de Beaumanoir, by his first wife, Tiphaine de Chemillé).

[59] *Monuments du procès de canonisation du bienheureux Charles de Blois, duc de Bretagne 1320–64*, ed. A. de Serent and Dom François Plaine (St-Brieuc, 1921), pp. 37–42, unless this is a case of homonymy, since this Morice du Parc, aged 50, gave his place of residence as Roslohen in the diocese of Tréguier and is thus possibly from the Du Parc de Locmaria family (cf. Potier de Courcy, *Nobiliaire*, ii, pp. 349–50) and to be distinguished from his better-known namesake, who haled from Rosnoën, diocese of Cornouaille (Potier de Courcy, *Nobiliaire*, ii, 350–51), unless the clerks responsible for recording his witness had become confused. Torchet, *Cornouaille*, p. 224, conflates the two Morices but the armorial evidence points to two distinct families.

his brother, Guillaume, was bishop of St-Malo (1359–75).[60] Beaumanoir, almost exclusively in ducal service, and Charruel, in both ducal and royal service, show that military and civil employment in equal measure was a routine characteristic of most of the careers that can be traced in some detail. In this respect that of Trésiguidy is again notable for its length and distinction: at one time or another not only had he been in Breton ducal service and that of Charles V[61] and Charles VI of France, but he had also been a counsellor or in receipt of fees and other favours from Louis, duke of Anjou, John, duke of Berry, Philip, duke of Burgundy and Louis, duke of Bourbon![62] Little wonder that Christine de Pisan, in a letter written on 2 October 1402, could cite him alongside Du Guesclin 'as an example of those who lived loyally.'[63]

As the Thirty approached the end of their lives, is there any evidence of them reflecting on their military careers, showing remorse or indicating how they wished to be remembered? Du Guesclin, for instance, left money to restore a church damaged during the battle of Chizé;[64] Geoffroy Tournemine, who died in 1264, had similarly left money to compensate innocent victims harmed by his private wars.[65] Unfortunately only two wills survive for the Thirty, though they are both of significant figures: Beaumanoir himself and Trésiguidy. Beaumanoir directed that his body should indeed be buried with those of his ancestors at Léhon, and there is a bequest of a horse, but none of armour. Most of his specific provisions were gifts to religious houses, with particular favour to mendicants although monastic houses and churches also benefited. There were also a few bequests to members of his household.[66] Trésiguidy elected to be

---

[60] *Recueil des Actes de Charles de Blois*, ed. Jones, passim for Pierre Poulard, who for a period acted as ducal treasurer; an Olivier Poulard, esquire, was also serving with Beaumanoir on 22 June 1351 (Morice, *Mémoires*, i, col. 1469).

[61] Among service for Charles V, Trésiguidy undertook a diplomatic mission to Aragon in 1379–80 (Morice, *Mémoires*, ii, cols 267, 283 and 410).

[62] In 1368 he received 2,500 francs with Hervé du Juch for bringing 300 combatants to serve Louis, duke of Anjou (Contamine, *Guerre, état et société*, p. 590), and in August 1381 he was one of Louis's councillors (*Journal de Jean le Fèvre, évêque de Chartres, chancelier des rois de Sicile, Louis I et Louis II d'Anjou*, ed. H. Moranvillé (Paris, 1887), p. 9). In October and November 1386 he received payment for service in the household of John, duke of Berry (BnF MS français 25765, p. 69). For service with Bourbon and Burgundy see n. 44.

[63] Cited by Brush, 'La Bataille', p. 522.

[64] *Letters*, ed. Jones, nos 544 and 913.

[65] Michael Jones, 'La vie quotidienne de trois nobles bretons au XIIIe siècle d'après leurs testaments', *Mémoires de la Société d'Histoire et d'Archéologie de Bretagne* 60 (1983), pp. 19–33 (reprinted in *The Creation of Brittany*, Ch. IV).

[66] BnF MS français 5842 no. 7, drawn up on 11 July 1363. Among the religious benefiting from his will were the Dominicans and Franciscans of Dinan, 10 l each, the Austin Canons of Lamballe, 100s, the Franciscans of Rennes, 100s, the Dominicans and Franciscans of Guingamp, 100s each, and Notre-Dame de Moncontour, 100s. A chapel was to be founded in the church of St-Jean de Montcontour with a rent of 30 l p.a. Any arrears of a rent due to the priory of St-Brede, near Merdrignac, were to be levied and used to repair it. Two friars

buried at St-Yves in Paris, a favourite among Bretons, but also left money to St-André-des-Arts, the parish in which he lived, to the four mendicant orders in Paris, to Ste-Catherine du Val des Écoliers (specifically in memory of his wife, Geneviève),[67] to the Celestins and Chartreux de Paris, the Hotel Dieu, the Saints-Innocents, the hospital of St-Esprit, the poor prisoners of the Chatellet and other prisons, and lepers (no less than 1000 l.), and then to no fewer than eighteen Breton houses as well as the parish church of his natal parish, Pleyben, in Cornouaille.[68] Hints of his military career are found in his legacy of two horses (*roncins*), one of which had been bought in Venice, to a nephew and fifty francs left to Even de Keroulas *qui fu a la bataille de Hongroie, si par aventure il revenoit ça*,[69] while the rest of *ses robes, son harnois, ses chevaux* were to be sold to pay for his other charitable benefactions and personal legacies to family members and servants.[70]

Finally, as far as physical remains are concerned, as noted at the start and Beaumanoir's will confirms, tombs of several of his relatives survive at Léhon; but none are known for the rest of the Thirty, although other family members are commemorated by tombs, some actually surviving, others now lost but recorded by antiquaries. Thus, those of Alain II de Montauban (d. 1359), probable father of Guillaume, and of Olivier VI de Montauban once reposed in the Dominican

---

were to go from Dinan to La Hardouinaye and Moncontour to inquire into any misdeeds and to make reparation and his executors likewise were to 'vaient touz mes conquestz que ge ay faiz tant en mon nom que ou nom de mes effanz' and repair anything done contrary to reason.

[67] It is usually stated that Morice married Jeanne de Ploesquellec/Pluscallec (cf. Contamine, *Guerre, état et société*, p. 590) but, as Du Breil de Pontbriand pointed out ('Maurice de Trésiguidy', p. 364), a quittance issued by Geneviève on behalf of Morice (Morice, *Mémoires*, ii, col. 267, 23 June 1380) and mention of her by name in his will (1399), by which time she was dead, as well as of at least three of their children, including his eldest son, Jean, who was also deceased, suggests that Morice was only married once and that if he married a Pluscallec, it was Geneviève not Jeanne.

[68] The Breton beneficiaries were: the Franciscans of Dinan, Rennes, Nantes, Vannes, Guingamp and Quimper; the Dominicans of Dinan, Rennes, Nantes, Quimperlé, Morlaix and Guingamp; the Carmelites of Nantes, Hennebont, Pont l'Abbé and St-Pol de Léon, and the Austin Canons of Lannion and Carhaix as well as the church of Pleyben 'où le manoir de Tresiguidi est assis', the current holder of which was a nephew, Jean, sire de Trésiguidy en Pleyben et des Salles en Plouisy, son of Morice's brother Eon/Yvon (d. 1396 and buried in the Franciscan friary at Quimper), who had been a staunch supporter of the Montfort family from the earliest days of the Civil War.

[69] Neither Keroualas nor Trésiguidy are listed by A.S. Atiyah, *The Crusade in the Later Middle Ages* (London, 1938), pp. 517–28, Appendix IV, List of Crusaders, Nicopolis, though at least two Bretons are: Thomas de *Kocrimel* (recte Kerimel) and Jean de Tremaugon, chamberlain to Louis, duke of Orléans. According to the *Chronicon Briocense* (Morice, *Mémoires*, i, cols 76–7), some 120 Bretons were killed and only three escaped (Jean, vicomte du Faou, Jean d'Acigné and Jean Le Manati).

[70] Pontbriand, 'Maurice de Trésiguidy', pp. 372–8, after the original in the Archives Nationales (but without mention of exact location).

friary at Dinan; that of Pierre Poulard and his wife, Constance de Kerraoul, was in the abbey of Beauport;[71] some fifteenth-century Rochefort tombs at La Haye-Fouassière (Loire-Atlantique) may belong to descendants of our Guy.[72] The only surviving late-fourteenth- to early-fifteenth-century group of Breton tombs close to rivalling that of the Beaumanoirs at Léhon is to be found in the Vieille-église de St-Lunaire, some twenty kilometres to the west, where several members of the closely allied Pontbriant and Pontual families lie, including some who served with Du Guesclin.[73]

Although not treated directly here, most of the characteristics which have been identified in that small handful of men who made up Beaumanoir's team in 1351 could have been placed on a firmer statistical footing had I taken the renowned Constable and his men and subjected them to a similar analysis. Some evidence for the composition of Du Guesclin's companies, for example, is presented in appendices to my edition of his *Letters, Orders and Musters* (2004).[74] But both in his thesis and in separate articles, Philippe Contamine had already revealed the broad outlines, not least underlining how Breton troops, especially in the 1360s and 1370s, made a quite disproportionate contribution to the make-up of many royal armies: those of Louis of Anjou as royal lieutenant in the Midi consisted of 40% and more of Bretons on some occasions,[75] and those led by Du Guesclin as Constable were very comparable. The tradition continued into Charles VI's reign with the second Breton Constable, Olivier de Clisson, also recruiting extensively in the duchy.[76] A generation later the same would be true, and the military recovery of France under Charles VII owed a similar huge debt to the third Breton Constable, Arthur de Richemont, and his entourage of Breton lieutenants and captains.[77] The surviving documentary material for the thousands of Bretons in royal military employment in the century between 1351

[71] Jean-Yves Copy, *Art, société et politique au temps des ducs de Bretagne. Les gisants haut-bretons* (Paris, 1986), p. 264 nos 37 and 38 for the lost Montauban tombs; p. 266 no. 71 for the lost tombstone of the Poulards; for their joint-will see Morice, *Mémoires*, i, cols 1554–5, 14 July 1362. Pierre is said to have died on 27 September 1364, but there is the possibility that he was killed at the battle of Auray on 29 Sept. 1364 (cf. *Anciens évêches de Bretagne*, ed. J. Geslin de Bourgogne and A. de Barthélemy, 6 vols (St-Brieuc and Paris, 1854–69), iv, p. 223).

[72] Copy, *Art, société et politique*, p. 266, no. 79.

[73] Copy, *Art, société et politique*, p. 273, nos 231–6. *Letters*, ed. Jones, p. 363, for Colin and Robin de Pontbriant serving with the Constable in 1370–71.

[74] *Letters*, ed. Jones, pp. 342–68; Morvan, 'Les hommes d'armes du duché de Bretagne', v, pp. 160–95, expands this list, and adds some notes on provenance; and pp. 196–203 for the Constable's companies in 1373–5, pp. 204–19 for 1378 and pp. 220–22 for 1379–80.

[75] Contamine, *Guerre, état et société*, pp. 153–4.

[76] J.B. Henneman, *Olivier de Clisson and Political Society in France under Charles V and Charles VI* (Philadelphia, 1996), pp. 211–21 for useful analysis and tables.

[77] É. Cosneau, *Le Connétable de Richemont (Artur de Bretagne) (1393–1458)* (Paris, 1886), remains the main account, but see also Contamine, *Guerre, état et société*, pp. 262 et seq.

and 1453 is overwhelming;[78] there is also a certain amount for their service to their own dukes which has been neglected here, other than that to Charles de Blois. Although inevitably partial, I would still like to suggest that the collective experience of that small handful of men who made up the Thirty and analysed here already encapsulates much of the contribution that would be made by their successors, and that not simply in the later fourteenth century.

Appendix I. Jean IV de Beaumanoir and his companions at the Battle of the Thirty, 26 March 1351[79]

Chevaliers

Beaumanoir, Jean IV de (1316–1366), lord of Merdrignac, La Hardouinaye, Moncontour and Beaumanoir en Evran (22, St-Malo diocese). Ancestry from Hervé, sire de Beaumanoir, fl. 1200; posterity: sons, Jean V (d. 1385) and Robert II (d. 1407). Arms: Azure, 10 billets argent (Fabre, no. 277, seals 1349, 1356).

Arel, Olivier II (c.1315/20–after 1351), lord of Kermarquer and Lézardrieux en Ploeumeur-Gautier (22, Tréguier diocese). Ancestry from Jean, sire de Kermarquer fl. 1240; posterity: male line continuing post-1500. Arms: Quarterly argent and azure (cf. Fabre, no. 187, seal of Yvon Arel, 1366).

Bodegat, Caro de (c.1315/20–after 1351), lord of Bodegat en Mohon (56, St-Malo diocese). Ancestry from Caro de Bodegat fl. 1255; posterity: male line continuing post-1500. Arms: Gules three *tourteaux* (hermit crabs) ermine (Fabre no. 366 after a roll of arms).

Bois (probably Bois-Ourhant or Coëtgourhant), Geoffroy du (c.1325–after 1351), Louannec (22, Tréguier diocese). Ancestry from Geoffroy de Boisourhant/Coëtgourhant fl. 1254; posterity: male line continuing post-1500. Arms: Or, a lion sable, a fess gules (Potier de Courcy, i, 267).

Charruel, Even (c.1310–1378 or later), lord of Ménez en Guerlesquin and Lezenor en Ploulec'h (both 22, Tréguier diocese). Ancestry from Henri de Charruel, chevalier, fl. 1294; posterity: male line extinct 1420. Arms: Gules, a fess argent (Fabre, no. 540, seal 1338/9).

La Marche, Geoffroy de (c.1310/15–1352), Bédée (35, St-Malo diocese) and lord of La Boëssière en Carentoir (56, Vannes diocese). Ancestry from Guillaume de La Marche, fl. 1306; posterity: male line extinct c.1430. Arms: Quarterly, 1 and 4, a

---

[78] A start for the period 1341–81 is made by Morvan's analysis of many surviving musters.

[79] These notes have mainly been compiled from Potier de Courcy, *Nobiliaire et armorial*. 'Ancestry' and 'Posterity' refer to the family in general terms. M. Fabre, *Héraldique médiévale bretonne. Images personnelles (vers 1350–1500). Armoriaux, sceaux, tombeaux*, 2 vols (Paris, 1993), provides much original material allowing refinement of the evidence provided by Potier de Courcy, notably for identifying the arms used by the Thirty or their nearest kin. Départements are identified by number: 22 (Côtes d'Armor); 29 (Finistère); 35 (Ille-et-Vilaine); 44 (Loire-Atlantique); 56 (Morbihan).

crosslet, 2 and 3 a *hie* (?or cross pattée), tinctures unknown (Fabre, no. 1857, seal 1352 and cf. Potier de Courcy, ii, 232).

Raguenel, Robin (Robert III) (*c.*1320–1352), lord of Châtel-Oger en Saint-Erblon (35, Rennes diocese). Ancestry from Robin Raguenel fl. 1260; posterity: male continuing post-1500. Arms: Quarterly argent and sable, a label of 4 points sable and argent (Fabre, no. 3097, seal 1352).

Rochefort, Guy de (*c.*1310–20–after 1357), lord of Henleix en Escoublac (44, Nantes diocese). Ancestry from Thibaut de Rochefort, fl. 1247; posterity: male line continuing post-1500. Arms: Vairy or and azure, a shell in chief (tincture unknown) to dexter (Fabre, no. 3157, seal 1357).

Rousselot, Jean (*c.*1315–20–1351), lord of Limoëlan en Sévignac (35, St-Malo diocese). Ancestry from Guillaume de Rousselot/Rouxelot fl. 1304; posterity: male line continuing post-1500. Arms: Argent, three axes sable, 2 and 1 (Fabre no. 3302 after Navarre roll of arms).

Saint-Hugeon, Huon de (*c.*1315–20–after 1351), Brélévenez (22, Tréguier diocese). Ancestry: not known; posterity: ?Guillaume, fl. 1395. Arms: Argent a cross sable with a cotice gules (Potier de Courcy, ii, 539 after 17th C. heraldist Guillaume Le Borgne).

Tinténiac, Jean de (*c.*1315–20–1352), lord of Tinténiac, Bécherel and Romillé (all 35, St-Malo diocese) and *iure uxoris* of Combourg (35, Dol diocese). Ancestry from Donoal fl. 1040; posterity: male continuing post-1500. Arms: Or two *jumelles* argent, a bend gules (Potier de Courcy, ii, 598, cf. Fabre, no. 3475 after Navarre roll of arms).

Écuyers

Beaucors/Beaucorps, Geoffroy de (*c.*1320–after 1351), Saint-Cast (22, St-Brieuc diocese). Ancestry: unknown; posterity: male line continuing post-1500. Arms: Azure, two fesses or (Potier de Courcy, i, 55).

Catus, Hugo/Hugues (*c.*1325–after 1351), Évran (35, St-Malo diocese). Ancestry from Maurice Catus fl. 1185; posterity: male line continuing post-1500. Arms: Gules, a leopard or, with numerous stars of the same (Potier, i, 210).

Du Parc, Morice (1321–1375/7), Rosnoën (29, Quimper diocese). Ancestry: cadet branch of the vicomtes du Faou (fl. 11th C.); posterity: male line continuing post-1500. Arms: Azure, a leopard or, a label gules (Fabre, no. 1092 after a roll of arms).

Fontenay/Le Fontenoys, Olivier de (*c.*1325–after 1351), Plédran (22, St-Brieuc diocese). Ancestry: unknown; posterity: male line continuing 1488. Arms: Or, a shield *en abyme* gules, eight martlets in orle of the same (Potier de Courcy, i, 393).

Gouyon, Louis/Thibault (*c.*1325–after 1351), lord of Launay en Ploubalay (22, St-Malo diocese). Ancestry from Étienne Gouyon, lord of Matignon, fl. 1200; posterity: male line continuing post-1500. Arms: Or, two fesses knotted gules, accompanied by nine martlets in orle of the same (cf. Fabre, nos 1337–1354).

Keranrais, Alain de (*c.*1325–after 1353), Plouaret (22, Tréguier diocese). Ancestry: claimed as cadet branch of Avaugour fl. 1150, otherwise from Alain de Keranrais, aged 72 in 1330; posterity: male line until 1432. Arms: Vairy argent and gules (cf. Fabre, nos 1546–50 after seals and rolls of arms).

Keranrais, Olivier de (*c.*1310–after 1351), Plouaret (22, Tréguier diocese), uncle of Alain. For Ancestry and Arms, see previous entry.

La Lande, Guillaume de (c.1320–?1396), lord of La Lande and La Grézillonaye en Guichen (35, St-Malo diocese). Ancestry from Guillaume de La Lande, fl. 1302; posterity: male line continuing post-1500. Arms: Azure, three shields argent (2,1), a cotice (cf. Fabre, no. 1843, seal 1366).

Lanloup, Geslin de (c.1325–after 1351), Plélo (22, St-Brieuc diocese) and lord of Lanloup (22, Dol diocese). Ancestry: claimed as cadet of Coëtmen family fl. 1200; otherwise Roland de Lanloup, chevalier, fl. 1260; posterity: male line continuing post-1500. Arms: Azure, six rings argent, 3,2,1 (Potier de Courcy, ii, 153).

La Roche, Geoffroy de (c.1325–after 1351), either Dinan (22, St-Malo diocese) or Cuguen (35, Dol diocese) or Plessis-Balisson (22, St-Malo diocese), knighted during battle. Ancestry: claimed from Brice de La Roche, alleged crusader in 1204; otherwise unknown; posterity: male line continuing post-1500 (Potier de Courcy, ii, 486–7). Arms: Gules, two leopards/lions or (Fabre, no. 1993 after Navarre roll of arms).

Mellon/Moëlon, Geoffroy de (c.1325–1351), lord of Mellon en Pacé (35, Rennes diocese). Ancestry: unknown; posterity: male line continuing post-1500. Arms: Azure, three crosses pattée argent (cf. Fabre, no. 2641, seals 1415–23).

Montauban, Guillaume de (c.1310/15–1352), lord of Bois-de-la-Roche en Néant (35, St-Malo diocese). Ancestry: cadet of Rohan family, fl. 12th C.; posterity: male line continuing post-1500 Arms: Gules, seven lozenges voided or, a label of four points argent (cf. Fabre, nos 2679–81, seals 1387–1427).

Monteville, Olivier de (c.1325–after 1351), Plouec (22, Tréguier diocese), lord of Launay-Monteville en Ploézal and Launay en Runan (both 22, St-Malo diocese). Ancestry: cadet of Quélen family, fl. 13th C., itself a cadet of Porhoët, fl. 11th C.; posterity: male line continuing c.1481 Arms: Argent, three ivy leaves sinople, with a bordure sable (Potier de Courcy, ii, 292–3).

Pestivien, Tristan de (c.1320/5–after 1353), Plougonvern (22, Tréguier diocese). Ancestry: Jean (I), sire de Pestivien fl. 1270; posterity: male line continuing post-1500. Arms: Vairy argent and sable (cf. Fabre, nos 2868–71 after seals and rolls of arms).

Pontblanc, Guyon de (c.1325–after 1351), Plouaret (22, Tréguier diocese). Ancestry: Geoffroy de Pontblanc, killed at Lannion, 1346; posterity: heiress takes to Trogoff family c.1370. Arms: Or, ten billets sable, 4,3,2,1 (Potier de Courcy, ii, 410).

Poulard, Geoffroy (c.1325–1351), lord of Kergolléau en Plouézec (22, St-Brieuc diocese). Ancestry: ?Elder brother, Pierre Poulard (d. 1364), treasurer of Jeanne de Penthièvre, married Constance de Kerraoul, 1339; posterity: male line continuing post-1500. Arms: Quarterly gules and sinople, 1 and 4, a rose argent (cf. Fabre, no. 3007, seal of Guillaume Poulard, bishop of St-Malo, 1365, Quarterly, 1 and 4, a cinquefoil).

Richard, Simon (c.1320/5–after 1381), lord of Kerjean en Plestin and Coëtléguer en Trégom (both 22, Tréguier diocese). Ancestry: Eudes Richard, alleged crusader, 1248, otherwise unknown; posterity: male line continuing post-1500 (Potier de Courcy, ii, 471). Arms: Six rings, 3,2,1, with bordure (Fabre, no. 3140, seal 1381)

Sérent, Jean/Jehannot de (c.1325–after 1356), lord of Tromeur en Sérent (56, Vannes diocese). Ancestry: Menguy, son of Marquis, chevalier, fl. 1115; posterity: male line continuing post-1500. Arms: Or, three cinquefoils sable (Fabre, no. 3408, seal 1356).

Tinténiac, Alain de (*c.*1320–after 1351), Bécherel (35, St-Malo diocese), brother of Jean de Tinténiac, knight. For Ancestry, see above. Arms: Gules, three fesses argent, a bend azure charged with three besants or (Fabre, no. 3476, after Navarre roll of arms).

Trésiguidy/Tronguidy, Morice de (*c.*1325/30–1402), Pleyben (29, Quimper diocese). Ancestry: Morice de Trésiguidy, alleged crusader in 1248, father of Morice, bishop of Rennes (1260–82); posterity: male line extinct *c.*1475. Arms: Or, three pine cones gules with a molet azure (Fabre, nos 3561–3, seals 1381–7 and rolls of arms).

Appendix II. Bretons serving with Robert de Bamborough, captain of Ploërmel, at the battle of the Thirty, 26 March 1351

Apremont, Raoulet d' (*c.*1325–after 1364), esquire, Renac (56, Vannes diocese). Ancestry: originally from Poitou; posterity: only daughter, Jeanne, marries (1) Jean Harpedanne (1390), and (2) Savary de Vivonne. Arms: Argent, three crescents gules (Potier de Courcy, i, 15 after Armorial of Guillaume Le Borgne)

Ardaine, Guillaume d', esquire (*c.*1325–1351), St-Georges de Reintembault (35, Rennes diocese). Ancestry: Juhel and his son, Olivier, fl. 1150–60; posterity: heiress takes to Romilley early 15th C. Arms: Argent, semé d'ancolies d'azure, à la bande chargée de feuilles de houx (Potier de Courcy, i, 16 after a seal of 1382, cf. Fabre, no. 799).

Comenan/Comellan, Perrot de (*c.*1325–after 1351), esquire, Sérent or Rieux (both 56, Vannes diocese). Arms: Gules, three molets argent (cf. Fabre, no., 746, seal of Maurice de Comenan, 1412), or Sable, three chevrons argent (Gicquel, 85).

Le Gaillard, Guillon/Guillemin/Hamon (*c.*1325–after 1351), esquire, Pommeret (22, St-Brieuc diocese). Ancestry: unknown; posterity: several Guillaume/Guillemin Le Gaillarts appear in muster for various parishes in St-Brieuc diocese in 15th C. including Ploeuc and Quessoy. Arms: 'de gueules à 3 besants mal ordonnés d'or, le champ chapé d'un fasce d'argent et d'azur' (Gicquel, 85).

8

Towards a Rehabilitation of Froissart's Credibility: The Non Fictitious Bascot de Mauléon

Guilhem Pépin

In the chronicles of Jean Froissart, one of the most famous passages is the interview by the author of the Gascon *routier* named the Bascot de Mauléon (given as Maulion in the text) which took place when Froissart was in Orthez to meet Gaston Fébus, count of Foix and vicomte of Béarn, in early December 1388. This passage in Book Three of Froissart's chronicles has been used many times by historians to illustrate the life of a typical mercenary of the fourteenth century as it provides the only contemporary coherent narrative of the *routiers'* history stretching from 1356 to the 1380s. But in 2001 Kenneth Fowler suggested in his book *Medieval Mercenaries* that the Bascot de Mauléon was 'possibly a figure of Froissart's imagination, created to tell the story himself', since Fowler did not find any record of the existence of the Bascot de Mauléon in archival sources.[1] Curiously enough, although it was only a supposition on Fowler's part, it seems that many medievalists have now begun to think that the Bascot probably never existed and that Froissart's interview was an elaborate forgery based on different testimonies. In fact, a clutch of reliable contemporary documents mention the Bascot de Mauléon holding a 'fortress' and acknowledging the authority of the king of England. This case study of his career will permit us to understand better the life of many Anglo-Gascon *routiers* of the second rank in the second half of the fourteenth century. It will also explain the meaning of some nicknames used by several Gascon *routiers*, including that of 'Bascot', and will try to establish whether statements made in Froissart's interview can be confirmed by other documents.

An undated list of 'places and fortresses of Guyenne' acknowledging the authority of the king of England survives in the British Library as Harley Manuscript 4763.[2] It puts on the same level places and fortresses situated in the

---

1 K. Fowler, *Medieval Mercenaries. 1: The Great Companies* (Oxford, 2001), p. 14, n. 53.

2 BL Harley MS 4763, fols 170r–172r.

recently contracted duchy of Guyenne or Aquitaine (stretching from Bordeaux to Bayonne) and fortresses held by Anglo-Gascon *routiers* outside this region. Its original author was obviously someone originating from Aquitaine-Gascony since, although the list is in French, some of its written forms are typical of this region. It was, at a later date, probably copied by an English scribe, as many names are evidently unknown to him and are badly misread. The surviving copy is contained in a manuscript probably written during the first half of the fifteenth century, but the original purpose of this list seems to have been as an ephemeral document intended to inform the Anglo-Gascon government at Bordeaux, and/ or the English government at Westminster, about the extent of English territory in Guyenne.

By checking the dates when some castles were taken or lost by Anglo-Gascon *routiers* it is possible to date the writing of the list to around 1383–4. For instance, the castle of Curvalle in the Albigeois was taken by *routiers* led by a certain Bourc de Galard in 1383. It was briefly given back to its lord in 1384 before being recaptured by the *routiers*, and then finally lost by them after a siege, conducted by the French knight Gaucher de Passat, which ended before 4 October 1384.[3] Our list says: 'Item, held in the Albigeois, the borc de Galard, Curvalle'.[4] Just after this mention may be read: 'Item, the men of the basco de Mauléon, Las Planques'.[5]

This simple sentence is quite explicit: the men of the basco de Mauléon hold for him the fortress of Las Planques.[6] This cannot be an invention of the author of the list, based, for example, on his reading of Froissart, because Las Planques is not mentioned in any versions of Froissart's Third Book. Froissart simply wrote there that the Bascot de Mauléon had taken and kept the castle of Thuriès in the Albigeois.[7] In fact, there is some truth in both of our sources, since Las Planques was a *routier* fortress held at the same time, situated near to Thuriès on the other side of the river Viaur. Both places were in the Albigeois at its boundary with Rouergue.

That the two *routier* garrisons of Thuriès and Las Planques were closely associated following their capture in 1380 is evidenced by the actions of the commune of Albi. For example, on 6 September 1381 the consuls of Albi sent a representative to the duke of Berry, then king's lieutenant in *la langue d'oc*, charged to 'explain

---

[3] L. Cabié, 'La Campagne de Gaucher de Passac contre les routiers du Sud-Ouest de la France, 1384–1385', *Revue du Tarn* 18 (1901), pp. 173–4. Cabié and other historians are mistaken in calling him Gaucher de Passac; he was in fact lord of Passat in the Bourbonnais (com[mune] St-Victor, arr[ondissement] Montluçon, c[anton] Montluçon-Nord-Est, dép[artement] Allier).

[4] BL Harley MS 4763, fol. 172r: 'Item ten' en Albiges lo bort de Galart, Cruballe' (Curvalle, arr. Albi, c. Alban, dép. Tarn).

[5] BL Harley MS 4763, fol. 172 r : 'Item la gent du basco de Maulion, Las Planques'.

[6] Las Planques, com. Tanus, arr. Albi, c. Pampelonne, dép. Tarn.

[7] Thuriès, com. Pampelonne, arr. Albi, c. Pampelonne, dép. Tarn. This castle was then a possession of the king of France.

to him the damages we suffer from the English of Thuriès and Las Planques.'[8]
It is recorded on 22 September 1381 that the consuls discussed whether to make
an agreement with the men-at-arms of Thuriès and Las Planques to permit the
inhabitants to pick their grapes safely, or to protect them with men-at-arms.[9]
The next day the consuls received a copy of a letter written by the count of
Armagnac to the men of Las Planques requesting them not to damage Albi.[10]
This tends to show that the command of the two associated fortresses was at
that moment based at Las Planques and not at Thuriès. However, none of the
texts from Albi of the period 1382–4 associate Thuriès and Las Planques again
and both garrisons are treated separately, maybe indicating that they were no
longer under the same command.

There are no remains of a castle or a fortified building at the now-deserted
hamlet of Las Planques apart from its church which has, as its church tower,
a real keep, formerly fortified. We can suppose that a simple fortress existed
around the church's keep. In comparison, Thuriès was a real fortress situated
on a much more impressive site. It is set on the ridge of an extremely steep hill
overhanging the river Viaur. Its only weak point was the side facing towards the
nearby *bastide* of Pampelonne, where a tower still remains.[11]

According to Froissart, the Bascot de Mauléon was captain of Thuriès, and,
according to our list, he was captain of Las Planques. Records of the personal
names of *routiers* in locally available sources are quite unusual, even with regard
to captains. However, on 18 July 1384 the town records of Albi name a certain
Arnaut-Guilhamet de Lustrac as constable of Thuriès.[12] Another source gives

---

8   A. Vidal, 'Les Deliberations du Conseil Municipal d'Albi de 1372 à 1388', *Revue des langues romanes* 7 (1904), p. 556: 'dissero que I bon home ane a moss. lo duc dessus dig per explicar a luy los dampnatges que prendem per los Engles de Thuria e de las Plancas'.

9   Vidal, 'Les Deliberations' (1904), p. 557: 'Sobre aisso que dissero los senhors cossols que estat era tractat per la provesio que hom pogues reculhir las vendemias, que hom aja certas gens d'armas, ho fassa accordi am las gens de Turia e de las Plancas, en tal manieira que hom puesca reculhir las vendemias segur, e que per pagar aquo que costaria … Sus aquo totz tengro que per aver las dichas gens d'armas, o per far l'acordi am las dichas gens d'armas de Turia e de las Plancas, aquo que seria may aprofechable, hom meta sus las vendemias la emposicio desus dicha.'

10   Vidal, 'Les Deliberations' (1904), p. 558: 'que dissero los senhors cossols que els aviau agudas letras de moss. d'Armanhac que se endressavo a'n aquels de las Plancas e que los pregava que no nos volguesso donar dampnatge'.

11   Thuriès was, and still is, on the territory of Pampelonne. The castle was sometimes called Pampelonne instead of Thuriès.

12   Arnaut-Guilhamet de Lustrac was obviously a member of the family of the lords of Lustrac, in the Agenais, who became famous with Arnaut or Naudonnet de Lustrac who fought the 'English' in the fifteenth century on the French side. P. de La Plagne-Barris, 'Naudonnet de Lustrac', *Revue de Gascogne* 18 (1877), pp. 297–311, and G. Tholin, 'Notes sur deux seigneurs de Lustrac', *Revue de Gascogne* 18 (1877), pp. 493–7. A. Vidal, 'Les Délibérations', *Revue des langues romanes* 8 (1905), p. 434: 'avia reportat que *Arnaut Guilhamet de Lustrac, conestable de Thuria.* … Item, Domergo de la dicha garniso de Thuria…' (my italics).

Johan Portal as captain of this castle for the same year.[13] Another text dating from 1381 confirms that there existed in Thuriès a captain and a constable who were two different people.[14] This organisation corresponds to that known in other Anglo-Gascon *routier* garrisons of the same period, and to a hierarchy described in 1912 by Marcellin Boudet and recently, in more detail, by Nicolas Savy.[15] As our list of 1383–4 specified that Las Planques was kept by the men of the Bascot de Mauléon, it suggests that the Bascot was absent most of the time.

Thuriès had been besieged twice by French armies, first by Colard d'Estouteville, lord of Torcy, from 15 October 1380, just a few days after its capture by the *routiers*, to 1 February 1381; and secondly by the troops of the count of Armagnac from June 1383 to 18 September 1384, the date of a treaty of evacuation with the captain of Thuriès, Johan Portal. Portal apparently evacuated the castle of Thuriès around 15 October 1384. We can mention here that Gaston Fébus, count of Foix, sent some help and victuals to the garrison of Thuriès when it was besieged by his family's enemy, the count of Armagnac,[16] having already sent to the garrison of Thuriès a reinforcement of fifty men on 23 May 1381.[17] Therefore, the Bascot de Mauléon's arrival in Orthez in December 1388 was probably partly due to an ancient connection with Fébus, who, furthermore, warmly

[13] V. Challet, 'Mundare et auferre malas erbas: la révolte des Tuchins en Languedoc (1381–1384)', unpublished thesis, Université Paris I – Panthéon-Sorbonne, 2002, pp. 62 n. 76, 63. Information based on an account of the county of Rodez for 1383–4 (Archives Départmentales de l'Aveyron, Rodez, C 1336). I am grateful to Dominique Barrois for his help on this matter. Portal is a family name essentially found in Velay, Gévaudan and the surrounding regions.

[14] *Inventaire Sommaire des Archives Départementales Antérieures à 1790. Tarn-et-Garonne*, ed. M. Maisonobe (Montauban, 1910), pp. 318–19. A 307, 13 September 1381. An agreement between Johan II, count of Armagnac, and Ysarn Ebral, squire of Gaillac, about the possession of Castelnau de Montmirail: 'de la finansa de mil sinq cens franxs d'aur et de las drechuras que degh *al connestable* et portier *de Turia*, et de un marc d'argent que degh al clerc *del capitani de Turia* don soy prizonier [Ebral requests that the count of Armagnac] me fassa donar et aver licencia de P. de Campanha, Angles de Turia, mon maestre, de qui sou prizonier…' (my italics). His name suggests Pey de Campagne was a Gascon from the Landes. He was mentioned as an 'English' of the garrison of Valon (com. Lacroix-Barrez, arr. Rodez, c. Mur-de-Barrez, dép. Aveyron) in 1390. The count of Armagnac sent him to Jean de Blaisy, the French official in charge of the evacuation of the *routiers* fortresses, in order to guide him in the country in avoiding the English garrisons, *Documents historiques relatifs à la vicomté de Carlat*, ed. G. Saige and C. de. Dienne (Monaco, 1900), i, p. 382.

[15] M. Boudet, 'L'histoire d'un bandit méconnu. Bernard de Garlan dit le Méchant Bossu, capitaine d'Alleuze', *Revue de la Haute-Auvergne* 14 (1912), pp. 97–9, and N. Savy, *Villes en guerre. La défense des villes et des bourgs du Haut-Quercy pendant la guerre de Cent Ans* (Cahors, 2009), pp. 104–11.

[16] M.Cl. Compayré, *Etudes historiques et documents inédits sur l'Albigeois, le Castrais et l'ancien diocèse de Lavaur* (Albi, 1841), pp. 326–7, letter of Charles VI of France dated January 1384.

[17] F. Lehoux, *Jean de France, duc de Berri, sa vie, son action politique (1340–1416)*, 4 vols (Paris, 1966–8), ii, pp. 37–8.

welcomed him, according to Froissart.[18] However, that does not mean that the Bascot and his companions had no contact with the count of Armagnac. In fact, the complex tangle of relationships between the Anglo-Gascon *routiers* and the political powers of their period still needs to be investigated and clarified.

In checking the accounts of the counts of Armagnac for their county of Rodez during this period, several unambiguous mentions of the Bascot de Mauléon have been found. These greatly enhance information on him and on his circle of companions. Johan II, count of Armagnac, was then officially in charge of the evacuation of the *routier* garrisons in Rouergue and the neighbouring regions. However, these accounts show him paying pensions to some *routier* captains of the Anglo-Gascon party, these being *patis* or *suffertes* paid to them in order to spare the Armagnac domains in Rouergue and payments to obtain the evacuation of the occupied fortresses. The first mention of the Bascot de Mauléon in these accounts is an annual pension of 100 *livres tournois* for life granted between All Saints 1381 and All Saints 1382.[19] There the Bascot de Mauléon is named as *basco de Malleo*, Mallléo being the Languedocian version of the Gascon word Mauléon.

On 22 January 1383 an Arnaut-Guilhamet is mentioned as companion of the Bascot de Mauléon. He is obviously the Arnaut-Guilhaumet de Lustrac found as constable of Thuriès in 1384, a reference just after the first mention of the Bascot in these accounts as captain of Thuriès.[20] This information confirms that Froissart was right in asserting that the Bascot was the captain of the castle of Thuriès. Chronologically, the first mention of the Bascot de Mauléon as captain of Thuriès is in a receipt of the count of Armagnac dated 8 April 1382, which is followed by another receipt dated 29 April 1382.[21]

Two further receipts of the count of Armagnac, the first dated 30 April 1382 and the second 23 May 1383, indicate that a certain Amaniu Leuger (*Leugier*) was the companion of the Bascot de Mauléon, the latter being named captain de Thuriès in the first receipt.[22] In a receipt of 4 June 1384 we learn that Amaniu Leuger was captain of Las Planques and that the count paid him on 11 February of that year sixty francs to evacuate this place.[23] Clearly Amaniu Leuger was an associate of the Bascot de Mauléon and shared in his destiny, so when the

---

[18] *Chroniques de Jean Froissart*, ed. S. Luce et al., 15 vols (Paris, 1869–1975), xii, p. 96: 'je l'oy nommer et vey que le conte de Foeis et chascun li faisoit feste'.

[19] Arch. Dép. Aveyron, C 1335, fol. 172r.

[20] Arch. Dép. Aveyron, C 1335, fol. 177v. There is another mention of the Bascot de Mauléon as captain of Thuriès on fol. 178r.

[21] Arch. Dép. Aveyron, C 1335, fols 181r and 183r.

[22] Arch. Dép. Aveyron, C 1335, fol. 184v. and C 1336, fol. 29r. It is possible that the 'Amanieu Brengier' mentioned on 24 September 1382 as a member of the garrison of Thuriès in the proceedings of the commune of Albi is in fact 'Amanieu Leugier'. Vidal, 'Les Délibérations' (1905), p. 268.

[23] Arch. Dép. Aveyron, C 1336, fol. 83r.

same accounts mention the fact that Leuger was a member of the company of
the Borc de Galard, it is permissible to suppose that the Bascot was also under
the authority of the Borc de Galard.[24] In all probability, the Bascot de Mauléon
and his companions, Amaniu Leuger and Arnaut-Guilhamet de Lustrac, held
Thuriès and Las Planques under the authority of the Borc de Galard, captain of
Curvalle, situated in the same region of the Albigeois. Though historians often
consider the Borc de Galard as a distinct person from Perrot de Galard, who was
one of the most prominent leaders of the Anglo-Gascon *routiers* until his death
during the summer of 1384, there is a possibility that they were one and the
same person. This would easily explain his authority over these fortresses and
these men.[25] Finally, we learn of the existence of another cousin of the Bascot de
Mauléon, besides the one cited in Froissart's narrative, through a payment dated
4 September 1384 to a certain Arnauton de Saint-Estèphe.[26] All mentions of
the Bascot de Mauléon disappear from these accounts after this date, coinciding
with the evacuation of the castle of Thuriès in October 1384. It seems that the
Bascot de Mauléon left the region after this event. Perhaps the recent death of
Perrot de Galard could explain his move.

How do we explain that the Bascot asserted to Froissart that he still held the
castle of Thuriès in 1388, and that he hesitated to sell it to the count of Armagnac, the king of France's representative? Was he lying to Froissart? Was this
an invention by Froissart? The sources for Albigeois history are not as good for
the years around 1388 as they are for the early 1380s, and it is possible, therefore,
that the castle of Thuriès was retaken by *routiers* after 1384, as often happened
in the case of other similar castles. Furthermore, we do not know the fate of Las
Planques in 1384 and in the years following. Since the French administration of
the Albigeois noted on 15 June 1387 that the castle of Thuriès had been occupied
by the 'English' for about four years this is unlikely, however.[27] Perhaps Froissart
mixed up the account of the Bascot with that of his cousin Arnauton, called the
Bourc of Caupenne, also present when Froissart interviewed the Bascot. This
latter, whose expanded name was Gassie-Arnaut de Caupenne, had been captain
of the castle of Carlat, according to Froissart, but in 1388 the captain of this castle
was Ramon-Guilhem de Caupenne, who was probably his brother, called by
Froissart the Bourc Anglés (the 'English Bourc'). Ramon-Guilhem de Caupenne

---

[24] Arch. Dép. Aveyron, C 1336, fol. 100v, payment of 120 francs to Amaniu Leuger on 13 July
1384.

[25] For the funeral of Perrot de Galard at Rodez: Arch. Dép. Aveyron, Archives Communales
de Rodez-Bourg, CC 128, an account which mentions that more 'English' (in fact *routiers*)
than usual were admitted into Rodez because of the funeral. No mention of the Borc de
Galard after the death of Perrot de Galard has been found.

[26] Arch. Dép. Aveyron, C 1336, fol.104v.

[27] *Histoire générale de Languedoc*, ed. Dom Dévic et Vaissett, new edition by E. Rosach, A.
Molinier et al., 16 vols (Toulouse, 1874–1904, reprinted Osnabrück 1973), x, no. 695, col. 1727
(original: AN JJ 133, no. 104), 'propter occupationem castri regii de Turea [...] quod Anglici
per quatuor annos et ultra tenuerunt occupatum'.

was in 1388 negotiating with the count of Armagnac to evacuate Carlat, but Gassie-Arnaut, alias Arnauton, was closely associated with Ramon-Guilhem. In fact, in a list of hostages given by the *routiers* to the French authorities in 1390 in order to secure the delivery of the castle of Carlat and two other castles, Arnauton de Caupenne was listed first, before Ramon-Guilhem de Caupenne.[28]

The possibility of a lack of comprehension between Froissart and his inter-locutors is rarely mentioned. Yet it is a likely explanation of a certain number of errors found in Froissart's narrative concerning his journey to Béarn and his stay in Orthez. Froissart's mother tongue was Picard, one of the languages of *Oïl*, while the mother tongue of Espan du Lion, the Bascot de Mauléon or the Bourc de Caupenne was Gascon, one of the languages of *Oc*. It is very unlikely that Froissart learned even snatches of Gascon or of another language of *Oc*, and it is more plausible that the Gascons whom he met knew some French or another language of *Oïl* because they had travelled and stayed for some time in places, and among people, speaking a language of *Oïl*. It would not have been surprising, however, if misunderstandings between them and Froissart had occurred, espe-cially if the Gascons had difficulties in pronouncing the language of *Oïl*. Frois-sart was really impressed by the quality of the French spoken by Gaston Fébus, although his mother tongue was Gascon;[29] but Fébus was a prince and great noble, and his mastery of French might be expected to contrast with that of more modest people such as the Bascot de Mauléon, Arnauton de Caupenne or Espan du Lion.

Can the Bascot de Mauléon be found in other documents apart from our list and the count of Armagnac's accounts? In February 1365, in the accounts of Charles II, king of Navarre, a certain 'Bourc de Mauléon', said to be a squire of Louis de Navarre, lieutenant of his brother in France and Normandy, was compensated for the loss of a horse at Carentan in the Cotentin, Normandy, when it was retaken by the Navarrese troops.[30] He is mentioned again in December 1365 following the loss of another horse.[31] Of course, since this Mauléon is not

28 *Documents historiques relatifs à la vicomté de Carlat*, ed. Saige and Dienne, i, no. CLXXV, p. 345.
29 *Œuvres de Froissart*, ed. K. De Lettenhove, 25 vols in 26 (Brussells, 1867–77), xi, p. 85, Gaston Fébus spoke to Froissart 'non pas en son gascon, mais en bon et beau françois'.
30 *Le Compte des recettes et dépenses du roi de Navarre en France et en Normandie de 1367 à 1370*, ed. E. Izarn (Paris, 1885), p. 82: 'Restor de chevaulx […] Au *Bourt de Maulion*, par un mandement de l'abbé de Cherebourg et messire Jehan de Tilli, lieutenant de monseigneur messire Loys de Navarre, donné XVIIe jour de Fevrier CCCLXV, pour le restor d'un coursier qu'il avoit eu mort au service de monseigneur, quant la ville de Carenten fut recouvrée de la main des Bretons, et par quittance dudit Bourt du XXIIIIe jour dudit moiz, VIˣˣ francs' (my italics).
31 *Le Compte des Recettes*, ed. Izarn, p. 414: 'Retor de chevaux, sont prins en deux clauses pour avoir été payé à Machin de St Johan pour le *Bourt de Maulion*, escuyer de monseigneur Loys de Navarre, frère de monseigneur et son lieutenant pour lors, donné XIIIe jour de novembre CCCLXV, pour restor d'un cheval que le dit Machin avoit baillé au dit Bourt,

named 'Bascot' he could have been another person, but we have to bear in mind that one version of Froissart's *Chronicles*, distinct from all the other versions, names the Bascot de Mauléon as 'Bastard de Mauléon'.[32] The word 'bourc' used in the Navarrese accounts came from the medieval Gascon word 'borc', which also meant 'bastard', so it makes it likely that this 'bourc de Mauléon' is our Bascot.

Furthermore, according to Froissart, the Bascot served on the Navarrese side at the battle of Cocherel with the Captal de Buch and was among the *routiers* allied with the king of Navarre occupying the town of La Charité-sur-Loire from 29 October 1363.[33] The Bascot asserted to Froissart that he himself occupied the castle of Le Bec d'Allier, situated around thirty kilometres to the south of La Charité.[34] Between August and October 1364 Louis de Navarre led a Navarrese army from Navarre to Normandy, passing by La Charité-sur-Loire in September. From there he added some *routier* troops from La Charité and its surrounding area to his own army, and then advanced against Normandy.[35] In this context, the presence of the Bascot de Mauléon in Normandy with Louis de Navarre's army under the name Bourc de Mauléon would not be at all surprising. This use of different nicknames necessitates a short digression on the real meaning and use of names such as *bascot* or *bourc* among *routiers*.

The word *bourc*, written in medieval Gascon as *borc* or *bord*, meant in Gascon bastard: that is, an illegitimate son.[36] It has as its origin the medieval Latin word *burdo* or *burdum*, which meant a mule or a hinny. The French equivalents to this word were *bordon* or *bardot*, which meant a hinny: that is, a hybrid animal bred from a horse and a she-ass, while a mule was bred from a donkey and a mare. Hinnies are far rarer than mules and have the reputation of having neither the strength of a horse nor the robustness of a donkey, contrary to mules. Conse-

---

lequel Bourt a eu mort un des siens ou service de monseigneur en Caresme CCCLXIIII, duquel mandement le dit trésorier ne peut pas bonnement enseigner, et pour ce rent cy ce qu'il en prent par les II dictes clauses, c'est assavoir IIII[xx] fr' (my italics).

[32] BnF MSS Français 2650, the only manuscript of the so-called second redaction used by the *Société de l'histoire de France* for its publication of the third book of Froissart. I thank Godfried Croenen for this information. See G. Croenen, 'La Tradition manuscrite du troisième livre des *Chroniques* de Froissart', in *Froissart et la cour de Béarn. L'écrivain, les arts et le pouvoir* (Turnhout, 2008), pp. 15–59. *Chroniques*, ed. Luce et al, xii, p. 95: 'Là vey venir ung escuier gascon, qui s'appelloit le *Bastard de Maulion*', and p. 98: 'Lors resprist le *Bastart de Maulion* sa parole et dist...' (my italics).

[33] Arr. Cosne-Cours-sur-Loire, dép. Nièvre.

[34] Le Bec d'Allier, com. Cuffy, arr. Saint-Amand-Montrond, c. Guerche-sur-l'Aubois, dép. Cher.

[35] R. Delachenal, *Histoire de Charles V*, 5 vols (Paris 1909–31), iii, p. 141 and notes.

[36] See the new edition by V. Lespy and P. Raymond of *Dictionnaire Béarnais Ancien et Moderne*, ed. J. Lafitte (Pau, 1998), p. 88. The title of this dictionary is misleading as different forms of Gascon were and are spoken in Béarn and, furthermore, this dictionary is also based on Gascon medieval texts from outside Béarn. See also F. Mistral, *Trésor dou Félibrige*, I (Aix-en-Provence, Avignon and Paris, 1979), p. 307. The term *bort* had the same meaning in Catalan.

quently, hinnies were and are still considered as bad crossbreeding, so maybe *borc*
meant originally in Gascony a 'bad bastard', which would have been even more
pejorative than the already insulting name of bastard. But we can also interpret
this as describing the status of a bastard: as a hinny issued from a stallion and
a female donkey, the horse being far more appreciated than the donkey, the *borc*
probably issued from a father with a higher status than his mother, since the
father was usually noble. There also existed in Gascony the term *bordat*, which
was apparently synonymous with *borc*.[37] In France north of the Loire, *bourc* was
considered an imported term from the South as a letter of the Parlement of Paris
of 1411 suggests: '*bourc* which means in the language of the country beyond, boy,
gangster, bastard'.[38] So *bourc* was a nickname indicating a status and was not the
real forename of the person described, while most often, but not all the time, his
noble origins were shown by his family name following his nickname. Thus, for
example, the *bourc* de Lesparre meant the bastard issued from the noble family
of the lords of Lesparre.

The Gascon name *basco* means Basque in the Gascon language and is perhaps
the second most common nickname after *borc* among the Gascon *routiers* during
our period.[39] For instance, we can find a *routier* simply known as *lo Basco* or
lo Bascol, which is the same word in Languedocian, active in Quercy during
the 1370s but dead by 1381.[40] More interestingly, a certain Guilhem-Arnaut de
Mauléon is nicknamed *lo Basco* in a letter of Edward I to the mayor and jurats
of Bayonne dated 1289 where he advised them to keep him in their service.[41]
Another nickname was *basquin*: the Basquin d'Astis and the Basquin de Sault, as
well as a Basque de Mareuil and a Basque de Chalois, occur in the accounts of
the king of Navarre concerning France and Normandy.[42] These latter appear to
have been Gascons from Béarn and not from the neighbouring Basque country

37 *Dictionnaire Béarnais*, p. 88.
38 AN JJ 165, no. 219: 'Icelui Pierre appellast le suppliant arlot, tacain, *bourc*, qui vault autant a dire en langaige du pays de par dela, garçon, truant, bastart' (my italics). Of course, this meaning of 'truant' is a consequence of the reputation of the *bourcs* being *routiers* and probably did not originally exist. F. Godefroy, *Dictionnaire de l'ancienne langue française et de tous ses dialectes du IXe au XVe siècle* (Paris, 1880), p. 703.
39 'Basco' is pronounced 'bascou' in modern Gascon.
40 This information was kindly provided by Nicolas Savy. See Archives Municipales de Gourdon (dép. Lot), CC 20, f. 12v and BB 5, fols 5v and 11r.
41 *Rôles Gascons II, 1273–1290*, ed. C. Bémont (Paris, 1900), p. 408, no. 1323 ; and J. de Jaurgain, *La Vasconie* (Pau, 1902), ii, pp. 475–6.
42 *Le Compte des Recettes*, ed. Izarn, pp. 287–9: 'le Basquin Datiz [or d'Atiz]' (le Basquin d'Astis, in Béarn), pp. 279 and 289; 'le Basquin de Sault' (le Basquin de Sault[-de-Navailles], in Béarn), pp. 134 and 408; 'le Basque de Mareul [or Maroil]' (le Basque de Mareuil), 'Basco de Maruel' (whose real name was Johan de Sault), 1361, in *Documents des archives de la chambre des comptes de Navarre (1196–1384)*, ed. J.-A. Brutails (Paris, 1890), p. 74, n. 2); p. 69 'le Basque de Chalois' (whose real name was Garcias-Arnaud de Charrat, that is probably de Charras (com. Lucq-de-Béarn), 1359, in *Documents*, ed. Brutails).

within France.[43] We can say the same thing for the Basco de Luc (Lucq-de-Béarn) or the Basquin de Miossens appearing in the muster of the army of Gaston Fébus in 1376.[44] Not all these Bascos were from Béarn, however, as is shown by the example of a certain Bascon de Rieux, maybe from Comminges, present among the troops of Naudonnet de Lustrac in 1435.[45]

This raises the question of the origins of the persons bearing these nicknames and the meaning of such nicknames. We can use the example of Arnaud-Gassie de Got, illegitimate son of the vicomte of Lomagne and Auvillar of the same name, who was nicknamed *lo basco* in Gascon, *le bascle* in French and most often *lo bascul* (or *bascol*) in Languedocian because he was lord of Puyguilhem in Southern Périgord where a Languedocian dialect was, and is still, spoken. Sometimes he was also named as '*lo bascul* de Lomagne', underlining his patrimonial origins.[46] Obviously his father was not a Basque but a Gascon and, in fact, a brother of Pope Clement V. However, he was married to Miramonda I de Mauléon, heiress of the family of Mauléon, which possessed until 1261 the vicomté of Soule in the Basque country. It is very plausible that he fathered the Bascul by a Basque woman from Miramonda de Mauléon's retinue, hence his nickname. We can suggest that these nicknames were given to illegitimate sons who had a Basque woman as mother while their father was a Gascon or, in some cases, to illegitimate sons who had older Basque ancestry. We must remember that until a recent period offspring with mixed Gascon and Basque ancestry were poorly regarded in Gascony and were called '*charnegou*': that is, half-breed. It is possible that their Basque ancestry was strongly underlined in medieval Gascony as these men combined the double defect of being illegitimate sons and half-Basque. However, it is probable that there were also some people nicknamed *lo Basco* just because they were fully Basques, or were half-breed Basco-Gascons living in the Basque Country, as was *lo Basco* de Saint-Palais, called Urtubie,

---

[43] During the fourteenth and fifteenth century only this area was named *Bascos* or *terra de Bascos* by both Gascons and inhabitants of Navarre. So, when the latter crossed the pass of Roncevaux from Pampelona, they said they went *en Bascos*. The inhabitants of other Basque-speaking areas (now in Spain) were sometimes named *Bascos* when they were Basque speakers, which was not the case of all the population, thus the entire populations of each province were then named after their province's name: Guipuscoanos, Alaveses, Biscayenos and Navarres.

[44] *Archives historiques de la Gironde* 12 (1870), no. CCXXI, pp. 151, 229, 235 and 237. For the Basquin de Miossens, *Archives historiques de la Gironde* 12 (1870), no. CCXXI, pp. 240 and 273.

[45] La Plagne-Barris, 'Naudonnet de Lustrac', p. 304. Rieux-Volvestre (dép. Haute-Garonne). There are other places with this name in the communes of Villeneuve-de-Rivière (dép. Haute-Garonne), Samatan (dép. Gers), Orgueil, Albas and St-Antonin-Noble-Val (dép. Tarn-et-Garonne), in Sainte-Colombe, Saint-Seurin-sur-l'Isle and Doulezon (dép. Gironde), but there are none in the départements of Pyrénées-Atlantiques, Hautes-Pyrénées and Landes.

[46] Mentioned in the Gascon Rolls between 1327 and 1349.

present in the army of Gaston Fébus in 1376.[47] But it had to be a nickname given only by non-Basque people: it would have been nonsensical if Basque persons called someone 'the Basque' when they were as much Basque themselves!

The case of the Basco or Bascot de Mauléon is perhaps slightly different. According to our list and the accounts of the count of Armagnac, his nickname was *basco*, but according to Froissart it was *Bascot*. Again, we could consider that Froissart himself added a 't' at the end of the common nickname *basco*. But we can speculate that the author of our list and the clerks writing these accounts were used to hearing about persons with the nickname *basco*, particularly among *routiers*, and that they misunderstood this peculiar nickname. If we follow the Gascon habit with names, the suffix 'ot' (more rarely 'et', 'on' or 'at') was often added to forenames of the younger members of a family when another older member (or other members) had the same forename, which happened very often in noble and non-noble families.[48] Following this pattern, Johan became Johanot, Guilhem Guilhemot, Aymeric Aymerigot, Auger Augerot, Bertran Bertranot, Gassie Gassiot, Hélias Héliot, Huc Hugot, Jacmes Jacmot, and so on. These 'younger' members of the family often continued to use this form of their Christian names throughout their lives, alternating it – or not – with the more correct form. The nickname *bascot* would in fact be the nickname *basco* transformed with a suffix 'ot' like a forename. It suggests that it came about when the future Bascot was born, at which time another illegitimate son in his family may have existed, labelled as *basco*, so he received the nickname of *bascot* de Mauléon. After all, we have already found in 1289 a member of the Mauléon family, Guilhem-Arnaut de Mauléon, who was nicknamed as *lo Basco*, but the Bascot is for the time being the only person we know who seems to have been nicknamed *Bascot* (with a t) and not Basco. This form is plausible as we know, for instance, the nickname of the grandson of Gassie-Arnaut de Got, who was known as *Bascol*, lord of Puyguilhem. The grandson, brother of Bertran, lord of Puyguilhem in 1401, was called the *Bascolat* probably to distinguish him from his grandfather the *Bascol*.[49] From which family, then, did our Bascot come?

The Bascot told Froissart that his 'heritage' was in the Bordelais, a statement that has presumably puzzled many people who generally call him a Basque.[50] In fact, a Mauléon family is documented in the Bordelais from around the middle

---

47 *Archives historiques de la Gironde* 12 (1870), no. CXXXI, 168.

48 For these suffixes and their uses, M.F. Berganton, *Le Dérivé du nom individuel au Moyen Age en Béarn et en Bigorre. Usage officiel, suffixe et formations, anthroponymie de la Haute Gascogne Centrale* (Paris, 1977), pp. 141–2, 112, 136–7 and 98.

49 In TNA C 61/108, m. 25: 'Bertran [de Got], seigneur de Puch Guillem, et le Bascolat sien frere' (Westminster, 14 April 1401). They were grandsons of the Bascol, and sons of Bertran de Got, lord of Puyguilhem. The nickname *Bascolat* is also found in Bordeaux in 1459 with '*lo Bascolat deus Castanhs*', an inhabitant of the parish of Baurech (arr. Bordeaux, c. Créon, dép. Gironde), AD de la Gironde, H 738, fol. 6v.

50 *Chroniques*, ed. Luce et al, xii, p. 107: 'Si ai-ge tousjours tenu frontiere et fait guerre pour le roy d'Engleterre; car mon hiretaige sciet et gist en Bourdelois'.

of the fourteenth century. We find several ecclesiastical members of this family mentioned in the accounts of the archbishopric of Bordeaux, and originating, in all probability, from Lévignacq.[51] Lévignacq was situated in the 'Pays de Born', the most southerly part of the diocese of Bordeaux, which was an enclave totally surrounded by lands of the diocese of Dax and the seneschalcy of the Landes.[52] Furthermore, Lévignacq was at the southernmost point of this region, and in 1659 there was at Lit (now Lit-et-Mixe), situated just ten kilometres west of Lévignacq, a noble farm of Mauléon.[53] This Mauléon family was probably a cadet branch of the main Mauléon family that had held the vicomté of Soule in the Basque Country before 1261.[54] In that year the Lord Edward (later Edward I) forced Auger de Mauléon to give up his *vicomté* of Soule in exchange for the lordships of Marensin and Laharie, both lordships surrounding the Pays de Born. When Miramonda II de Mauléon, lady of Marensin, died c.1354, the Mauléons of the Pays de Born remained the only surviving branch of the Mauléon family in Anglo-Gascon Aquitaine.[55] So, the Bascot had almost certainly received this nickname because of the origins of his family in the Basque Country, though they had probably left the Basque Country around seventy years before his birth (c.1338). The Bascot himself was, however, a Gascon of the South Bordelais. Thus Froissart was almost certainly right to describe him as a 'Gascon squire'. Since by the time of the Bascot's birth his family was based on the borders between the Bordelais and the Landes, it is now understandable that he had ties

---

[51] *Archives historiques de la Gironde* 21 (1881): Arnaut de Mauléon, keeper of the seal of the Curia: 207 [1355]; Pey de Mauléon, keeper of the seal of the officiality: 292 [1355], 381 [1356]; Ramon de Mauléon, chamberlain of the cardinal of Montesquieu: 222 [March 1355], 236 [after 25 April 1356]; Per-Arnaut de Mauléon, priest, keeper of the seal of the archbishopric, 1354–58, 172, 187, 249, 264, 314, 351, 386, 423, 432, 460, 474, 641; chaplain of Mimizan, 1361–2, *Archives historiques de la Gironde* 21 (1881), 661, 668. Notes of Léo Drouyn on this family of Mauléon in *Archives historiques de la Gironde* 22 (1882), 683: 'Les de Mauléon étaient probablement de la paroisse de Lévignac dans l'archiprêtré de Born. Mre. Pierre Arnaud de Mauléon était scelleur de la cour de l'officialité en 1355; il paya des arrérages, en 1354, au nom du curé de Lévignac, des Prêcheurs de Bayonne et de Comtor de Montausier. Il se trouve au nombre des bénéficiers invités à dîner à l'archevêché lors de la tenue du synode d'octobre 1361. Mre Raymond de Mauléon, ancien valet de chambre du cardinal de Montesquiou, vint à l'archevêché en 1355.' Com. Lévignacq, arr. Dax, c. Castets, dép. Landes.

[52] Now in dép. Landes.

[53] Arch. Dép. des Landes, 2 F 1750. Seizure of the noble goods of Mauléon on 2 January 1659. The noble farm of Mauléon and Capdet is now known as Pavillon landais or maison Fabas. I am grateful to Jacques de Cauna for this important information. Com. Lit-et-Mixe, arr. Dax c. Castets, dép. Landes. Lit was in Marensin on the borders with the 'Pays de Born'.

[54] The castle which was the centre of this vicomté was Mauléon (now Mauléon-Licharre, arr. Oloron-Ste-Marie, ch.l. c., dép. Pyrénées Atlantiques), hence the name of this family. See their (incomplete) genealogy in Jaurgain, *La Vasconie*, ii, pp. 476–88.

[55] There was also another branch of the Mauléon which had separated from the main branch in the early twelfth century: the Mauléon-Barousse, lords of Mauléon-Barousse (dép. Hautes-Pyrénées). There is also the locality of Mauléon-d'Armagnac (dép. Gers).

with Landais noble families like the lords of Caupenne.[56] It could be supposed
that the Bascot de Mauléon himself was a member of the Caupenne family, as
some of its members were captains of the castle of Mauléon for the kings-dukes.
However, the dates at which they held this office do not match the approximate
birth date of the Bascot we can conjecture according to Froissart (c.1338) and the
period of his childhood when the nickname of 'Bascot de Mauléon' could have
been given to him. Thus, when Arnauton, Bourc de Caupenne, is called a cousin
of the Bascot by Froissart, we do not need to doubt this fact.

Other individuals with the name of Mauléon can be found in the Gascon
Rolls and the Gascon petitions, and are probably to be related to the Mauléons
of the 'Pays de Born'. Thus, we know the existence of an Arnaut-Guilhem de
Mauléon, who had been provost of Bazas for the king-duke at the beginning of
the fourteenth century, and of Johan de Mauléon, called Moneder, mentioned in
Anglo-Gascon sources between 1326 and 1332.[57] The latter is implicitly connected
to the elder branch of the Mauléon, as he requested the king-duke to allocate
him the wages owed to him on the Landais lands of Marensin and Laharie
which had been granted in 1261 to Auger de Mauléon, former vicomte of Soule.[58]

The data discussed here supports the narrative of Froissart and tends to
demonstrate that he really met the Bascot de Mauléon at the inn of the Moon
in Orthez. But we still do not know the real forename of the Bascot, and we need
to locate him in sources where his nicknames of Bascot or Bourc are not specified. Contrary to what is usually believed, *routier* captains were not systematically
recorded with their nicknames, when they had one, in contemporary documentation. Gassie-Arnaut de Caupenne and Ramon-Guilhem de Caupenne, for
example, who were both captains of Carlat, never had their nicknames of *Bourc*
written into the treaties to evacuate the fortress of Carlat in which they were
involved. Similarly, when Ramon-Guilhem de Caupenne appears in the registers
of the commune of Saint-Flour he is never identified by his nickname of *bourc*,
yet he was so named by King Richard II in 1393[59] and was called 'the Bourc

---

56 Bidau de Caupenne was captain of the castle of Mauléon c.1268–88, then his nephew
Hélies, lord of Caupenne, between 1289 and 1295 and the great grandson of this latter, Ramon-
Guilhem II, lord of Caupenne, between 1350 and c.1390. This office probably created family
links between the families of Caupenne and Mauléon. J. de Jaurgain, 'Les capitaines châtelains
de Mauléon, gouverneurs de la vicomté de Soule', *Revue de Béarn, Navarre et Lannes* 2 (1884),
pp. 116–17, 124–7; and J. de Cauna, *Cadets de Gascogne. La maison de Marsan de Cauna*, 2 vols
(Pau, 2004), ii, pp. 120–21 and 123–4.

57 The petitions of Arnaut-Guilhem de Mauléon are in BL Cotton MS, Caligula D III, nos
11 and 12 and TNA SC 8/278/13862.

58 TNA SC 8/281/14031 (reply in C 61/41, m. 6, 20 August 1329) and SC 8/63/3127 (reply
in C 61/44, m. 5, 10 September 1332).

59 TNA C 61/103, m. 2 (11 June 1393): 'Rex dilectis et fidelibus suis Galhardo de Durfort,
domino de Duras et de Blankefort, Johanni Trailly, maiori Burdegale, Willelmo Elmham,
chivaler, et *Reymundo Guylliam de Caupen dicto Bourt*' (my italics) and m. 1: '*Reymond
Guilliam de Caupen dit Bourt*' (my italics), the latter document being published in *Foedera*,

anglés' when he was received as burgess of Bordeaux in 1406.[60] We can also point to Perrot de Fontans alias Perrot the Béarnais, captain of Châlucet, who introduced himself in a document he issued himself by his real name, 'forgetting' to mention his nickname. Clearly, the use of such nicknames was not always deemed appropriate.[61]

In fact, we have found a Mauléon who was a *routier* captain and was active in the same year that the Bascot met Froissart at Orthez. It is a certain Galhardet de Mauléon, who was closely associated with another *routier* captain named Vita de Blois who was active during the years 1387–8 in the county of Provence. The context there was highly favourable to *routiers* in these years, as the county of Provence witnessed a war of succession between the Valois dukes of Anjou and the kings of Naples from the Capetian Durrazzo branch. As is well known, the count of Savoy, Amédéus VII, took advantage of this situation to annex Nice and some other eastern Provençal lands to his domains in 1388.[62] On 25 October 1388 he bought the castle of Gattières for 2000 gold florins from 'the noble squire Galhardet de Mauléon from the regions of Gascony', who had previously taken it from its legitimate owner, the bishop of Vence, in 1384.[63] It appears that this Galhardet de Mauléon secretly acted there on behalf of the count of Savoy, as there is a receipt from February 1389 showing that fifteen gold florins were paid for the expenses that Galhardet had incurred during a stay in Chambéry, the capital of the counts of Savoy. It is curious to notice that this Galhardet de Mauléon appears at Gattières in 1384, the same year the Bascot de Mauléon disappears from the Albigeois.

In 1396 a certain Alégret de Mauléon was captain and bailiff of Barcelonnette, a Provençal town united to Savoy in 1388, at the same time as Nice. He was said to be nephew of Denis de Vaugrigneuse, vice-seneschal of the lands of Provence annexed by the count of Savoy.[64] This Alégret de Mauléon is usually considered to be the same person as Galhardet de Mauléon, but he could also be a relative

---

Conventiones, Literae et Cujuscunque Generis Acta Publica inter Reges Angliae et alios, ed. T. Rymer, 20 volumes (London, 1704–35), vii, p. 747.

[60] *Registres de la Jurade. Délibérations de 1406 à 1409. Archives municipales de Bordeaux* (Bordeaux, 1873), p. 14 (7 August 1406): 'fo recebut en borgues de la bila *Ramon-Guilhem de Caupena apperat lo Borc angles*' (my italics).

[61] M. d'Abzac de la Douze, 'Quittance de Pierre de Fontaines, capitaine de Chalusset, à Elie La Roque, 3 septembre 1393', *Bulletin de la société historique et archéologique du Périgord* 13 (1886), p. 185. Castle of Châlucet, in com. St-Jean-Ligoure, arr. Limoges, c. Pierre-Buffière, dép. Haute-Vienne.

[62] See '1388, la dédition de Nice à la Savoie', *Actes du colloque international de Nice, septembre 1988* (Paris, 1990).

[63] J.-A. Durbec, 'Le Chanan et ses environs, aux confins des Alpes Maritimes et de la Haute Provence. Première partie: l'Antiquité et le Moyen Age', *Annales de la société scientifique et littéraire de Cannes et de l'arrondissement de Grasse Cannes* 30 (1983), pp. 30–31.

[64] E. Caïs de Pierlas, *La ville de Nice pendant le premier siècle de la domination des princes de Savoie* (Turino, 1898), p. 42 nn. 2–6. Com. Barcelonnette, dép. Alpes-de-Haute-Provence.

or perhaps even his son. We can underline here that Alégret is again a nickname, meaning in Gascon 'perky' or 'cheerful', not a real Christian name, and therefore it is possible that he could be the same person as Galhardet de Mauléon.[65] The implication is that Galhardet de Mauléon had settled in the domains of the count of Savoy. Of course, nothing formally proves that this Galhardet de Mauléon is our Bascot de Mauléon. He is, however, the only Gascon *routier* with the name of Mauléon we have found active in 1388 and it seems he followed the same path as the Bascot in taking the castle of Gattières as the Bascot had taken Thuriès.[66] The Bascot also said to Froissart that he did not want to talk to him about some of his adventures,[67] so we can suspect he had some recent business in mind that had to be kept secret, as was the sale of Gattières to the count of Savoy by Galhardet de Mauléon. The association of the counts of Savoy with Gascon *routiers* can be traced back to 1380, when Amédéus VI, at war against Edouard, lord of Beaujeu, secretly sent a certain *damoiseau* named Sibuet de Briord to Gascony to make 'certain treaties and agreements with the counts of Foix and Comminges, with other barons of the said land of Gascony, and also with some captains of companies'.[68] To conclude on this matter, it is curious to find that the only French *département* where the family name Bascot is present in the period 1891 and 1915, the oldest systematically recorded period for French family names, is precisely the département of Savoie.[69]

As we now know that the Bascot de Mauléon was a real person, I think we cannot find any realistic reason to deny that he met, and was interviewed by, Froissart in the inn of the Moon at Orthez in December 1388. Of course, that does not mean that everything in the Bascot's testimony reported in Froissart is totally accurate. I have suggested that Froissart's understanding was possibly impaired by differences of language between him and the Bascot. Nevertheless, if some inaccuracies may still be found in the Bascot's account that does not condemn it as a whole, especially as other details mentioned by the Bascot

---

[65] Alégret was the nickname of a twelfth-century Gascon troubadour whose real name is unknown, like those of his compatriots Marcabru and Cercamon. Alégret became a family name.

[66] We have to mention Pèr-Arnaut de Mauléon, called 'Le Gallois', who fought on the Navarrese side in the Anglo-Gascon army led by Thomas Trivet in the war against Castile in 1378. He was paid by Charles II of Navarre in 1379. B. Leroy, 'D'un règne à l'autre: politique et diplomatie des souverains de Navarre dans les années 1380–1390', *Principe de Viana* 46 (1985), p. 726 n. 9. His nickname 'Le Gallois' shows he is not the Bascot, but its derivation is unclear.

[67] *Chroniques*, ed. Luce et al, xii, p. 109: 'J'ay encore eu assez plus d'aventures que ne vous ay dis, desquelles je ne puis ne ne vueil pas de toutes parler'.

[68] J. Cordey, *Les Comtes de Savoie et les rois de France pendant la guerre de Cent Ans (1329–1391)* (Paris, 1911), p. 235 n. 2: 'tractando de mandato domini certa pacta et conventiones cum dominis comitibus de Fuys et de Cuminges et aliis baronibus dicte terre Gasconie et etiam cum aliquibus capitaneis societatum'.

[69] See http://www.geopatronyme.com/cgi-bin/carte/nomcarte.cgi?nom=bascot&submit=-Valider&client=cdip.

about his own life are confirmed by other historical sources. The stories he told to Froissart are still invaluable for historians as they describe many important military events from the second half of the fourteenth century from the point of view of a *routier* captain, not from that of an outsider. Of course, historians have to be cautious with narrative sources like Froissart's chronicles, but being systematically hyper-critical may lead us to forget that Froissart gives us much valuable information we simply would not know without him. Nor would our understanding of the Hundred Years War before 1400 be so lively without Froissart's account!

Addendum

After the completion of this article, another reference of the Bascot de Mauléon was found in M. Ménard, *Histoire de la ville de Nismes*, 3 (Paris, 1752), p. 52. In this well documented work we learn that there was a conflict between Tetbaut, lord of Budos (cant. Podensac, arr. Bordeaux, dép. Gironde) and Portes (cant. Génolhac, arr. Alès, dép. Gard) and Ramon VIII, vicomte of Turenne, about the possession of this barony of Portes (on this conflict, see Jean-Bernard Elzière, *Histoire des Budos* (Portes, 1978), pp. 49–51). Some of Turenne's men, the bastard and the lord of Cailar (com. le Cailar, cant. Rhôny-Vidourle, arr. Nîmes, dép. Gard), made a treaty in 1384 with Bertran, lord of Montferrand (com. St-Louis-de-Montferrand, cant. Lormont, arr. Bordeaux, dép. Gironde), a captain of the English party who was then in Gascony, through Bernat Foulc, a noble from Posquières (now called Vauvert, ch.-l. cant., arr. Nîmes, dép. Gard). They had an examination carried out of the castle of Portes by the bastard de Mauléon, who asserted that it was possible to take the castle by assault. But this scheme came to nothing. This information fits completely with what we know of the Bascot de Mauléon. We know that he left the Albigeois in 1384, and that a Galhardet de Mauléon took the castle of Gattières in Provence the same year. Furthermore, we know that the vicomte of Turenne conducted a war in Provence with *routier* troops from 1384 onwards. It seems that the Bascot de Mauléon, under the name of Galhardet de Mauléon, followed him, starting a new phase of his career in Provence.

9

The English Reversal of Fortunes in the 1370s and the Experience of Prisoners of War

RÉMY AMBÜHL

In the debate over the costs of the Hundred Years War, Postan famously considered that until a complete tally of prisoners (and ransoms) on both sides had been compiled we should consider profits and losses to be in balance.[1] McFarlane and M.K. Jones did not share this opinion. According to them, the balance was undoubtedly highly favourable to the English.[2] Adding to the debate, however, M.C.E. Jones carefully remarked that the misfortunes of English prisoners in the 1370s remain relatively obscure.[3] Building on this comment, the purpose of this essay is to explore the fate of English (and English-obedient Gascon) prisoners of war during this period of French recovery. To what extent did they suffer from the reversal of fortunes in the 1370s? There is some clear evidence of English prisoners in trouble during this decade, which will be presented in the first part of this essay. However, the close scrutiny of various well-documented individual

---

[1]   M.M. Postan, 'The Cost of the Hundred Years War', *Past and Present* 27 (1969), p. 49.

[2]   'But one has only to begin looking into the periods of English retreat after 1369 and 1429 to realise how overwhelmingly French gains then were outweighed by French losses earlier in terms of financial advantage. As for the pitched battles, the English did not lose at Baugé what they had won at Agincourt, nor at Jargeau, Patay and Castillon the rich harvest of Verneuil': K.B. McFarlane, 'War, the Economy and Social Changes. England and the Hundred Years War', *Past and Present* 22 (1962), p. 10; see also idem, *The Nobility of Later Medieval England* (Oxford, 1973), pp. 127–8. M.K. Jones agreed with the opinion that 'the possibilities of success far outweighed the risks', but he acknowledged that 'as the war entered its last stages men became aware of the catastrophic effect that imprisonment and ransom could have on the fortunes of the families of English soldiers': M.K. Jones, 'Ransom Brokerage in the Fifteenth Century', in *Guerre et société en France, en Angleterre et en Bourgogne, XIVe–XVe siècle*, ed. P. Contamine, et al. (Lille, 1991), pp. 222, 225.

[3]   M.C.E. Jones, 'The Fortunes of War: The Military Career of John, Second Lord Bourchier (d. 1400)', *Essex Archaeology and History* 26 (1995), translated as 'Fortunes et malheurs de guerre. Autour de la rançon du chevalier anglais Jean Bourchier (†1400)', in *La guerre, la violence et les gens au Moyen Age. I: Guerre et violence*, ed. P. Contamine and O. Guyotjeannin (Paris, 1996), pp. 189–208.

cases slowly shifted my focus from the debate on the extent of this reversal of
fortunes and its impact on the issue of prisoners of war to the factors involved in
the ransoming of these prisoners. These factors will be examined in the following
two parts of this paper, in which I will investigate and assess the involvement
of the crown and the warrior community in the liberation of prisoners. How
particular was the context of the 1370s for the fate of English and Gascon prisoners? This last question will be addressed in the conclusion.

Signs of reversal

The following three cases involving prisoners of war vary in time, scale and
depth. Taken together, they vividly illustrate the difficulties encountered by the
English during the French reconquest in the 1370s.

Alan Buxhill's accountancy for the first six months of his appointment as
captain of the fortress of Saint-Sauveur-le-Vicomte (Normandy) shows early
signs of the English reversal of fortunes in 1370–71.[4] Buxhill's expenses were
greatly inflated by the mass of men-at-arms, archers and other Englishmen who
had been expelled from different Norman castles and towns,[5] and who took
refuge in Saint-Sauveur.[6] The refugees arrived there in two waves, on 15 February
and 25 March 1371. In Buxhill's first account, covering the first two and a half
months of his captaincy, from 1 December 1370 to 15 February 1371, he claimed
to have spent 3,034 francs 'for the payment of the ransoms of several bankrupt
prisoners who had been captured by the French on different occasions'.[7] Some
of these prisoners may have been in the first wave of refugees. Interestingly, the
second wave included William Nevill, John Clanvow and Edmund Daumarle.
These three knights had been captured at the battle of Pontvallain, which had
been fought just a few months before, on 4 December 1370.[8] Therefore, it is

---

[4]   K.A. Fowler, *Medieval Mercenaries. I: The Great Companies* (Oxford, 2001), p. 297 and
n. 64, drew attention to these pieces of accountancy preserved in the National Archives. He
consulted TNA E 101/30/38 and 39. The account referenced E 101/30/38 runs over the whole
six months of Buxhill's captaincy, from 1 December 1370 to 3 June 1371, while E 101/30/39
includes just the first two and a half months, from 1 December 1370 to 15 February 1371. There
is a third piece of accountancy, E 101/31/18, which directly follows E 101/30/39, including the
last three and a half months, from 15 February to 3 June 1371.

[5]   Namely, Tinchebray, Gavray and Mortain.

[6]   These English retreats most probably resulted from a confrontation with the troops of the
French constable Bertrand Du Guesclin, whose presence in Lower-Normandy in April–May
1371 is testified in the sources. The Constable and his men were in Saint-Lô, Dreux and
Pontorson in April–May 1371. *Letters, Orders and Musters of Bertrand Du Guesclin, 1357–1380*,
ed. M.C.E. Jones (Woodbridge, 2004), pp. xxvii, xlix, nos 398–400, 403.

[7]   '...diversis solucionibus per ipsum factis pro redemcionibus diversorum prisionarium
impotencium qui in servicio regis per inimicos Franciae per dives vices capti fuerunt': TNA
E 101/30/39. These expenses are also mentioned in E 101/30/38.

[8]   *Chroniques de Jean Froissart*, ed. S. Luce et al., 15 vols (Paris, 1869–1975), viii, p. vii, n. 2;

probably not going too far to assume that the forty-seven men who arrived at Saint-Sauveur under their command were prisoners too, as well as the other nine men-at-arms and three archers who arrived the very same day.[9]

The situation had certainly not improved by the time of the Good Parliament in April 1376. It was then that the commons of England endorsed an alarming petition in which they prayed the king to come to the aid of numerous English soldiers who had been taken prisoner by the enemy and could not afford their ransom.[10] Such a petition presented by the commons and seeking assistance for a large number of prisoners is unique in the Hundred Years War and needs to be put in context. First, the parliament had not met during the two previous calendar years.[11] This unusual fact may partly explain the singularity of this larger-scale appeal to the crown, many prisoners having been captured in the meantime. Secondly, it is interesting to note that the commons of the Good Parliament were composed of a majority of knights who were militarily active.[12] The promotion of their own interests was hardly disguised, as their petition concerned, in particular, soldiers of high renown, held by the enemy to be 'of great estate'.[13] Eight soldiers are named in the document, all of them knights.[14] Sir Thomas Fogg was one of them and this is significant, for he had had his first appointment as a knight of the shire at the time of the Good Parliament.[15] This was no coincidence; the petition was most probably his own initiative. Fogg tried to obtain assistance for himself and his friends. Nevertheless, the commons' endorsement shows that the more general issue of prisoners raised conscience, interest and need for action amongst the parliamentary class.

On an individual level, the case of Geoffrey Worsley is probably the closest example that we can find to illustrate a reversal of fortunes. The Lancastrian

---

Chronique normande du XIVe siècle (1294–1376), ed. A. and E. Molinier (Paris, 1882), p. 197; *The Anonimalle Chronicle, 1331–1381*, ed. V.H. Galbraith (Manchester, 1927), p. 64; Cuvelier, *Chronique de Bertrand du Guesclin*, ed. E. Charrière, 2 vols (Paris, 1839), ii, pp. 484–6; Fowler, *Medieval Mercenaries*, pp. 294–5.

9   The men-at-arms were Robert FitzRauf, John Ceggeshale, John de *Seinlee*, Richard Gorleye, William Rokwell, John Sankrell, Alan Ohmaler, John Parkerell and Aleyn de la Chivalerye.

10   *PROME*, v, pp. 344–5, item 129.

11   W.M. Ormrod, 'Parliament of April 1376, Introduction', *PROME*, v, pp. 289–94.

12   J. Sumption, *The Hundred Years War. III: Divided Houses* (London, 2009), pp. 255–6.

13   On the promotion of the parliamentary class's own interests, see G. Dodd, *Justice and Grace. Private Petitioning and the English Parliament in the Late Middle Ages* (Oxford, 2007), pp. 148, 150.

14   Sir Matthew Gournay, Sir Matthew Redman, Sir Thomas Fogg, Sir John Harpenden, Sir Gregory Sais, Sir Geoffrey Worsley, Sir Robert Twyford and Sir John Bourchier.

15   Fogg had been taken prisoner during Lancaster's *chevauchée* in France in 1373. He may have been a prisoner a second time in 1375, but regained his freedom that same year. The petition suggests that a part of or his whole ransom had remained unpaid. *Anonimalle Chronicle, 1331–1381*, ed. Galbraith, pp. 63–4; *The History of Parliament. The House of Commons, 1386–1421*, ed. J.S. Roskell, L. Clark and C. Rawcliffe, 4 vols (Stroud, 1992), iii, pp. 95–7.

knight is supposed to have reaped handsome profits during the 1360s which were swallowed by his trials and tribulations in the next decade. The story of his rise and fall is recounted in a petition of the commons on his behalf in around 1381,[16] which is corroborated and followed up by other sources. To summarise, Worsley is said to have long served Edward III, the Prince of Wales and Richard II in their wars in France. We also know that he was leader of a free company in the 1360s and is meant to have made considerable profits during that period.[17] However, fortune did not always smile on him. The commons claimed that Worsley had often been captured during the war. There is evidence, for instance, that he was one of the prisoners of Pontvallain in 1370.[18] He had regained his freedom by 1375, when he served in Brittany.[19] His mention as a prisoner in the Good Parliament's petition may suggest that he had been again captured at that time.[20] According to the commons, his several ransoms considerably burdened his finances and, as he had never received any grant, he was seriously in debt at the time of the petition. His disastrous financial situation is substantiated by other sources. He was forced to borrow heavily and parts of his estates were eventually sequestrated and awarded to his creditors.[21]

The petition also refers to Worsley's marriage with Mary Felton, one of the daughters and heirs of the distinguished soldier and administrator, Sir Thomas Felton,[22] in 1376, which marked an improvement both socially and financially for him. On this level too, however, the hopes of the unfortunate knight eventually fell and the disastrous epilogue of their divorce was, in fact, at the core of this petition.[23] During his service in France Worsley had entrusted his wife to the care of Thomas Pulle, who had abused his trust and induced her to seek

[16] TNA SC 8/103/5109 (c.1381). The great council of Reading which is mentioned in the petition is very likely to be that which met at Reading in August 1381; A. Goodman, 'Richard II's Councils', in *Richard II. The Art of Kingship*, ed. A Goodman and J. Gillepsie (Oxford, 1999), p. 77.

[17] Fowler, *Medieval Mercenaries*, pp. 18, 235.

[18] *Chroniques*, ed. Luce et al., viii, p. 4.

[19] He received several letters of attorney on 8 January 1373, 8 January 1374 and 14 September 1374 while in France. However, it is not specified whether or not he was prisoner of the enemy: TNA C 76/56, mm. 33, 57, mm. 4, 12.

[20] There is, however, no firm evidence of this and we know, on the other hand, that he was at large in May 1376, when he was commissioned by the king to arrest a confederacy of felons in the county of Derby: CPR 1374–7, p. 320 (20 May 1376).

[21] TNA PL 14/154/3, nos 33, 34; CP 40/462, m. 98; quoted in S. Walker, *The Lancastrian Affinity, 1361–1399* (Oxford, 1990), p. 75.

[22] For Thomas Felton, see P. Morgan, 'Sir Thomas Felton (d. 1381), soldier and administrator' [http://www.oxforddnb.com/view/article/9275], in O.D.N.B., online ed., 2006. The (unsubstantiated) date of the marriage is provided in W.G. Davis, *The Ancestry of Mary Isaac, c.1549–1613, Wife of Thomas Appleton of Little Waldingfield, co. Suffolk, and Mother of Samuel Appleton of Ipswich* (Portland, ME., 1955), p. 315.

[23] Davis provides curious details about their divorce on the ground of bigamy: *Ancestry of Mary Isaac*, p. 316.

a divorce. Worsley and Pulle met afterwards at the great council in Reading in August 1381 and, after strong words came to blows, Thomas was wounded. He died, later on, and Pulle's friends tried to make Worsley responsible. The commons, however, claimed that Pulle had recovered from his wounds, as it appeared to many, for he had been seen horse riding and had married Mary Felton. For all these reasons the commons asked the king to grant his pardon to Worsley. Interestingly, the latter's several misfortunes did not prevent him from being active in the late 1370s and the beginning of the 1380s.[24]

Worsley's misfortunes were, however, not necessarily the norm. The most detailed cases in the sources, which inevitably concern higher-ranking soldiers, offer a large variety of fates. Some prisoners, such as Simon Burley, knew a relatively long period of captivity and possibly hard conditions of detention.[25] On the other hand, the capture and ransom of some others seem to have been a bracket in their long career at the service of the crown, as was the case for Matthew Gournay.[26] It is not even uncommon to see captives, such as John Cresswell and John Devereux, released almost on the spot, or within a few months.[27] Beyond all their difficulties, many prisoners show this remarkable capacity to recover and rearm, sometimes even after several captures.[28] These observations urge the need to investigate different ways of regaining freedom and the factors involved in this process.

[24] Walker sees the signs of a decline in Worsley's career after 1376 as that 'an increasing amount of his time was spent on the unglamorous, and hardly lucrative, business of garrison duty', but these signs are far from obvious. Worsley was lieutenant of the Channel Islands in 1377. He bore the title of 'warden of Guernsey and of the castle Cornet'. He participated in Buckingham's expedition in 1380. The duke of Lancaster first retained him in August 1381. Worsley was also acting as Thomas Holland's lieutenant at Cherbourg in 1379 and just before his death in 1385: J. Le Patourel, *The Medieval Administration of the Channel Islands, 1199–1399* (London, 1937), p. 64. According to this indenture of service, he received for himself and his esquires £20 a year both in time of peace and war: *John of Gaunt's Register, 1372–1383*, ed. E.C. Lodge and R. Somerville, 2 vols, Camden Soc., 3rd ser., 56–7 (1937), nos 38 (1 Aug. 1381), 581 (2 Aug. 1381), 799 (24 Jan. 1383); Walker, *Lancastrian Affinity*, p. 75.

[25] The trials and tribulations of the capture and captivity of the English knight Simon Burley are described in P.-C. Timbal et al., *La Guerre de Cent Ans vue à travers les registres du Parlement, 1337–1369* (Paris, 1961), pp. 322–9. He was eventually ransomed in 1373: TNA C 76/56, m. 33 (18 Feb. 1373).

[26] About this capture in the 1350s and 1360s, see TNA SC 8/103/5114; 113/5629. He was again captured in 1373: *Anonimalle Chronicle, 1331–1381*, ed. Galbraith, p. 73. For his long career, see M.C.E. Jones, 'Sir Matthew Gournay [Gourney] (d.1406), soldier', in *ODNB*.

[27] Their case will be discussed later.

[28] See the case of Matthew Redman, who had been captured twice in the 1370s: *Anonimalle Chronicle, 1331–1381*, ed. Galbraith, pp. 64, 73. See also the petitions of Gournay (three times), Jean Jodrell (several times), Guillaume de Balansac (twice). The record is held by the Gascon knight Bernard Montet, whose grant in 1383 specifies that he had been taken prisoner six times: TNA SC 8/118/5878 (*c*.1372–*c*.1377); 34/1655 (*c*.1375); C 61/96, m. 15 (23 Aug. 1383).

The Crown's Assistance

A case study: John Harpenden and the prisoners in Castile

John Harpenden was one of the many prisoners taken by the Castilians at the battle of La Rochelle in June 1372.[29] He was taken to Castile and handed over to King Henry II.[30] Several petitions at the beginning of the reign of Richard II reveal that Harpenden's fate was then closely linked with that of Alfonso of Aragon, the son and hostage of the count of Denia, who had been captured by the English at the battle of Nájera, in 1367.[31] A project of exchange dating back to the last years of Edward III had seemingly been agreed by the king and his council but not carried out, according to the Gascon lord Florimont de Lesparre, Harpenden, and several other knights who were prisoners in Spain.[32] Lesparre had been captured during the Anglo-Franco-Castilian truces toward the end of 1375.[33] He himself, as well as his friends, family and servants, seem to have been particularly proactive in the process of petitioning the authorities.[34] However, the intricate entanglements of private interests in the ransom business of the count of Denia prevented any quick move.

In December 1380 Richard II sealed an agreement with Guy Bryan and John Shakel in which he sold his rights over Denia's ransom (which included the rights of various other claimants) to John Shakel, who would enjoy the whole

---

[29] *Chroniques*, ed. Luce et al., viii, pp. 42, 299. About Harpenden, his wife and Anglo-French progeny, see the biographical note in *Recueil des documents concernant le Poitou contenus dans les registres de la chancellerie de France. V: 1376–1390*, ed. P. Guérin (Poitiers, 1888–91), pp. 203–6; and G. Dupont-Ferrier, *Gallia Regia, ou Etat des officiers royaux des bailliages et des sénéchaussées de 1328 à 1515*, 7 vols (Paris, 1942–65), v, pp. 289–91, 299, 349, nos 20080, 20090, 20117 and 20454.

[30] His presence in the Castilian prison, together with 6 other English knights and 16 esquires, in 1377, is reported in *Anonimalle Chronicle, 1331–1381*, ed. Galbraith, pp. 115–16. His surrender to the king is mentioned in Rabanis, 'Notice sur Florimont de Lesparre', *Actes de l'Académie de Bordeaux* 5 (1843), p. 161, n. 28.

[31] TNA SC 8/121/6049, 122/6051, 151/7547, 199/9909, 212/10597. About the capture and ransom of Denia, see E. Perroy, 'Gras profits et rançons pendant la guerre de Cent Ans: l'affaire du comte de Denia', in *Mélanges d'histoire du Moyen Age dédiés à la mémoire de Louis Halphen*, ed. F. Lot, et al. (Paris, 1951); A. Rogers, 'Hoton versus Shakell: A Ransom Case in the Court of Chivalry, 1390–5. Part I', *Nottingham Medieval Studies* 6 (1962), pp. 74–108, and 'Part II', *Nottingham Medieval Studies* 7 (1963), pp. 53–78.

[32] TNA SC 8/122/6051 (*c.*1378–1380).

[33] The fact that Florimont de Lesparre is included in it suggests that this agreement did not precede 1375, as we know that Lesparre was captured during the Franco-Castilian truces (June 1375–June 1376): TNA SC 8/151/7547. A letter of remission granted to Huet le Boeuf on 11 January 1376 reveals that the latter had been captured upon the sea while he was sailing to England in the company of Florimont de Lesparre. AN JJ 108, no. 78, fol. 51; published in *Recueil des documents concernant le Poitou*, ed. Guérin, xix, p. 388, no. 590.

[34] TNA SC 8/151/7547 (*c.*1378); SC 8/122/6049 (*c.*1378–*c.*1380).

ownership of the prisoner, for a huge 40,000 francs.[35] Half this sum was to be paid directly to Lesparre in aid for his ransom.[36] Whether Harpenden and the other knights and esquires in Spain would benefit from this sum is far from certain, but, either way, these steps taken by the crown liberated neither Lesparre nor any other captives in Spain nor the Aragonese hostage in England. The latter regained his freedom only nine years later, in March 1389.[37] In the meantime, Lesparre, Harpenden and others found their way out of prison through the intervention of the earl of Cambridge, William Beauchamp and Matthew Gournay, who pledged their release on parole while they were themselves leading an expedition in Portugal, in 1382.[38] Two later petitions from Lesparre and Harpenden show that their definitive release was still pending on the liberation of Denia, but apparently they did not return to prison.[39] Harpenden was ultimately ransomed but found it difficult to raise the money, as is revealed by a grant of an annuity of 100 marks made by Richard II in July 1384.[40]

What does the case of these men tell us about the attitude of the crown toward the question of prisoners of war? The changes on the political scene provoked by the deaths of Edward III, in 1377, and of Henry II of Castile, in

35 CCR 1377–81, pp. 482–3 (17 Dec. 1380); see also Perroy, 'Gras profits et rançons', p. 579.

36 CCR 1377–81, pp. 482–3; CCR 1381–5, p. 487 (28 Oct. 1384).

37 On 1 March 1389 Queen Iolanda of Aragon sent a letter to Charles VI, asking him to deliver a two-year-long safe-conduct to Dom Alfonso, son of the marquess of Villena, prisoner in England, whose terms of his ransom had been settled with the duke of Lancaster; L. Mirot and J. Vielliard, 'Inventaire des lettres des rois d'Aragon à Charles VI et à la cour de France, conservées aux Archives de la Couronne d'Aragon à Barcelone', *Bibliothèque de l'École des Chartes* 103 (1942), pp. 99–150, p. 115, no. 42.

38 Florimont de Lesparre stated in a petition that 'mon seigneur de Cambruga qui par sa courtoisie et par sa noblesse lez [Lesparre, Jean Courson and John Harpenden] a aplegez li et autres chivaliers de sa compagnie qui estoient en Portugal'. Courson and Harpenden are said, in this document, to have suffered a ten-year-long captivity. According to Walsingham (*The St Albans Chronicle. The Chronica maiora of Thomas Walsingham. I: 1376–1394*, ed. J. Taylor, W.R. Childs and L. Watkiss (Oxford, 2003), p. 398) and the *Anonimalle Chronicle, 1331–1381*, ed. Galbraith, p. 188, John Karpele (Harpenden?) was released in 1383 after an eleven-year-long captivity. A later entry in the *Inventaires de Lesparre*, in 1386, mentions that Cambridge 'and others' committed themselves to pay the ransoms of Lesparre, Harpenden and Curson, if the prisoners failed to honour their debts within nine months, or to hand them over to the Spanish. Rabanis, 'Florimont de Lesparre', p. 161 n. 28. In 1388 Cambridge and the other English knights had sworn to obtain the release of Alfonso de Denia and we can see them trying to accelerate the process of his liberation: TNA C 61/100, m. 6 (26 Mar. 1388); also quoted in *The Diplomatic Correspondence of Richard II, 1377–1399*, ed. E. Perroy, Camden Soc., 3rd ser., 48 (1933), p. 237.

39 TNA SC 8/199/9909; 212/10597.

40 CPR 1381–5, p. 447 (12 Jul. 1384). Harpenden also seemed to have encountered further difficulties. On 12 May 1385 the king ordered to deliver to him a barge called the 'Seint Jake of Seynt Andreu of Spain', which had recently been seized in Southampton, as damages for his 'being taken at sea by the king's enemies of Spain in the said ship contrary to a safe conduct of the king of Spain which was shown to them, it is said': CPR 1381–5, p. 543.

1379, may have played a part in the fate of the prisoners. The government of the minority in England, which had opened negotiations of alliance with the court of Aragon, was probably more inclined than Edward III had been to see the release of the hostage.[41] It is surprising, therefore, that it did not make more efforts to claim the count of Denia as a king's prisoner and organise the liberation of his son. Instead, it sold its own rights over the captive to Shakell. What should we deduce from this? Either the release of the captives in Castile was not a priority in the royal agenda, or the king simply did not have the authority to ignore the private interests of the captors. Finally, the government's withdrawal might well have been the result of a combination of these two factors and its underlying explanation may have been essentially financial.

In reality, the role of the crown in the release of these prisoners was very small. The fate of the captives was very much in their own hands. They found a way to make their case known to the authorities,[42] thanks largely to Lesparre and his connections.[43] The fact that the project of an exchange with Denia was first submitted to the English crown in the last year of Edward III may simply show that Lesparre, who was captured toward the end of 1375, was its architect and promoter. Harpenden and the others, who had been languishing in prison for four years, joined in and thereby added an extra weight to Lesparre's plight. Following this logic, it is less surprising to see Lesparre as the only beneficiary of the 20,000 francs from the ransom of Denia. This grant, however, did not liberate the prisoners. As we have seen, the prisoners regained their freedom thanks to the assistance of the leading members of the Portuguese expedition, the presence of whom in the Iberian Peninsula must have carried a lot of weight in negotiations. This highlights the precarious situation of captives detained in distant countries. Harpenden and his higher-ranking companions managed to find their way out. One wonders, however, what happened to such common people as the mariners from Cornwall who had been taken in war at La Rochelle and who were still languishing in prison in Spain in 1380.[44]

[41] *Diplomatic Correspondence of Richard II*, ed. Perroy, pp. 180–81.

[42] As Tuck put it, 'the importance of the petition in medieval government can hardly be over-emphasised', and this was certainly true insofar as the issue of prisoners of war was concerned: J.A. Tuck, 'Richard II's System of Patronage', in *The Reign of Richard II. Essays in Honour of May McKisack*, ed. F.R.H. Du Boulay and C. Barron (London, 1971), p. 4.

[43] There was apparently another project of release in which Lesparre was involved. According to Froissart, a clause of a treaty between the English and Castilians toward the end of 1378 anticipated the liberation of Philip Courtenay and the lord of Lesparre, but this never happened. *Chroniques*, ed. Luce, et al., viii, pp. xcviii, 165–6.

[44] For the petition of Thomas Collan, collector of the subsidy in Cornwall, see TNA SC 8/40/1954. In response, the king sent a writ to the sheriff of Cornwall to lead an inquiry: *Calendar of Inquisitions Miscellaneous*, vol. iv. *1377–1388* (London, 1957), no. 126 (26 Apr. 1380).

Royal grants

The adoption of the system of thirds in the sharing out of gains of war was a consequence of the withdrawal of the *restauro equorum* – a system of compensation for the loss of warhorses – which took place in the 1360s. This was a way to alleviate the budget of war.[45] The fact that the king asked for less return on profits from the ransoms of prisoners taken by his men could only contribute to detaching him from any form of moral obligation towards his subjects captured by the enemy. The strong need for savings in the early 1380s would even lead the authorities to deduct the time passed in prison in service of the king from the wages of the soldiers who went to Brittany under the command of the earl of Buckingham.[46] This said, the king, however, was not necessarily unwilling to assist on an individual basis, and some important knights and commanders occasionally benefited from generous grants towards their ransom. Sir Matthew Redman and Sir Gregory Sais, who both appeared in the petition to the Good Parliament in 1376, received a significant amount of money to help them pay their ransoms: the former, twice captured in 1370 and 1373, received £1,000, while the latter was granted an annual pension of £200 for life in 1378.[47] But, in general, evidence of financial contributions towards ransoms is relatively rare and these grants could be very small.[48]

There were alternative forms of assistance which did not necessarily require the king to draw on the treasury coffers. Exchanges of prisoners were one such way to obtain the liberation of a prisoner. Ideally, two French and English captors had in their hands two prisoners of similar value, whom they were willing to exchange. Not surprisingly, these conditions were very rarely fulfilled – the reason why these exchanges often proved to be rather complicated and sometimes failed, as in the case of the prisoners of Castile who hoped to be

---

45 Before this, when the *restauro equorum* was included in the indenture, the superior contracting party asked for half of the profits of his retainer: J.W.M. Bean, *From Lord to Patron. Lordship in Late-Medieval England* (Manchester, 1989), pp. 238–44; A. Ayton, *Knights and Warhorses. Military Service and the English Aristocracy under Edward III* (Woodbridge, 1994), pp. 127–37.

46 TNA SC 8/19/928 (May 1382).

47 J.S. Roskell, *Parliament and Politics in Late Medieval England*, 3 vols (London, 1981–3), iii, p. 206; A.D. Carr, 'A Welsh Knight in the Hundred Years War: Sir Gregory Sais', *Transactions of the Honourable Society of Cymmrodorion* (1977), pp. 40–53. Quite surprisingly, however, Edward III was not among the lords and barons who bound themselves to making the payment of the ransom of his step-son, John Hastings, earl of Pembroke, captured at La Rochelle, in June 1372. The contract between Hastings and Bertrand du Guesclin sealed on 11 January 1375 is published in *Letters, Orders and Musters*, ed. Jones, pp. 236–7, no. 633.

48 For instance, Edward III's grant towards the ransoms of six prisoners and their retainers in St-Omer barely amounted to £20: *Issue Roll of Thomas de Brantingham, Bishop of Exeter, Lord High Treasurer of England*, ed. F. Devon (London, 1835), p. 344 (31 Oct. 1369). The gesture of Richard II was larger, when he agreed to contribute half the ransoms of the esquire Raymond de Misanz, the lord of Châteauneuf, and his brother, which in total amounted to £250: TNA E 404/10 (27 Dec. 1378).

exchanged with Denia.[49] The case of Thomas Felton was more successful. This English knight was captured at the battle of Eymet in 1377.[50] His captor, a French esquire called Jean de Lignac, handed him over to Gaston de Phébus, count of Foix.[51] Felton and his wife addressed a series of petitions to the king in 1379–80, asking him not to release the count of Saint-Pol, captured in 1375, until Felton's own release, and asking as well for his assistance to help Felton out of prison.[52] Felton's ransom was fixed on 12 August 1380 at 30,000 francs and 1,000 florins.[53] The count of Saint-Pol was a much more valuable prisoner, whose ransom amounted to 100,000 francs.[54] There was no question of exchange, but Felton hoped that his ransom would be paid out of that of Saint-Pol. This was agreed on 16 August but withdrawn on 30 August.[55] Instead, the king granted Felton, Guillaumes des Bordes, another French prisoner in his hands, with the power to set his ransom at the highest possible price – that is, 30,000 francs – provided that he satisfied John Harleston and others in respect of any claim in the said prisoner. It was, however, the king who eventually paid Harleston's claim, which amounted to a third of the ransom, in October 1381.[56] In the meantime, des Bordes had received a safe-conduct to raise the money for his ransom in 1380 and benefited from a very generous grant from Charles VI in December of that year.[57]

[49] The case of Simon Burley is another example of a failed exchange. Charles V, who had acquired the English soldier following his capture at Lusignan in 1369, handed him over to the wife of Hugues de Châtillon, lord of Dampierre, who had been captured near Abbeville at about the same time and surrendered to Edward III. Charles V hoped that Lady Dampierre could organise an exchange of prisoners. We do not know whether or not Edward III was favourable to this project, which never materialised because Châtillon managed to escape his prison in the castle of Nottingham. *Chroniques*, ed. Luce et al., vii, 194–5; viii, p. 182; TNA E 404/10 (9 Feb. 1370); *Issue Roll of Thomas de Brantingham*, ed. Devon, p. 445 (16 Feb. 1370); *PROME*, v, 364 (Apr. 1376); *CPR 1377–81*, p. 276 (1378); Timbal et al., *La Guerre de Cent Ans*, pp. 322–7.
[50] *Chroniques*, ed. Luce et al., ix, 10, 139–40; *Chronique des règnes de Jean II et de Charles V*, ed. R. Delachanal, 4 vols (Paris, 1910–20), ii, p. 187; *St Albans Chronicle*, ed. Taylor et al., pp. 167–9.
[51] P. Tucoo-Chala, *Gaston Phébus et la vicomté de Béarn, 1342–1391* (Bordeaux, 1960), p. 299, n. 61.
[52] TNA SC 8/21/1018; 111/5513, 5114; *PROME*, iii, 256 (24 Apr. 1379).
[53] Tucoo-Chala, *Gaston Phébus*, p. 299, n. 61.
[54] TNA E 30/1686 (17 Jul. 1376); *Foedera, conventianes, litterae, etc.*, T. Rymer (ed.), 20 vols (London, 1704–35), vii, p. 224.
[55] *Issues of the Exchequer; being a collection of payments made out of his majesty's revenue, from king Henry III to king Henry VI, inclusive*, ed. F. Devon (London, 1837), p. 212 (16 Aug. 1380); *CPR 1377–81*, pp. 271, 543 (30 Aug. 1380).
[56] TNA E 404/12 (10 Oct. 1381).
[57] For the safe-conduct, see TNA SC 8/169/8424. He received 20,000 *livres tournois* from Charles VI on 15 December 1380 and another 1,500 francs from the duke of Burgundy on 13 May 1383; AN JJ 117, no. 85; quoted in P. Contamine, *Guerre, État et Société à la fin du moyen âge. Études sur les armées des rois de France, 1337–1494* (Paris, 1972), pp. 567–8; Archives

In around 1376 the king received a long petition from the lord Mussidan which asked him, among other things, to grant the *bailliage* of Sainte-Foy to one of his men, Guillaume de Motes, considering the loss of his castle and his capture by the enemy.[58] Edward III replied that he wished to be informed about Motes's case, after which he would take advice from his council. If the king was satisfied with the results of this inquiry, Motes stood a good chance to be made *bailli* of Sainte-Foy. Indeed, it was quite common to see the crown granting offices to his subjects who were in trouble in compensation for their losses. Following the Good Parliament, Matthew Gournay was made captain of Dax in 1377 and seneschal of Landes in 1378,[59] while as compensation for his alleged six captures Bernard Montet was granted the castellany of Saint-Macaire in 1383.[60] Marriages were valuable commodities which could also be granted to former prisoners in order to help them pay their ransoms. This was the case for Peter Courtenay, who was granted the marriage of Richard Poynings in October 1379, in consideration of his capture at sea by the Spanish in 1379.[61] The king's esquire Walter Whitors was not only given the marriage of the daughter and heir of Simon de Rauvill, but also received the wardship of her lands.[62] This grant was made in aid of the payment of the ransom of his son Ralph.[63]

There was no royal obligation towards the assistance of prisoners and probably not even a moral one, since the soldier was remunerated for his services. This was apparently well understood and acknowledged, for we can see elsewhere prisoners exploiting all their possible resources and connections before ultimately resorting to the authorities.[64] The significance of the process of petitioning, in this context, surely contributed to keeping humble men away from the crown. It even raised difficulties for higher-ranking lords to obtain assistance while they were in prison.

départementales de la Côte-d'Or, B 1460, f° 116 v° (I owe this last reference to Prof. Bertrand Schnerb). A safe conduct provided to certain merchants to procure the ransom of Thomas Felton on 20 February 1381 may suggest that the payments made by Des Bordes were not sufficient; *Foedera*, vii, p. 283.

58   TNA SC 8/262/13069.

59   TNA E 101/181/1, no. 45; Dupont-Ferrier, *Gallia Regia*, iii, no. 13855 (I owe these references to Prof. Michael Jones).

60   TNA C 61/96, m. 15.

61   *CPR 1377–81*, p. 392 (15 Oct. 1379). About his capture at sea, see *St Albans Chronicle*, ed. Taylor et al., p. 223.

62   *CPR 1374–7*, p. 394 (20 Dec. 1376).

63   Prisoners could also benefit from releases of payment owed to the crown. See, for instance, TNA E 159/156 (13 May 1380).

64   R. Ambühl, 'Prisoners of War in the Hundred Years War: The Golden Age of Private Ransoms', unpublished PhD thesis, University of St Andrews, 2009, Ch. 8.

The warrior community

Investigating the channels of assistance beyond that of the crown is a rather difficult task. The private nature of the assistance between individuals makes it and them far less visible in the sources than is the government. We see, through the process of petition, how important the role of families, friends and servants was. In particular, Fogg's petition and its endorsement by the commons is one clear sign of cohesion within the warrior community. But to what extent could the prisoner rely on his captain and his companions-in-arms?

Solidarity v. private interests

It was mentioned earlier that Buxhill's account included a large sum of 3,034 francs devoted to the payments of ransoms of prisoners. Significantly, this is the only mention of a captain who claimed such expenses in his account that I have come across. As these expenses would ultimately be taken care of by the Exchequer, it is, in fact, the crown who paid for these ransoms. However, there is reason to believe that the government had nothing to do with this generous initiative. The contracts of indenture for Knowles' expedition did not anticipate the payment of the ransoms of prisoners.[65] What also seems clear is that there was no general agreement through which the leaders of the expedition, including Buxhill, would pay for the ransoms of their men, as there is evidence of other prisoners captured during the campaign who did not benefit from such largesse.[66] Therefore, it would seem that this gesture towards the prisoners who took refuge in Saint-Sauveur was an initiative of Buxhill's, clear evidence of assistance from the captain to his subordinates. One could wonder, however, whether Buxhill would have been as generous if the money had to come out of his own pocket.

Evidence of captains who paid the ransoms of their men is scarce. During the 1370s there are a couple of references in the works of Froissart and Cuvelier relating to Bertrand du Guesclin and his brother Olivier.[67] One must, however,

---

[65] The unusual financial organisation of the 1370 expedition anticipated that the king would pay the wages and regards of the soldiers for only 13 weeks, or, if it were longer, for the period between the departure of the soldiers from their homes and their arrival in France: J.W. Sherborne, 'Indentured Retinues and English Expeditions to France, 1369–80', in J.W. Sherborne, War, Politics and Culture in Fourteenth Century England, ed. A. Tuck (London, 1994), reprinted from EHR 79 (1964), p. 7.

[66] The knight John Gurney led the smallest retinue during the expedition: Sherborne, 'Indentured Retinues', p. 7. His capture is attested in several letters of protection, which also show that he had been kept in captivity for at least four years, unless he was recaptured in 1372 or 1373. See TNA C 76/54, m. 5 (15 Jul. 1371), C 76/56, m. 8 (18 Oct. 1373); C 76/57, m. 6 (28 Nov. 1374). John Meriet, son of John Meriet, who was in the retinue of Robert Knowles, is also mentioned as a prisoner in France in the letter of protection which he received on 28 November 1371: TNA C 76/54, m. 1. See also T. Moore, 'Walter, Fifth Lord Fitzwalter of Little Dunmow (Essex)', at http://www.icmacentre.ac.uk/soldier/database/May2008.php, accessed 15 May 2009.

[67] Cuvelier, Chronique, ed. Charrière, p. 207; Chroniques, ed. Luce et al., ix, p. 98; C. Given-

be careful in handling these sources. Apart from these, I have found only one reference taken from administrative records. In his petition to the king in the late 1370s Matthew Gournay claimed that, following his third capture in Poitou, he paid his own ransom and that of all the men of his company 'to the great impediment of his condition'.[68] How should we interpret this testimony? Is it evidence that captains usually paid for the ransoms of their men or, on the contrary, is the fact that Gournay highlighted his generosity toward his men and its impact on his finances a sign that such generosity was exceptional and praiseworthy? Given the relative silence of the sources on this issue, it is tempting to believe that Gournay's action was more the exception than the rule.

This does not mean, however, that soldiers would not find any support within the warrior community. Soldiers lent money to each other or stood as sureties for the payment of a ransom. The earl of Cambridge and other knights pledged the release on parole of Lesparre and Harpenden. In the aftermath of the battle of Pontvallain John Bourchier and Thomas Warde lent 640 marks to William Flete for 'his great need for saving his body from the hands of the enemies'.[69] Invariably, the creditors would ask for their money back and do whatever was necessary to get it. In the late 1370s, for instance, Thomas Percy asked the king and his council to bring before them some people in England to whom Percy had paid a lot of money to get them out of prison, so that he could obtain justice.[70] Surprisingly, the knight specified in his petition that he used the royal channel because there was no court of constable or marshal in this realm. Financial issues could be far more disruptive than this, however. In the 1370s Walter Ferrefort wrote a despairing letter to his captain Sir John del Strother from his prison in Saint-Brieuc begging him to pay the 120 francs he was obliged to pay to his captor. Ferrefort had pledged the release on parole of a certain John More, who failed his word and disappeared.[71] Whether or not Strother came to the assistance of his man will probably remain unknown, but there is reason to be sceptical. The fact that the main concern of such captains as Strother or Hugh

Wilson, 'The Ransom of Olivier de Guesclin', *Bulletin of the Institute of Historical Research* liv (1981), p. 18.

68   TNA SC 8/113/5629 (c.1377–c.1380).

69   Muniments of the Marquess of Bath, Longleat House, Wiltshire, Longleat MS 116; quoted in Jones, 'Fortunes of War' (5 Jun. 1371). Flete received a letter of attorney valid for a year on 19 November 1371: TNA C 76/54, m. 7.

70   'Supplie … Thomas de Percy que luy please ordeigner ascuns de son counsaille devant quelx poent comparoire certeins gentz qui sont en Engleterre pour quelx il ad grauntment paiez de soen si bien pour leur acquiter de prison come pour autre chose, auffyn qu'il poet de eux avoir droite et justice si come il n'y a courte de conestable ne de marescall en ceste roialme': TNA SC 8/65/3247.

71   S. Walker, 'Profit and Loss in the Hundred Years War: The Sub-Contracts of Sir John Strother, 1374', *Historical Research* 58 (1985), p. 105 n. 39.

Hastings, when recruiting and sealing contracts, was to make a profit at the expense of their retainers does not point to their generosity.[72]

Treaties of surrender

It should not, however, be deduced from this observation that the world of the combatant was essentially individualistic. Assistance also took other forms. The numerous treaties of surrender sealed in the 1370s offered good opportunities to save companions or retainers from the hands of the enemy. It is true that the parties involved in the negotiation for the evacuation of a town or fortress did it on behalf of the sovereign authority, but the terms of these treaties were commonly the result of private negotiations between commanders on each side. Not surprisingly, the crown sometimes disagreed with the decision of their captains, who were compelled to justify their actions and the terms of the treaty of capitulation in front of the parliament.[73]

In general, the treaties of capitulation sealed in the 1370s were particularly advantageous to the English defenders, who could leave the place safely, without being ransomed. Furthermore, the French besiegers often made substantial concessions to obtain the evacuation of towns or fortresses. In 1372 the treaty of surrender of the fortresses of Breteuil and Conches authorised the Gascons to leave these places with their captives, unless the besiegers paid their ransoms.[74] Similarly, Jean de Vienne agreed in the treaty of surrender of the fortress of Saint-Sauveur to pay the ransoms of all the French prisoners who had been captured during the siege.[75] In several cases, the English besieged also required

---

[72] A. Goodman, 'The Military Subcontracts of Sir Hugh Hastings, 1380', *EHR* 95 (1980), pp. 114–20; Walker, 'Profit and Loss'. The retinue of a great host seems to have given less opportunity for the soldiers to bond than did garrisons. What Bell's figures show about the English campaigns of 1387 and 1388 is that, as we go down the hierarchy, soldiers seem less and less willing to serve under the same captain in different campaigns, and it is striking for our purpose that in fact 62% of the esquires and 71% of the archers did not serve under the same captain. Therefore, out of the low percentage of soldiers (20%) from the first expedition who participated in the second one, only 38% of esquires and 29% of archers fought in the same retinue. In this particular case, it is quite clear that the expeditions were not propitious to the development of an *esprit de corps*. Soldiers did not seem inclined to join the expedition to France a second time and, above all, not under the same leader: A. R. Bell, *War and the Soldier in the Fourteenth Century* (Woodbridge, 2004), pp. 98–100, 245.

[73] See, for instance, the justification of William Weston for the surrender of the castle of Audruicq and John, lord Gommegnies for Ardres, in October 1377; Peter Cressingham and John Spikesworth for the surrender of the castle of Drincham, Sir William Elmham, Sir Thomas Trivet, Sir Henry Ferrers, Sir William Farringdon and Robert FitzRalph for the surrender of Bourbourg, in October 1383. *PROME*, vi, pp. 21–6, 331, 338–40. The commons sentenced Weston and Gommegnies to death, but the king subsequently pardoned William Weston and released him on 28 December 1377: *CPR 1377–1381*, p. 124.

[74] The treaty is published in Cuvelier, *Chronique*, ed. Charrière, ii, pp. 408–9 (31 Jan. 1372).

[75] The treaty is published in L. Delisle, *Histoire du château et des sires de Saint-Sauveur-le-Vicomte* (Valognes, Paris and Caen, 1867), pp. 198–200, 242–8 (21 May 1375).

the release of their comrades taken prisoner by the French during the siege or previous confrontations. The terms of the treaty for the evacuation of the fortress of Thury in April 1371 anticipated that two English prisoners detained in Caen would be released without paying any ransom and that, at the same time, the soldiers of the garrison would be brought to Saint-Sauveur or Bécherel with their goods, horses and prisoners.[76] The marshal of France, Jean de Sancerre, agreed to pay 1,700 francs to the English of the castle of Esse. In addition to this he would also release several English prisoners whose ransoms had been valued at 1,400 francs.[77] In some instances the liberation of English captives was the main or only clause of the treaty. For instance, the English garrison of the castle of La Roche-sur-Yon, which surrendered in August 1373, requested the release of the prestigious English captain John Devereux and several others.[78] In October 1374, finally, the English agreed with the duke of Berry to evacuate the fortress of Lusignan in exchange for the release of John Cresswell and Thomas Percy, the former having been captured in June 1374 and the latter at Soubise in 1372.[79] The two prisoners cost 52,000 francs to the duke of Berry who had to buy them from their respective captors, Jean de Sancerre and Charles V.[80]

Conclusion

The limits of source materials that tend to focus on the higher-ranking prisoners must be highlighted. They give only occasional glimpses into the fate of lesser prisoners which suggest that many a commoner may have met his end in captivity.

[76] BnF MSS français 26011, no. 1282 (31 Apr. 1371). For the quittance of payment for the purchase of the two prisoners to their captors, see BnF pièces originales 2876, Trémagon, no. 3 (25 May 1371).

[77] BnF pièces originales 2624, Sancerre, no. 25, also published in *Mandements et actes divers de Charles V, 1364–1380, recueillis dans les collections de la Bibliothèque Nationale*, ed. L. Delisle (Paris, 1874), pp. 434–5, no. 846.

[78] *Chroniques*, ed. Luce et al., viii, pp. 113–14; Cuvelier, *Chronique*, ed. Charrière, ii, p. 311; F. Lehoux, *Jean de France, duc de Berri. Sa vie, son action politique, 1340–1416*, 4 vols (Paris, 1966–8), i, pp. 313–14. His ransom was estimated at 10,000 francs. At the very least, this was the sum that several French lords were bound to pay to the masters of Devereux, Du Guesclin, Jean Macé and Alain du Parc; *Letters, Orders and Musters*, ed. Jones, pp. 214–15 (no. 577), 223 (no. 597), 226 (no. 608), 262–3 (no. 709), 265 (no. 715).

[79] About this treaty of surrender, see Lehoux, *Jean de France*, i, 337–43. Berry provided a certificate to Percy in which he released him from his oath as a prisoner, on 2 October 1374. See also TNA E 101/178/20.

[80] Treaties of capitulation of French towns may well include the release of English prisoners too. In May 1373 Robert Knowles included the liberations of John Lakyngeth, on the English side, and Hervé de Saint-Goüeno, on the French side, in the clauses of the treaty of capitulation of Brest in July 1373. Lakyngeth had been captured a few months earlier at Conques: *Chroniques*, ed. Luce et al., viii, pp. 113–14, 140–41; Cuvelier, *Chronique*, ed. Charrière, ii, p. 311.

That said, we have seen that a striking feature of the various higher-ranking cases is the capacity of the prisoners to recover and rearm. But to what extent were these recoveries due to the particular context of the 1370s? The stories of English fortunes made out of profits of war in the three previous decades, which are abundantly reported by the chroniclers, may have been true.[81] If so, the wealth accumulated by soldiers in that earlier period of success may have absorbed the impact of their misfortunes in the 1370s. It is also possible that the capacity for quick recovery was due to the changing nature of warfare in the 1370s. The French carefully avoided big confrontations with the English at that time; the slow and methodical recapture of French towns and fortresses in the hands of the English was often negotiated. And we have seen how the English seized this opportunity to obtain the liberation of their captains and comrades. There is a final political factor which should be taken into account. More than any other period, the particular context of French reconquest may have offered a greater opportunity for Gascon prisoners to change allegiance, avoiding long periods of captivity and the eventual payment of a ransom.[82]

On the other hand, there is reason to believe that the particularity of the 1370s should not be overstated. First, it is important to note that sustained military activities, very often made up of small-scale operations, exposed soldiers as much in the 1370s as in the previous decades. For instance, Matthew Gournay claimed to have been captured three times in 1359, and it was to these misfortunes that the English knight referred in his petition to Richard II in the late 1370s.[83] This observation highlights the gap between the overall political or military success of a kingdom and the harsh reality of warfare in the field. Secondly, this investigation of the fate of the English prisoners in the 1370s simply illustrates some aspects of the ransom system at work at any time during the Hundred Years War. One defining characteristic of this system was the lack of ready cash. This prevailing issue explains, at least partly, the relative disengagement of the crown

---

[81] About these stories of fortunes, see J. Barnie, *War in Medieval Society. Social Values and the Hundred Years War, 1337–99* (London, 1974), pp. 33–6. This dream of fortunes was at the origin of the 'gold rush' in France in the 1360s, as described by Sir Thomas Gray in his *Scalacronica (1272–1363)*, ed. A. King, Surtees Society, ccix (2005), pp. 153, 157.

[82] See the case of Guillaume Aramon de Madaillan, lord of Rauzan, Bérart d'Albret, lord of Langoiran, Raymond de Montaut, lord of Mussidan, and Galhart de Durfort, lord of Duras who had been captured at the battle of Eymet in 1377 and acquired by the duke of Anjou in order to 'yceulx tourner et faire venir a l'obeyssance de Monseigneur et de nous', as is mentioned in the contract of purchase of three of them. BnF, PO 2624, Sancerre, no. 28; as cited in R. Delachenal, *Histoire de Charles V*, 5 vols (Paris, 1909–31), v, p. 54, n. 6 (8 Oct. 1377). The four men wisely agreed to give their oath to the French king, but Duras and Rauzan deserted from the French cause very shortly afterwards. *Chroniques*, ed. Luce et al., ix, pp. 20–21. On the other hand, Jean de Grailly's refusal to become a liege man of Charles V resulted in his death in prison in 1376 after a four-year-long captivity: F. Bériac-Lainé and C. Given-Wilson, *Les prisonniers de la bataille de Poitiers* (Paris, 2002), p. 163.

[83] TNA SC 8/103/5114.

in the rescue of prisoners of war. We have seen how kings were not always keen to respond to some pressing demands from their subjects in trouble. There is also reason to believe that, to some extent, the lack of money also put a strain on the support that the prisoner could gain from his captain and companions-in-arms. If, in general, the prisoner could not expect to have his ransom paid by the latter, on the other hand, captains and companions were inclined to act as sureties for the payment of the ransom and this enabled many a prisoner to regain his freedom, even if it was temporary. The solidarity within the company expressed itself even more clearly through the exploration of alternative ways to release prisoners. In this respect, I believe that the exchange of prisoners for prisoners or in return for the evacuation of a town or fortress is a clear indicator of solidarity, rather than patronage, within the warrior community.[84]

---

[84] In his investigation of ransom brokerage M.K. Jones dwells on the significance of patronage which took place between the broker and the prisoner: Jones, 'Ransom Brokerage', pp. 229–35.

10

The soldier, 'hadde he riden, no man ferre'[1]

Adrian R. Bell

The later fourteenth century is blessed with sources enabling historians to create portrayals of colourful careers in arms. The testimony of deponents before the Court of Chivalry gives the soldiers' own accounts of their activities,[2] while the portrait of the knight in the Canterbury Tales delivers an image of (allegedly) perfect military accomplishments.[3] To this, we can now add the online database produced during the 'Soldier in Later Medieval England' project, which provides evidence of both actual and intended service for the English crown.[4] Combining these sources, we can reconstruct a number of detailed case studies of soldiers and where they chose to fight. We can also test the depositions in the Court of Chivalry against the royal records of military service, and consider if the witnesses were braggards, or, by contrast, were modestly understating their level of military service. Finally, can we find out which soldier was 'best': who had the longest record of service; who took part in the most varied campaigns; who was the youngest; who was the oldest; and, of course, as the title suggests, taking the line from the description of Chaucer's Knight, who rode the furthest? This essay is limited to a set of case studies, drawing mainly from cases heard before

---

[1]   Line taken from the prologue to the Canterbury Tales, describing how well travelled the knight was. *The Riverside Chaucer*, ed. L.D. Benson (Oxford, 3rd edn, 1992), line 48, p. 24. I am grateful to Anne Curry, Tony Moore and David Simpkin for reading and commenting on an earlier draft.

[2]   The most famous is *The Scrope and Grosvenor Controversy*, ed. N.H. Nicolas, 2 vols (London, 1832), but there are also Lovell v. Morley and Grey v. Hastings, neither of which is published. An overview is, however, provided in Andrew Ayton, 'Knights, Esquires and Military Service: The Evidence of the Armorial Cases before the Court of Chivalry', in *The Medieval Military Revolution: State, Society and Military Change in Medieval and Early Modern Europe*, ed. A. Ayton and J.L. Price (New York, 1995), pp. 81–104, and Maurice Keen, 'English Military Experience and the Court of Chivalry: The Case of Grey v. Hastings', in *Guerre et société en France, en Angleterre et en Bourgogne, XIVe–XVe siecle*, ed. P. Contamine, C. Giry-Deloison and M. Keen (Lille, 1992), pp. 123–42.

[3]   *Riverside Chaucer*, lines 43–78, p. 24.

[4]   Online database available at www.medievalsoldier.org.

the Court of Chivalry and expanded with further information from the medieval
soldier database. Although they cannot be said to form a truly representative
sample of the medieval English soldiery, nevertheless, this self-selected sample
does indeed allow us to paint a dynamic portrait of what an average, as well as
an exceptional, career in arms could involve in the later fourteenth century.

It is well known that the fourteenth-century soldier travelled widely and
visited all kinds of exotic places.[5] Hundreds of English soldiers travelled to
Prussia to crusade with the Teutonic knights, though these numbers are perhaps
skewed by the men travelling in the large parties with Henry of Derby in the
early 1390s.[6] Soldiers are known to have gone on pilgrimage to Jerusalem, been
involved at the siege of Alexandria in 1365, fought at the battle of Nájera with the
Black Prince in 1367 and travelled to Milan with the marriage party of Lionel of
Clarence. Closer to home, though perhaps no less challenging, a soldier would
have gained experience in France, Ireland, Scotland and Wales. So, if these
form the geographical boundaries of the medieval English soldier's world, how
common was geographically extensive soldiering experience, or were other less
travelled careers more normal and expected?

An obvious starting point is the Scrope v. Grosvenor case. One of the most
interesting deponents was Nicolas Sabraham. His example has been used by
a number of historians to highlight the wealth of experience that an ordinary
English soldier could gain in the later fourteenth century. In his own words,
on the day of his deposition (17 September 1386) he was 'aged 60 and upwards
and had been armed 39 years'.[7] He recounted an extensive career fighting in the
early years of the Hundred Years War, taking in the battle of Crécy, the siege
of Calais and service in Brittany, Gascony, Spain and Scotland. Sabraham had
also served 'beyond the great sea' (the Mediterranean) and had seen action in
Prussia, Hungary, Constantinople and Messembria (now Nessebar, on the Black
Sea coast of Bulgaria). But, above all, he was also, alongside Chaucer's knight, at
the sack of Alexandria led by Peter of Cyprus in 1365, where he was witness to
the knighting of Stephen Scrope by King Peter himself upon their landing. It
may well be that much of Sabraham's travels can be assigned to the 'wanderlust'
of his patrons, the de Bohun earls of Northampton and Hereford, who, as we
shall see, also had lengthy crusading credentials. Nevertheless, it does show how
a soldier 'of unknown origins', according to his biographer, was able to travel far
and wide.[8]

What can the Soldier database add to Sabraham's own lengthy account of
his career? We can introduce one previously unknown nugget of information,

[5] C. Tyerman, *England and the Crusades 1095–1588* (London, 1988).

[6] *Expeditions to Prussia and the Holy Land made by Henry, Earl of Derby, in the years 1390–1
and 1392–3*, ed. L.T. Smith, Camden Society, new series, lii (London, 1894).

[7] *Scrope and Grosvenor*. 323. Thanks to Andrew Ayton for the dates of depositions.

[8] T. Guard, 'Sabraham, Nicholas (b. c.1325, d. in or after 1399)', *ODNB* (Oxford), May 2005,
at http://www.oxforddnb.com/view/article/92452, accessed 23 November 2010.

as there is a record of him taking a letter of protection on 29 April 1371 for one year's service with Alan del Strother in the garrison of Roxburgh Castle.[9] The ability to discover military service in this way demonstrates the limitations of the Scrope v. Grosvenor case as a comprehensive source for military careers, as the deponents may not have mentioned service where they had seen neither Scrope or Grosvenor in action.

The next example frequently used by scholars to demonstrate the wide-ranging nature of military service is the career of Sir Richard Waldegrave, also renowned as Speaker of the House of Commons. Indeed, some have gone so far to propose him as a possible real-life model for Chaucer's knight.[10] Roskell demonstrated that Chaucer was at the same deposition hearing in the Scrope–Grosvernor case as Waldegrave, and suggests that Chaucer may have picked up some of his details for his description of the knight from hearing Waldegrave's tales of overseas travel and adventure.[11] Sir Richard's own deposition stated that he was aged 48 and had been armed for twenty-five years. He described a mixed career of service in France and Scotland, while also campaigning further afield in Satalia (Turkey) in 1361 and in Prussia in 1363. It should be noted that all this service (apart from Scotland) was, in common with Sabraham, with the de Bohun earls of Northampton and Hereford. The *History of Parliament* entry embellishes his own statement of his career with attendance at the sack of Alexandria alongside Sabraham and Scrope: 'Waldegrave was not only present at Attalia when the treaty was signed in 1364, but also party to the taking of Alexandria in the following year. It was during this eventful campaign that he won his spurs.'[12] This thesis rests on the well-travelled earl of Hereford (d. 1372) being at Alexandria and having a number of his close followers with him, as reported in the *Anomimalle Chronicle*.[13] This may be a possibility, but it is impossible to prove. Anthony Luttrell has questioned the assumptions behind the placement

9 Information on soldiers has been taken from the AHRC-funded 'The Soldier in Later Medieval England' online database, www.medievalsoldier.org, accessed 23 November 2010. TNA C 71/50 m. 4, 'Nicholas Sabrame'. See Ayton above for discussion, including his possible service with the White company in Italy.

10 J.S. Roskell, *The Commons and their Speakers in English Parliaments 1376–1523* (Manchester, 1965), p. 129: 'there is, in fact, a remarkable resemblance between Sir Richard's careers and that of the knight of the prologue to Chaucer's *Canterbury Tales* (which may not have been entirely adventitious)'. This debate still rages and a recent paper has suggested Philippe de Mézières as the exemplar: Stefan Vander Elst, '"Tu es pelerine en la sainte cité": Chaucer's Knight and Philippe de Mézières', *Studies in Philology* 106 (2009), pp. 379–401.

11 J.S. Roskell, 'Sir Richard Waldegrave of Bures St. Mary, Speaker in the Parliament of 1381–2', *Proceedings of the Suffolk Institute of Archaeology* xxvii (1958), pp. 154–75 (158). Both appeared on 15 October 1386.

12 J.S. Roskell, L. Clark and C. Rawcliffe, *The History of Parliament: The House of Commons 1386–1421* (Stroud, 1992), vol. iv, p. 736. The date of the visit to Satalia is variously given as 1361 and 1364 and Luttrell argues that it should be dated 1367: Anthony Luttrell, 'English Levantine crusaders, 1363–1367', *Renaissance Studies* 2 (1988), pp. 143–53 (150).

13 *The Anonimalle Chronicle, 1333–1381*, ed. V.H. Galbraith (Manchester, 1927), pp. 51 and 170.

of these English soldiers on this crusade, using evidence to suggest that the earl was in London in January 1365 and again in 1366,[14] thus making his travelling to Egypt and back nigh impossible without the use of modern forms of transportation. This provides a lesson for historians using the statements of chroniclers as their only basis for attributing military service. Waldegrave does not mention service at Alexandria in his deposition (unlike Sabraham) and yet the 'fact' of his attendance has become a repeated truth. This instance indicates that caution should be taken when using such sources and that other supporting evidence should also be found to confirm the full details of a military career.[15]

Governmental records can be used to fill in some of the gaps in Waldegrave's career. He took out a letter of protection and appointed attorneys with the intention of joining the earl of Hereford on campaign in France with John of Gaunt at the reopening of the war in 1369[16] and he is listed on the muster rolls for the naval expeditions of 1371 and 1372, again in Hereford's retinue.[17] Using the issue rolls we can also see that on the royal campaign of 1385 to Scotland Waldegrave was paid for leading twenty-seven soldiers, including two knights, seven men-at-arms and eighteen archers.[18] Utilising the government sources, therefore, provides an even richer picture of the Speaker's service at war.[19]

The crusading activities of Sir Lewis Clifford provide a good example to follow up. Many historians refer to his interest and activities on crusade, some citing his membership of Phillippe de Mézières' Order of the Passion. It is also claimed that he served on the Bourbon Crusade to Tunis in 1390. When the original reference for this is tracked down, it can be traced to a mention of the leader of the English forces as *Le Sire le Cliffort* in the Chronicle of Caberet d'Orville.[20] This could just as easily refer to Thomas, Lord Clifford, who crusaded with the Teutonic knights and died 'on an unidentified Mediterranean island' on his way

---

[14] Luttrell, 'English Levantine crusaders', 150. Luttrell does provide evidence for attendance at Alexandria by John de Grey of Codnor, Sir Miles de Stapleton of Bedale in Yorkshire, Sir Stephen Scrope, Sir John de Argentine of Suffolk, and of course Nicholas Sabraham. In addition he demonstrates that two English members of the Hospitaller order were also present, the turcopolier William Middleton and Robert Hales, later prior of England: Anthony Luttrell, 'The Hospitallers at Rhodes, 1306–1421', in *History of the Crusades*, vol. iii, ed. H.W. Hazard (London, 1985), pp. 278–313 (299n).

[15] For a case study see Adrian R. Bell, 'Medieval Chroniclers as War Correspondents during the Hundred Years War: The Earl of Arundel's Naval Campaign of 1387', in *Fourteenth Century England VI*, ed. Chris Given-Wilson (Woodbridge, 2010), pp. 171–84.

[16] TNA C 76/52, ms. 18, 22.

[17] TNA E 101/31/15, m. 1; /32/20, m. 1.

[18] He was paid £40 on 19 August 1385: TNA E 403/508, m. 21.

[19] Anne Curry, 'Speakers at War in the Late 14th and 15th Centuries', in *Speakers and the Speakership: Presiding Officers and the Management of Business from the Middle Ages to the 21st Century*, ed. P. Seaward, *Parliamentary History*, vol. 29 part 1 (2010), pp. 8–21.

[20] J. Cabaret d'Orville, *La chronique du bon duc Loys de Bourbon*, ed. A-M. Chazaud (Paris, 1876), pp. 222, 238, 248.

to the Holy Land on 4 October 1391.[21] This demonstrates again that, in all such cases, the original source should always be found and scrutinised.

Another Bohunite, Sir Alexander Goldingham, was also a deponent at Scrope v. Grosvenor, although his account of his own exploits is less detailed than those previously discussed.[22] It is with such a soldier that the details taken from governmental sources can really extend a career in arms. In his testimony before the Court of Chivalry in 1386 he mentioned his service in Italy in 1366, which can be confirmed from his accompanying de Bohun for the marriage negotiations between England and Milan regarding Lionel of Clarence.[23] Further, he also stated that he served on the Scottish expedition of Richard II in 1385. However, Goldingham does not appear in any of the governmental records from this campaign and his word in the court case is our only evidence that he did go to Scotland. His deposition provides no further details about the rest of his military career.

From the Soldier database we can demonstrate that Goldingham was a regular attendee on English expeditions throughout the period, between and beyond the two journeys mentioned in his testimony. First, he took out a letter of protection as intending to serve with the earl of Hereford in 1369;[24] then he had a protection and appointed attorneys in preparation for serving with John de Montfort, duke of Brittany, in 1374–5.[25] In 1378 Sir Alexander intended to serve in the retinue of Sir Robert Knolles, on John of Gaunt's expedition,[26] and two years later he was probably back in France as part of the expeditionary force led by Thomas of Woodstock, earl of Buckingham (who had inherited the Bohun lands in Essex), as he had again secured a protection and appointed attorneys.[27] In 1384 he joined a standing force for the Scottish borders led by Walter, Lord FitzWalter (a close associate of Buckingham), and he appears on the muster roll for this retinue, having also taken out a protection for his service.[28] It seems he also took a protection to serve overseas with Sir John Cheyne, captain of Marck castle, later in the same year, though this was revoked as 'he is not going.'[29] He joined the expedition of John of Gaunt to Castile from 1386 to 1387 (on which FitzWalter served), and his protection was renewed as he was staying longer in

[21] H. Summerson, 'Clifford, Thomas, sixth Baron Clifford (1362/3–1391)', *ODNB* (Oxford, 2004); online edn January 2008 at http://www.oxforddnb.com/view/article/5662, accessed 14 December 2010.
[22] *Scrope and Grosvenor*, ed. Nicolas, p. 227.
[23] *CPR, 1364–1367*, p. 303, for letters of attorney.
[24] TNA C 76/52, m.9.
[25] TNA C 76/57, m. 13; /58, m. 25.
[26] TNA C 76/63, m. 18.
[27] TNA C 76/64, m. 7; /65, m. 27.
[28] TNA C 76/63, m. 6; E 101/39/38, m. 3.
[29] *CPR, 1381–1385*, p. 532.

Spain.[30] Finally, he served in the retinue of Sir Thomas Ponynges on the naval expedition of the earl of Arundel in 1388, as we can tell from the muster roll and the protection he took out prior to this service.[31]

In the preceding paragraph I have been very careful with my language, depending upon the source material providing the service record. For instance, when mentioned on a muster roll (which would be presented at the Exchequer as justification for payment), we can be very sure that the named solder did indeed serve, unless a marginal observation is made to the contrary or his name is deleted. With letters of protection and appointment of attorney, however, we need to be much more considered. It may be that such legal instruments were taken and then not used, as Goldingham had done in 1384; on other occasions, they were extended as the soldier was still overseas, and so can be strong evidence of service. It is the historian's duty to be clear about what evidence they are using and also to point out the pitfalls of relying too heavily on some types of evidence, even when produced by the royal government.

A good test of the stories produced at the Court of Chivalry is the evidence provided by Sir Hugh Browe on behalf of Grosvenor. Browe seems to have enjoyed a most eventful career. His connection with his probable uncle, Sir Robert Knolles, involved him in the struggle of John de Montfort, duke of Brittany, against the French. It is reported by Froissart that he was entrusted with the custody of Derval castle during Knolles' time as lieutenant of Brittany. The castle was besieged by the French and Browe therefore offered hostages and agreed to capitulate if he was not relieved within forty days. Knolles managed to enter the town and then claimed that the bargain Browe had made did not apply to him, as it had been made without his knowledge. The French besiegers therefore executed the hostages, and Knolles, in retaliation, killed a matching number of prisoners held in the town and threw their bodies over the wall.[32] Such a story reminds us of the reality and indeed brutality of the war between England and France.

In his testimony before the court, however, Browe denied taking part in any major actions, stating that he was 'aged forty and armed twenty years and upwards … he had been employed in garrisons during the wars … and never in the wars in great expeditions … '[33] However, from the surviving military administrative records we can confirm that he was in Edmund, earl of March's planned retinue in 1374 and was with Knolles and John of Gaunt on the expedition of 1378, where he is listed on the muster roll under the retinue of the earl of Arundel. His

---

[30] TNA C 76/70, m. 11; 71, mm. 11, 15.

[31] TNA C 76/72, m. 7; E 101/41/5, m. 7d.

[32] *Dictionary of National Biography*, vol. xxxi (London, 1892), p. 284; story briefly retold in M. Jones, 'Knolles, Sir Robert (d. 1407)', *ODNB* (Oxford, 2004); online edn at http://wwww. oxforddnb.com/view/article/15758, accessed 21 January 2008. Both appear to take the story from *Chroniques de Jean Froissart*, ed. S. Luce et al., 15 vols (Paris, 1869–1975).

[33] *Scrope and Grosvenor*, ed. Nicolas, p. 266. See Ayton above for discussion.

military fame was such that Froissart mentions him by name in his description of the siege of St Malo during this campaign:

> The siege of St. Malo was directly commenced, for they were in sufficient numbers to undertake it: they overran the country, and did much damage. Those who were most active in this business were sir Robert Knolles and sir Hugh Broc [sic] his nephew, who were well acquainted with these parts. These two made excursions daily, and the canon Robesart in company with them. Some days they lost, and at others gained: they however, burnt and destroyed all around St. Malo.[34]

Further, in 1380 Browe took out letters of protection as he intended to accompany Thomas of Woodstock on his Breton expedition – another major expedition. It can also be shown from muster roll evidence that Browe later renewed his acquaintance with Arundel and served once again in the earl's retinue in 1387 before leading his own retinue in the follow-up campaign of 1388. It is perhaps ironic to note that local rivals would have noticed Browe's absence overseas, and indeed it seems that during his period of military service his manor house was robbed.[35]

Browe, therefore, maybe deliberately, did not mention his involvement in these significant expeditions. This could have been a legal ploy in support of Grosvenor. It is possible that Browe and, perhaps, other deponents, may have been consciously editing their military careers and choosing not to mention campaigns where they may have seen the Scrope family bearing the disputed arms. The depositions given in the Scrope v. Grosvenor case have been used uncritically by some scholars as an accurate record of the careers of the deponents, but Browe's evidence should remind us that these depositions were part of a legal process and were produced to support one of the claimants.[36]

Another deponent in the Scrope v. Grosvenor case was Sir John de Brewes. He served with the earl of Arundel in 1387 and jointly captained his own retinue with Sir Andrew Hake in 1388.[37] Brewes testified that he was 54 years old and that his service had begun at the siege of Calais in 1347, making him just 15 years old at that point if he had given his age accurately. He also mentions that he was present at the siege of Mauron in Brittany in 1352 and that he served on the crusade to Flanders of Bishop Despencer in 1383 and with John of Gaunt in Spain in 1386.[38] He had therefore only just returned from Spain just prior

---

34 J. Froissart, *Chronicles*, ed. and trans. T. Johnes (2 vols, London, 1874), vol. 1, p. 544–5.
35 P. Morgan, *War and Society in Medieval Cheshire* (Manchester, 1987), p. 155, citing TNA CHES 25/8, m. 23.
36 Thanks to Dr Tony Moore for discussion on this paragraph.
37 TNA E 101/40/33, m. 1, C 76/71, m. 12; E 101/41/5, m. 12d, C76/72, m. 7. Hake was executed in 1400 for his support of the Epiphany plot; C. Given-Wilson, *The Royal Household and the King's Affinity: Service, Politics and Finance, 1360–1413* (New Haven and London, 1986), pp. 224–5.
38 *Scrope and Grosvenor*, ed. Nicolas, p. 208.

to joining the campaign in 1387. Using the Soldier database, we can confirm some of his service from the official record and also extend his service record to include other expeditions which he did not mention in his testimony. We can add his service on a naval expedition under the command of Humphrey de Bohun, earl of Hereford, in 1372.[39] In 1373 he took the precaution of securing a letter of protection for his intended service with Edward, Lord Despencer, in France.[40] We can see that his relationship with John of Gaunt had already begun by 1378, when he joined him on a naval expedition at Christmas of that year,[41] and his involvement in Bishop Despencer's crusade of 1383 is also backed by his appointing attorneys while he served overseas on this campaign.[42]

William Plumstead, esquire, a deponent in another case before the Court of Chivalry – that of Grey v. Hastings (1408–10) – claimed an extensive career in English expeditions. He said that he had served in Gascony in 1370; with Gaunt in 1378; with Sir John Arundel in 1379; with Buckingham in 1380; and in Portugal with Gaunt in 1386.[43] He then continued this service by joining the expedition of the earl of Arundel in 1388.[44] Once again, using the database, we can see that he also served at sea with Buckingham in 1377–8, and we can confirm his service with Gaunt in 1378.[45] We can also add that he intended to serve with Edward, Lord Despencer in France in 1375.[46] What is intriguing about the case studies of Brewes and Plumstead is that, although chosen randomly for this paper, they appear to have had a very similar service record. Both men served with Gaunt in 1378 and again in 1386, and also in the expeditions led by Arundel in 1387–8. In addition, they both served with Lord Despencer in the early 1370s. The ability to link unconnected soldiers in this way perhaps demonstrates that we still have a lot to discover about the shared experience of the English military community.

The final example is not drawn from a case in the Court of Chivalry. Instead, our entry point into this career profile is through the account of a pilgrimage to the Holy Land undertaken by Sir Thomas Swynburne in 1392, as recounted by his companion on this journey, Thomas Brygg. The document begins: '1392, on Tuesday the sixth of August, I, Thomas Brygg, departed from the fort of Guines for the Holy Sepulchre of the Lord, in the company of my Lord, Lord Thomas of Swynburne, a soldier of England ... '.[47] Brygg then recounts a journey

[39] TNA E 101/32/20, m. 1.

[40] TNA C 76/56, m. 31.

[41] TNA C 76/62, m.1.

[42] TNA C 76/67, mm. 8, 17.

[43] Keen, 'English Military Experience and the Court of Chivalry', pp. 132–3.

[44] TNA E 101/41/5, m. 3d.

[45] TNA E 101/37/10, m. 1; 38/2, m. 1.

[46] TNA C 76/57, m. 7, enrolled in 1374 for intended service the following year.

[47] My thanks to Henri Gourinard who told me about the Brygg account whilst walking across Nicosia in June 2009. P.E. Riant, 'Voyage en Terre-Sainte d'un maire de Bordeaux au XIVᵉ siècle', *Archives de l'Orient Latin* II (1884), pp. 378–88; E. Hoade, *Western Pilgrims: The*

from the fort of Guines in the Calais Pale all the way to Jerusalem. They travelled overland to Venice (where they joined a company of other soldiers from Bohemia and Germany) then by sea to Alexandria before travelling again overland to Cairo (including the Pyramids), Mount Sinai, Gaza and Bethlehem. The return journey took them to Nazareth, Tiberius, Damascus, Beirut and Rhodes. It seems from the description that Swynburne took in all the known holy sites, including the Holy Sepulchre, and Brygg accompanied him and totted up all of the indulgences gained and how much each part of the visit cost.

To reconstruct the career of Sir Thomas Swynburne we are aided comprehensively by the soldier database. We have over twenty service records for him drawn from musters, letters of protection and appointments of attorney. This evidence can be supplemented by looking at payment information recorded on the issue rolls and appointment information from indentures. His career is very complicated to recount, but, simply put, he served in leading (and overlapping) military positions including mayor, garrison captain, lieutenant and keeper: in the garrison of Roxburgh from 1385–1390;[48] the garrison of Guines from 1391 to 1394;[49] on pilgrimage from 1392 to 1393; in garrison at Calais Castle in 1395;[50] he had a protection that was revoked for an intended expedition into Picardy in 1397;[51] from 1397 to 1403 in the garrison of Hammes;[52] from 1405, mayor of Bordeaux;[53] Hammes from 1406 to 1407;[54] received reinforcements to Gascony of 50 men-at-arms and 100 archers in 1408;[55] garrison of Fronsac from 1409 to 1411;[56] garrison of Hammes again in 1412.[57] Thomas's service as an important military officer, therefore, spanned the change of regime from Richard II to Henry IV and in this, in fact, he is far from unique.[58] He was, in effect, a career soldier, with his recorded service spent mainly holding militarily important posi-

Itineraries of Fr. Simon Fitzsimons (1322–23), *a Certain Englishman* (1344–45), *Thomas Brygg* (1392), *and Notes on Other Authors and Pilgrims* (Jerusalem, 1952), pp. 77–86.

48 TNA C 71/65, m. 5; /68, m. 4; /69, m. 1.

49 TNA C 76/75, ms. 3, 7; /76, m. 8; /77, m. 7; /78, m. 10; E 403/553, m. 14.

50 TNA C 76/79, m. 4; E 101/69/1/282.

51 *CPR, 1396–99*, p. 166.

52 TNA C 76/81, m. 2; /82, m. 11; /83, m. 13; /84, m. 24; /85, m. 15; /86, m. 12; /87, m. 19; E 101/69/1/295.

53 TNA E 101/69/2/313; /101/44/8, m. 2; E 403/587, ms. 12, 1.

54 TNA C 76/91, m. 6; E 403/598, ms. 2, 8, 13.

55 TNA E 403/595, m. 9.

56 TNA E 101/69/2/326; C 61/112, m. 7; E 403/605, ms. 3, 10; /403/608, ms. 7, 9.

57 TNA E 403/610, ms. 5, 16. See also M. Wade Labarge, 'Swynburne, Sir Thomas (d. 1412)', *ODNB* (Oxford, 2004); online edn at http://www.oxforddnb.com/view/article/47046, accessed 9 December 2009, for a summary which also mentions that Froissart reported that he was involved in the jousts at St Ingelvert in 1390.

58 For other examples see: Anne Curry, Adrian R. Bell, Andy King and David Simpkin, 'New Regime, New Army? Henry IV's Scottish Expedition of 1400', *EHR* CXXV, 517 (December, 2010), pp. 1382–413.

tions for the Crown. Despite this continued service, and thanks to Brygg, we also know that he managed to travel across the Mediterranean and made an extensive perambulation of the Holy Land.

As an epilogue to this tale – what of Thomas Brygg? It seems that the Soldier database can also give us access to some details of his later military career. A certain Thomas Brygg, archer, served in the expedition that Henry IV led to Scotland in 1400, in the retinue of Sir Henry Riddeford;[59] and he also served as an archer in the retinue of Lord John Clifford in the expedition to France in 1417.[60] What is especially intriguing about this later service is that another Thomas Swynburne, esquire, also served on this campaign, in the retinue of Lord Henry FitzHugh – both retinues being under the overall command of Humphrey, duke of Gloucester.[61] This could therefore be an indication that Brygg continued his service with a relative of Sir Thomas after the latter's death in 1412.

While it would be possible to add numerous other examples demonstrating interesting and extensive careers in arms, the case studies presented have covered the major campaigns and theatres of war available to soldiers in the later fourteenth century. This survey has shown that, although it is possible to construct partial career profiles without reference to official governmental records, using evidence from the Court of Chivalry, chronicles and other materials, the Soldier database greatly enhances our ability to reconstruct these careers, even when such careers seem richly detailed from other sources. We have been able to note that English soldiers in the later fourteenth century would travel widely in search of military adventure and such journeys occurred perhaps more regularly than we might have expected. We have also seen that such far-flung travels were always based around a core of repeated military service for the English crown, in Scotland, Ireland and France – which reaffirms some earlier conclusions made with much more limited access to the data.[62] So, who was the best soldier? The answer is perhaps rather counter-intuitive given the argument followed in this paper, for the soldier with the widest and most far-ranging travels, in his own words anyway, was Nicholas Sabraham. He appears on the database only once, serving at Roxburgh in 1371. But this one additional instance of service, even if it is not very exotic, was not previously known.

59 TNA E 101/41/1, m. 39.
60 TNA E 101/51/2, m. 21.
61 TNA E 101/51/2, m. 3.
62 A.R. Bell, 'The Fourteenth Century Soldier – more Chaucer's Knight or Medieval Career?' in *Mercenaries and Paid Men: The Mercenary Identity in the Middle Ages*, ed. J. France (Leiden, 2008), pp. 301–15.

Index

Warfare in History

Printed and bound by CPI Group (UK) Ltd, Croydon, CR0 4YY

09/06/2025

14685776-0001